GLOBAL
GODS

GLOBAL GODS

Exploring the Role of Religions in Modern Societies

Second 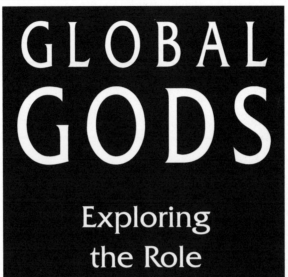 Edition

David W. Shenk
Foreword by Kenneth Cragg

Herald
Press

HERALD PRESS
Scottdale, Pennsylvania
Waterloo, Ontario

Library of Congress Cataloging-in-Publication Data
Shenk, David W., 1937-
  Global gods : exploring the role of religions in modern societies
/ David W. Shenk : foreword by Kenneth Cragg.
        p. cm.
  Includes bibliographical references.
  ISBN 0-8361-9006-8 (alk. paper)
  1. Religions. I. Title.
BL80.2.S484 1995
291—dc20

                                                    95-2233

GLOBAL GODS
Copyright © 1995, 1999 by Herald Press, Scottdale, Pa. 15683
    Published simultaneously in Canada by Herald Press,
    Waterloo, Ont. N2L 6H7. All rights reserved
Second edition, 1999
Website: www.mph.org
Library of Congress Catalog Number: 95-2233
International Standard Book Number: 0-8361-9006-8
Printed in the United States of America

08 07 06 05 04 03 02 01 00 99 10 9 8 7 6 5 4 3 2

Dedicated to our children
Karen
Doris
Jonathan
Timothy
who have lived among diverse societies and religions
within the global village.

Contents

Foreword by Kenneth Cragg 15
Preface 18
Introduction 20

1 The Gods and Global Community 29
Religion and the Philosophers
Quest for a Universal Faith
Comprehending the Gods
Distortions of the Gods
The Problem of Evil Gods
Conversion and Change
The Gods Are Persistent
Ten Faiths and Ideologies
People and Their Gods

2 The Gods and Human Well-Being 53
Global Interdependence
Development and Ecology
Human Rights and Pluralistic Society
Right and Wrong
Freedom and Responsibility
Technological Transformation
War and Peace
The Family
Global Urban Culture
The Global Village

3 God Went Away: *African Religions* 72
   African Religion and Religions
     God and the Gods
     The Golden Age
     Hierarchy and Harmony
     Hierarchy and Modern Societies
     Peace and Justice
     The Person in Community
     The Witch
     The Family
     The Local and Global Village
   Interaction with Islam and Christianity
     Scriptures and Culture
     Children and Family
     Local and Universal Community
     Development and Change
     Spirits and Powers
     Forgiveness and Reconciliation
   Discovering the Global Village

4 All Is Brahman: *Hinduism* 96
   That Art Thou: Brahman
   What Is Hinduism?
     Caste and Pluralism
     Karma and Relativism
     Brahman and Maya
   Paths to Salvation
   Hindus Living Within the Global Village
     The Person and Destiny
     Righteousness and Truth
     History and Development
     Justice and Peace
     Minorities and Secular Society
     Soul Force and Gandhi's Legacy
     Hinduism and the Global Village
   The Gods in Collision with Allah

5 Peace Without God: *Buddha* 125
   A Missionary Movement
   Siddhartha Gautama Buddha
   The Person and Suffering

The First Refuge: The Buddha
  Compassion and Salvation
  History and Progress
  Nature and Science
The Second Refuge: The Dharma
  Peace and Nonviolence
  Ego-Negation and Tolerance
  Intercommunity Peace
The Third Refuge: The Sangha
  Mission
  Politics
  Pluralism
  Buddhist Nations
  Ethics
  Family
  An International Community
Global Issues
The Lotus

6 Ignore the Gods: *Confucius and Plato* 156
Chinese Philosophy
  P'an Ku
  Yin Yang
  Wu-Wei
  The Emperor and the Cosmos
  Government and Well-being
  Li
  Shu
  The Higher Type of Human
  Modernity
Plato's Problem
  The Gods Also Sin
  Godless Government Might Be Good
  Seeking Universal Truth
  The Gods Won't Die
  A Home for Philosophy
Confucius, Plato, and Marx

7 Yahweh Against the Gods: *The Bible* 177
The First Theme: Creation
  Yahweh Versus the Gods

Secular Development
The Seedbed of Science
Wrong Choices
Renewing the Earth
Wrap-up
The Second Theme: History
Joyful Community
Broken Community
A Call and a Promise
A Free People
A New Community
The Prophets
A People with Hope
The Bible and Global Issues

8 The God of Abraham: *Israel* 212
The Covenant
  Abraham and Sarah
  Ishmael and Isaac
  Freedom and Land
  Righteousness and Generosity
  Jubilee and Joviality
  The Covenant and War
  The Covenant and the State
Judaism
  Exile and Renewal
  A Scattered People
  The Talmud and Peoplehood
  Promise and Hope
The State of Israel
  Zionism and Palestine
  Painful Peacemaking
Israel and the Nations

9 The Wounded God: *Messiah* 246
Jesus of Nazareth
  The First Believers
  The New Testament Account
  Immanuel
  Son of Adam
  The Surprise

The Church
  The Family and Singleness
  The Church and Culture
  Different Christian Communities
  The Church and the State
  The Church and Pluralism
  The Church and Mission
  The Church and the Poor
  The Church and Reconciliation
  The Person and the Eschaton
The Church and Global Issues

10 **Allah Without Associates:** *Islam* 279
  Submission to Allah
    Origins
    The Hanif and Abraham
    The Prophet and the Qur'an
    The Miraj and Jerusalem
    The Problem of Suffering
    The Flight from Suffering
    The Creation of the Ummah
    Pillars of Belief and Practice
    Muslims, Christians, and Jews
    Islam and Culture
    The Way of the Prophet
    Consensus and Change
    The Shi'ah
    The Mystics and Their Way
  A Witness to the Nations
    The Region of Peace and the Region of War
    The Ummah and Pluralism
    The Ummah and the State
    The Ummah and the Secular
    The Ummah and Israel
    The Muslim Nation and the Nations
    The Ummah and the Family
    The Ummah and the Earth
    The Ummah and Progress
  Global Issues

11 **Freedom from the Gods:** *The Enlightenment* 317
Taproots
Reason Replaces Revelation
  Nature
  Ethics
  Religion
  Truth
  The Person and Government
A Global Philosophy
  The American Experiment
  Western Hegemony
  Global Secularization
  Global Secularism
  Free Enterprise
  The Problem of Evil
  The American Crisis
Is the Enlightenment Helpful?
A Secular Gospel

12 **Utopia Without the Gods:** *Marxism* 349
A Discredited Global System?
Marxist Ideology
  Revolution the Solution
  Religion an Illusion
  A Global Plan
  Dangers of Compassion
Global Utopia
  Justice for Exploited Nations
  Peace Among the Nations
Marxism and Other Faiths
  Christianity
  Buddhism and Confucianism
  Maoism in China
  Islam
  A Great Debate
Disaster in the Global Village
Faith for the Future?

13 **Global Gods and Human Choice** 377
One Global Village
Religions and Modern Societies

Welcoming the Good
Worrying About Evil
Alternatives and Commitments
A Confession

Notes 387
Select Bibliography 394
The Author 400

Foreword

ONE WONDERS what forewords are for, since a good book commends itself best by its contents. "Good wine," as the proverb goes, "needs no bush"—bush in this context being the sprigs of ivy that vintners hung outside their premises to draw attention to their vintage (for ivy was the emblem of Bacchus, the god of inebriates). So a good book does not need the "bush" of a foreword.

Yet while an author's friend wisely leaves a work to the readers' judgment, he may well ruminate it to offer them some sort of introduction. In this case there are several sprigs in the "bush." One is that *Global Gods* has behind it *a caring mind*. The adjective is important. Some interreligious studies—and much sociology and anthropology —are dryly academic. In its proper concern for objectivity, much Western scholarship in the field of religion and culture has tended to be overly analytical and cold, sometimes as if it were dissecting a corpse rather than wondering at the living. It is always possible, as the poet said, "to peep and botanize upon one's mother's grave."

As a consequence, there is much legitimate resentment in cultures and societies studied by researchers who do not share the ethos of those they dissect. *Pagan* was all too readily a pejorative word with which to summarize rites and meanings that distance failed to register aright. The Hebrew psalmist, for his part, was sometimes too ready to dismiss "heathen" practices with gibes about carpenters who used part of a tree for fuel while carving the other part into deity. That superficial perception failed to understand that the carved piece was no longer "fuel" at all, but symbol, withdrawn altogether from utility and sacralized for wonder, mystery, and awe. There may well have been unworthy superstition in the whole transaction, but even these were not properly handled by the lofty and dismissive theist. Some Western orientalism, too, has disturbed Easterners who have experienced such scholarship as treading on their dreams, passing verdict on their religious story.

To be sure, those critiqued may sometimes benefit as well from self-criticism. If so, the truly relational question is how best to evoke this. The caring mind of David Shenk contributes to the likelihood that this book will generate appropriate critique on all sides. This study handles exacting themes, not only with thorough insight, but also with a gentleness drawn from life experience and personal devotion. When autobiography enters wisely into such a study, personal experience can enable the sort of exposition not attainable through the visitor's notebook or computer.

There is a tragic progression in Psalm 1 from "walking in the counsel" to "standing in the way" and finally "sitting in the seat." That is the pattern of the cynic as well as of the sinner. Happily one can imagine a reverse sequence that leads through initial interest to personal concern and so, at length, to intimate perception. David Shenk's writing, the rich fruit of a caring mind, exemplifies this.

We can appreciate that this has led to what I would characterize as the second "bush" of *anxious wisdom*. Interfaith studies are truly a minefield for the unwary—or perhaps a better metaphor would be the need for "a sailor's negotiation of winds and waters." One has to be responding all the time to tantalizing clues that perhaps one is misreading. Often the "other" religion has reason to complain that our verdicts are awry. Christians may deplore what they see as "extinction" in the Buddhist reckoning with selfhood when, rightly seen, the *Dharma* is saying that "no thing" was (truly) "ever there" to become "extinct." It is our ultimate "nothingness" we are being called on to appreciate and concede. Paradox, to be sure, persists. But we have not wrestled with meaning if we have not rightly taken it for what it means to say.

On the other hand, the Christian may see all issues revolving around "salvation" and become preoccupied with whether (and if so how) salvation may be available to one ignorant of the "only" saving "Christ crucified." The urgent issue here is not helped if we overlook that we have contained it in a term and significance which are themselves disparate and, therefore, cannot—unexamined—be the territory of agreed decision.

Whatever global gods entail, they do not allow us either the satisfaction of sheer dogma or the comfort of a complacent confidence. We must always be interrogating our assumptions and perceptions, aware of the dangers of a little knowledge, the confusions in hasty conclusions. If "forewording" is forewarning, readers must be alert to their temptations and be grateful for an authorship that does not play into their temptations or oversimplify. An author who brings an anxious mind is reassuring for those who realize they need to share it lest they be lulled or soothed or blandly satisfied.

The caring heart and anxious wisdom of *Global Gods* belong with the third "bush" of *careful intention*. The writer is avowedly Christian. There is an intention to clarify, with such honesty as love can bring, what others believe. There is also the hope to commend what Christians find through "God in Christ reconciling the world." Genuine religious interconcern cannot be neutral, for neutrality is never religious. One cannot be noncommittal about the transcendent, except for the time being. Faith is not finally about pondering but about participating and belonging because choosing neutrality is itself a decision.

Christian writing does not remain such if it acknowledges no will to witness. Yet that intention has to renounce all arrogance and know itself for what it is—being in trust with the self-expending love of God in its "on-behalf-ness" in relation to creation, grace, fellowship, and peace. In a world yearning for human community under the constraints of growing population, technological change, and tragic economic disequilibrium, it is urgent that religions renounce the agelong will to contend, to divide, and to alienate. The religions are all surely required to show cause for their separateness, to offer to the world that which by its distinctiveness warrants their continuing separate identity. The Christian identifies that distinctively Christian meaning in divine *kenosis*, in a transcendent compassion which retrieves the tragic in history by the vicarious love which, through Jesus crucified, is "the place of the Name" whereby we must be saved.

With that careful intention, the author wants to discern, celebrate, and mutually esteem all that can yearn with him for the peace of the world and hope for humanity. *Global Gods* must mean "territorial gods"—even "tribal" deities. Those territories are cultural, psychic, temperamental, and spiritual, as well as geographical. David Shenk's careful intention is that "God so loved the world" of territorial theologies and that the one world of this multiplicity must be known and loved by us in that same measure.

—Kenneth Cragg
  Assistant Anglican Bishop of Oxford (Retired)
  Oxford, England, 1994

Preface

I WAS BORN in the village of Shirati, Tanganyika (Tanzania). Except for my family, my most intimate childhood friends were Zanaki Africans living in the hill lands twenty miles east of Lake Victoria. We hunted, worked, played soccer, and fought together.

Most Zanaki venerated ancestral and nature spirits. They called their creator Murungu. Some were newly Christian. A few were Muslims. These friends helped form me. Sungura, Nyakitumu, Wambura, Mirengeri, Butenge—I could never name them all. They helped me appreciate the importance of faith in the affairs of humankind.

My East African childhood was an introduction to interaction between church, traditional African community, Islam, and Hinduism. My adult career in education, anthropology, and administration in over fifty countries has provided opportunities for considerable involvement with all the religions and ideologies explored in this book. Much of what I describe comes from personal experience of global issues through living or working on all six continents.

I have also been formed by the academic disciplines of this exploration through more than a decade of teaching comparative religion and courses related to the history and phenomenology of religion in colleges and graduate schools. I have enjoyed teaching comparative religion in the context of a Western worldview. Yet the years invested in the philosophy and religion department of Kenyatta University College of the University of Nairobi in Kenya, East Africa, have been especially noteworthy.

In that East African university community, diverse religions and ideologies competed for a hearing—African traditional religion, Islam, Christianity, Asian religions, Marxism, capitalism, and other secularisms. Even the phenomenon of the far-off state of Israel affected the

18

quality of community relationships in East Africa, and so Judaism also provided lively interest. The themes of this book were planted in my spirit during those intense years of interaction with African people who perceived that their very survival depended on developing fresh forms of faith compatible with modern global realities.

Many others have also influenced my perspectives and created in me a desire to understand and empathize with peoples of diverse cultures, religions, and ideologies. As an international educationalist, I have worked with Marxists, secularists, Sikhs, Christians, Hindus, Muslims, Buddhists, Confucianists, agnostics, Jews, and people of other perspectives as well. My colleagues have included Australians, Europeans, Asians, Africans, South Americans, North Americans, and others from islands of the seas.

I have experienced hospitality and conversation with people of great diversity, from the Chengdu University president in the heartland of China to the illiterate barefoot K'ekchi farmer of Alta Verapaz in Guatemala. I have often walked, slept, and eaten with those in regions of the global community who live with the pain of poverty, injustice, and violence. This book is a reflection on insights of many of these friends and colleagues.

A number of people with whom I have enjoyed academic, spiritual, or professional fraternity have informed my thinking. Others have invested many hours reading and critiquing the manuscript. Several acquaintances and friends who have influenced my thinking or who have read and critiqued the manuscript include Said Sheikh Samatar, Ross Bender, Janet Kreider, Mohammed Omar Mohammud, Peter Lee, Christoph Melchert, Donald R. Jacobs, Harold Reed, Cathrine Leatherman, Kamuyu wa-Kangethe, Kenneth Cragg, Calvin E. Shenk, Badru D. Kateregga, James N. Pankratz, Fatuma Omar Hashi, Gerald Shenk, Roelf Kuitse, Lamin Sanneh, Ahmed Haile, and Wan Phetsongkhram.

Eastern Mennonite Missions encouraged my beginning this effort during a sabbatical. Leaders of the agency such as Paul Landis, Norman Shenk, Jay Garber, and Carlton Stambaugh encouraged me with their affirmation.

Grace, my wife, has cheered me onward even though I have spent too many evenings writing. Our children have applauded the effort and so have my professional colleagues. I am grateful!

—*David W. Shenk*
Salunga, Pennsylvania

Introduction

IN DECEMBER 1992, the world's largest democracy was aflame. India's eight hundred million people looked into the abyss of possible disintegration as a nation. The fabric of nationhood was tearing apart; one thousand people were killed in a week of interreligious mayhem.

The match which lit the conflagration happened in Ayodhya on Sunday, December 6. Two hundred thousand Hindu worshipers of the god Ram destroyed a four-hundred-year-old mosque. Ram devotees believe the mosque was perched at the place where their god Ram had been born over five millennia ago.

The Indian convulsion projects disturbing questions about the role of religion in modern societies. Within every community the debate goes on. Is religion helpful? Is it obsolete? Is religion harmful? Whatever our answers might be to those questions, religions are thriving everywhere.

Eighty-five out of every hundred people on earth are adherents of a religion. As the twentieth century merges into the twenty-first, the global village includes more than five billion religious people. The religions are not dying out; they are pervasive, powerful, influential, and growing.

There is global debate concerning the role of religions in modern societies. The differences in opinion are startling. Compare the opposite ideas concerning religion expressed by John Lennon and Hazrat Sahib Sibgatullah Mojadedi.

In his lyric, "Imagine," Lennon invites us to imagine that there is neither heaven nor hell, themes that religions sometimes use to encourage obedience through fear of future judgment. By abandoning worries of future reward and punishment we are freed to focus only on the present; it is not difficult imagining no heaven in the blue beyond.

Lennon nuances the observation that nationalisms and religions often intertwine; the mix can produce wars. People fight and kill and die defending their nation; religion justifies the war. Religion and nation cooperate, robbing people of peace. Therefore imagining into oblivion both country and religion could create peace.

Lennon imagines a peaceful world where people have abandoned religion and live in harmony with one another. His quest for peace in a world without religion is attractive. "Imagine" has ignited the imagination of a generation convinced that religions are divisive and irrelevant.

In contrast from Afghanistan we hear the counsel, "The reason we have suffered from fourteen years of war is because we have not adequately submitted to the religion of Islam." (Hazrat Sahib Sibgatullah Mojadedi, interim president of Afghanistan, in his inaugural statement, April 30, 1992.)

John Lennon and Hazrat Sahib Sibgatullah Mojadedi expressed enormously different views of the role of religion.

Lennon believed religions undermined human well-being. Mojadedi is convinced that true religion is the only way for peace in his nation of Afghanistan and in the global community. This book explores that kind of debate. It is an investigation of the riddle of world religions in modern global human affairs.

The modern debate about religions has ancient roots. For example, Greek philosophers, viewing the world twenty-five hundred years ago from their perch on the Acropolis, were bemused and sometimes horrified by the ways the gods affected human community. From their lookout astride the crosscurrents of religious pluralism in the Mediterranean societies, these philosophers were sobered by the realization that societies formed their divinities and were then ensnared by these same gods. They observed that the gods did not create moral society.

One Greek writer, Xenophanes, lamented,

> Homer and Hesiod have ascribed to the gods all things that among men are a shame and a reproach—theft and adultery and deceiving one another. . . .

> If oxen or horses or lions had hands and could draw with
> them and make works of art as men do, horses would draw
> the shapes of gods like horses, oxen like oxen, each kind
> would represent their bodies just like their own forms.
> The Ethiopians say their gods are black and flat-nosed, the
> Thracians that theirs are blue-eyed and red-haired.

Xenophanes and many of his colleagues were dismayed by the immorality of the gods and the way they fostered moral relativism and division in the human community. They were concerned that the gods never critiqued society, for they were merely the reflection of culture. Too often the gods prevented the development of wholesome relationships between peoples. The Greek philosophers yearned for that universal good which could nurture quality relationships and culture throughout the community of humankind.

This book continues the quest of the ancient Greek sages by exploring the various ways faith, religion, and ideology affect modern global societies. It describes the phenomena of the gods of tribe, nation, and culture, both in their ancient and modern expressions. It explores the visions of Israel, Christianity, and Islam with their respective expressions of a mission among the nations based on the conviction that there is one God, one humanity, and one morality. It probes the universal mission of Buddhism which invites people to discover the way of enlightenment.

Are such religions helpful? Ancient and modern philosophers have often critiqued religion while pursuing a quest for universal truth providing a nonreligious basis for comprehending unity and diversity in global community. We reflect on several philosophical critiques of religions. We explore ways some such philosophies have become ideologies possessing a religious-like aura of supreme authority. Our exploration reveals that ideologies can also become gods.

This exploration has developed in the context of considerable international discussion about the relationships between the religions and wholesome community. In recent years there have been numerous interreligious global conferences on themes such as peace, justice, or the care of the earth.

A close colleague of mine participated in one such interreligious peace conference convened by Pope John Paul II on October 27, 1987, in Assisi, Italy. There were sixty present. Thirty were Christians and thirty represented from fifteen to twenty other religions, including Sikhism, Buddhism, Hinduism, Islam, and Native

American traditional faiths. The assembly respected the integrity of the religious diversity of the group; they did not worship or pray together as one assembly.

Each religious community had its own separate prayer or reflection experience. Yet they met to converse about the role of religion in the quest for peace in the global village. Each contributed to the conversation from within the perspective of her or his own faith community. This was an authentic dialogue, in which all were enriched, challenged, and critiqued.

The nine-day Chicago Parliament of the World's Religions was a more exuberant event (August 28 to September 5, 1993). The six thousand participants represented 125 religious groups, ranging from Sunni Muslims to moon-worshiping Wiccans. The seven hundred seminars and lectures were a spectrum of global religious diversity. The organizers sought consensus on a nine-page manifesto entitled, "A Global Ethic."

Alas, it was unexpectedly difficult for the Chicago Parliament to achieve agreement. Nevertheless, this brave effort to find an ethical consensus among these experts and practitioners of religion dramatized that we are one humanity living in one global village. Global issues put all religions on trial. Responsible religion must create responsible ethics for responsible global living. Are the religions up to the challenge of creating an ethical foundation for modern global community?

Books exploring aspects of religions and global community have attracted considerable attention. Theologian Robert McAfee Brown has written *Religion and Violence* (Westminster, 1973), which describes positive as well as negative contributions of the global church in the quest for peace in modern times. Denise Lardner Carmody and John Tully Carmody describe interreligious peace and justice themes in *Peace and Justice in the Scriptures of the World Religions* (Paulist, 1988).

Harold Coward explores human rights and pluralism in his book, *Pluralism: Challenge to World Religions* (Orbis, 1985). The issue of pluralism is analyzed from a philosophical perspective in Allan Bloom's best-seller, *The Closing of the American Mind* (Simon and Schuster, 1987). *Habits of the Heart*, by Robert N. Bellah and team (University of California Press, 1985), is an equally provocative book which critiques the individualism of the post-Enlightenment North American worldview.

In the meantime, psychiatrist and author M. Scott Peck is calling for radically fresh perspectives on the issues of faith and global community in *The Different Drum: Community Making and Peace* (Simon and Schuster, 1987). Dutch theologian Hans Küng observes that there can be no global peace without religious peace in *Global Responsibility: In Search of a New World Ethic* (Crossroad, 1991). A more comprehensive bibliography is included at the end of this book.

thesis

This particular book, *Global Gods,* is a comparative exploration of specific world religions, including several philosophical critiques of religion. We reflect on ways these belief systems contribute to or detract from quality global well-being. Tension is present throughout this exploration, for all religions and ideologies are challenged, confronted, and sometimes transformed by the realities of modernity.

Global Gods is written in the conviction that we should all take responsibility for building quality global community. Dynamic, healthy local societies are the building blocks for authentic global community. The two interrelate. Wholesome local and global community must include a commitment to constructive engagement with modern issues.

Universal modern issues which touch all humanity include:

• human rights and personal freedom
• family and children
• the role of women
• integrity and ethics
• economic, community, and personal development
• ecology
• ethnic, national, and global relationships
• religious and ideological pluralism
• peace and justice
• urbanization and mobility

These are modern issues which any commitment to global well-being must address.

Should not our religions and ideologies be critiqued and evaluated in light of their contributions to the issues affecting the modern global village? On the other hand, should not healthy religions possess the resiliency and power to critique and transform societies in ways which build personal and community well-being?

A letter from a dear Somali friend illustrates the urgency of our quest. He laments, "I am almost naked. I am often beaten. I am tired and ill. The bullets go over my head many times. I am separated from the family, but they are also in detention. They call me the offspring of a pig. I am hungry. My city of Mogadiscio is destroyed by this horrible war. This place is like hell. Please send me food if you can!" (July 1991)

My friend is a religious man. He is also a good man. Those who have detained him are also a religious people, and so are the soldiers who have destroyed his city and home. They all utter the name of God as they shoot one another and as they die.

A later communication from this same devastation describes peacemakers crossing the lines of battle, trying to weave a fragile fabric of understanding between the hostile clans. These peacemakers are also inspired by their faith in God. At awesome personal risk, they function with the unshakable conviction that peace is the will of God.

One of these peacemakers had his leg severed by a mortar. Yet as soon as he had recovered, he sought to return to the arena of conflict as a one-legged peacemaker. His religious faith inspires hope in him that his efforts will someday be fruitful.

Our global community is critically ill. Have the global gods done us in? Are the religions or ideologies of humankind of any help? Is God or are the gods impotent? Where are the indications that religion is helpful? Where do we discover religious communities engaged in constructive critique of modern society? What are the qualities of those faith communities which genuinely undergird human well-being? What can these healthy communities learn and receive from one another?

These are the questions this book explores.

GLOBAL
GODS

1

The Gods and Global Community

"R ELIGIONS are dangerous; philosophy is useless," deadpanned the young Punjabi Sikh.

Story →

I was astonished!

The bearded and turbaned Sikh was my seat companion on a Kenya Airways flight from Nairobi to Athens. Kenya had always been his home. He was a bit fatigued from all-night partying with his friends before his departure from Nairobi. This was his emigration flight to England.

He learned that I had been a lecturer in the Department of Philosophy and Religious Studies at Kenyatta University College, and I tuned in to the fortunes of his family's Nairobi-based truck body manufacturing business.

He was surprised when I told him that my students and I occasionally visited the Sikh temple in the center of Nairobi. We would converse with temple leaders as we sat on the colorful matted floor before the opened Gathas (part of the Sikh scriptures) lying in sacred dignity on the ornamented bed at the front of the sanctuary.

My companion volunteered, "The son of the head priest is one of my best friends. He is an atheist. His parents grieve for their son's loss of faith."

"Why has your friend become a person without faith?"

"Actually, many of my friends have become atheists, not just the son of the priest. The violence in the Punjab makes us become atheists. Even in our most holy golden temple at Amritsar, there is violence in the name of religion. Perhaps atheism is the better way."

After an uncomfortable pause, I ventured, "You'll be interested to know that I am on my way to Cyprus for a Christian consultation on peace in the Middle East."

"May God bless you!" my companion exclaimed. "The Christians, Muslims, and Jews have been arguing with each other for fourteen hundred years. And they all claim to be the true spiritual descendants of Abraham."

"Are you an atheist?" I prodded gently.

"No, I want to be a believer. Neither Marxism nor atheism have helped to build understanding between peoples."

He continued slowly. "I have read the Qur'an of the Muslims, the Bhagavad Gita of the Hindus, some of the teachings of Gautama Buddha, and the Bible, especially the New Testament. I have also read the writings of some of your Western philosophers, such as Immanuel Kant, Georg Hegel, Karl Marx, and Bertrand Russell."

I glanced in surprise at the turbaned youth. This technician who built trucks amazed me by being so intelligently in touch with the spiritual and intellectual streams which nurture modern commitments.

Tentatively I ventured, "Did your high school teachers in Nairobi require your reading so widely?"

"Oh, no," he responded breezily. "I am very interested in why people behave in different ways, and so I read the religions and philosophies which guide their lives."

After a pensive pause, he continued, "Also, I must say that I am seeking the truth."

"What will the truth look like when you find it?"

"The truth will replace hate with love."

The spiritual roots of my airline companion extended into the fifteenth-century Punjab in northwestern India, where the Sikh faith originated. Now as a cosmopolitan world-citizen youth anticipating the twenty-first century, he was in a quest for a faith which nurtured intercommunity peace.

His name was Singh, for all Sikhs have the surname "Singh," which means lion. They are to be lions in the defense of their faith and community. The sensitive, wise spirit of this "lion" resisted the easy avoidance of the issues which agnosticism offers.

Singh's faith in the Creator nudged him away from the tempting options of atheism or humanism. Yet so much of human religiosity sows discord rather than harmony. This turbaned youth perceived the nature of the problem more keenly than many, with his spiritual moorings anchored in the heartland of Asia, his impressionable childhood and youth nurtured in African community, but his destiny unfolding in Western society. No wonder this youth, whose livelihood was sustained by his welder's torch, had sought wisdom from books during the cool Nairobi evenings after the shop was closed. He sought a faith able to transcend the animosities which divide the human community.

This gentle, thoughtful Singh helped to crystallize the themes of this book, for he put his finger on a matter whose urgency cannot be exaggerated. The issue is this: in what ways do our belief systems affect the quality of our global community? Do the religions equip us for modern issues? Are the religions relevant?

That question is not new. It is the same question which fueled the philosophical quest of some of the ancient sages of Greece and the Orient. They also sought relevance. What can our contemporary modernity learn from the ancient quest for relevant belief systems? In what ways do their discoveries continue to affect the perspectives of modern societies?

Religion and the Philosophers

My Sikh companion and I parted in Athens, the very city in which Socrates had once debated the role of the gods in human affairs. It seemed to some of the Greek philosophers that the gods which people worship are really the creations of the human mind. Xenophanes cynically observed that if oxen, lions, or horses could form the gods, then the gods would resemble oxen, lions, or horses.

The notion of these ancient Greek philosophers that the gods are the extension of human imagination is also incredibly modern. Twentieth-century anthropological and psychological research has demonstrated that the notions of the divine in different cultures are mostly a psychoprojection of the values and felt needs of a society. This consensus emerges from various disciplines.

For example, Emile Durkheim, the father of modern sociology, developed an anthropological analysis of the relationship between religion and society in his classic *The Elementary Forms of the Religious Life*.[1] The research demonstrates that religion is the mirror of primal society. His case studies among primal societies in Australia and North America led him to the conclusion that religions are the expression of a people's own social ideal.

Sigmund Freud's *The Future of an Illusion*,[2] published only about a decade and a half after Durkheim's classic, comes to much the same conclusion. Freud used the tools of psychoanalytic research. He believed that religion is a need-based projection of a person's father. The person invents a god to worship who fulfills the role of the father figure within her family.

Both Durkheim and Freud perceived that the gods people worship function as a mirror of culture. This is the universal inclination of all human cultures across the continuum from small-scale tribal or national societies to more universal global cultures. In subsequent decades anthropological research has mostly supported these pioneer insights of Durkheim and Freud.

The anthropological consensus is that all societies are inclined to form God or gods in the image of their own society. That is the essence of tribal religions or national religions such as Shintoism. However, even the universal religions such as Islam, Christianity, or Buddhism are often seduced into ethnocentricism.

The outbreak of the Gulf War in 1991 illustrates the inclination of societies to equate God with national agendas. After President Bush announced the commencement of the war, the news media reverently revealed that the president would be spending the evening in prayer. Television revealed not only President George Bush at prayer, but also President Saddam Hussein prostrating in prayerful submission to God.

All sides in the conflict seemed confident that God supported their goal of victory in battle. As the war progressed, several leaders in the world Muslim community called the war a *jihad*, or holy war sanctioned by God. However, these calls for jihad came from Muslim leaders representing communities on opposite sides of the conflict. In the Christianized West, some Christian theologians dusted off the nearly forgotten criteria for a so-called just war which Christians could support. The political leaders of predominantly Muslim, Christian, or Jewish nations encouraged their people to pray for victory.

Among the Greek philosophers, there were expressions of resistance to the ethnocentrism and moral relativism which the gods encouraged. The gods reinforced the divisions in the global community by fostering ethnic or national egoism and were a quite immoral cluster of beings. The philosophers, therefore, sought elsewhere for the clue to authentic human transnational relationships and a universal moral perspective. Socrates was a pioneer who questioned the appropriateness of worshiping divinities whose behavior was scandalous and divisive. He was condemned to death for sharing such thoughts, corrupting youths, neglecting the gods, and practicing religious novelties.

Socrates and his disciple, Plato, helped set the tone for the developing consensus of many of the Greek sages. Plato believed there is one universal ideal good which is the key to authentic relationships among the peoples. For Plato and his disciples, the universal glue capable of transcending the petty divisions of culture is the enlightenment (*logos*) within the person which provides insight into the universal good. Through a process of intellectual testing and consensus, the universal truth can be realized and applied in the political and social order.

Plato and his colleagues were excited about this vision of an ideal which would free people from the particularities and immorality of the gods. They sought an intuitive and rational enlightenment which would be the universal good in which all particulars found meaning and unity. This was the vision of the Greek worldview which permeated the eastern Mediterranean region through the spread of Hellenistic culture during and after the reign of Alexander the Great.

While the Greeks were reflecting on the Acropolis, Buddha was also in contemplation about suffering under the Bodhi tree in northeast India. And Confucius was thinking about political injustice in the province of Lu in China. Like their Greek European contemporaries, these Asian sages of India and China also developed skepticism concerning the role of the gods in human community. Both Buddha and Confucius looked beyond the gods for the key to universal human well-being; they perceived the gods to be irrelevant to solving the human condition. They were certainly irrelevant for the hard realities of community well-being.

For Buddha, like the Greek Platonists, enlightenment was paramount. Yet the enlightenment which he championed took him and his disciples away from serious engagement with the global community. The right-mindedness of Buddhist salvation was for the individual. Buddhism provided a monastic community (*sangha*) for transmitting the life and insights of the enlightened one. Buddhism equipped people to experience suffering with the psychological fortitude which transformed the suffering into nonsuffering.

Confucius, on the other hand, had little patience with such types of reflection. For him right government which gladly received counsel from the philosophers was the key to human happiness. Within the Chinese worldview, right government in that country, which is the Middle Kingdom, would also contribute to harmony within the entire global community and the cosmos as a whole.

All three of these philosophical themes—Platonist, Buddhist, and Confucianist—diverse as they are, continue significantly to affect the well-being of the global community. Although all three of these philosophical movements attempted to turn away from the influence of the gods, all three have in themselves become awesome, godlike powers in societies. Both Buddha and Confucius have been deified and worshiped by many of their admirers.

It is not shocking for the beloved founder of a movement to be divinized in societies where ancestor veneration is a prominent feature. Although Western culture has not divinized Plato or the other Greek sages, the West has embraced its own ideologies in such a way as to make them like gods possessing unchallengeable power.

Western culture lives within the long shadow of the Acropolis. Especially attractive is the notion that humanity is capable of perceiving and achieving the universal ideal good through the tool of enlightened reason. Whole philosophical systems have developed around the effort to discern the universal reality which gives all particulars their meaning. Occasionally these philosophies have become the ideologies to which people commit themselves.

Sometimes these ideologies have become the new gods. Like the ancient gods whom the Greeks maligned, the ideologies themselves become unchallengeable masters of societies who condemn to death any Socrates who resists their authority or morality. In modern times some of these ideologies have become powerful movements affecting the whole global community. Nazism was such an ideology; it was a god which threatened death to an entire civilization.

Marxism is also such an ideology. This ideology announces that the ideal good is the universal classless society led by the authentic workers. For much of the twentieth century, Marxism provided a program for the unification of the entire global community within one universal philosophy and political system. Its competitor has been capitalism, which also claims to be the ideal good capable of saving the global community from poverty. These dual ideologies and systems tended toward an absolutism which gave them an aura of godlikeness as powerful as the ancient and unchallengeable Marduk of Babylon or the god-king, Pharaoh, of Egypt.

Quest for a Universal Faith

For a millennium before Buddha, Confucius, and Plato raised their philosophical objections to the gods, there had been another people emerging who also derided the divinities. These people had historical and cultural roots within the cultures of the Tigris, Euphrates, and Nile valleys. In time they developed an alternative society in the lands of the eastern Mediterranean between nations of Mesopotamia and Egypt. Israel was their name.

The Israelites were a people not given to philosophy but rather to history, for they believed that the Creator* of the universe and all humanity reveals himself through his acts in history. Israel had no philosophers, but their prophets confronted and confounded them. Jeremiah was one of these prophets and an approximate contemporary to the three just mentioned sages of China, India, and Greece.

Jeremiah of ancient Israel derided the gods of the nations, exclaiming,

> For the customs of the peoples are worthless;
> > they cut a tree out of the forest,
> > and a craftsman shapes it with his chisel.
> They adorn it with silver and gold;
> > they fasten it with hammer and nails
> > so it will not totter.
> Like a scarecrow in a melon patch,
> > their idols cannot speak;
> they must be carried
> > because they cannot walk.
> Do not fear them;
> > they can do no harm
> > nor can they do any good.[3]

The prophet Jeremiah and his contemporary, the Greek philosopher Xenophanes, would have agreed on the futility of worshiping divinities who are the creations of people. Yet the way of the philoso-

---

* Contemporary Christian theologies remind us that the Creator of biblical faith is characterized by both feminine and masculine qualities. The use of the masculine gender for God does not suggest maleness. Rather it is an affirmation of his personhood and otherness. The neuter is not satisfactory, for God is personal. Referring to God as "Mother" suggests nature worship or pantheism. To use both masculine and feminine gender would erode the biblical concept of I-thou or bipolarity between God and humankind.

phers diverged from that of the prophets of Israel. The philosophers sought universal truth through enlightenment. The prophets of Israel never spoke of enlightenment. Rather they called for people to *shub* (repent, return).

Shub means turning around. Shub is a response to the conviction that the people God has created should never create a god. The prophets explained that shub is a U-turn away from loyalty to the divinities which are the creation of culture, and a turning toward the righteous personal God who has created one universal humanity.

Shub involves moral choice, an act of the will. The gods whom a people or nation create never call for shub, for they are the mirror of the culture. On the other hand, the biblical writers described God as the one who encounters the people whom he has created, calling them to make a U-turn away from false gods of culture toward the one God who is their Creator.

The philosophers sought truth through the instruments of reflection and reason. In contrast, the prophets of Israel were historians, not philosophers. They perceived that God reveals himself through his acts in history. Their mission was to remind people of what God, the righteous one, has done and is doing, and to confront them with the personal implications of these acts.

The prophets proclaimed that God is calling forth a people to be his righteous, covenant community among the nations. For over a thousand years, the voice of the prophets was heard intermittently but persistently in the streets of Jerusalem and the byways of Palestine calling, "See what God has done. He has chosen you to be his people. Therefore, *shub* and rejoice!"

Ancient Israel, this inauspicious little community of faith in ancient Palestine, has influenced the global community in astonishing ways. From this people other movements have developed, notably Christianity, Islam, and Marxism, which perceive that theirs is a global mission. Although the effectiveness and attractiveness of these mission movements have varied from era to era, their respective missions have significantly influenced most of the modern global community.

My Kenya Airways companion was particularly appalled by religious violence—Sikhs and Hindus in the Punjab, Shiite and Sunni Muslims in the Iran-Iraq war, Christians and Muslims in Lebanon, Buddhists and Muslims in Thailand, Catholics and Protestants in Ireland, the Jewish state and Muslim states in the Middle East, Hindus and Buddhists in Sri Lanka. Every faith system or ideology contributes either positively or negatively to the need for collegial relationships between different ethnic groups and religious communities in the local and global community.

The global influence of religions and ideologies is poignant in our age of instant communication, massive mobility, urbanization, pluralism, and economic interdependence. These movements intensify relationships and interdependence within the global community. There is no escape. Even the adherents of a tribal religion, which by its very nature provides no mandate for global relationships, are often pressed by modern realities to reconsider their whole faith system in the interests of transtribal relationships.

For example, recently when Luo and Maasai societies in Kenya were engaged in violent clashes, their elders determined that the heart of the problem lay in the ethnocentricity of their respective tribal religions. They determined that peace could come only when they began to worship together. That would require commitment to a universal faith, a transtribal religion. The pragmatics of modern life pushed them to this conclusion. In this case they called in a Christian pastor who could lead them into a new faith, worship, and community.

Comprehending the Gods

Any exploration of the gods encounters problems. The gods we describe sometimes undergo metamorphosis. Religions and philosophies do adapt and change, some more than others. Our discoveries reveal that no system of belief and practice is fully consistent. All religious and ideological systems involve distortions of the so-called true original belief. Faith systems often include paradoxes and even contradictions. All partake of both evil and good. the glasses on looks

Then there are personal biases; we each view the world from our thru own perspectives. We often distort. If the system is in competition with our own perspectives, it is tempting to accent the worst in the opposing religions or ideologies. None of us is capable of achieving complete objectivity. It is impossible fully to understand the inside perceptions of another's faith system. Nevertheless, any commitment to global understanding demands that we try to understand and empathize with the faiths of people. We must learn to celebrate the good wherever it is found.

Some assert that objectivity is only possible from an agnostic stance. Is this really so? One of my sad experiences in graduate school was with a professor who claimed he was an agnostic. He argued that this stance enabled him to look at all faith systems with objectivity. Yet he was unkind in his comments against those in class who cherished faith. Agnosticism does not assure objectivity!

Neither does faith assure objectivity. Nevertheless, it is often true that a person of faith is best equipped to understand the yearnings and perspectives of the other who lives within an alternative religion. However, this can be so only if one's faith inculcates humility, with a listening and learning spirit.

"I have never heard Islam presented with such empathy and insight!" a Muslim exclaimed in his formal response to a lecture I had presented on Islam and Christianity in a college assembly. I had spoken with candor about core convictions which divide and unite Christians and Muslims.

I walk life's journey within the Christian faith. That commitment has planted within me a yearning to really hear those who walk with other commitments. I seek to listen until I also experience the inner attraction, the spiritual tug, of the alternative faith which I am exploring. At the same time I strive for honesty concerning the issues which divide and unite us in our different religious or philosophical commitments. It is in that spirit that we commence this exploration of the positive and negative ways religions and ideologies affect our well-being.

Religious and ideological systems are a complex and intricate fabric. For example, how does one discern and describe modern Islam as a global faith and community, this religion which includes over nine hundred million adherents scattered to all the continents? That kind of descriptive analysis is beyond the scope of this book.

This exploration focuses on the primal vision of each faith or ideology. We do not probe the many dimensions of the modern expressions of the different faith systems. Neither is this primarily an exploration of the historical development of religions. However, the narrative does discern the dialogue between the primal norms of a religion and the changes history creates. We reflect on the frequent dissonance between actuality and the ideal.

The question behind our quest is this: What is the ideal vision of this faith community? What norms and beliefs does a community of faith consider ideal? All religious or ideological systems live and develop within the long shadow of the original vision; religious people are conversant with the norms of their heritage.

The primal vision and norms have a source. That source might be a nature myth such as Shintoism. Frequently the norms derive from an anecdote, such as Krishna in the Hindu Bhagavad-Gita. The norms might be derived from the teachings of a sage such as Confucius or a philosopher such as Marx. The Jewish theologian, Emil Fackenheim, demonstrates that within biblical faith the primal vision is nurtured by a "root experience" or event that creates an "abiding astonishment."[4] Israel's deliverance from Egypt at the time of Moses is that kind of root experience; the event is reenacted among Jewish people in the annual Passover festival. In some religions scriptures transmit the primal vision and norms from generation to generation.

Distortions of the Gods

However, there are often discrepancies between the primal gods and the practices of a people. Within Christian experience an astonishing contradiction between their original vision of Christ and Christian practice transpired in a catalytic event on the evening of October 26, 312. The Roman general Flavius Valerius Aurelius Constantine allegedly saw a vision commanding him to paint the sign of the cross on the shields of his soldiers who faced the army of his rival, Maxentius, in battle on the outskirts of Rome.[5]

The cross is the Christian symbol which represents Christ crucified. The cross reminds Christians that Christ offered his life in non-violent, suffering, redemptive love. Now the cross was painted on weapons of violence. Constantine won the battle and secured his position as head of the Roman Empire, fighting under the sign of the cross!

The Constantinian distortion of Christ was epitomized in the Crusades which began seven hundred years later. Christian armies from western Europe marched east under the sign of the cross to capture from the Muslims the lands where Jesus had lived. This was a grievous Christian violation of the New Testament meaning of the cross. To this day Christian-Muslim relations are often peppery because of the long memory of the Crusades.

Nevertheless, the authentic vision of the cross was never totally obscured. Especially within the monastic movement in the post-Constantinian church, a lifestyle developed which was in many respects consistent with the way of the cross of Christ. That witness became a conscience within a society which often falsely equated violence with the way of the cross.

Just as some expressions of the monastic movement and some other Christian renewal movements invited the broader Christianized society in medieval Europe to return to a more New Testament understanding of the way of the cross, so it is in all religious systems. There is always a tug, a witness to retrieve the original vision.

It is never completely lost and is always present as a latent current and sometimes powerful force within society. The primal norms and beliefs are always in dialogue with modernity and sometimes in confrontation with it.

We note several modern examples of intense conversation between modernity and the primal norms of religions.

The powerful worldwide resurgence of so-called Islamic fundamentalism is an urgent call to all Muslims to return to the original seventh-century vision of the Islamic community under the prophet Muhammad's leadership.

Many expressions of the "independent church movement" in sub-Saharan Africa are explicit efforts to retrieve and preserve enduring aspects of the original vision of pre-Christian African religion.

Shinto resurgence in Japan contributed significantly to the propulsion of Japanese military power and patriotism into the World War II arena.

Confucian, Buddhist, or Hindu renewal are significant influences in most Far East Asian societies. One expression of Hindu renewal propelled masses of devotees of the god Ram to destroy the mosque at Ayodhya in 1992.

Within many of the republics of the Commonwealth of Independent States and countries of Eastern Europe, there is renewed interest in the Christian roots of these societies. For example, in Romania following the collapse of the communist regime, Christian Scriptures were freely distributed to school children, and the authorities urged churches to teach the Bible in the public schools.

In societies around the world, the original visions which formed religious or ideological systems continue to inform communities of believers. At times the influence is overtly and powerfully present.

The Problem of Evil Gods

Evil is persistently present in all cultures. What is the source of evil? Religions and philosophies attempt to answer that question. Yet wholesome faith should do more than conjecture on the root causes of evil. We also need to deal with evil, to address the root causes.

It might surprise us that religions are not always helpful in combating evil. The primal norms of a religion or philosophy are not always good. The primal vision might nurture harmful inclinations within the person toward uninhibited pleasure, the will-to-power, or unhealthy ego abdication. Religions may be prone to nurture evil rather than address evil.

Witchcraft is an example of evil religion. The function of the witch is to kill and harm through the use of demonic or extraordinary magical powers.

Witchcraft was the topic in a public assembly on the Kenyatta campus of the University of Nairobi in Kenya, East Africa, in 1975. Probably 75 percent of the university community was present, testimony to intrigue with the subject. The internationally recognized Kenyan philosopher and author John S. Mbiti was the speaker.

After Mbiti's lecture on witchcraft and the manner in which Christian faith and African traditional religion address the issue, there was a response time.

"How dare you say you don't believe in witchcraft," chided a student, testing his intellectual prowess with quizzical Mbiti. "This is a thoroughly African belief which you don't accept!"

In a flash Mbiti was at the chalkboard. He drew a picture of a tank with the gun turret aimed at a house. "I know that military tanks are for real, and they can destroy houses and people. They are dangerous killers."

Mbiti continued, "I also know that witchcraft is real and exceedingly powerful. It kills. It destroys people, communities, and families."

Then turning to the audience, he exclaimed, "And all of you know that it is evil."

There were no rejoinders. The audience went on to query the professor on more comfortable topics.

It is unusual for the primal vision or norms of a religion to be as starkly evil as witchcraft. Nevertheless, a vision may have served a community quite well for centuries, yet in the light of modern global realities, the vision may become inimical to human well-being. For example, as the 1980s came to a close, it was the tough issues of survival in the modern global community which dramatically and unexpectedly exposed the inimical dimensions of Marxism, especially in Eastern Europe.

Do the norms of a religion or ideology enable a community to respond adequately to the hard issues of modern global community? When tested by the expectations of modern societies, Marxism was exposed as an ideology which justified the cruel repression of people and horrible ecological disasters.

Returning to the primal vision or norms of the past may actually be the worst thing a society or person could do. For example, some societies have always believed that many children are needed to assure a good life after death. In an era of overpopulation and inadequate food for their families, the well-being of such societies requires a change in perspectives on children. The well-being of the community demands that parents stop believing they must have many children to secure immortality when they die.

The primal vision is not always good. The norms and values of a people do not always provide adequate perspectives for modern global realities.

Conversion and Change

Some religions or ideologies contribute more positively than others to the realities of global community. And religions or religious people respond in varied ways to a world in transformation or to the expectations of a global village in crisis.

The agony of the young Singh on the Nairobi-Athens flight was his suspicion that the Sikh religion at its core, in its ideal primal version, was incapable of rebuilding wholesome intercommunity relations within the ashes of Punjabi violence. He believed that the primal norms of the Sikh community nurtured a spirit of vengeance in response to the massacre at the Sikh temple of Amritsar in 1984, when Indian troops attacked.

Intercommunity peace was Singh's criteria for truth; by that measuring rod, Sikhism fell short. However, there are mystical themes within Sikhism which encourage the cultivation of enlightenment as a basis for interpersonal peace. Yet he questioned whether mystical insight could provide a solid foundation for peace. Because the Muslim, Hindu, and Sikh religions of the Punjab had not broken the cycle of violence, Singh sought an alternative faith or philosophical orientation which could provide a framework for peace in the Punjabi and global community.

It might be that Singh's quest will lead him to **conversion**—to another faith or ideological system which seems more compatible with the demands of global community. Conversion to an alternative faith is the option the Maasai and Luo elders chose when they perceived that their traditional religious systems were inadequate to bring harmony between their peoples. Within their microcosmic local setting, they perceived that the macrocosmic demands of global community were pressing them to accept a new expectation: tribes must live in peace with each other.

The Maasai also recognized that the food needs of the community, the nation, and the world required better use of their land. Agricultural development of their fertile soil was urgent. They surveyed their nomadic and warrior tradition. They examined the present and took a long look forward. Then they decided that they needed to convert to a new faith. The old was an inadequate resource for the new day.

"We have come to the *lengo* (point) of decision in the road of life," a Maasai elder told me. "We know that our traditional religion is not adequate for the new day."

Then turning toward the east, facing the verdant rolling pasturelands of his people, he gestured with his hand. "That is the reason all of my people have now made a turning in our minds. There will be no going back. We have chosen to join the universal tribe, the church."

Of course, conversion never means that a people are henceforth completely cut off from the primal vision which has nurtured their peoplehood for generations. Nevertheless, conversion does mean that a people now invite into their perspective a new vision, a fresh faith perspective. They begin the process of rearranging their community in response to the alternate faith.

The new ferments with the old, sometimes cleansing away inadequacies and at other times affirming ancient perceptions. The ferment can excite incredible creativity. Conversion of a people means that the old and the new will enter into a creative dialogue of judgment and affirmation, of transformation and reaffirmation. Conversion introduces a people to a dialogue which never ceases.

However, change in the religion of a people is not always due to conversion to another faith. Frequently modifications of religion occur subtly through **osmosis**—as peoples of different traditions intermingle. Recently I traveled by Land Rover in Kenya with a wise African bishop. We were discussing Islam.

The bishop commented, "Every morning the Muslims awake at four o'clock with their prayers. Recently I began arising the same time the Muslims do for prayer. This commitment has changed my prayer life, and my ministry as a servant of Christ has been enriched."

Sometimes the transformation may involve **syncretism**—the fusion of two different religious streams. Hinduism is particularly adept at syncretism, for Hinduism welcomes and attempts to embrace all faith streams. Syncretistic universal movements such as the New Age movement are spawned by Hindu spirituality. In vigorously syncretistic milieus it is difficult to discern the primal themes. Nevertheless, a syncretistic vision such as that of Hinduism is one approach to pluralism; one accepts all beliefs as truth.

Occasionally the demands of modernity force a radical change in the fabric of belief and practice within a religious system. A memorable modern example is Japan, where the Shinto religion combined the nation and divinity in ontocratic union. Central to this convergence of deity and nation was the emperor, who was supreme both politically and religiously because "his line goes back unbroken to the sun-goddess Amaterasu and behind her to the all inclusive spirit that is 'the great life of the universe.' "[6]

This meant,

> The center of this phenomenal world is the Mikado's land. From this center we must expand this Great Spirit throughout the world. . . . The expansion of Great Japan throughout the world and the elevation of the entire world into the Land of the Gods is the urgent business of the present and, again, it is our eternal and unchanging object.[7]

This Shinto vision propelled Japan into World War II. At the end of the war, the emperor of a defeated Japan renounced his divinity. The constitution of the reconstituted Japanese government was a secular document. The stubborn realities of global community have forced Shintoism to undergo radical internal reassessment. Yet the primal Shinto myth persists and continues to provide powerful inducements to Japanese patriotism.

The radical change within the soul of Shinto patriotism is an example of a **paradigm shift**—which refers to a profound change in worldview. The physicist Thomas S. Kuhn introduced the helpful notion of paradigm shifts in the physical sciences. He has demonstrated that as scientific data accumulates, periodically the entire scientific community experiences a major reconstruction of their conceptual and theoretical framework so as to accommodate the new data.[8]

The Copernican revolution in astronomy is an example of a paradigm shift. For 1,400 years people had assumed that the Egyptian astronomer, Ptolemy, was correct: the universe revolves around a stationary earth. Then in the sixteenth century, the Polish astronomer Nicolaus Copernicus demonstrated that the earth revolves around the sun. Now that required a paradigm shift of immense magnitude!

Kuhn's observations concerning paradigm shifts in the physical sciences are a helpful way of understanding conceptual revolutions in social sciences and in the realms of religion and philosophy. For example, when the Japanese emperor gave up any notions that he was divine, that was a profound paradigm shift for all Shinto devotees. Yet Shintoism has survived. In a similar manner, global realities often press a faith system to undergo a paradigm shift. Sometimes that is extremely difficult or perhaps impossible.

A paradigm shift might actually result in the destruction of the religious or philosophical system itself. That happened in the communist regimes in Eastern Europe. Gorbachev hoped to preserve communism by introducing the paradigm shift known as *perestroika*. The economic decay and malaise within these societies required such a paradigm shift. Yet the change in the paradigm led to the self-destruction of the communist system in Eastern Europe and the former Soviet Union.

During the first half of 1990s, it was not just communism that cracked. Other seemingly unshakable political-theological paradigms yielded to the yearning for justice for all peoples in the global village. In May 1994, the world was astonished to behold the mostly peaceful overthrow of the 350-year-old socioreligious system of apartheid in South Africa. In the same month, Israeli hegemony over the Palestinians of Gaza and Jericho came to a negotiated end.

Both these political transformations demanded amazing religious and theological paradigm shifts that were unthinkable even five years earlier. The shifts were largely a response to a global village that could not endure the suffering created by apartheid and a Zionism that repressed Palestinians.

Our exploration will reveal that global realities create enormous stress in all ideological and religious systems. Modern cultures often press a faith system to undergo a paradigm shift. Yet can the religion or ideology survive the conceptual changes which modernity urges? Can the faith system survive radical change?

No system is exempt from the challenge. Let us note a few specifics.

Modern secular societies consider the Buddhist *sangha* (monasteries) irrelevant. Occasionally governments have closed the sangha. Can Buddhism survive a paradigm shift of a Buddhism without the sangha?

Modernity challenges any notions of the extraordinary, including the resurrection of the dead. Can Christianity survive a paradigm shift of a Jesus who has not risen from the dead?

Islam believes that the Qur'an came from God. Modern approaches to the study of history are critical of any historical accounts which cannot be supported by evidence. Can Islam survive applying the tools of historical analysis and criticism to the Qur'an?

Caste is central to the Hindu worldview. Modern mobility and human rights concerns profoundly challenge caste. Can Hinduism survive in a society without caste?

The European Enlightenment believed that human reason will bring about goodness. Can such optimistic philosophies survive in a world increasingly dismayed by Western amorality and hedonism?

It might be that any of the above possible paradigm shifts would lead to the self-destruction of the system itself, as happened within Soviet and Eastern European communism. In most circumstances we will discover tension, sometimes acutely so, between modern realities and the norms, ideologies, or faiths of people. Healthy paradigm shifts enable religions or ideologies to survive new circumstances and to contribute to the well-being of human community.

Often internal adjustments to modernity take place subtly, and do not require a major paradigm shift. The faith experiences a **reformation**. Note two examples, one from Christianity and the other from Islam.

The worldwide church is appalled today at the thought of slavery, yet this has not always been so. In fact, within the early church some Christians had slaves. The institution of slavery is noted, although not condoned as ideal, in the New Testament. Over time the church became convinced that slavery was inconsistent with the Spirit and the teachings of Christ. Some Christian communities gave significant leadership to the move to abolish slavery in the entire global community.

Islam has always taught that a man may have a maximum of four wives, providing he treats them all equally. In modern times the interrelationships of global community raise disturbing questions about the propriety of such polygyny. The worldwide women's rights movement has touched Muslim communities. Consequently in a few Muslim societies, the teachings of the Qur'an concerning polygyny are being reinterpreted.

It is recognized that multiple wives may have been appropriate in seventh-century Mecca-Medina because wars had killed so many men. Polygyny provided care for widows. In more normal circumstances, it is doubtful that these same practices should apply.

"Furthermore," Muslims sometimes comment, "the Qur'anic text says the man must treat all his wives equally. That is impossible. So the real intention is to command monogamy!"

It is evident that conversion to another faith system is not the only option that a people or a person may take when the realities of our modern global village reveal inadequacies in one's faith moorings.

Modern exigencies may nudge a person or community to reevaluate and possibly reinterpret the faith system. This process may include the gentle, unobtrusive inculcation of new perceptions through osmosis or even syncretism. It may also include a radical and revolutionary reinterpretation of faith, as happened in post-war Japan. Sometimes change involves a more reformist approach, such as that taking place today in some Muslim communities in light of the feminist movement. Alternatively, the religious community may seek to change society rather than to conform. We need to be aware of ferment and change within religious communities.

Frequently religious people embrace **renewal** as their response to the challenges of modernization. Rather than acquiesce to modern pressure, they nurture faithfulness to the primal vision. They might confront the changes in society and culture, seeking to form the culture into the vision of their primal norms. If society resists their influence, they might choose to retreat and become an island of faithfulness within a sea of indifference or worldliness. Renewal movements that seek to influence local and global society are a significant feature of the modern global village.

The Gods Are Persistent

All change in a faith system requires a conversation, a dialogue between the past and present. To understand that dialogue, we need to comprehend both the present realities and the primal vision of that faith.

We must never underestimate the enduring significance of the original vision and the norms which that vision has nurtured. For example, modern Japan has struggled with how the imperial line should be carried forward into the succeeding generations if the traditional coronation ceremonies proclaiming the emperor divine are disregarded. Interestingly, within biblical faith the original vision is an invitation to change. The vision is of a future hope more excellent than the present. Such a faith system encourages cultural critique and change.

Sometimes the original vision is written in scripture or tradition as with the Qur'an and Hadith in Islam. Yet even when not written as scripture or tradition, the oral mythology carries the vision from generation to generation.

I once asked a youth of nomadic background to describe his family for me. With a proud smile he began to recount his genealogy for twenty generations. For a patriarchal polygynous society, that may extend between eight hundred to one thousand years into the past!

Mohammed,
the son of Omar,
the son of Ahmed,
the son of Fidow,
the son of Robleh,
the son of Abubakar,
the son of Odowa,
the son of Guled,
the son of Halane,
the son of Samatar,
the son of Yusuf,
the son of Gu'ug-Addeh,
the son of Gurey,
the son of Baso-Gab,
the son of Hussein,
the son of Mohammed,
the son of Abdallah,
the son of Samo-Talis,
the son of Hawadleh,
the son of Mohammed,
who is my clan father!

He then continued from the clan father, concluding with a triumphant victory emphasis, ". . . the son of Fatima, the daughter of the prophet Muhammad, peace be upon him!"

Was this proud prince from the deserts of Africa really a descendant of the prophet of Islam? Yet the conviction that his genealogy linked him to the Muslim prophet was exceedingly significant. The oral traditions which communicate the ancient spirituality of a people are as significant as scripture in defining the archetypical vision which nurtures the faith and life of a people.

This exploration describes conversations between the primal vision and modern global realities. The religion of a people often equips them to confront and transform those dimensions of modernity that are alien or inimical to their traditional values. We shall explore ways the worldview and norms of people speak to the issues of modernity. These conversations are impressed on societies today with unprecedented urgency, precisely because all of us, whether we like it or not, are being drawn into the phenomenon of the universal global village.

Ten Faiths and Ideologies

This book describes ten religious, philosophical, or ideological systems which have global significance. Some are case studies of tribal or national religious systems. Others are worldwide faith movements. Here is a brief introduction of the faith or philosophical systems we shall explore.

African religions are a case study of primal religion. Each society in sub-Saharan Africa has participated in its own system of religion. Although these hundreds of clan or tribal religions are specific to each society, they also enjoy commonalities with all other African traditional religions. There are also similarities with other non-African primal or so-called tribal religions. Focusing on African traditional religions is therefore one way of gaining clues to the manner in which religions in small-scale or tribal societies function.

There is richness and wisdom within the African religions, as is true of all primal religions. Nevertheless, as tribal societies begin participating in global community, a quest usually develops for inclusion in a universal faith or ideological community.

In the twentieth century, Islam, Christianity, and Marxism have been especially attractive alternatives to the peoples who are participants in primal religions. In some arenas, such as the African continent, the movement from tribal religions into a universal faith community has been phenomenal. Within one century, most of the people of sub-Saharan Africa have sought inclusion in the Muslim or Christian global communities. Why is this? Our exploration of African traditional religions includes reflection on the interaction between these African traditional faith systems and the universal communities of Islam and Christianity.

Hinduism is a case study of an intricate national sociology and a universal philosophy. A person cannot convert into Hinduism, for it is interwoven within the national fabric. Hinduism is an intriguing example of the tensions between a universal philosophy and national religious system.

The tension is an enigma, for while Hindu religion and sociology are a national system, aspects of Hindu philosophy have universal appeal, especially as a rejoinder to any universal faith systems which are based on perceptions of universal "truth." Thus the exploration of Hinduism will include observations of Hindu interaction with the global faith systems of Buddhism, Christianity, and Islam.

Buddhism is one of the world's three missionary religions. The other missionary faiths are Islam and Christianity. (Marxism may be considered a secular missionary movement.) The believers in these missionary faiths are persuaded that they have a message for all people. They invite people from all societies to believe in their teachings and become participants in the transnational communities which they form.

These missionary faiths are especially relevant to the themes of this book, for these systems are by their very essence transtribal and transnational. They are the only truly global communities.

Buddhism is a Hindu reform movement which has broken away from the shackles of Indian national identity and sociology to become a universal missionary movement. As a transnational philosophical community, Buddhism is compelled to respond to the issues of global community. Some Buddhist philosophers have been particularly forthright in attempting to address the issues of war and peace and the ecological crisis.

4 + 5   The philosophies of **Confucius** and **Plato** developed within the same era, about two and a half millennia ago. Both these philosophers critique the divinities. Both the Far East and the West continue to live within the intellectual shadow of these philosophical developments and the approaches to global issues which these systems suggest. They have been the harbingers of secularism.

6   The **Christian** church, as mentioned above, is a missionary movement, as are Buddhism and Islam. A third of humanity are professing Christians, which means that the church has become the most universal global community with at least small communities of believers in every nation-state on earth.

The universal spread of the Christian church places on this community special obligations and responsibilities to address modern global realities effectively. Does the Christian gospel equip the church for such a global responsibility? Two chapters are devoted to the interaction of biblical faith and the church with the issues confronting modern global community

7   The spiritual roots of **Judaism** are within the first portion of the Bible known as the Torah. The state of Israel exists as an expression of modern Judaism. Although Israel is a relatively small nation, its significance among the nations is enormous, especially as it relates to the issues of war and peace.

8   **Islam** is the faith of the Muslim community. Islam competes with Buddhism and Christianity in being a missionary movement. Nearly a fifth of the earth's people profess the Islamic faith.

The Muslim community is universal and very significant in the affairs of the global community. To what extent does the primal vision of Islam equip the Muslim community for this responsibility? The function of Islam within the global community is crucial to this exploration.

Finally, there is a chapter each on the philosophies and ideologies 9 ⅃10 of the European **Enlightenment** and **Marxism**. These are secular philosophies and ideologies which have powerfully influenced the global community. These ideologies proclaim the failures of the religions to create wholesome responses to the crises of modern times.

For multitudes secularism has become an attractive alternative to faith in any god. What are the consequences for the well-being of the global community of turning away from faith and embracing a secular ideology? The last two chapters explore that question.

In summary, the ten religions and ideologies we explore are African traditional religion, Hinduism, Buddhism, Platonism, Confucianism, Christianity, Judaism, Islam, the European Enlightenment, and Marxism.

People and Their Gods

We explore how each particular primal vision contributes to various dimensions of local and global community. Not all of the issues confronting modern humanity are discussed. As we walk through this exploration, we discover that the gods do not relate to the various issues with equal relevance. For example, our exploration of Buddhism will expand around the themes of personal peace. African traditional religion is especially relevant to the quest for creating healthy local community but is largely mute on the issues of global relationships. Thus each exploration will expand within the areas in which that religion or ideology seems to be especially relevant.

It also might be that a system appears to be inimical to commitments necessary for the well-being of human community. When dysfunctions seem to be present, the exploration expands to probe the reasons for this apparently negative streak within the god or gods. We probe the characteristics which seem unable to address particular modern issues or are a negative influence on society.

Terms such as "negative influence" or "inimical to the well-being of the human community" or "creative contribution" suggest value judgments. That is a correct observation. The issues of human well-being and even survival now confronting the global community are so urgent that value judgments are necessary. Issues such as AIDS, soil erosion, hunger, or human rights invite commitments to values which enhance the healthy functioning of both the local and global community.

The next chapter describes global issues which modern humanity must face with integrity and creativity. The alternative is the erosion of quality community and eventual death. These issues include economic interdependence, development and ecology, human rights and pluralism, ethics, freedom and responsibility, cultural transformation, war and peace, the family, and the city.

This is a comparative study of religion and ideology from the perspective of the issues we experience in modern times through our membership in global community. The exploration reveals that there is an intricate web between the health of the local community and the well-being of the global community. We discover that the many-sided faiths and ideologies of humankind are a core reality within all global community relationships.

Reflection

1. What are the strengths and liabilities of exploring religions and ideologies from an agnostic perspective? From within a faith perspective?

2. Describe ways the religious or ideological perspectives of a person or society can change. What role does the primal vision play in a changing world?

3. Both Plato of the Greeks and Jeremiah of the Hebrews opposed the gods. On what basis did they do so?

4. Reflect on a religious community you know of which has undergone a paradigm shift within the last half-century. In what ways has modernity influenced that shift? In what ways has the paradigm shift weakened the religious community? In what ways has the change strengthened the community?

5. Consider specific examples of ways in which religious faith forms and influences societies.

2

The Gods and Human Well-Being

I T WAS a dark Monday!
The American Wall Street stock market had crashed. A trillion
dollars of assets vaporized in only a day, October 19, 1987. I was
in Hong Kong. That city quaked.

The day after the crash, I visited a theological school nestled in a
quaint village on Cheung Chau Island, about an hour's ferry boat
ride from the metropolis. At lunch time scores of students filled the
public lounge and outside walkway. They were peering at the television console.

"Why are these students so interested in the noon television
broadcast?" I queried the principal.

"Your president is going to speak in a few minutes," he responded. "Our future is in his hands!"

These Hong Kong theology students 12,000 miles from Washington knew that policies made in Washington ripple around the
world, affecting their prosperity!

In recent years the term "global village" has slipped into our vo-
cabulary, helping us understand the kind of global interdependence
revealed on that Monday in 1987 when stock markets around the
world were shaken. Communication theorist Marshall McLuhan
has conceptualized our world as an interdependent village.[1] Perhaps it would be more accurate to describe our world as a global
city. Yet most of the earth's new cities still have a village ethos. We

shall stick with McLuhan's term—global village.

Our exploration accepts McLuhan's thesis that the millions of varied local communities around our world comprise one interdependent global village. Furthermore, quality local communities who have a generous commitment to the well-being of other communities are vital to the survival of the global village. This chapter explores dimensions of our cultures and religions that are especially pertinent to the well-being of the peoples everywhere who inhabit the global village.

As the twentieth century becomes the twenty-first, we observe that our global village has become quite ill.

State of the globe?

Every day the debt burden of the poor nations increases by U.S. $250,000,000. This is mostly uncollectable interest on old debts, which was added to a debt burden of $1,500,000,000,000 by the close of the 1980s.

Every day global financial institutions glean U.S. $150,000,000 in interest payments from the poor nations.

Every day forty thousand children die of avoidable disease or malnutrition.

Every night one hundred million teenagers seek sleep in homeless conditions.

Every day a precious plant or animal species vanishes from the earth.

Every day the nations of the earth spend U.S. $2,500,000,000 in arms (based on late 1980s figures).

Every year global population increases by 90 million people, 87 million of them born in poor countries.[2]

During the mid-1990s, forty wars ravaged the global village. Ethnic wars raged within a number of nation states such as Turkey, Armenia, Ethiopia, or Mexico.

Global Interdependence

We have become interdependent communities in crisis. How do the religions of humankind inform our response to the deepening global crisis? How do our faiths and ideologies relate to the urgent need for a spirit of genuine global interdependence, cooperation, and responsibility?

Sometimes it takes a disaster to push us toward genuine inter-community partnership and an assessment of the faiths that inform our commitments. That happened during the late summer of 1988, when Bangladesh experienced the worst floods in historical memory.

Three-fourths of this land of 110,000,000 people was under water.

In the midst of the emergency, the prime minister of Bangladesh, Maudud Ahmed, announced that he was calling for a tri-national conference with India, Nepal, and Bangladesh to plan for joint flood control measures, including the reforestation of Himalayan mountain slopes. The religious pluralism of the region indicates that the participants included Muslims, Hindus, Buddhists, Jains, Sikhs, Christians, and Marxists. Together they discussed international plans to alleviate the plight of Bangladesh.

The faiths of participants in such a conference inform the responses to disaster. Is the earth real or an illusion? Is human history meaningful or meaningless? Is the source of the disaster an angry God, aggrieved ancestral spirits, fate, bad karma, human irresponsibility, capitalists, or the laws of nature? Are some groups of people more worthy of help than others? Do secure communities have any responsibility for disadvantaged communities? What responsibility do Hindus cutting trees on the mountainsides have for Muslims living in the Bangladesh flood plains? The responses to such questions inform our perspectives on our community's relationship and responsibility to nature and to other communities.

Commitment to interdependence is urgent, not only for the survival of human civilization in Bangladesh but worldwide. By the turn of the millennium, six billion people will reside in our global village. Our survival depends on the fragile interrelationship between human community and the earth's resources of fertile land, forests, water, energy, minerals, and even fresh, wholesome air. We must also learn to cooperate as a worldwide human family.

The religious communities of humankind have a special responsibility for enhancing wholesome community in the global village. That influence can be constructive; however, sometimes religions have a destructive influence.

Too often we use our religions to feed intolerance and even hate—Muslim versus Buddhist in Burma, Catholic versus Protestant in Northern Ireland, Sikh versus Hindu in the Punjab, Shiah versus Sunni Muslim in Iraq, Buddhist versus Hindu in Sri Lanka, Marxist versus Buddhist in Tibet, Muslim versus Christian in Lebanon, Jew versus Muslim in Jerusalem, Muslim versus Christian in Nigeria, papal Christians versus Orthodox Christians in Yugoslavia, Marxism versus the church in China. Any commitment to global well-being gives a mandate to all religious and ideological communities: live in peace with one another.

It is not surprising that UNESCO convened a symposium "No World Peace Without Religious Peace" (February, 1989, Paris). The United Nations perceives that it is urgent for the religious communities of humankind to meet one another in the kinds of constructive conversation and actions which build understanding and cooperation.[3]

This is not to say that cooperation demands agreement on our respective faith commitments. That is impossible and would represent distortions of the core commitments of faith. A Sikh community and Shinto community cannot remain Sikh and Shinto and at the same time genuinely embrace the perspectives of the alternative community. Furthermore, missionary faiths will always seek to invite people into their respective faith communities. Nevertheless, modern global community realities reveal that responsible faith needs to respect alternative perspectives and communities.

UNESCO is right when it declares, "There is no world peace without religious peace."

Development and Ecology

Some years ago I was a teacher in a society which was generating about $50 per capita annually. A Western development expert joined our team.

During an afternoon get-acquainted tea, I commented, "Development is a theological issue!"

The teacups almost jumped off the table. The expert patiently explained that development is a technological enterprise. It is applying appropriate technology to the need at hand, getting pesticides and fertilizer to the farmer, and instructing him or her on how to use these inputs.

At a farewell tea for this same expert a few years later, he commented, "I have not forgotten that conversation about faith and development when we first arrived. Development *is* a theological enterprise!"

The worldview of a people is foundational to their perception of the relationship between human community and nature. This particular society had a strong dose of fatalism. The spirits and divinity capriciously determined everything. The best the community could do was submit to the mind of fate. The threshold of expectancy was just about zero. There was no anticipation that the future could be any better than the present or the past. These religious worldview attitudes permeated the community's understanding of their responsibilities and possibilities.

Europeans who settled in North America during the era of the frontier expressed a vastly different worldview. For many of them, nature was an expendable commodity to be used and then discarded. Millions of square miles of fertile land were ruined through exploitative agricultural practices. The buffalo were nearly eradicated from the North American continent. Subdue, dominate, and use with no thought for future generations is the legacy of too many North American homesteaders. Theirs was a worldview which enabled them to plunder the good earth with no apparent qualms. Many believed in a divinity who provided unlimited resources for them to exploit and destroy.

Only a century ago, most of the earth's peoples embraced the illusion of unlimited resources for human consumption. As early as 1798, Thomas Malthus had warned of disasters ahead as population growth overwhelms earth's resources. Yet his classic *Essay on the Principle of Population* did not significantly affect the ecological agenda for the nineteenth century.

In previous centuries the way people related to nature seemed of little long-term consequence for the well-being of the global community. However, population growth and the depletion of natural resources compel modern people to take a new look at their personal responsibility for the well-being of this planet. During the last half of the twentieth century, the myth of unlimited resources has been exploded.

Today global population trends and our intimate worldwide interrelationships mean that ecological irresponsibility in a particular community becomes the concern of the wider community of humankind. Felling the hardwood forests in the Amazon Valley may jeopardize weather patterns globally. Acidic smoke from Ohio's chimneys is destroying the forests of southeastern Canada. Deforestation of the Himalayan slopes may eventually destroy a great nation on the flood plains of the Brahmaputra, Ganges, and Meghna rivers. The goats grazing in Sehelian Africa help thrust the Sahara Desert southward; the desert destroys societies as it advances. Denuding the hills of Haiti creates perennial hunger, forcing waves of hungry refugees to flee to neighboring countries. Fluorocarbons used by northern industrial societies may contribute to an increase in skin cancers in Australia, South Africa, and South America. When human community in one region of the world lives irresponsibly with nature, we all suffer.

The global community must not continue to ignore the delicate relationship between human community and nature. We need to be sensitively aware of the religious or ideological commitments which undergird and inform those relationships.

Human Rights and Pluralistic Society

We have observed that the faiths of humankind inform our approaches and commitments to intercommunity relationships and our interaction with nature. These are only two dimensions of the role of religion and ideology in global human relationships. The person in community is also a significant consideration and relates to issues such as human rights and pluralism.

For several years my family and I lived in Mogadishu, Somalia. One evening a *hodi* at my door brought me into an acquaintance with Muhammad. He was the handsome son of a camel-herding family from the barren Ogaden of the Somali interior. After the spiced tea had been served, we sat in the roped chairs of our living room, delicately exploring interests. Finally the purpose of his visit became clear.

"Religion should be a good thing. But for me religion has been hurtful. It has not respected my dignity, my freedom and rights as a person."

I prodded, "There are many Marxist teachers from Russia contributing to the educational growth of the high school students in this city. Are you suggesting that Marxism is a preferable alternative to Islam, that you believe you would experience more personal dignity in an atheistic environment than in a Muslim community?"

"Oh, no!" he broke in. "I will never become an atheist. I know that God is the creator. But I long for a faith, a religious system, in which the person is treated gently, where persons can develop their full potential."

Muhammad recognized that religious people and societies often abuse the rights of the person. He was also aware that secular philosophies can encourage abuse as well.

Too often the gods people worship condone attitudes or actions which violate human dignity. Tragically, even when a people do worship one whose scriptures uphold human dignity, under test those commitments are frequently distorted. Too often people interpret their creator as the one who justifies their abuse of others, particularly when their self-interest is threatened.

Associated with the issues of human rights is the response of a religious or ideological community to the phenomenon of pluralism. Modern mobility and communication mean that most persons in the global village have some contact, often intimate and intense contact, with people of alternative ideological or religious commitments. *Pluralism*

The modest metropolitan area in eastern Pennsylvania in which I now live is an example of what is happening globally. Half a century ago, our Pennsylvania community was almost exclusively Christian. No one had ever met a Hindu, Buddhist, or Muslim. In contrast, today most people among our acquaintances know people of other faiths. Not only in my community, but nearly everywhere it is so, whether in Beijing, Moscow, Chicago, Munich, San Salvador, or Dar es Salaam.

Particularly in hitherto relatively homogeneous societies, the toleration of pluralism is often difficult or even impossible. David Livingstone, the pioneer Christian missionary in Central Africa during the mid-nineteenth century, was dismayed by the inability of homogeneous African societies to tolerate diversity. They were not elastic enough to tolerate alternative communities such as the church.

Livingstone believed that trade would loosen the tight cohesion of tribal societies, thereby making room for a pluralism that would have space for church. This was one reason he became the river explorer, hoping that navigable rivers would open the African interior for international commerce. He believed that commerce would relax the tight bonds of homogeneity, thereby creating the sociological dynamics which could accept a pluralism large enough to welcome the church.

Livingstone died in Central Africa still looking for navigable rivers. As for converts forming churches, his mission in Africa was a failure. These societies did not yet have room for the church or any other alternative community. However, Livingstone was right; in later years, as trade expanded throughout the continent, African tribes became more tolerant of diversity, and the church found a welcome home within tribal societies throughout the continent.

Yet the very Christianity which Livingstone proclaimed has sometimes also functioned as the adversary of pluralism. It is ironic in the North American experience that the Massachusetts Bay Colony pilgrims became notorious for their persecution of people whose religious commitments diverged from those of the Puritans themselves. Thus those who fled to the New World for religious freedom became the persecutors of others who also sought religious freedom.

Only sixteen years after the first pilgrim settlement formed, Roger Williams, a Baptist, journeyed 100 miles south to escape persecution from the Puritans. He began a new settlement called Providence. No wonder the separation of church and state are such prominent themes in Baptist thinking in the North American context. It was Roger Williams's experiences of persecution in the Massachusetts theocracy which led the Baptists in North America to determine to oppose forever any other trends towards theocracy.

The Massachusetts Bay Colony experience is only one example of the struggle a religiously grounded political system experiences when needing to cope with alternative religious communities. We note several other modern examples of the difficulties a politico-religious system can experience when meeting pluralism.

In modern times the Protestant control of the political system in Northern Ireland has contributed to havoc in relationships with the minority Catholic community.

Orthodox Judaism is the constitutional basis of the state of Israel. Ever since the creation of this religious-political system, there has been a perplexing struggle over how to incorporate Muslim and Christian Palestinians into the system.

In Lebanon the experiment of balancing Christian and Muslim political systems exploded in a civil war which commenced in 1975. Beirut, the commercial and banking nerve center of the Middle East, was pulverized by a decade and a half of intermittent shelling.

In Sri Lanka the supposedly harmless tilt towards Buddhism by the state alienated the largely Hindu Tamils, thus triggering endemic violence.

Sudan has experienced only a few years of peace since independence in 1956. The core of the conflict is the inability of an Islamic oriented government really to accept southern Christians as equals within the political system.

These are only a few examples of the problems pluralism creates for religiously controlled political systems.

Secular ideologies are not exempt from the temptation to oppose authentic pluralism. We note several examples.

Probably the most hideous example is Nazism. This is a racist secular ideology which has drunk from the philosophical streams of evolutionary theory. The Nazis taught that Aryans are the pinnacle of human evolution and as the fittest race are destined to dominate or liquidate other races. During the second third of the twentieth century, a Nazi-controlled Germany committed genocide against an entire people and sucked the whole world into a war in which tens of millions died.

Marxism under Josef Stalin's guiding hand was horribly repressive of dissenters in the Soviet Union. Many years after Stalin's death, torture, banishment to Siberia, or mind-changing drugs administered in insane asylums were still included in the Soviet Union's approach to the perplexing challenge of ideological or religious pluralism.

Capitalist ideology, with the sometimes heavy-handed guidance of the United States, has been horribly repressive in some Central and South American states. In some settings in this region, even the pluralism suggested by ministering to the poor is considered unpatriotic, and steps are taken to eliminate these forms of dissent.

The ultimate irony may be that in the liberal and secular tradition of the U.S. public school system, even the discussion of a religious perspective on issues is often prohibited. In liberal, enlightened France, Muslim school girls have created a furor when they came to school veiled. Secular liberalism does not necessarily view alternative perspectives kindly.

Religious or ideological jargon is often only a camouflage, a way to justify the grasp on power and privilege. For example, when the last white prime minister of Rhodesia, Ian Smith, proclaimed that the war to maintain white dominance in Rhodesia was to defend Christian civilization, the camouflage was obvious. He was using a Christian mask to deflect criticism of his racist government.

Even African Muslims with whom I was living at the time explained to me that the war in Rhodesia could not protect Christian civilization because the war was racist and contrary to Christian faith. It is more palatable to proclaim that the purpose of a people's struggle against others is to defend Christianity or Islam or Sikhism or democracy than it is to admit that this struggle has to do with power, greed, and selfishness.

Authentic pluralism requires power sharing and affirmation of the legitimacy of diversity. Religions and ideologies in the global village are under test. Do these systems respect pluralistic society? Or do they seek to dominate and control those who believe differently? Especially critical is the way a religion or ideology relates to ethnic diversity.

Right and Wrong

One of the most delicate issues in coping with pluralistic society is ethics. How does a pluralistic society develop moral norms which provide a basis for social interaction? This issue permeates modern societies at every level—the village, the city, the nation, and the global community.

A tempting solution in societies in which Muslims are a significant influence is to subscribe to Islamic *Sharia* law. Yet non-Islamic communities chafe under Islamic law, which circumscribes rather precisely their place in Muslim society.

Sudan is an example of the problems a government can experience when attempting to legislate morality. The central government has tried to homogenize social relationships by imposing Islamic law throughout the country. Alternative groups consisting of Christians and the practitioners of African traditional religion chafe at these efforts by the central government to assume that an Islamic ethical consensus should be the norm for the whole society.

Another example is the abortion issue plaguing the conscience of people in the United States of America. Most churches generally oppose abortion. To what extent should the instruments of law be recruited to impose the conscience of the church on society as a whole? In recent years every presidential campaign has been shadowed by this issue. For many people other issues pale in significance. Candidates' views on this one issue automatically determine their standing with a large portion of the electorate.

The Moral Majority and Christian Coalition movements have given the antiabortion forces strident support. The tactics of such movements in the United States lead their detractors to complain that they seek to impose their conscience on everyone. "A recent poll reveals that one in three academics now view evangelicals as a `serious threat to democracy,' " observes John N. Akers in an editorial for *Christianity Today*.[4]

Leslie Newbigin struggles with these issues of truth and moral consensus in a pluralistic world in two books, *Foolishness to the Greeks* and *The Gospel in a Pluralistic Society*.[5] From whence can modern pluralistic society receive the gift of moral consensus and cohesion? Newbigin calls on the church to reassert its role as a conscience—although not an arbitrator—of morality in society.

Perhaps faith communities such as Islam or Christianity can function best as conscience rather than arbitrators when they are a minority with no power base. India is an example. Although the caste system is at the core of Hindu values and worldview, both Islam and Christianity as minority communities offer an alternative social system. So does the tiny Buddhist community. The alternatives demonstrated by these minority communities have contributed to changes in Hindu attitudes towards caste.

Occasionally the global community of nations develops a clear moral consensus on a particular issue. Consider these examples of a developing global conscience.

During the last half of the twentieth century, the community of nations spoke with one voice in condemning apartheid in South Africa and sought ways to sharpen the conscience of that regime. The April 1994 nonracial elections in South Africa was, to some extent at least, an affirmative response by the white minority in that country to a global ethical consensus concerning apartheid.

There is overwhelming agreement that the use of poison gas in any circumstances must be prohibited, except for capital punishment. Iraq's use of poison gas in the Iran-Iraq War was widely condemned.

United States troops landed in Mogadishu, Somalia, on December 9, 1992. No Somali government had invited these troops. Yet there was no international outcry against this invasion. In fact, the U.S. action was mostly applauded. A global moral consensus had developed, asserting that the leaders of a people do not have a right to use starvation as a political weapon. Shortly after the invasion to assure food deliveries, at least a dozen other nations joined in the effort, all sanctioned by the United Nations Security Council. However, the failure of the mission to establish peace in Somalia raises questions about the wisdom of outside military intervention to stop a civil war.

Another example of global ethic is the June 1992 Earth Summit in Rio de Janeiro. This was an astonishing statement regarding the global consensus for a universal ecology ethic. One hundred seventy-eight nations were represented; over 100 heads of state participated. There was not much sympathy for nations or religious communities who appeared ambivalent in their support for an emerging global ecology ethic. The United States was stridently criticized for refusing to sign a bio-diversity treaty. Perhaps unfairly, a global religious community was cited for its stance in regards to artificial means of birth control.

The globalization of human community sometimes creates an astonishing moral consensus. Modernity can sharpen our ethical perspectives. Global relationships often nudge the whole world toward universal ethical commitments. Even religions are evaluated in the light of their ethical stance in relationship to global moral consensus.

No nation is an island. The world community helps bring fresh perspectives into the local situation. The fact that the earth's approximately six billion people now live in one global village nudges the whole community of humankind toward the quest for universally relevant moral principles. To what extent can or do the religions and ideologies of people contribute to that quest?

The 1993 Parliament of the World's Religions in Chicago sought consensus on a global ethic. Ecology was a special concern. The Parliament demonstrated that religions everywhere are on trial. Are the religions capable of forging a global ethic which nurtures the well-being of the global village?

Freedom and Responsibility

All societies struggle with the tension between freedom and responsibility. We have described how over a century ago David Livingstone discovered that Central African societies emphasized the integrity of community so strongly that the individual experienced very little personal freedom. He believed this was the reason his missionary work was never crowned by conversions. The African societies he met did not permit the person enough freedom to enable personal faith choices.

Even the daily diet in these African societies was precisely defined. Mother never had to worry about the menu for supper; it was always the same. I grew up in East Africa in that kind of community. By contrast, in the community in which I now live, the local grocery store carries 100 different breakfast cereals. Even something as routine as breakfast involves selection and choice.

A century ago a herdsboy in East Africa probably had only one vocational option—to be a herdsman. Today aspiring children in that same society are faced with several hundred thousand job possibilities, many in their own community, but the worldwide community also beckons.

The freedoms and opportunities which modernity provides place a confusing array of choices in front of people. These choices and modern mobility provide persons with enormous opportunities either to use or misuse the gift of personal freedom. The choices which the traditional community used to make for the person have become personal choices in modern society.

"There was no premarital pregnancy in the whole land, when I was a young man. Not one. Our so-called pagan communities taught sexual morality, and we protected our young people," a Kenyan pastor explained to me. "Our sisters entered marriage as virgins."

Modern mobility has frayed the fabric of the pastor's community.

The aroma of personal freedom is in the air. And premarital pregnancies blight families and young people with sadness. Although in that pastor's community church life has largely replaced the traditional community practices, the church has never succeeded in communicating and securing the values which it believes in as effectively as the traditional community transmitted its values.

Recently at an orientation for parents bringing their freshmen youth to a U.S. church college, this same issue of sexual morality was raised for discussion.

One parent commented, "If your child has not yet decided to live a chaste life, there is no way that the college or even your home or community can prevent her from experimenting sexually. The only real defenders of chastity are the personal decisions of our sons and daughters."

Modern mobility and the values communicated through the mass media provide unprecedented challenges to communities everywhere. These communities must attempt to nurture a sense of personal responsibility in the face of the incredible freedoms and divergent values which people in many communities experience today.

Imagine the impact on traditional values in conservative Egypt, where most people have access to television, and where much of the programming is relayed from Hollywood via satellites. In a metropolis like Cairo ten million people jostle. Slowly the metropolis strangles the intimate relationship between the person and the Christian or Muslim village along the banks of the upper Nile or the delta region in which she had been born.

One of the most urgent challenges to religion in the global community is the inculcating of responsibility in the individual amidst the incredible freedoms which modernity provides.

Technological Transformation

As a son of the East African hinterland, I saw my first telephone when I was nine. Today I dial East Africa directly via satellite from my own living room in eastern Pennsylvania. My father growing up in eastern Pennsylvania remembered running to the road past the family farm to see the first autos chugging along the muddy track which was the main highway. In a few decades, my father flew in jets which whisked him to distant continents in less than a day. Technology has introduced astonishing changes in twentieth-century communications and transportation.

Other modern technologies are equally significant.

"There it is!" exclaimed my Filipino companions.

I was startled when my companions poked my ribs and pointed toward the manicured Laguna rice fields flitting by us as we zoomed along the expressway just south of Manila.

"What is there?" I responded looking blankly into the horizon.

"This is where the genetic engineering was performed which led to the development of miracle rice!"

I knew immediately that indeed this was where IT IS. This astonishing development in crop production has alleviated hunger for some of the world's most impoverished nations. Even Bangladesh, with 110,000,000 people in an area about the size of Greece, can now export rice when the harvest is optimum. What a miracle!

These revolutions in communications, transportation, and crops are only examples of momentous developments within the human community during the twentieth century. They affect the whole global village. Consider these transformations.

Jama is a jet pilot. As a lad he herded camels and goats in the Somali Ogaden.

Agane is a director of the international finance department of a major North American banking firm. His boyhood was invested in petty merchandising in a steamy East African port town.

How do religions contribute to and respond to the pace of change in this era of megatrends? Is faith always conservative, or does it also sometimes urge change and guide the directions of change? Do the gods of the peoples within the global village thwart progress, or are they sometimes a catalyst for development? Do they keep people shackled to impotent or demeaning superstition and divinities, or free people for an open-ended search for objective truth which is the mainstay of the scientific approach? Do religions shackle change or lead change?

These are dramatically relevant questions in this era when the pace of change seems to propel humankind from one crisis to another. What is the role of faith in times like these?

War and Peace

It was August 1945. We knew something horrible had occurred, for Father was in a grave mood. He had just arrived home on his little Wanderer motor bike, having been to the Lake Victoria port town of Musoma for the day. Even before entering our home, he called his family around him, with several of our Zanaki friends and neighbors.

We clustered beneath the eucalyptus in our front yard. The late afternoon August air had the tang of coolness typical of East African highlands. We knew there was a war elsewhere in our world. Yet we were not greatly affected, except for the inconvenience of not having access to an auto.

Then in grave tones my father described how Little Boy, dropped from a lonely B-29, had pulverized Hiroshima. With a little stick scratching on the flinty earth, he tried to picture the radius of the destruction from the epicenter of the blast. In Zanaki fashion we crowded close, shaking our heads and grunting gently in amazement and horror, "Unh! Unh! Unh! Unh!" as the picture of ghastly tragedy grew.

Nearly four decades later, I visited Hiroshima. I invested much of a day at the peace museum. I tried to relive the horror and wickedness of that awful August 6, when in an instant over one hundred thousand people died. I wept as I witnessed hundreds, yes thousands, of little children alighting from buses and walking through the peace park with the bunches of cranes on sticks which they had prepared. They placed the cranes on the monuments in the park as a memorial for the thousands of children who died on their way to school that sad morning in 1945. I stood before a dark silhouette in the concrete where a human body had vaporized into the cement sidewalk, leaving only a shadow-like imprint.

In my spirit, I joined with these beautiful Japanese children at the peace park. I prayed with them that this wickedness will never happen again. In my idealism I dared to hope that the United Nations would require every head of state who has access to nuclear weapons to visit this museum and park and see for themselves the horror which is recorded here. Let them see the children coming to this place from all over Japan with their symbols of peace, the cranes. Let the leaders of the nations join with these children in prayer and commitment that such a calamity shall never happen again.

The global community was investing a trillion dollars a year in arms and the mechanisms of war by the end of the 1980s. At that time one hundred million youth were homeless. Forty thousand babies were dying daily from hunger or lack of basic medical care. Our cultures are turned too much toward war and too little toward life and peace. Even in the most tranquil communities, violence and the celebration of violence lurk beneath the facade of peace. *a moral dilemma*

The cozy suburban community in which I now live is an example
Story

of the violence which lurks in human societies. Ours is a fine town of about five thousand people. On any Sunday the six churches in our community are well filled.

There is a factory on the edge of town, new and trim, with ornamental trees and manicured flower beds. In that factory are manufactured the components for cluster bombs. The soul of these bombs are multitudes of plastic pellets which penetrate the body of the victim.

At one time the pellets were made of metal. The problem with metal is that X-rays can detect them. Plastic pellets cannot be found, unless the surgeon feels them inside the body with his fingers. So the experts who study how best to kill have recommended plastic pellets, in the confident anticipation that the victim will die before the surgeon can find the pellets.

The triggers for these devices of death are timed. First comes the explosion on impact. The plan is that hundreds of pellets will penetrate the genitals and abdomen of the victims. In moments there is a second explosion of pellets to catch friends who may dash to the rescue of the wounded and dying. A third explosion of pellets some minutes later will kill or wound the medics and rescue team. These are tiny bombs that possess three cycles of death.

The chairman of the board of directors of this weapons factory had been an active lay leader in a respected local Christian congregation. Yet not everyone in our community acquiesces to this evil. When a young woman secretary was offered a job in this factory, she turned down the offer after learning what the factory produces. In some ways we are a divided community. Most do not object to the presence of the factory; many welcome the jobs which it creates. Yet there are those few who grieve that hideous instruments of death are produced in our tranquil community.

The Family

Human sexuality and family life are urgent issues facing the global village. An Asian woman told me recently, with deep emotion, that all the teenage girls in her home town have gone to the city for prostitution because there is no economic future for them in their community. She added that 40 percent of the teenage prostitutes in the city are carriers of the AIDS virus. The virus has entered her beloved country and people through visitors who come from countries abroad on sex tours. What a catastrophe for a beautiful people and culture!

In many regions of the global community, family stability is eroding. Factors contributing to the fracturing of the family include urbanization with the mobility which the city demands, a global erosion of the traditional sexual mores of folk societies, a developing worldwide ethos of individualism, and economic pressures which induce spouses to move in divergent directions for employment.

In many societies the expectations for marriage have increased, especially the expectations of women. On all six continents, the stresses which modern marriages and families experience are similar. The modern global village is creating universal challenges to the fabric and health of the family.

AIDS is forcing all societies to take a new look at sexual norms. The disease has been thoroughly researched. Millions yearn for a medical solution to end this virus of death. Yet researchers warn that people must not trust in a medical cure. Prevention is the way to stop AIDS.

The experts inform us that a monogamous sexual life is the best prevention. For most modern societies that would indeed require an astonishing transformation in sexual mores. Nevertheless, sexual monogamy had been an ideal tradition in many communities. AIDS is forcing peoples everywhere to listen more seriously to the wisdom and counsel of the grandmothers and grandfathers who have always cherished that tradition.

Global Urban Culture

This chapter has reviewed some of the hard realities which affect the quality of modern global community. Modernity means that none are really exempt, perhaps especially so because the entire global village is experiencing the modern global city. The year 2000 is a watershed. At that time half the earth's peoples will be urban. That is three billion city dwellers compared to a quarter billion urban people at the beginning of the twentieth century. The city facilitates the spread and cohesion of global culture.

The exploding growth of cities during the twentieth century and the phenomenal development of communication systems are creating a global urban culture which affects all humanity. English is the language which links the decision makers within the emerging global urban culture. The youth wear blue jeans; they listen to North American pop songs; they watch MTV. Individual freedom is the ascendant value.

Global urban culture assumes that technology can bring salvation. For example, in this universal culture, AIDS is considered a medical rather than a lifestyle issue. Ecological considerations are sidelined if those concerns collide with technological development; the pollution of the earth and air and water are assumed in most cities. Technology is considered the savior of humankind.

The global urban communication network means that the dinner table conversation in Tokyo, Nairobi, or New York will be similar. When Mount Pinatubo blew in the Philippines, people in a billion homes were talking about that volcanic explosion during their evening mealtime conversation. Even the most remote rural homestead is within reach of the global urban communication network.

Television is everywhere. In modern China, even in lonely rural villages, it is almost impossible to find a home without television. Global culture cascades upon television screens everywhere from satellites in the skies.

The Global Village

This chapter has surveyed nine major themes in modern societies. In the following chapters we shall consider the role of ten religions and ideologies in relation to these major global themes. However, this exploration does not probe each global issue with equal intensity. The particular belief and practice profile of each faith, philosophy, or ideological system indicates which issues should be probed with the greatest depth in the context of a particular belief system.

Other unexpected issues emerge from time to time during the course of the exploration. These are issues which acquire global significance and beg for attention in the context of a particular system. An example is the relationship of faith to land in the experience of Israel. That question becomes a war-and-peace issue in the Middle East, and therefore invites careful assessment in the discussion on the faith of Israel.

The exploration expands in areas where a belief and practice system seems to be either inimical or especially constructive to the well-being of the global village. Although only several modern issues in the global community are focused, the realities described are urgent—economic interdependence, including the juxtaposition of wealth-hunger-poverty; development and ecology; human rights and pluralistic society; ethics; freedom and responsibility; cultural change; war and peace; the family; and the city.

The following chapters describe ways the gods people worship and venerate influence their responses to the experience of living in an interdependent world.

Reflection

1. What are the most urgent issues in global community?

2. In what ways do the realities of global community invite you to an evaluation of your religious or ideological orientation?

3. In what ways does modernity intensify the interdependence between the global village and local community where you live?

3

God Went Away

African Religions

TEN PERSONS are intertwined within my *muntu*. It is a black hardwood carving which stands at my office door. This muntu is an intricate weaving together of persons culminating at the apex in a solemn human head. My muntu is a symbol of the soul of African traditional religion and philosophy. Muntu is the Bantu root word which means human.

Philosophically inclined African colleagues explain the meaning of this muntu: "I am because we are, and we are because I am."

The person can exist only in community, and community can thrive only through the harmonious involvement of the person. The relationship between the person and community is reciprocal, creative, and life enhancing.

African Religion and Religions

This African spirituality is not only significant for the African continent. There are continuities between African traditional religions and primal religions everywhere, as a study of the primal religions of the Americas, Europe, Asia, Australia, or Oceania will reveal.

There are intriguing similarities among the tribal faiths of the ancient Ashanti of Ghana, the Incas of Peru, the Celts of England, or the Dravidians of India. There are different nuances, but the similarities are significant. There is value, then, in understanding African traditional religions for their enduring modern relevance and because they help us appreciate the early faiths of small, tribal, oral societies everywhere. A case study of African traditional religions is helpful in understanding the primal spiritual roots of us all.

Today the African peoples are largely Christianized. Islam is a second major faith. Yet both these missionary faiths have been built on the enduring heritage of African traditional religion and philosophy. This chapter focuses on the experience of the sub-Saharan region, where the conversation between African traditional religions and these two missionary faiths is relatively recent, fresh, dynamic, and intense. Even though they may be Christians or Muslims, hundreds of millions of Africans live in the shadow of the traditional perceptions and values of their ancestors.

Each of the eight-hundred-some language groups in the African continent developed its own religious system. Therefore we frequently speak of African traditional religions. These were not universal or missionary faiths. They were local faiths, tribal religions.

However, there are significant commonalities between all African religions. An example is the understanding of the interrelationship between the person and community. The major themes of African religions are so similar that we can also refer to them collectively as African traditional religion.

God and the Gods

All African religions believe in God the creator who is the lifegiver. Although African traditional faith agrees with Islam and Christianity that God is the creator of the earth, most believe that our creator is no longer dynamically present sustaining the earth and life. Those functions are carried forward by spirits or lesser deities.

Some societies perceive that there is little or no difference between divinity and nature. I refer to this worldview as "ontocratic." This is the perception that divinity, nature, and social institutions participate in oneness.[1] Pantheism perceives that there is no difference between divinity and nature. That would be the ultimate expression of an ontocratic worldview. In that case nature or expressions of nature are worshiped.

Anthropologists usually refer to the ontocratic worldview as "mythical." However, the term *myth* is used with a variety of meanings by theologians, philosophers, and anthropologists. For this reason I prefer the term ontocratic when referring to a worldview which perceives that social institutions or natural phenomena are at one with divinity. Nuances of an *ontocratic* worldview pervade primal religions everywhere; it is not only or primarily an African phenomenon.

The primal religions of ancient Greece are a classic and well-researched example of the ontocratic worldview. The Greeks believed the death and resurrection of the divinity caused the cycle of the seasons. The annual cycle of nature was an expression of the annual cycle of death and rebirth or resurrection of a god or gods. The Greek view was typical of most peoples in the northern hemisphere.

For the ancient Greeks as well as other expressions of primal religion, the fusion between divinity and nature is intimate. However, most African religions have some nuances of a transcendent view of divinity; that is to say, they perceive that there is an otherness between the Creator and creation. Yet all African traditional religions believe that supernatural spirits, powers, and forces pervade nature. Their ontocratic worldview provides a basis for spirit veneration, magic, and worship or veneration of ancestral or nature divinities.

The ontocratic worldview is fertile ground for magic. Magic develops in a culture which believes nature is permeated with divine force which can be bent and manipulated through magical devices such as incantations. Anthropologists refer to this vital force as *mana*, a term which comes from South Pacific islanders. Mana is impersonal divine-sacred power which permeates all phenomena. It is believed that experts can bend or manipulate this power for good or harm.

Mana contrasts with spirits in that they are personalized powers who can be entreated, perhaps through sacrifices. Spirits can be benevolent, malevolent, and like mana, are often present in phenomena. Experts also specialize in spirit manipulation. The magicians and spiritists are the same people, for both expressions of power need attention, and in reality these powers converge.

These powers form the spiritual bedrock of witchcraft which is the manipulation of the powers for evil. The powers can also be used beneficially. Although all African traditional religions are aware of God the creator, he is too busy to be bothered with ordinary problems. Thus these lesser divine powers are the most immediate reality.

Nevertheless, God the creator and lifegiver does provide the community with all gifts needed to sustain life. This includes land and livestock. Land is an especially precious gift which provides life for the entire community. Therefore, a person cannot own land. It belongs to the entire community for it has been given to sustain the life of all.

A century ago Europeans arrived and sometimes took land from

Africans. That created a serious theological problem. Africans believed that God gave each group of people ample land to sustain their peoplehood. Why God had not provided the Europeans with ample land in Europe to sustain peoplehood was a theological enigma.

The Golden Age

The myths of origins in African societies picture a golden age in the past when people lived in a tranquil, harmonious relationship with nature. The myths are ambivalent concerning the place of work in the ideal past. Some of the myths describe God as the one who does the work for the community. A Luo myth pictures the primal community placing their gardening tools in the doorway of the house before retiring for the night. When morning appears, lo, God has completed the garden work. Others describe God being very present and assisting with the work. The myths suggest a fairly laissez-faire, live-and-let-live relationship with nature.

Hundreds of myths across the continent also picture a disruption in the primal harmony. Something went wrong in the distant past. Consequently the close relationship between God and humanity is now distorted. This distortion affects every area of human life but is especially evident in the relationships of the community to nature. Work now becomes a universal necessity with little or no assistance from God.

Frequently nature refuses to cooperate, so sacrifices are offered to attempt to pacify God and the spirits. The sacrifices are offered in the hope that aspects of the lost golden age can be recaptured. The sacrifice must always represent the best the clan possesses, usually a perfect animal from the household of an upright family. In dire circumstances some societies offered humans, a practice condemned everywhere today.

All myths agree that the golden age will never be retrieved. It is gone forever. The breach between God and community will never be healed. Devices such as sacrifices at best can only recapture aspects of the lost harmony enjoyed in the golden age. The future is hopeless.[2]

So society faces the past while living in the present. The goal of life is to participate fully in the present while facing the past. The person anticipates moving toward that golden past through the process of old age and eventually death. Change is from the present to the past, from the baby toward the elderly and eventually the ancestors.

Hierarchy and Harmony

One can also view this process of movement hierarchically. God, the source of all life, is the apex of the hierarchy. Life flows down the hierarchy from the life-giving source, down through the ancestors who have passed from this life, through the elderly chiefs and counselors, through the grandparents and mature married, through the young married, the unmarried youth, the adolescents, and the children. Eventually this downward movement touches even the unborn with life. Conversely, the moment of conception begins the process of a person moving up the hierarchy with his or her age mates.

The process of moving up is ritually institutionalized. Examples include naming the child, giving a second name to the child, circumcising the youth, or entering marriage. For men with a well-established household, the process includes receiving the first cow tail with his worthy age mates. In old age the man who is truly wise and gentle in spirit will receive the symbols of inauguration into the council of elders. It is important that life flow comfortably down through the hierarchy and the process of moving upward through the hierarchy also be preserved.

Disharmony in the hierarchy sabotages the flow of life. For this reason traditional African societies have a fixation on preserving the integrity and harmony of the hierarchy. The persons or spirits above one in the hierarchy must remain invulnerable from challenge or disruption from those below. Power flows downward, not upward. This concept is grounded in theology—God himself is securely invulnerable and never affected by what we do.

In a university class in East African history, an experienced student teacher was presenting the function of democracy to his classmates. "In a democracy," he explained impressively, "the job of the parliamentary representatives is to listen carefully to the wisdom of the president. Then when they go home from the parliamentary session, their job is to explain to the people the wisdom of the president so everyone can follow the mind of the president faithfully."

This description of democracy was consistent with both the worldview and reality in most African democratic political systems. For many decades in sub-Saharan Africa, presidents ran for office unopposed. Alternative political parties were anathema. The hierarchical worldview made multiple political parties or a challenge to an incumbent president incomprehensible.

Many dimensions of the hierarchical system have been beneficial to human dignity and growth. The attitude toward strangers is an outstanding example. Although the hierarchical system is tribal, it normally functions with great courtesy and concern for the guest or the stranger. The presence of a guest at meal time is cause for celebration. The Gikuyu of Kenya used to place a small granary at the intersections of the foot paths which crisscrossed the land. At harvesttime people put portions of grain in these granaries, so the strangers who journeyed their land could find food.

This same spirit of courtesy to the guest was extended to the European explorers and settlers. Violence against the European settlers was rare. When it did occur, it was usually as a countermeasure against the violence of the Europeans or due to a misunderstanding. Even in times when war did occur, this sense of propriety toward the stranger was often present.

During the Ashanti wars in West Africa, the Ashanti army regularly lifted the siege of Kumasi—where the British soldiers were trapped—to permit them to come through the lines to find food and water. Sadly, such genteel Ashanti wartime proprieties toward their British soldier "guests" were not reciprocated by the British when they finally gained the upper hand in that war.

Proprieties toward the stranger include adoption for the permanent guest. These rituals involve sacrifice, vows of commitment, and ritual feasting. These covenants of adoption incorporate the guest into the tribal structure; they bring her into the encompassing securities of the hierarchical system.

These gentle sensitivities toward the outsider are precious and are probably one reason why an Arab proverb says, "He who has once drunk from the streams of Africa must return again and again for refreshment."

Hierarchy and Modern Societies

In modern societies the power hierarchy undergoes intense strains.

The first stress point is the **localism** of the hierarchy. Each society has its own hierarchy. Although Africans have always believed that God is the creator of all peoples, the manner in which each society participated in the life-giving blessing was through maintaining harmony in its own hierarchical system. Each system developed its own pattern of mores, ritual, and proprieties. Each system was tribal and local. None had a universal vision.

Consequently these tribal hierarchical systems come under serious strain and disruption in an age where nation-states usurp the primacy of tribal identity. Massive mobility invites people away from the traditional village settings into urban areas, where hundreds of diverse societies intermingle in new cosmopolitan communities and internationalization prods people to think globally.

Occasionally the strain created between different hierarchical systems by modernization results in an explosion of violence. That is what happened in Rwanda in 1994. For many centuries the Tutsi and Hutu tribal systems found a way to live together. However, the modern nation-state of Rwanda disrupted those traditional systems. After the Hutu president was killed, when a rocket allegedly hit his plane as it approached Kigali, the consequence was a genocidal conflagration between the Hutu tribe seeking revenge and the Tutsi tribe. Even those churches in Rwanda that renounced war for peacemaking were overwhelmed.

Nevertheless, modernization has compelled Africans to seek a global faith community as an alternative to the traditional tribal hierarchy. The need is urgent. People want to avoid the chaos that Rwanda or Liberia have experienced. This urgent modern need for a universal faith and community has helped to propel over 250,000,000 Africans into the Christian faith in the twentieth century. The Muslim community has also grown, although less rapidly than the church. There is an urgent need for a transtribal and transnational faith community which also enthusiastically affirms local culture and idiom.

A second problem with the hierarchy is **human rights**. The commitment to maintaining harmony in the hierarchy stifles dissent. The one who challenges authority is anathema. The hierarchy is an ontocracy. This is to say, there is a unity of divine and political power. In traditional systems, a challenge to the authority of the hierarchy is really a challenge against the sacred powers. That must not happen!

The perceived sacredness of the hierarchy has occasionally been the grounds on which detractors are harmed. An example from Uganda illustrates the point. In 1886, shortly after Christian witness began in Uganda, there was intense persecution of the first believers by the *kabaka* (king). The fuse which ignited the persecution was the refusal of some of his page boys who had become Christians to cooperate in his homosexual practices.

The refusal of the page boys to submit to the whims of the king was unprecedented. Those lads threatened the stability of the whole hierarchical system. In the firestorm which followed, thirty-two youths were burned to death at Namugongo.[3] This account is a worst case. Yet the persecution of the page boys was not out of harmony with the notion that the hierarchy was sacred and should not be challenged.

Normally the hierarchical system worked harmoniously. Yet in the cosmology and the system there was little room for detractors. Modern African political systems often mirror this reality. Normally they work well and harmoniously. Yet the human rights record in some settings has been heartbreaking.

Peace and Justice

In traditional societies there are correctives against the abuse of power. These correctives are the consensus process and the careful thought which goes into the selection of the higher councils of elders or chiefs. The mechanisms of counsel and leadership selection prevent gross abuses of power.

This restraining spirit is nurtured by the widespread belief that God as the life-giver bestows through the hierarchy all the gifts needed to sustain life. Those gifts include more than land, which we have already mentioned. Justice, truth, wisdom, empowerment, and peace are also necessary to sustain life. God generously bestows these gifts. Therefore, the hierarchy should function in a manner consistent with these qualities.

"The one true God for the Gikuyu, and the African people generally, is and always has been above everything else, the God of sociopolitical justice," writes Samuel Kibicho of the University of Nairobi.[4]

Kibicho goes on to point out that in Bantu languages the root word for justice is also the root for truth, wisdom, empowerment, win, or victory. All these gifts undergird the peace which sustains life.[5] This conviction gives African peoples incredible patience and persistence in the face of injustice. Because God is, justice and peace will eventually prevail.

All Africans I ever talked with about that dark night of apartheid in South Africa believed the system would not endure.

When I asked, "Why are you so sure apartheid will go?" the confident reply I heard was, "Because God is!"

Western systems of court trial do not sit well with African views of justice. In Western courts the attorneys for the prosecution and the defense battle out the case on the basis of legalities. Although the truth may be known to the attorneys, their presentations in court may have little or nothing to do with the real truth. The game plan is to impress the jury.

In contrast, in the traditional African courts the council of elders meet with protagonists and question them together and individually until a "truth" consensus is achieved. Wisdom, truth, and justice all belong together. The wise elder who demonstrates these godlike qualities is eventually admitted to the highest tribal council, which in many African societies is appropriately called the council of peace.

Since the gift of God is peace, warfare is anathema to the wise elder. So is murder. The destruction of life is completely contrary to the life-giving powers. In times of war, prayers might sometimes be offered to lesser divinities or the ancestors beseeching victory. However, it is hard to discover prayers to God seeking victory. Rather the prayers to God in time of war mostly seek reconciliation. "Turn our enemies to be our friends," prayed General Dedan Kimathi of the Mau Mau freedom fighters in Kenya during the 1950s.

In traditional society the elders of clans at war meet to arrange peace. The leaders review the issues leading up to the conflict. Steps are taken to bring reconciliation. Confession and restitution are required. An animal is sacrificed. Opponents seek cleansing and forgiveness from the ancestral spirits and from God for their violation of the land through contaminating the precious earth with blood spilled in warfare. They eat the sacrificial animal together, sometimes sprinkling the blood on one another as a covenant of peace.

That is traditional society; however, modernity has eroded many of these practices. "In the old days, we knew how to bring reconciliation when intertribal war happened. Today all of that is lost. We do not know how to establish the peace any more," lamented a Turkana elder in the deserts of northern Kenya.

The Turkana sage was only partially correct. For multitudes of Africans, the communion service in church has literally replaced the traditional sacrificial system. In this manner many celebrate and reaffirm regularly a covenant of peace which unites people from all tribes and nations. In the church as well as in Muslim communities, many of the traditional themes of peace endure. The traditional insights on peace influence both Muslims and Christians.

Occasionally in the political arena there are astonishing expressions of the ancient prayers: "God, make our enemies to be at peace with us." Zimbabwe is an example. From 1972 until 1979, civil war devastated the country. Whites and blacks battled, the whites to maintain their hold on to power, and the blacks to gain independence. After years of tedious negotiations, an open election was finally held. One of the African leaders in the war for independence,

Robert Mugabe, won the election.

The night before the election results were to be announced, Mugabe invited his archenemy, Prime Minister Ian Smith, to meet with him in his home. In that meeting he pledged to work for reconciliation and asked Ian Smith to join him in the quest. Immediately after he was installed as the new prime minister, Mugabe asked General Walls, who had led the white armies during those horrible years of civil war, to become commander of the new united Zimbabwean army. What an amazing olive branch for peace that was!

Admittedly, Christian people, including Ian Smith's own son, were praying and working vigorously behind the scenes to encourage and facilitate this reconciliation. Nevertheless we also recognize that the ancient wellsprings of African values and spirituality influenced Mugabe.

"Tomorrow we are being born again; born again not as individuals, but collectively as a people, as a viable nation of Zimbabweans" the prime minister broadcast to the nation on the eve of Independence Day.[7]

The Person in Community

These themes of peace have always contributed to the development of well-integrated, whole people. Although traditional structures did not provide much opportunity for the expression of personal freedom, the system was nevertheless impressively person-affirming. The community recognized the gifts of the person and encouraged the use of those gifts. After all, the Life-Giver does provide society with all the gifts for the creation of life, and those gifts include diversities of talents. Even the fool is a gift from God to provide the community with humor.

Naming a newborn child reveals this sensitivity to the person and the gifts which characterize the new person. The name must fit the person; therefore, it is unthinkable to name the child before she is born. It may take weeks before the name is finally chosen, for family and friends need to become acquainted with the person as part of the process of deciding on the name. As life develops, new names may be given in addition to the original name given by the parents when they first became acquainted with the newborn.

Decision-making processes affirm the person. For this reason voting is never practiced in traditional settings. When issues are decided through a vote, the minority group feels defeated. That is dehumanizing. It may even sow seeds of bitterness or divisiveness.

In contrast to voting, the consensus approach compels the consultants to listen to one another and to bend hardline opinions so a common mind can be achieved. Chiefs or leaders of palavers need to listen to and then summarize all dimensions of discussion. Their statements are reviewed and modified until all heads begin nodding in assent. Persons leave that kind of decision-making counsel feeling that they have been heard and affirmed.

hospitality
↓

Handshaking permeates African society. Even the infant child is included. When the guest is departing, handshaking won't happen just once, but again and again. Often the hosts accompany the guest for a short distance before the final handshake. Even a casual drop-in for an item of business usually requires drinking at least a cup of water or tea before departure. These proprieties are saturated with laughter. Even work is often oiled with humor and song.

Recently in a rural African homestead, I observed two teenage girls pounding grain with a mortar between them and a pestle for each. As they faced each other, rhythmically swaying back and forth in unison pounding the grain, they sang. The exuberant, rhythmic song helped unite them in the mutual ebb and flow of their bodies.

The person is more precious than things. The viewpoint of Mother Mirengeri is in harmony with traditional values. She told her pastor, an American Caucasian, "You are a good man, and so we are praying that God will bless you with more children."

"Oh," her amazed pastor exclaimed, "we already have four children, and they are a sufficient blessing!"

A cloud crossed her face as she responded, "Has the disease of the Europeans also begun to spoil you, my pastor? I have heard that in Western lands the streets of the cities are full of cars, but the children are very few. That is a great poverty, for cars are only metal; they are not human or eternal. In our land we are rich, even though we have few cars, for our streets are full of children."[8]

Julius Nyerere, the father of the Tanzanian nation, developed the concept that community is development. Personal growth has little to do with material possessions; however, the person is fulfilled in the context of quality community. Nyerere perceived that authentic human development is largely unrelated to growth in the gross national product. This is because development is wholesome relationships between people and with the land. His philosophy is popularly described as African socialism.[9]

Riding a Land Rover through the Tanzanian countryside, I asked a question which astonished my hosts. "How much does an acre of land sell for these days?"

My Tanzanian colleagues were amazed. "What do you mean? How can anyone buy land? The earth is God's gift to all humanity. The community loans people land at no charge. People may build on the land and sell the building, but we must never make profit on land, for the land belongs to the Creator. It is his gift to us. We Tanzanians believe it is wrong to make a profit on the gifts God has given such as water, air, or land!"

These ideals grounded in African spirituality have undergirded a number of flirtations with socialism in modern Africa. In some instances, such as Mozambique, Angola, Somalia, and Ethiopia, this course was avowedly Marxist. Others, such as Tanzania and Guinea, attempted a path of African socialism which was less ideologically alien to African values and spirituality than is Marxism. While ideally all these socialist commitments sought roots in African traditional spirituality, too often the mechanisms for implementation developed a coerciveness which was alien to the African spirit.

The Witch

Traditional society seeks to protect the person from forms of coercion which may create broken relationships and bitterness. This is necessary to protect the flow of life in the hierarchy.

Maintaining harmony is necessary for another reason. The bitter person becomes a cancer in society. The one who will not forgive shrivels and becomes small. This bitter and unforgiving attitude breeds malevolence. The person may become a witch, an evil person whose life is devoted to manipulating the powers of the spirits and *mana* for destructive purposes. That kind of malevolence kills.

An African sage once told me, "In my childhood witchcraft was the scourge of the whole land. Fear often paralyzed our communities and development was impossible."

The witch was and is the most feared evil in African societies. For this reason traditional society has always sought social and spiritual devices which can minister healing before the wound of hurt feelings becomes the deep anger which spawns witches. We have already described the consensus process, which institutionalizes person-affirming, decision-making procedures. Equally significant is the confessional. When a break in relations occurs, elders meet with the aggrieved person to listen and counsel. The elders work with the offended person to plan for restitution. Usually a reconciliation meal consummates the healing of relationships.

Yet these bold efforts to excise bitterness before it becomes malevolent have never been fully adequate. In modern times witchcraft has not vanished; probably this malevolence is increasing. There are several reasons for this growth in witchcraft.

First, the traditional approaches to dealing with the one troubled with inner anger are often not available. Mobility and urbanization have removed people from their traditional communities, where ancient therapies for dealing with personal anger were known.

Second, urban living makes neighbors of people who do not want to be neighbors. In the traditional rural setting, where land was ample, one could simply move to avoid neighborly tensions. For many urbanites that is impossible. Consequently tensions build up and anger is internalized.

We have observed that in the traditional cosmology, the golden age is in the past. That was when God was truly present with his creation. Community was life-creating, and work flowed in a comfortable harmony between humanity and nature. However, all the traditional myths agree that this golden age is gone forever. This fact is the root cause of the broken relationships which are the seedbed of witchcraft.[10] Nevertheless, the elders in the hierarchy function in an attempt to retrieve hints of the lost golden age; they seek to maintain life-nurturing harmony.

The Family

There are other devices too which have been developed in an attempt to retrieve glimpses of the lost harmony. The most significant social device is the quest for progeny. To understand the importance of children in African traditional religion, we need to identify with the malaise experienced because of the lost golden age. The distancing of God from human community nudges people to seek other routes to acquire islands of joy, snatches of the lost immortality, glimpses of the golden age, and a secure community.

Children provide all of this. Ideally the family homestead is an island of security. As the parents grow older, the children will provide for them. Most significantly the children will remember the parents when they pass on to join the ancestors.

God, who is distanced from humanity, is most likely not concerned about the tranquillity of people in the next life. However, one's children will always desire peace for their beloved, departed parents. That peace is assured as long as the children remember the ancestral parents through offering oblations of food and drink when the family gathers for meals and on other occasions as well. It includes reminiscing about the life of the departed. Children are the only assurance of tranquil life after death.

Since children are the only guarantee of immortality, having abundant progeny is urgent and necessary. To die without children is to be cut off forever. Many children provide for a more ample next life than do few children.

These beliefs affect practice significantly. Traditional values make marriage mandatory. Singleness is incomprehensible, for it is only through marriage and the creation of progeny that salvation is experienced. A childless marriage is a terrible tragedy and shame.

Practices have been developed to rectify the tragedy of infertility. Some practices are similar to that of biblical Abraham and Sarah. Abraham had a conjugal relationship with Sarah's maid, Hagar, because Sarah was barren. In this way Sarah hoped the reproach of her childlessness would be removed. Similar practices to cope with the tragedy of childlessness have been institutionalized in the African environment.

The desire for the salvation which children bring creates the spiritual environment in which polygyny thrives. Even though a household in which several wives are living together is prone to suffer from jealousies and tensions, the truly wise man who desires peace in the next life will often surrender the comparative tranquillity of monogamy in favor of the headaches of polygyny. He does this to have more children than one wife could bear.

Children are the true wealth of the person, the household, the community, the tribal society, and the nation. This theme runs deep in traditional spirituality.

Several years ago a church community in central Kenya asked a partner church community in Canada to send a family planning expert. In this farming region in central Kenya, there seemed to be no space for more people. So in compassion the Canadian church sent a family planning expert. The community prepared a goat feast as a welcome to this nurse who was the fulfillment of their prayers.

She was appalled when the chairperson at the welcome banquet proclaimed, "Praise God! Our prayers are answered. A family planning expert has arrived who will teach our women how they can have more children!"

The desire for children produces severe population pressures in some modern African societies, where available land, resources, or job opportunities are insufficient to support exploding population growth. Annual population increase in some African societies is well over 3 percent, which is unprecedented anywhere else. The coalescence of modern medical service, improved agriculture, and better diet with the traditional value placed on children creates the milieu for astonishing population growth. In many African societies, half the people are under sixteen years of age; the population in Africa will double in one generation.

Modern African participation in the global community raises new and urgent questions concerning the function of children. Modern realities invite a reassessment of the traditional worldview concerning the role of children in assuring peace in the next life. In an earlier era, when the land was ample, the traditional worldview concerning children blended comfortably with the realities of life.

However, in many communities that comfort has ended. This is especially true in urban centers where children are a severe economic burden. Views of the role of children in providing well-being for parents in the next life need to be modified as African societies are drawn into the web of global urban community.

Polygyny, which has always undergirded the perceived need for many children, is undergoing intense debate. Modern economics and urbanization force the debate. At another level, African women are also participants in global community. They share in the worldwide concern for women's rights. I have conversed with hundreds of African university women; I believe all of them considered polygyny demeaning to the integrity of the womanhood they sought.

In most traditional societies, female circumcision (surgical removal of the clitoris) is practiced. The blood spilt on the ground in male and female circumcision mystically bonds the adolescent youth to the life flow of the hierarchy.

For girls the rite also has observable practical implications. By reducing their capability for sexual pleasure, it is hoped that they will not seek sexual adventures. Sexual activity for women is for progeny, not pleasure. This view of sexuality lends itself to the institution of polygyny. The woman enters marriage for the supreme purpose of bearing children.

Many modern African women challenge these values. In the traditional society singleness is never an option. Some modern men and women prefer to forego marriage to focus on the professional or service opportunities available to them. They seek a worldview which affirms the option of singleness. And in marriage many women desire to be accepted as much more than a field for the planting and growing of children. They seek marriage relationships which honor their full

personhood and sexuality and which value them as equal companions with their husbands.

The Local and Global Village

Much of the African continent today is in the throes of transformation. The movement is from the largely small-scale societies and
language groups of only a century ago to modern dynamic involvement in national and global community. A perusal of any African
newspaper will reveal the presence of an intense conversation in African communities as their societies struggle with the divergences
and convergencies between traditional spirituality and modern realities. Conversation, challenge, confrontation, change, and conformity permeate the interaction between traditional African societies and
contemporary global community.

Womanhood, marriage, and children are not the only issues in Africa. Here are some of the most-pertinent issues:

- God and his relationship to society and all creation
- The relationship between natural laws as understood by mod-
  ern scientific investigation, and traditional understandings of
  the role of spirits and mana in affecting the material world
- Effective ways to cope with or end witchcraft
- Change and futurism in tension with the traditional focus on the
  past
- The use and abuse of power
- The function of the church and the Muslim *ummah* (community)
- Ethnicity, racism, peace and war, poverty and justice
- African tribal society, the modern nation-state, and the world
  community

The conversations concerning such issues reveal a quest for religious or ideological foundations which can equip the local community to participate in national and global community in a wholesome, mutually beneficial manner. African peoples seek a faith and
values which can more adequately equip them for participation in
global community, while at the same time affirming and deepening
the helpful values of their traditional spirituality.

This quest, which develops in the context of global community
awareness, seeks fresh spiritual or ideological foundations. Secularism or nihilism are not attractive options for most Africans. Where
can a fresh spirituality be found capable of nurturing the values

needed for authentic personhood in the modern global village?

Interaction with Islam and Christianity

A century ago, as African peoples south of the Sahara began the pilgrimage toward participation in global community, Islam provided a fairly attractive option as a universal faith system. The Muslim ummah invited participation in a universal community where all believers stood as equals before God. Islamic theology had many commonalities with African beliefs concerning God and spirits. Especially in Sahelian Africa and along the east coast, Islam has developed an enduring synthesis with African traditional values and spirituality.

However, as the twentieth century progressed, the movement toward Islam slowed considerably as Africans turned to Christianity. Of course, Christianity had serious liabilities as the religion of the Western colonizers. Nevertheless, even in the face of those liabilities, the contemporary movement of African people toward the Christian faith has created the most dramatic church growth experience in the history of Christianity. By the last quarter of the twentieth century, Africa had become a predominantly Christian continent.

Apparently the Christian faith has made good sense to Africans. Why? The little pulls and tugs in a society which nudge people toward a new faith system are always complex. We can never comprehend the process fully. Nevertheless, we will tentatively explore some of those apparent attractions. We will also consider several dimensions of the Islamicic interaction with African peoples.

Scriptures and Culture

The church provided a community of faith which *both* introduced the person to a worldwide family of believers *and* affirmed continued participation in the development of local culture. It is true that there are embarrassing accounts of critical attitudes some Christian missionaries had toward African culture. Nevertheless, it is also true that the church in Africa has taken deep root in local culture. Central to this development is the translation of the Bible into vernacular languages.

Muslims have been very cautious about translating the Qur'an into African or other languages. This is because the Qur'an is Arabic. Muslims accept the Qur'anic witness concerning itself—God revealed an Arabic Qur'an. When translated it ceases to be the word of God. Therefore, every faithful Muslim needs to attempt to learn Arabic to read and hear the word of God.

Admittedly, in recent years Muslims have published several translations of the Qur'an in other languages. However, in Islamic orthodoxy these publications are interpretations, not translations of the Qur'an.

On the other hand, the church has steadfastly worked toward the goal of publishing the whole Bible or portions of it in the eight hundred languages Africans speak. The church believes that the very nature of the Christian faith means the biblical accounts should be available to everyone in their mother tongue. This conviction has often propelled the church in mission to put tribal languages in writing, and then develop schools to teach mother-tongue reading to the society. Often the first book a newly literate person possesses is the Bible. Imagine the exuberance and surprise of a people receiving what they believe to be the written Word of God in their own language.

Just as Muslim and Christian approaches to translating scriptures differ, so also their evaluations of traditional culture in Africa are quite different. A genius of the Christian faith in the African continent has been its ability to embrace Africanness and diversity as authentic expressions of church in the global Christian family. The nature of the Christian gospel encourages the church to communicate faith in the idiom of the heart and the culture. This is why, across the continent, Christian African theologians invite the church in Africa to become more fully clothed in African culture.

The burden of Muslim theologians is different. They are concerned that Africanization will erode the right practice of Islam. For many Africans, Islamization is synonymous with Arabization. Although Muslims invite people into the global community of Islam, the parameters of that community are defined by Islamic law. This may be a bothersome constraint on a people proud of their African culture.

Children and Family

Neither Islam nor Christianity believe that children contribute to immortality. Nevertheless, Islam in Africa is not noted for encouraging restraint in the number of children. Both faiths teach that children are a blessing.

However, in folk Islam, distortions of the Islamic view of progeny do appear. This is because of a desire to be genealogically linked with the prophet Muhammad.

In an island community off the coast of Kenya, men blessed by a genealogical linkage with the prophet make themselves available to father a child or children in a family not linked with the prophet. A temporary marriage is arranged which will conclude in divorce after the child is born. In this way the bereft family will have the blessing of having a child who is the descendant of the prophet. In a mystical way, descendants of the prophet link the local family and community to the rich spirituality of the global Muslim community.

In relation to the function and role of family and womanhood, Islam in Africa struggles with modernity. This is surprising, especially since Islam seems to be in harmony with traditional African values in accepting polygyny. The Muslim community was a liberating movement for women during its origin in seventh-century Arabia. But in most traditional African societies, Islamization seems to contribute to a decline in the status of women and the eroding of marriage stability. African university women have frequently told me that they perceive Islam to be less than an ally in their quest for monogamy, marriage stability, and the dignity of womanhood.

In traditional society, divorce is rarely tolerated. This provides stability and a degree of security for women. Paradoxically Christianity, which allegedly champions the sacredness of marriage, seems to be an ally with Islam in introducing divorce as an acceptable option for African marriages. The Christian church is partly responsible for the instability of family in some African societies. Often the church, in its witness against polygyny, recommended divorce from all but the first wife when a man had more than one wife.

Nevertheless, strange as it may seem in light of the above comments, many African women see the Christian gospel as their ally in the quest for dignified womanhood and a faith that affirms enduring, monogamous marriage.

Local and Universal Community

Islam and the Christian faith also help build the foundations for modern intertribal states. This is because the Muslim community and the church are the most authentic transtribal communities in modern African nations. These communities are the glue which more than any other phenomena provide authentic intertribal community.

An example occurred in Kenya in 1967, when the assassination of a popular political leader pushed that nation near the abyss of intertribal civil war. At the height of the danger, tens of thousands of Christians from tribes all across Kenya met in the central highlands for a festival of reconciliation. They proclaimed to the nation that they would never fight against one another. That astonishing demonstration of intertribal community helped to ameliorate the tensions and salted the nation with a more reconciling spirit.

In contrast, I was intimately acquainted with a painful division in a church in Tanzania. The fracture was along a sociological fault line between rival tribes. In that case the Muslim president of the nation met with leaders of this church and demanded that they act like Christians and heal the breach. Why was the president so concerned? He recognized that if the church fractured because of tribal allegiance, the nation could not survive in peace. The health of the nation rested on the ability of the church to function as an authentic community comprising many tribes.

The same is true of the Muslim community. Transtribal political parties build on the good will and trust nurtured by the intertribal communities of Muslim and Christian faith.

Development and Change

Authentic participation in global community requires change. In this respect the Christian gospel has been effective as a change-agent. The most obvious changes have to do with customs and rites which, in the light of the Jesus story, seem to be dehumanizing. Once that story becomes available in the language of a people and those people begin to interact with the account of Jesus' life, fundamental changes begin to take place in that culture.

Of course, Islam also introduces change. It bends a culture toward conformity to the Muslim *shari'ah*. Marxism and other secularisms also foster change. Islam, Christianity, and Marxism have fomented significant change in African societies during the twentieth century.

An account from the Chagga of Tanzania about a century ago illustrates the change function of the Christian faith in African societies. When an early missionary among the Chagga returned to his homeland in Germany for a leave, he wrote a book about effective missiology. His thesis was that the gospel gets people ready for heaven but does not affect the culture.

While the missionary was away, the Chagga Christian leadership convened a conference to draw up a list of evils in their society from which Jesus would liberate them. Practices they decided to reject included witchcraft, alcoholism, female circumcision, polygyny, and lack of cleanliness around their homes. Later they arranged regular inspections of Christian homesteads to check on whether the home was tidied and clean! They also recognized that much in their culture was good. They believed Christianity would cleanse and vitalize their Chagga culture.[11]

Change in Africa has included a reorientation of worldview. Whereas the traditional society faced the past, modern global community invites movement toward the future. The Christian faith has helped encourage that change in perspective.

Jesus is a great surprise. Africans who believe in Christ perceive that the God the ancient African myths believed would never again become fully present among people has surprised humanity. Christian believers affirm that in Jesus an event has occurred which is more excellent than the golden age. That event is present now, yet also leads toward future fulfillment. For this reason the Jesus event breaks the binding allure of the past for African Christians.

Jesus promised to return in the future and to establish the kingdom of God forever. Fulfillment is in the future, not in the past. Suddenly themes like progress and development make sense and seem completely right aspirations. Cultural growth, change, and humanization become expectations, for Jesus has promised to establish his kingdom. Christians believe that in the church that kingdom is already beginning; it will be fulfilled in the future. That is an invitation for hope and transformation.

The biblical teaching that God is Creator and sustainer of the earth, that the spirits and powers are under authority of the risen Jesus, that humankind is commanded to care for and subdue the earth in a way which blesses both the human community and creation—these themes are incentives for responsible economic development. It is no wonder that, in tens of thousands of communities across sub-Saharan Africa, church and development are considered almost synonymous.

The revolution created by the gospel moves in many directions. While releasing a society from fixation on the past or undue concern for the power of evil spirits, it also frees from the compulsion to have children. If the risen Christ remembers and saves the dead, then children are not necessary for immortality. It is not surprising that these various themes in the gospel provide for millions of traditional small-village Africans a faith which supports constructive responses to the demands of participation in a modern global village.

Spirits and Powers

In traditional religion the spirits are considered benevolent, but sometimes mischievous or even evil. Witchcraft is a sellout to the evil powers. Traditional religion seeks ways to pacify the spirits and control the evil powers. The ritual and social devices used to control and pacify the spirits and other powers are complex and awesome.

Both Islam and Christianity have responded to the need not to be overwhelmed by the spirits or powers. These faiths have brought hope for the exorcism of evil spirits and freedom from the curse of witchcraft, because Muslims and Christians believe the spirits are under the authority of the Creator.

Islam provides various talismans and Qur'anic incantations to protect from or cajole these evil powers. The Muslim community brings with it expertise for dealing with the spirits. Attempts to exorcise spirits from possessed people have been a Muslim vocation in African societies. However, some literate opinion observes that the disease of possession seems to increase with the presence of these curative experts. That observation merits further research.[12] *J has the last word*

The church ministers in the confidence that the powers do not have the last word. The Christian gospel proclaims that the spirits and the powers have been brought into submission through the life, death, and resurrection of Jesus. Therefore, the church claims authority to command the powers, in Jesus' name.

Secularism and Marxism have been less helpful; such ideologies deny that supernatural spiritual powers exist. Yet few Africans believe that!

Forgiveness and Reconciliation

Recall that witchcraft has always been the great fear in African communities. The root of witchcraft is an inner unforgiving spirit, which leads eventually to bitterness and malevolence. Traditional society developed precious and beautiful proprieties which create an aura of person affirmation. These proprieties help to soften interpersonal relationships and provide opportunity to deal with hurt feelings so that healing may come. These winsome relational qualities of African society are enduring. They will never vanish.

Nevertheless, in spite of all the laudable efforts to keep relationships harmonious, witchcraft has always persisted, with sometimes heartbreaking damage. In this context the Christian gospel has been a special gift. Jesus suffered without bitterness, and while dying he forgave even the enemies who had crucified and were taunting him.

That depth of forgiveness is the death knell to witchcraft. African Christians believe and are grateful that the Spirit of Jesus is available to his disciples. Witchcraft cannot survive or develop in a person or community filled with the Spirit of Jesus which forgives enemies.

Shortly after the horrible Mau Mau war for independence in Kenya, Christians gathered for a large conference in central Kenya. At *Story on forg?*

that meeting a former Mau Mau freedom fighter arose and turned toward a widow seated near by.

Then he confessed, "I killed your husband."

With tears of sorrow and forgiveness, the widow cried out, "Because of Jesus I forgive you!"

That spirit is the death of witchcraft. That spirit of forgiveness and reconciliation helps to provide some of the glue which holds modern African nation states together. Many Africans wistfully hope that the day will come when the whole African continent and the entire global village will be permeated with more of that spirit.

For many years Africans wept for South Africa, where so many white Christians seemed oblivious to the inner meaning of the gospel. They ignored the best in African spirituality, which longed to be reconciled and live in peace and justice with their white neighbors. Yet millions of Africans lived in the confidence that someday the barriers of race would come down.

Why? Because God is!

The 1994 inauguration of Nelson Mandela as the first black president of South Africa was an astonishing vindication of that hope. The whole world was grateful; 150 nations were represented giving their blessing to the new South Africa.

Mandela had experienced twenty-seven years of prison because of his opposition to apartheid. He says he was in church every Sunday but one during those years. For many years he and multitudes of others had prayed for the healing of South Africa. At his inauguration the peoples of our earth were filled with joy and wonder to hear this man inviting forgiveness and reconciliation between the black and white races. The healing had begun.

Discovering the Global Village

This chapter has explored some of the remarkable ways modern Africans have drawn from the wells of their traditional spirituality as they have entered the universal global community. We have discovered precious resources in that traditional heritage which undergird an African approach to such modern global issues as human rights, family, children, war and peace, pluralism, or justice.

We have also found inadequacies in the traditional religious system when viewed from a global perspective. Some of these inadequacies are significant. This is especially so because the traditional faiths were honed for the needs of a tribal small-scale society. Consequently, as Africans began their pilgrimage of discovering the global village, they also commenced a faith journey, a quest for involvement in a universal faith community.

Islam and Christianity and to a lesser extent Marxism have provided spiritual or ideological homes for Africans searching for universal community. For this reason, any exploration of African traditional religions from the perspective of global community issues must include a description of how these universal faiths or ideologies have provided attractive alternatives to traditional faith. The attraction is especially strong because there are so many areas of agreement and complementarity between African religions and the universal monotheistic faiths.

In their respective ways, Islam and Christianity have provided alternative faiths and communities which have facilitated African discovery of and participation in the global village. African Muslim and Christian communities have nurtured enduring qualities in traditional African spirituality; the African heritage has also enriched both Muslim and Christian peoplehood.

As we go from the twentieth century into the twenty-first, 600 million people consider themselves either African Muslims or African Christians. These are people who celebrate both the richness of their African heritage and the exuberance of participation in universal faith communities as they discover their place and make their contribution in the global village.

Reflection

1. What enduring values in African culture are especially helpful in enabling these traditional small-scale societies to participate in global community?

2. Consider the positive and negative aspects of the hierarchy in traditional African society. In what ways is the reality of the hierarchy felt in modern national societies?

3. In light of modern global realities, what are some functional and dysfunctional aspects of the traditional African perspective on progeny? On polygyny?

4. Reflect on witchcraft and its negative implications for healthy involvement in modern community.

5. Discern the respective ways Islam and Christianity contribute to the African quest for involvement in global community.

6. In what ways does Jesus affect the traditional perspective on the past, the present, and the future?

4

All Is Brahman

Hinduism

Y OU are god!" the Hindu priest exclaimed.
The swami in the Hindu temple near the Nairobi, Kenya, bus station was explaining the meaning behind the various images and creatures in the temple—the turtle, the cow, the monkeys, the phallic and female images, Rama and Krishna, and even the doves flitting around on the floor, rafters, and icons.

"Everything in the universe is divine. Even you are god. Even your sexual organs. So are the animals, also the doves. For that reason we worship everything as god."

Then in an extraordinary burst of enthusiasm, the swami began pointing in turn at one object or person at a time exclaiming in disjointed syntax, "This god. This god. This god. This god. This god. This god. Everything only god, god, god, god, god, god, god, god, god, god, god, god, god!"

This gentle Hindu priest was accurately interpreting the most basic philosophical and spiritual foundation of ancient Hinduism, the belief that all phenomena are Brahman.

That Art Thou: Brahman

"Tat tvam asi (that art thou),"[1] exclaimed an ancient Hindu when instructing his student.

Any phenomenon which you perceive as being "that" is in reality perfectly one with "thou." I and my typewriter are in essence and quality one, for both I and my typewriter are expressions of the one universal divinity which is Brahman. The gods, nature, and humanity are a divine unity. Yet *"Tat tvam asi"* must be seen alongside *"Neti, neti* (not that, not that)," meaning that no one phenomenon is fully identifiable with all that is Brahman.

Recall in the previous chapter that some expressions of African traditional religion flirt with the idea that divinity and natural phenomena experience a oneness. This was described as an ontocratic worldview. We observed that nuances of the ontocratic perception have been present within all primal religions. Evidence for this is that some forms of magic are universally practiced in primal religions, and nature spirits are revered. In Africa and elsewhere, nature spirits sometimes take on identity as gods. Nature and the divinities participate in a unity.

The Hindus also consider nature and divinity as a unity. However, Hinduism takes the ontocratic worldview further than do most primal cultures. In classical Hinduism nature and divinity are identical; there is no distinction between creator and creation. This is pantheism, the complete fusion of divinity and nature. Hindu Brahman philosophy is grounded in the conviction that all phenomena are divine, yet no one phenomenon is fully Brahman. *Tat tvam asi. Neti, neti.*

What Is Hinduism?

The worldview that all phenomena and divinity are one is the bedrock for Hindu participation in the global village. All Hindus believe that all is Brahman. That conviction informs the Hindu response to such global issues as economic development, pluralism, human rights, peace and war, community, the quest for truth, cultural change, ecology, or justice. This chapter explores Hindu engagement with these modern concerns.

In our exploration we shall discover the extraordinarily intense engagement Hindus, Muslims, and Christians experience in their relationships with one another in the Indian subcontinent. Although Christians comprise only 3 percent of the people of India and Muslims about 9 percent, the nature of the encounter between the ashram, the mosque, and the church in India is critically important for the health of India and the well-being of the global village. Over the centuries the incompatibilities between Brahman and the God of Abraham have sown seeds of sorrow in many regions of India.

Hinduism is an amorphous kaleidoscope of beliefs and practices. How does one grasp the complexities of a religion in which some sages claim at least 330 million gods? How does one probe the heart of a faith which abounds with ancient and often apparently contradictory scriptures?

The most authentic way to grasp the essence of Hinduism is to ask this question: What are core Hindu beliefs?

1. Hindus everywhere participate in the caste system.
2. Hindus are acquainted with the law of *karma* or retribution.
3. Hindus believe that universal divine soul is the reality within all phenomena.[2]

We shall describe these three beliefs and practices briefly, with special awareness of the way they contribute to modern Hindu involvement in both the local and the global village. We shall especially explore specific modern global issues to which Hinduism relates with poignancy.

Nevertheless, we explore Hindu beliefs, acknowledging that to do so represents a touch of temerity. Hindu scholars will likely question the wisdom of attempting to define any core Hindu beliefs and practices. Commenting on the three dimensions of Hinduism mentioned above, Dr. K. B. Rokaya of Nepal observes,

> I myself have never come across a definite or specific definition of Hinduism by Hindus themselves. In other words, what does a person need to be or do in order to be a Hindu? From the many definitions given by Hindus themselves, they seem to indicate that a person does not need to be or to do any specific thing in order to be a Hindu. They seem to suggest that Hinduism is so broad, so wide, so deep, and so high that anyone can be accommodated within Hinduism.[3]

Hindu scriptures are voluminous, diverse, and complex. It is not necessary to detail these scriptures, for a description would be included in any elementary text on Hinduism. We shall be eclectic in our selection of scripture, choosing special mention for the Bhagavad-Gita and Upanishads. These scriptures have special attraction for many outside Hindu culture, and they do significantly nurture the enduring worldview of Hinduism.

Caste and Pluralism

Caste is the universal experience of all Hindus. It is likely that the early beginning of caste was about thirty five hundred years ago, which is about the same time Moses was leading the Hebrews out of slavery in Egypt. An invasion created a felt need for caste.

About 1500 B.C. nomadic, Aryan invaders swarmed across the mountains on the northern periphery of the Indian subcontinent. They began the long process of military and political subjugation of the peasant agriculturalists settled in the river valleys of India. These indigenous agriculturalists, known as the Dravidians, had developed an advanced civilization which the Aryans absorbed and benefited from even while they were in the process of extending their power throughout the region.

The newly arrived Aryans were white. The indigenous Dravidians were dark brown. Intermarriage commenced. The conquerors began to lose their color as the children of mixed marriages were various hues of brown. To preserve racial purity, regulations were developed to prohibit marriages between Aryans and Dravidians. In time the rules also prohibited marriages between those of various hues of color.

To guard against possible intermarriage, each group began to develop their respective social and cultural distinctives. Intergroup proprieties developed which regulated the manner in which these various social clusters could relate to one another. Within five centuries of the Aryan invasions, the caste system was well developed.

The castes were known as *varnas*, referring to genus or color. Aryans occupied the upper castes and Dravidians the lower ones. Four principal castes developed, ranked in this order: (1) *Brahman*, the priestly caste; (2) *Kshatriya*, the warrior and ruler caste; (3) *Vaisya*, the merchant and farmer caste; (4) *Sudra*, the servant caste. The outcastes might be considered as a fifth major caste. The caste system eventually became a wall prohibiting cross-cultural marriages.

Multitudes of subcastes and sub-subcastes also developed. These form the *jati* system. Today there are some fifty thousand groupings, based on considerations such as occupation or ancient clan taboos about clean and unclean groups. Even trade guilds became part of the caste system. The sub-subcastes cluster within the thirty-six overarching subcastes and the four major castes or varnas.

Within a thousand years of the Aryan invasions, written codes regulating caste practices were developing. These were collected in the Code of Manu about the third century B.C. The caste system meant that everyone had his place. However, any children born through a liaison between persons of different castes were outcastes with no place in the system.

Hindu scriptures support the conviction that caste is a sacral social system, for its origins are divine. The four varnas are first mentioned in the Rig Veda, which describes the castes coming forth from the body of the divine primal giant, Purusha. The Brahmans came from his mouth, the Kshatriyas from his arms, the Vaisyas his thighs, and the Sudras his feet.

The social order as expressed in caste is ontocratic. Divinity and caste society are a unity. Therefore, one cannot critique caste. It is divine. The Nepali scholar Dor Bahadur Bista refers to the system as "fatalistic hierarchy."[4] He views the fatalism as an obstacle to cultural and economic development.

In India maintaining caste purity became a fixation. The upper caste Brahmans marshaled religion and philosophy expressed in beliefs such as karma and reincarnation to support and interpret the system. Caste became the core value of the Hindu worldview. Caste laws reinforced the commitment to caste integrity. Dor observes the same incipient development within Nepal, India's northern neighbor.

Social institutions developed to guarantee caste purity. Parents betrothed their children for marriage before the youngsters could think about marrying someone outside their caste. Girls could be given in marriage before they were mature. Parents often viewed marriage as a contract on behalf of their children, a contract which would protect their children from the horrible possibility of marrying outside of their caste, thereby becoming outcastes. In modern times Indian governments have worked persistently to outlaw these excesses. Child marriages are prohibited.

There seem to be similarities between the emergence of caste in India and the development of apartheid in South Africa. Over three centuries ago, an Aryan nation began immigrating to southern Africa. These were the Dutch, who were one of many Aryan groups, according to nineteenth-century linguists. Intermarriage developed between them and the dark-complexioned indigenous peoples. To preserve the status and purity of their race, the European immigrants imposed regulations controlling relationships between South African societies.

Consequently, in modern times four main classes became recognized by law in the South African apartheid system—white, Indian, colored, and black. Religion was marshaled to support apartheid, even though the global Christian community decried these beliefs and practices as a distortion of biblical faith. In the early 1990s, the government of South Africa began the process of dismantling the apartheid system. Participation in the modern global village had exposed apartheid as an unworkable system.

The modern development of apartheid in South Africa when Aryan and black peoples met may have parallels to the dynamics which created varna in India over 3,000 years ago. In both settings religion was molded and used to support the racial purity of an immigrant community. However, the class systems in both South Africa and India have been changing because of the realities of modern global community, especially the reality of horizontal and vertical mobility. For example, universal secular education is a powerful force for the equalization of peoples.

Caste in India is astonishingly elastic in its ability to absorb new communities—but always within the caste system. Caste is the manner in which Hinduism most comfortably deals with pluralism. The worldview seeks to place each new community into the category of another caste.

Immigrant communities such as the Buddhists of Tibet or new religious movements such as the Muslim Ahmadiyya all have a place in Hinduism as subcaste communities (*jati*). Each functions within its own ethos; the new caste is expected to adhere to the proprieties in relationships with other castes. Hindu pluralism protects the ethos of each group while discouraging the development of a cultural melting pot in India.

Caste is both a frustration and challenge to the Muslim ummah (community) and the Christian church, because both religions resist the caste system as being contrary to their understandings of the nature of human sisterhood and brotherhood. Over two millennia ago, caste also frustrated and finally contributed to the smothering of the Buddhist *sangha* (monastic community) in India. The instinct of Hinduism is to incorporate the ummah, the church, or the sangha as new castes within the Hindu system. That kind of incorporation is contrary to the missionary vocation of these three communities.

The soul of both the Christian and Muslim faith requires invitation to people to believe in the one transcendent Creator God and become participants in their respective faith communities. Both the Muslims and Christians believe that the ummah and the church must transcend caste; they are intercaste, or noncaste communities. The same is true of the Buddhist sangha. The essence of these communities requires that they receive people from all castes.

However, once Hinduism has domesticated a missionary community such as Buddhism by defining that community as a caste, then further movement of new recruits into the community is impossible. If the Buddhist sangha, the Christian church, or the Muslim ummah become castes, then movement from other castes into any of these communities cannot happen. Caste is caste. It is impossible to move from one caste into another.

The sociological and religious inclination of Hinduism is a roadblock to the mission of Buddhist, Muslim, or Christian commitments. Furthermore the ummah, the church, or the sangha as castes would cease to be bridges between the castes. These intercaste missionary communities function as bridge builders among the castes by including people from all strata of society.

Karma and Relativism

Caste in India is formed and supported by the Hindu religious and philosophical system. A core concept supporting caste is the philosophy of karma that, with the belief in reincarnation, provides a worldview in which caste can thrive. The law of karma is one of the three universals among all Hindus. Reincarnation and karma are like different sides of the same coin. Reincarnation is the conviction that after death a person's soul is reborn into another being.

The *atman*, not the person, is reincarnated. At each reincarnation, the atman will reside in a body and status of life which is an appropriate compensation for the actions of the atman in the previous existence. The cycle of reincarnations includes the animals. Thus in the next life the atman of a person whose karma was not so good could reappear in the form of an animal such as a jackal or lizard. Likewise the atman of a good animal could be reincarnated in a human being.

This notion that the animals are included with humans in the reincarnation cycle provides Hinduism with considerable respect for animal life. There are strong inhibitions against killing animals; the Jains in India point out that the gnats in one's yard just might be the reincarnation of an ancestor. Many Hindus are vegetarians because of their reincarnation convictions. In this context, nutritionists develop protein-adequate diets that do not depend on meat. Nutritional pragmatism must be based on the sensitivities toward animals that a reincarnation worldview nurtures.

The deeds or karma of a person in this life determine the body, condition, and caste in which the person will be reincarnated in the next life. One's present caste has been determined through one's karma in a previous life. Movement from a lower to a higher caste can only happen after death through reincarnation into a higher caste. The person's actions form the soul into the shape which determines the status and body into which it will be reincarnated in the next life.

According to the Upanishads, karma is a law of nature that cannot be bent or altered in any way. The Christian belief in forgiveness of sin or the Mahayana Buddhist teaching that one can receive merit from others, seems to Hindu sages to be a disastrous abrogation of moral law. The sages have always taught that there is a direct relationship between the deed and the consequence. Forgiveness would break the cause and effect relationship between deed and destiny, between the act and its consequence.

Karma is like the arm swinging the tennis racket, and the ball is like the soul. Once the ball is hit, there is no altering its course. A person's present life is the arm and racket swinging at the ball. That is karma. Forgiveness cannot alter the consequences of a person's actions.

Nevertheless, within popular Hinduism, ways are found to soften the cause-and-effect consequences of karma. Forgiveness is a theme within the Bhagavad-Gita. Religious rituals prevail as people seek merit. Folk Hindu practices convey the belief that the virtue of one person can be transferred to another.

Good karma is obeying the laws of one's own caste. Thus the way to improve one's lot is not to chafe at one's circumstances but to subscribe to the expectations of one's caste. Thereby is gained good karma to propel the soul into a better state in the next life. This belief system ingeniously supports community stability and well-defined social relationships, even in a pluralistic society. Each group has its own mores, and the people in each group are expected to obey the respective mores of their own group; that is *dharma*, their code for conduct.

The Hindu fusion of caste and karma provides a firm philosophical foundation for communal moral relativism, but not personal relativism. Each society should function in the parameters of its own moral code; that is good karma.

The epic of Arjuna described in the Bhagavad-Gita is a brilliant defense of Hindu communal moral relativism. Although Hindus believe that the Bhagavad-Gita is not *sruti* (divinely revealed scripture), they do accept it as *smriti* (the teaching of a divine incarnation). It is short, a small booklet of about sixty pages. This smriti, probably written about the second or third century A. D., was Mahatma Gandhi's favorite scripture. However, he drew from other spiritual wells for guidance in his commitment to nonviolence.

The Bhagavad-Gita is a response to the moral crisis of war. Two clans, related through kinship ties, are entering battle on the plains of Kuruksetra. Arjuna with his charioteer, Krishna, is leading the Pandava clan into battle against their kinsmen. Arjuna is distraught at the prospect of killing his own kinspersons in battle. The moral ambiguities of warfare oppress him. It is then that he discerns that Krishna is an *avatar* (incarnation) of the god Vishnu, who is the divinity who preserves life and the moral order. The Bhagavad-Gita (Song of God) is a poetic narrative of the conversation between Arjuna and Krishna as the battle is about to commence.

As Arjuna and his charioteer entered the war zone, Arjuna recognized people on both sides of battle: friends, grandfathers, cousins, brothers, fathers, uncles, teachers, and acquaintances. In anguish he turned to Krishna for counsel:

> Krishna, Krishna
> Now as I look on
> These my kinsmen
> Arrayed for battle,
> My limbs are weakened,
> My mouth is parching,
> My body trembles,
> My hair stands upright,
> My skin seems burning,
> The bow Gandiva
> Slips from my hand,
> My brain is whirling
> Round and round,
> I can stand no longer:
> Krishna, I see such
> Omens of evil
> What can we hope from
> This killing of kinsmen?
> . . . Evil they may be,
> Worst of the wicked,
> Yet if we kill them
> Our sin is greater.
> How could we dare spill
> The blood that unites us?
> Where is joy in
> This killing of kinsmen?
> . . . What is this crime
> I am planning, O Krishna?
> Murder most hateful,
> Murder of brothers!

Am I indeed
So greedy for greatness?[5]

Krishna replied with the wisdom of the divine Vishnu:

In the beginning
The Lord of beings
Created all men
To each his duty.
"Do this," He said,
"And you shall prosper.
Duty well done
Fulfills desire. . . .
If a man plays no part
In the acts thus appointed
His living is evil
His joy is in lusting.
Know this, O Prince:
His life is for nothing.[6]

Krishna goes on to explain the importance of duty. Duty is one's assigned work which contributes to the wholesome functioning of society. If a people cease to perform their assigned duty, chaos would en-
sue, caste purity would be defiled, and society would be destroyed.
Krishna continues,

The ignorant work
For the fruit of their action;
The wise must work also
Without desire
Pointing man's feet
To the path of his duty.[7]

On the battlefield of Kuruksetra, fighting was the path of right
duty. Deviation from the battle would be an abrogation of the duty
which Arjuna's caste regulations required. Not all castes are kshatriya, or warrior castes. Yet each caste has its duty which is divinely
defined, and each person needs to subscribe to that duty. For Arjuna
in this situation, battle was his required duty, even if in fulfilling that
duty he slew his kinsfolk.
Although Hindu communal moral relativism provides clear pa-

Problems of the caste system ↓

rameters of conduct for each caste, it is difficult to discern a basis upon which to critique those caste practices, which are inimical to human well-being. On what basis can the government outlaw child marriages when caste practices condone such marriages? What about the once-universal practice of the widow committing suicide by throwing herself on the burning funeral pyre of her dead husband? What about the practice of the bride's parents paying a dowry to the groom, especially exorbitant dowries that can drive a family into debt and impoverishment?

What about human rights for some 200 million outcastes? On what basis can society or individuals muster the authority to critique, evaluate, and transform caste practices? Does the government have authority and power to impose a morality that caste mores do not support?

The Bhagavad-Gita is concerned about righteousness and justice. Yet these concerns are expressed in the context of caste law. Nevertheless, in modern times Hindu reformers seeking a more just society have sometimes attempted to build upon the Gita's concern for justice by expanding those themes beyond the confining parameters of caste law. This was Mahatma Gandhi's vocation.

Yet like Gandhi, in their quest for justice, modern reformers such as Swami Anand Thirth are often significantly nurtured by non-Hindu models of righteousness, such as Jesus of Nazareth. There is no inconsistency in this. Hinduism is open to all truth from all sources.

Other youth reform movements simply ignore the scriptures of any religion, drawing rather on the inspiration of the Siddhas of a millennium and a half ago who defied religious institutions in their challenge to the domination of India by the Brahman caste.[8] A quest for a more just society among the *dalit* (200 million outcastes) shatters ancient social institutions. It is astonishing that some of the pressure for reform is inspired by dalit women, who have been described as "the dust of the dust!"[9]

The Hindu worldview provides a religious and philosophical foundation for communal moral relativism. Yet Hinduism is hard put to discern an authentic basis for reforming caste mores. Actually, most societies in the global community agree with the Hindu perspectives that moral action is relative to one's particular society. Moral relativism is a fairly common conviction of ancient as well as modern societies. Like the Hindu castes, most communities resist critique of their traditional mores.

In *The Closing of the American Mind,* U.S. philosophy professor Allan Bloom describes the modern experience of moral relativism:

> There is one thing a professor can be absolutely certain of: almost every student entering the university believes, or says he believes, that truth is relative. If this belief is put to the test, one can count on the students' reaction: they will be uncomprehending. . . . The relativity of truth is not a theoretical insight but a moral postulate, the condition of a free society, or so they see it. . . . That it is a moral issue for students is revealed by the character of their response when challenged—a combination of disbelief and indignation: "Are you an absolutist?"[10]

Hinduism would provide these students with a philosophical and religious perspective which would nurture any inclination toward communal moral relativism. However, Hinduism would oppose any embracing of individual moral relativism. The individualism of Bloom's American students would have no truck with the communal commitments of the Hinduism of the Bhagavad-Gita. Yet they would embrace the basic moral relativism which Krishna expounded.

Of course, there are alternative perspectives to be found in the global village. Biblical and Islamic faiths, when compared with Hinduism, present dramatic alternatives. On the one hand, these monotheistic prophetic faiths insist that there is one God, one humanity, and one morality. On the other hand, Hindu philosophy and spirituality embraces group relativism. The prophetic missionary religions are in acute tension with Hindu relativism.

Hinduism dogmatically insists that all beliefs and practices are equally true if the group accepts them as true. In recent years Hindu philosophies are received with favor by many Western people who believe that relativism is the best way to cope with modern pluralism.

Brahman and Maya

The Hindu caste system is sustained by the belief in karma and reincarnation; it is also nurtured by the belief that all apparent phenomena are Brahman. Recall that caste is the first belief we have explored; karma is the second. Now we explore a third dimension of Hinduism, the conviction that all reality is Brahman. The Bhagavad-Gita is permeated with the worldview that the divine soul which is Brahman is the essence of all phenomena and the only reality.

Krishna explains to Arjuna as he prepares for battle,

> Can such acts bring evil?
> Brahman is the ritual,
> Brahman is the offering,
> Brahman is he who offers
> To the fire that is Brahman,
> If a man sees Brahman
> In every action,
> He will find Brahman.[11]

"In every action, he will find Brahman!" There is therefore no qualitative, essential difference between the acts of killing or not killing one's kinsfolk if the law of caste places a person in battle with one's kinsfolk. Brahman is equally in every action. Krishna further expounds that since all phenomena are Brahman, apparent reality is an illusion. Hindu sages refer to apparent reality as *maya*. Any apparent phenomenon is an illusion; only the universal Brahman is reality.

Thus death is an illusion. Warfare is justified if the norms of one's society propel a person into battle. Death releases the divine atman (soul) which is entrapped in the illusion of individual personhood. This release is a mercy, for it will hasten the process of reincarnation or perchance may free the atman for absorption into the universal Brahman. In that case, the sad cycle of reincarnations will be broken for the atman will cease existence as differentiated individuality; it will be absorbed in the universal sea of life.

What do Brahman, atman, and maya have to do with caste or with one's personal life situation? There are several implications.

First, since all is Brahman, the caste system is also divinity. There is no word of divine authority or critique from outside the system. Krishna assures Arjuna that a function of the god Vishnu is to help people not neglect or forget the system.

Second, since the goal of the atman (individual soul) is to cease the meaningless cycle of rebirth through absorption into Brahman, then one should faithfully practice the dharma (way) of one's caste. In that way one develops good karma which will help to propel one off the cycle of rebirth into personal oblivion through absorption into the universal Brahman.

Third, since all apparent phenomena are maya, the inconveniences and tragedies of life are really an illusion.

These three perceptions affect approaches and attitudes toward human development. It is therefore not surprising that Hinduism has never developed history writing as a serious enterprise. Why should human enterprise which is meaningless be recorded? Rather the energies of the Indian subcontinent were turned toward contemplation, which has been highly developed in the disciplines of yoga.

During our visit to a Hindu ashram, the swami impressed us with his profound spirituality. He reverently explained some Hindu insights on Brahman and maya. Then there was a time for dialogue.

"It seems to me," I ventured, "that *vedanta* philosophy would not encourage the development of hospitals."

"Of course not!" he exclaimed.

The agitation and energy with which this pious swami responded surprised me. "You Christians are far too interested in the illusive material world. You build hospitals to prolong life, which in turn creates overpopulation. Your emphasis on the material world creates tragic problems for humanity. By focusing on elusive material phenomenon, you detract from the essence of reality which is that all is Brahman."

The pious swami had no apology for his conviction that a brahmanistic worldview does not encourage economic development. In *Fatalism and Development: Nepal's Struggle for Modernization*, Nepali anthropologist Dor B. Bista describes the encroaching caste and Hindu worldview on Nepali society. He observes,

> The most important effect of this has been the absolute belief in fatalism; that one has no personal control over one's life circumstances, which are determined through a divine or external agency. This deep belief in fatalism has had a devastating effect on the work ethic and achievement motivation, and through these on the Nepali response to development. It has consequences on the sense of time, and in particular such things as the concept of planning, orientation to the future, sense of causality, human dignity and punctuality.[12]

The Hindu worldview insists that personal individuality is a tragic accident, an illusion to be overcome. All history and creation is a sad accident. Just as the person's atman is affixed to the cycle of birth and rebirth, so all history and natural existence is involved in a great cycle of meaninglessness called *kalpa*. Each kalpa is millions of years long.

These great cycles of existence and non-existence involve four respective eons of time, each with distinctive characteristics—creation, preservation, destruction, and the oblivion when all phenomena are at rest in Brahman. Then again tragically, accidentally, inexplicably, a new creation and history emerges from Brahman. Each stage in the cycle is divine, with Brahman for creation, Vishnu for preservation, and Shiva for the destructive phase. Each person is a manifestation of the cycle, with the reincarnations of each soul being a mini-cycle within the great wheel of kalpa.

Hindu yoga is intended to help the person escape from this wheel of individual existence which is tragedy. The Bhagavad-Gita encourages yoga as an effective approach to the salvation which is escape from individual existence. The goal of Hindu yoga is to assist the individual in the process of becoming absorbed into the universal Brahman. The intention is to help the person lose the false sense of individual personhood. Cessation of personal existence should be the goal of the person.

Several years ago one of my university classes met with Hindus who described the disciplines of yoga as the path to tranquillity. Suddenly, in the midst of the lecture, the group leader exclaimed, "Life is hell, isn't it!" In vedanta philosophy individual existence is tragedy, for Brahman is the essence of reality.

Paths to Salvation

The Bhagavad-Gita supports the three dimensions of Hinduism we have reviewed: caste, karma, Brahman. Within the context of these three dimensional faces of Hinduism, the Gita also describes three paths of salvation. Occasionally we have alluded to one or another of these paths for salvation in our exploration; a brief summary description will be helpful.

Salvation (moksha) is escape from the tragic cycles of rebirth. The three paths leading to salvation are pyramidal.

First, the path of devotion to the deity of one's choice (bhakti) is at the base of the pyramid. This path is achievable for everyone. Amazingly the Gita alludes to the forgiveness one can receive from the chosen deity. We have already found that such notions run counter to alternative Hindu notions concerning the unbending laws of karma. It is not surprising that hundreds of millions of Hindus welcome the Gita's astonishing invitation to seek forgiveness from a god.

Second, there is the path of obedience to the laws of one's caste (dharma); that is the way a person acquires the good karma necessary for salvation. Within the Bhagavad-Gita, dharma is perceived as good action, the sort of action which strives for righteousness and justice. However, the Gita perceives of that righteous action within the context of one's own caste laws. Yet some Hindu reformers, such as Gandhi, expanded the invitation to righteousness within the Gita. We have noted that they used the Gita as an inspiration for a struggle for justice within Indian society.

Third, the path of yoga is at the peak of the pyramid leading toward salvation. Yoga is the discipline necessary to experience enlightenment (mukti), that is, to realize that the person is one with the universal Brahman.

The Bhagavad-Gita invites Hindus to seek salvation through one or all three of these paths: bhakti, karma, yoga. The Hindu quest for salvation happens within the three-dimensional worldview which embraces all Hindus—caste, karma, Brahman. We have observed ways these three beliefs inform Hindu responses to global issues such as pluralism, ethics, and the visible world.

Hindus Living Within the Global Village

With these three core Hindu themes in mind, we explore ways Hinduism affects the well-being of the person, the local community, and engagement within the global village. We give special attention to (1) the person and the life stages, (2) right conduct and truth, (3) history and development, (4) justice and peace, (5) secular society, and (6) nonviolence.

The Person and Destiny

First, we explore further the implications of the Brahman worldview for the person. The oldest and most influential Hindu scriptures are the Vedas, hence the term Vedanta philosophy. *Veda* means knowledge. The central theme of the Vedas is salvation through knowledge.

Among these ancient Vedic scriptures, the Upanishads, written about 500 B.C., have been especially significant as interpreters and communicators of Brahmanism and true knowledge. These scriptures have been very influential in communicating Vedanta philosophy and spirituality century after century for over 25 hundred years. *Upanishad* means "sitting near devotedly." They portray the student and teacher conversing concerning the meaning of life.[13]

One of the Upanishads describes a conversation between Svetaketu and his father, Uddalaka. When Svetaketu was twelve years old, his father sent him away for twelve years to learn the knowledge of the Vedas. Thereafter Svetaketu returned puffed up by his knowledge. The wise father invited his son into conversation concerning the essence of the self.

Uddalaka describes the bees who get nectar from many flowers, yet all that sweetness is combined into one honey. The rivers flow from many directions, yet when they enter the sea all their waters from millions of raindrops are merged into the universal oneness of the ocean. He takes salt and pours it into water in a container until all the saltiness is dispersed throughout the liquid.

"*Tat tvam asi* (that art thou)!" exclaims Uddalaka at the conclusion of each parable. There is no difference in essence between the self and the universal Brahman; the intention of apparent personal existence is to be absorbed into the universal sea of Brahman.

This poem from the Upanishads describes Uddalaka's worldview and that of Hinduism.

G in
e'thing

O Brahman Supreme!
Formless art thou, and yet
(Through the reason none knows)
Thou bringest forth many forms;
Thou bringest them forth, and then
Withdrawest them to thyself,
Fill us with thoughts of thee!

Thou art the fire,
Thou art the sun,
Thou art the air,
Thou art the moon,
Thou art the starry firmament,
Thou art Brahman Supreme:
Thou art the waters—
The creator of all!

Thou art woman, thou art man,
Thou art the youth, thou art the maiden,
Thou art the old man tottering with his staff;
Thou the faces everywhere. . . .

Maya is thy divine consort—
Wedded to thee.
Thou art her master, her ruler.
Red, white, and black is she,

Each color a *guna*.
Many are her children—
The rivers, the mountains,
Flower, stone, and tree,
Beast, bird, and man—
In every way like herself.
Thou, spirit in flesh,
Forgetting what thou art,
Unitest with Maya—
But only for a season.
Parting from her at last,
Thou regainest thyself.[14]

These scriptures show that the Upanishads have a different view of a person's place in the universe than do faith systems such as African traditional religion, Judaism, Islam, or Christianity.

In African religions the person is significant. Africans have relied on devices such as progeny or sacrifice, hoping that these may provide a peaceful existence for the person after death.

In biblical faith the entire person—body, soul, mind, spirit, personality, life—is created in God's own image. Christians believe that the bodily resurrection of Christ is the guarantee by God that at the conclusion of history there will be a universal bodily resurrection of the whole person.

Islam also believes the person is eternal. In Islam the significance and eternal integrity of the person comes into sharp focus.

As Hinduism and Christian or Islamic faith seem to represent opposite poles in relationship to moral relativism versus moral universalism, so these different worldviews also represent opposite perceptions concerning the nature and the significance of the person.

This contrast is especially true between Hinduism and biblical faith. In Hinduism identity with and absorption into the impersonal universal Brahman is the ultimate goal of human existence. In the Bible a right and joyous relationship with the Creator and with others is the ultimate purpose of human existence. One Christian creed says that we are created to glorify God and enjoy him forever. The contrasts are startling. In the range of world religions, views on personhood are nuanced somewhere on the continuum between the perceptions represented in these two different understandings.

These perspectives significantly inform the manner in which the respective faith communities, society, and the nation relate to the person. For example, in many Indian communities, church and hospital seem to belong together. The church develops hospitals because it believes that the whole person is eternally significant, for God who created the person in his own image is eternal and personal. Therefore, the goal of the church is to be a community of people becoming full and complete persons now and eternally.

Hindu ashram communities are characterized as meditation centers. This is an expected response of a cluster of people who believe that peace can only come through developing attitudes and disciplines which enable the person to cease individual existence by becoming absorbed into the universal. The goal of the ashram is to help the person cease existing as an individual by providing opportunities and instruction for developing meditation skills. These skills are known as yoga, and Hindus believe they open the door for absorption into the universal.

When a person experiences the truth of *tat tvam asi* (that art thou), she has acquired moksha (liberation). Moksha is the realization that the person is fully one with the universal, that the atman of personhood is the Brahman of universality. This experience of moksha releases the person for absorption into the universal Brahman. Such release means that person may now cease the cycles of reincarnation by being absorbed into the universal Brahman like the streams of water from the land are absorbed into the ocean.

The ideal Hindu life stages are intended to facilitate mukti which can lead to moksha. The four ideal stages are student, householder, ascetic, and then *sannyasi*. The student learns the laws of caste and Vedanta wisdom. The householder raises a family. When gray hair appears or the first grandchildren are born, the householder may leave home to become an ascetic, seeking mukti. Once this enlightenment is acquired, the ascetic enters the final stage of life, that of sannyasi, a wandering person awaiting the release (moksha) from existence.

The ideal life stages invite the devotee to escape from responsibilities in the phenomenal world, which is maya (a distracting illusion). However, the negative implications for family life and community development is significant. Indian society is secularizing; the ideal life stages are not the ideal upheld by the modern mainstream of Hindu culture.

In the book *The Death of a Guru,* a Hindu lad describes the day his father achieved mukti. From that day on, he could never converse with his father again, for the householder lived in a state of perennial trance. This trance was evidence that the father was on the verge of moksha. Although his relational involvement with the family was nil, he was becoming fully identified with the universal soul.[15]

Serious interaction with the phenomenal world, including one's family, is a distraction which a person who is in quest of release from the cycles of rebirth must avoid. This idealization of escape from community relationships is why modern Hindus are becoming skeptical about such inclinations to disengage from earthly responsibilities.

Nevertheless, Hindus have informed me with conviction that the Himalaya mountains are the ideal location to acquire mukti, for these mountains radiate cosmic emanations. These mountains are indeed the favorite haunts of the ascetic in quest of mukti. The New Age movement which has been influencing Western societies draws on the perceptions of these Hindu Himalayan ascetics. The so-called cosmic convergencies of New Age thinking seems similar to the Hindu notions of divine emanations.

There is a difference, however. The Hindu ascetics invest years absorbing the emanations. Western New Age thinkers, for the most part, seek instant convergencies. Yet the New Age call for right thought focused on universal mind is a Western expression of Hindu philosophy. Absorption into the universal is the essence of human existence, rather than personal growth through synergistic inter-personal relationships.

Righteousness and Truth

We have discovered that karma and caste inform and undergird Hindu ethics. The system of right and wrong is anchored In Vedanta philosophy and provides the cohesion and stability of caste. The essence of communal morality is therefore quite evident; it is the mores and ethical commitments of one's caste. However, the ethical tension point comes whenever the person begins participating in the life of societies other than those of his own caste. How does caste equip the person for participating in national or global community?

One might anticipate that the gods would help provide ethical moorings for the person caught in the maelstrom of modern mobility. That is hardly so. The function of the gods is more that of empowerment than providing moral tone to the community or the person. The Hindu gods are not necessarily celebrated for their morality.

Village Hinduism is vigorously polytheistic. The deities and avatars (incarnations of divinity) which Hindus worship are interpreted by the sages as manifestations of the eternal Brahman; it is therefore not surprising that there are millions of gods. In the Bhagavad-Gita, Krishna invites Arjuna to worship any god of his choice. In the Gita this worship of Vishnu takes on a personal I-thou relationship.

Recall that Krishna is an avatar of the god Vishnu. In the conversation Vishnu describes himself as the god who loves people, and occasionally reveals himself so as to reestablish the moral order. Vishnu even promises forgiveness for those who have bad karma.

These perceptions of divinity as personal, righteous, loving, and as one who relates to people personally seems discordant with Brahmanism and Vedanta philosophy. They also seem in tension with the foundational worldview of the Gita, which is that Brahman is the impersonal universal vitality of the universe.

The description of a god appearing to establish righteousness on earth is exceptional in Hinduism. On the whole the morality of the gods and avatars is like that of humans. Unlike biblical faith, where God calls people to repentance, in Hinduism repentance does not fit the worldview. This is because the moral behavior of the gods is similar to that of humans; they are capable of both good and evil. In fact even Vishnu did not call Arjuna to repentance; rather he was encouraged to submit to the practices of his caste, even though that meant killing his own relatives.

Sometimes the gods behave with civility, but sometimes also with deeds which society frowns upon. For example, some legends of Krishna describe him cavorting on the hillside pastures seducing the milkmaids. An amoral view of the divinities is consistent with the worldview which perceives Brahman as the essence of all phenomena, both good and evil.

During the last two centuries, Hindu reformers have attempted to interpret Vedanta philosophy for the modern era. These reforms have been a response to the interaction between Hinduism and the Christian faith and Islam as well as a response to secularism. Sarvepalli Radhakrishnan has been one of the most influential twentieth-century interpreters of Hinduism both for India and the global community. His classic and widely read book, East and West in Religion, boldly attempts to reinterpret Vedanta philosophy for modern reality.

Radhakrishnan insisted that all religions are one in essence. Various doctrines have developed from that basic core of truth. These doctrines may differ, but the teachings are not the significant reality. Only the religious core is the soul of reality. However, doctrinal differences do make it possible to consider religions on a continuum, with higher and lower belief patterns.

First, the polytheists are at the bottom of the continuum, for they *a* need idols and spirits to assist them in identifying with the universal core of truth.

Second, there are religions such as Christianity which worship a *b* person who helps Christians comprehend the core of truth.

Third, in the hierarchy are faiths which believe in a personal God, *c* but need no person or idol to symbolize that reality. Islam is such a religion.

Finally, there are religions such as Vedanta Hinduism, which *d* needs no idols, person, or personal God to assist the devotee in identifying with ultimate reality, the universal impersonal Brahman.

Although religions can be classified as higher and lower systems, no religion or belief is false, for Brahman is the essence of all phenomena, and all religions are expressions of the universal Brahman. Hinduism insists that all religions are true, no matter how contradictory the beliefs, for all originate in Brahman. In Hinduism, we meet pluralism of religion and truth in addition to moral pluralism.

Radhakrishnan summarizes the Hindu perception of religious pluralism by exclaiming, "As a result of this tolerant attitude, Hinduism itself has become a mosaic of almost all types and stages of religious aspirations and endeavor."[16] The Upanishads state in veneration of Brahman, "Of all religions, thou art the source."[17]

This form of Hindu universalism is a persistent challenge to Islam and Christianity as they meet Hinduism. Hindus are incredulous that any faith could claim a missionary mandate. Mahatma Gandhi never overcame his dismay with the Christian commitment to invite people into the community of faith known as the church. Although Gandhi appreciated the ministries of the church and honored Jesus Christ, he strongly opposed any commitment to inviting people into the community of Christian faith. Hindu tolerance for pluralism is often transformed into vigorous intolerance when confronted with a universal faith and community such as Islam or Christianity.[18]

History and Development

Modern Hindu participation in global community raised new questions about the quality of human life and the meaning of history. For more than twenty centuries, Vedanta philosophy has insisted that history has no meaning and all phenomena is maya. Hindu sages nurtured within the Indian subcontinent a spirit which did not encourage human progress and development. If all apparent phenomena is illusion, why change anything?

However, in modern times large-scale mobility has brought many Hindu communities into dynamic interaction with Muslim, Christian, and secular perspectives, all of which believe the present reality is serious business. How does the Vedanta concept of maya connect with these modern perspectives within India which invite people to join for development in all aspects of the human situation?

Radhakrishnan attempted to help the process of Hindu transformation into a more this-worldly religion. He did this by setting a new tone for Hinduism in his prolific writings. He surprised the Hindu sages by interpreting the Vedanta philosophies as affirming that, although history is maya, it is nevertheless an arena in which real and genuine human achievement can happen.[19]

Has Radhakrishnan distorted the Vedanta scriptures in this radical reinterpretation of maya and history? That is a question which only Hindus can answer. Radhakrishnan seems to be encouraging a fundamental paradigm shift within the soul of Hindu Vedanta philosophy.

Justice and Peace

When Radhakrishnan and other twentieth-century reformers were seeking to reform Hinduism from within while at the same time interpreting Hinduism winsomely to societies outside of India, Mahatma Gandhi emerged as probably the most powerful and influential moral voice of the twentieth century. Although the British prime minister Winston Churchill may have attempted to dismiss him as an irrelevant nuisance, this man through his single-minded commitment to integrity and justice helped move India away from entrapment in the mighty British Empire.

Throughout the struggle for independence, Gandhi nurtured the wellsprings of Christian conscience in the British people. He effectively appealed to their Christianized principles. Gandhi could not have been as effective functioning in a closed or autocratic political system, such as those in Nazi Germany, Stalinist Russia, or Communist Kampuchea (Cambodia).

Mahatma Gandhi was always a Hindu. He always functioned in the worldview of Brahmanism. That worldview enabled him to borrow insights from many sources, even those which did not originate in Hinduism. He could affirm his conviction that he was Muslim, Christian, Jain, Sikh, or Buddhist because his Hindu worldview nurtured that sort of universalism. For Gandhi all truth, phenomena, religions, or ideas were expressions of God. Yet God was not person-

al. Gandhi's dogmatic universalism and eclecticism is in harmony
with Hinduism.

Gandhi was committed to right action. The Christian belief in forgiveness seemed to him to be a disturbing doctrine, for he feared
that forgiveness could deflect people from the urgent need to take
personal responsibility for their actions. He was perplexed by the
nature of the transcaste communities called the church or the
Muslim *ummah*. Gandhi was enthusiastic about the teachings of Jesus, especially the Sermon on the Mount. These are only a few examples of his eclectic borrowing or rejecting from non-Hindu
streams of spirituality.

Although Gandhi claimed to receive spiritual nurture in the
Bhagavad-Gita, his commitment to nonviolence came from other
spiritual streams, for these scriptures condone violence if justified
by one's community. His nonviolence was greatly influenced by
Tolstoy's interpretation of Jesus Christ and the Sermon on the
Mount, in which Jesus taught simplicity, integrity, humility, and love
for one's enemies. Yet the spirituality for nonviolence also came
through the perceptions of the Jain community in India who for
many centuries had taught ahimsa or nonviolence to all creatures.
Thus various streams converged in this man to nurture his commitment to non-violent resistance to injustice.   *indictment of Christianity*

Gandhi was dismayed that so few Western Christians took the life
and teachings of Jesus seriously. He was appalled that, in violation of
Jesus' clear teachings, Christians accumulated wealth in a world filled
with the hungry and exercised violence although Jesus commanded
his followers to love their enemies. His mission to the Western
churches was to beseech them to receive the life and teachings of Jesus as the right model for responsible living in the global community.

Gandhi's own lifestyle demonstrated that he sought to practice the
biblical Sermon on the Mount. This highly trained lawyer, the spiritual leader of several hundred million Indians, traveled third class on
congested trains, while most of the Christian missionaries from Western societies who had come to India to tell of Jesus rode first class.
Gandhi complained that too many Christians divided their deeds and
words. In Jesus, he believed, deed and word converged.

Gandhi urged Christians to be more like Jesus. He believed that
kind of commitment would transform the global community for
good. Many Christians didn't know how to cope with this Hindu fa-
kir who pled with them to be more faithful to Jesus.

5   **Minorities and Secular Society**

Gandhi was committed to religious pluralism and desired an India which would be open to all religions. Nevertheless, he believed that the missionary commitment of Christianity and Islam were inimical to harmonious community relationships and authentic pluralism. He believed that the caste system was a reasonable basis on which to establish a pluralistic society in which all minorities would be respected. This meant that each community needed to function with integrity as self-contained social systems and needed to avoid receiving people from other communities.

As India moved toward independence, intense dialogue developed on the nature of the government in the new Indian state. Should the government be a kaleidoscope of communities, each with their representation in government, or a secular government? The Christian community encouraged the secular option of a government which attempted to function without being beholden to religious interest groups. Christians were grateful that the outcome of the debate resulted in the formation of a constitution for independent India which established a secular state.

One of Gandhi's keen disappointments was the division of the subcontinent into India and Pakistan. Gandhi was striving for an independent India where all would have full rights and privileges: Muslims, Hindus, Christians, Sikhs, Jains, Zoroastrians, Buddhists, Ahmadiyyas, and secularists. Side by side under Gandhi's leadership, the whole kaleidoscope of Indian peoples struggled for independence.

Yet as independence came into view, the Muslim community under the leadership of Muhammed Ali Jinnah worried about their status in a secular or Hindu state. Gandhi worshiped the god Rama, which seemed to the Muslims a nod of affirmation for polytheism. Nevertheless, Gandhi dreamed and worked for a pluralistic India with a heart large enough to incorporate all religious communities. Yet the Islamic view of Muslim community in global society did not fit Gandhi's vision.

A later chapter describes the Islamic worldview. The Islamic ideal is a pluralism which thrives in the administration of an Islamic state. The Muslim approach to pluralism was not compatible with Gandhi's commitment.

Thus under Jinnah's leadership, Pakistan was created in 1947 as a Muslim state. A minimum of ten million Muslims and Hindus were displaced as throngs of Muslims moved from India to Pakistan and many Hindus emigrated from Pakistan to India. This was likely the most massive displacement of people in the history of humankind.

Yet Gandhi's dream was not completely obliterated. Forty million Muslims remained in India. Nevertheless, horrible intercommunal violence exploded between Muslims and Hindus during the upheavals caused by the partitioning. Gandhi fasted nigh unto death as a witness to his commitment for peace between Muslims and Hindus. The fasting was an effective witness, and the communal violence between Muslims and Hindus ceased, at least for a time.

Gandhi's commitment to pluralism and justice for all also led him into concern for the plight of the outcastes in Indian society. One of Gandhi's commitments was to incorporate these dispossessed people into the caste system. Many outcastes were converting to Islam and Christianity. Inclusion into Hinduism as a caste would give them a place in the Hindu system, making it less attractive for them to seek an alternate religious and social home.

Gandhi strove for a new India which would embrace all peoples, including outcastes and other religious communities such as the forty million Muslims who had remained in India after the partition. This vision cost him his life. He insisted on including the outcastes in the Hindu system. His sacrificial quest for an India whose heart was large enough to include every group of people, was likely the reason an assassin pulled his gun on Gandhi when he was going to his customary place of prayer in New Delhi on January 20, 1948.

Soul Force and Gandhi's Legacy

Gandhi practiced *satyagraha*, soul force. His life revealed the best in Hinduism. He marshaled diverse spiritualities in a Hindu worldview. Through satyagraha he became a powerful moral conscience in India, the mighty British Empire, and the global community.

Perhaps Gandhi's spirituality was too eclectic and consequently lacked an enduring foundation and focus. Although Gandhi struggled for the equality of all castes, no intercaste ashram movement developed in India. Even those ashram communities which nurtured the springs of Hindu spirituality conformed to the profiles of caste. No continuing Hindu community emerged with the energy and consistent focus needed to cultivate satyagraha, ahimsa, and healthy intercaste relations in Indian society and the global community.

Yet the constitution of independent India declares the government secular. The politicians who formed the government hoped that secular perspectives would best preserve the ideals of interreligious and intercaste cooperation that Gandhi supported. These Gandhian perspectives were vital for national well-being and cohesion.

In some settings the global church has attempted to embrace Gandhi's commitments to nonviolent confrontation in the struggle against injustice. This Hindu sage opened the eyes of Christians to dimensions of the message of Jesus which Western culture had obscured. We note several examples.

Gandhi's ahimsa powerfully influenced Martin Luther King Jr., and other leaders of the civil rights struggle in the United States during the 1950s and 1960s.

Christian commitment to nonviolent resistance to apartheid in South Africa, as expressed by such leaders as Archbishop Desmond Tutu, was influenced by Gandhi's example.

The founding father of the Zambian nation, Kenneth Kaunda, was explicit in his recognition of Gandhi as helping him discover nonviolence as a truly Christian vocation.[20]

Gandhi's example is also embraced by some streams of the liberation theology movement in Latin America.

Although Gandhi never became a confessing Christian, his legacy endures in the conscience of many Christian communities, especially those who experience oppression and injustice.

Mahatma Gandhi demonstrated that unflinching integrity and compassion are powerful weapons in the struggle against injustice. The soul force of this man moved a nation and an empire. Moral power is also effective in the humdrum of home, job, or community.

Hinduism and the Global Village

Our exploration of Hinduism has revealed qualities attractive to the global community. Many have discovered in the Hindu caste system and relativism a neat response to the enigmas of global sociological, moral, and religious pluralism. We have seen that these themes are grounded in universal Hindu perceptions of caste, karma, and brahman. Our exploration has probed the implications of this socio-religious system in the context of the global village as well as the Indian subcontinent.

The survey focused especially on five themes—the person, righteousness and truth, history and development, justice and peace, pluralism and secular society. We have discovered expressions of modern Hinduism drawing from wells of Vedanta spirituality in response to the new realities of modern global community. None did this better than Mahatma Gandhi.

The Gods in Collision with Allah

In the 1990s, caste and interreligious tension in India seriously threatened the delicate fabric of nationhood. The eleven-month 1990 leadership of Prime Minister V. P. Singh was marred by tensions in the Hindu community which escalated when he pushed the secular mandates of the constitution further than the upper-caste Hindus would tolerate. The issue was his affirmative action plans for job placements for lower-caste Hindus, who comprise 43 percent of the population. India exploded in rage. Some upper-caste youth gave their lives in protest through self-immolations.

Then the town of Ayodhya, in Uttar Pradesh, became a focus of further rage. This is the place where, according to Hindu legend, the warrior god Ram was born. Four and a half centuries ago, the first Mogul emperor of India, Babar, built a mosque on the spot where Ram had been born, thereby showing disrespect for Hindu sensitivities.

The caste crisis provided Hindu leaders with a perceived opportunity to redress the wrong committed by Emperor Babar in 1528 against the god Ram and the Hindu community. Lal Kishen Advani, a leader of the Hindu political party, Bharatiya Janata Party (BJP), boarded a Toyota van. He headed across India to Ayodhya to destroy the mosque. Confrontation between Muslim monotheism and Hinduism was inevitable.

In early November 1990, hundreds of thousands of Hindus converged to destroy the mosque. Police responding to protect it left over thirty dead and hundreds wounded. Hindu-Muslim violence spread across the nation and even infected adjoining Bangladesh.

V. P. Singh lost a vote of confidence in parliament, which he perceived as a defeat for the secular commitments of the government in the face of intercaste and interreligious tensions. Several months later, amid the volatile atmosphere in which the subsequent parliamentary elections took place, India experienced a further convulsion when Rajiv Gandhi, the head of the Congress Party, was assassinated.

Two years later, 200 thousand Hindu worshipers of Ram converged again at Ayodhya and overwhelmed security arrangements. On December 6, 1992, they destroyed the mosque and began building a temple to Ram. India exploded. In one week a thousand people died in violence between Muslims and Hindus. The world's largest democracy of 800 million perched at the abyss of disintegration.

Religious and caste loyalties were eroding the secular foundations of the Indian nation. The well-being of India was threatened by pluralism. Religious and caste loyalties usurped the secular ideals of the state. Allah of Islam and the gods of Hinduism were in collision.

The Islamic vision of a universal noncaste or intercaste community of faith was in dramatic collision with the Hindu worldview of a nation comprised of many societies defined by caste systems. A few influential leaders of the 700 million Hindus of India were determined to confront and undermine a secular approach in dealing with religious pluralism in India.

However, multitudes of Hindus and Muslims strove to bring an end to the violence. Across India, Muslims gathered at Hindu temples to protect those shrines from attack by overzealous Muslims. Hindus likewise stood guard at Muslim mosques. In the town of Malappjram in Kerala, local Muslims rebuilt two Hindu temples which had been destroyed by Muslim troublemakers from outside the town.

Heroic Muslim and Hindu efforts at reconciliation helped tame passions following the Ayodhya disaster. Multitudes of Hindus and Muslims recognized that respect for one another was right. These reconcilers sought to preserve an India founded on healthy pluralism.

The 1990 and 1992, Ayodhya crisis in India was only one event of many convulsions through India's tumultuous decades of experimentation as a secular pluralistic state, which comprises a mostly Hindu society. Yet multiparty democracy had survived. That was a remarkable achievement.

Reflection

1. What are the strengths and weaknesses of the Hindu approach to pluralism? Why would Muslim and Christian communities in India prefer a secular approach to pluralism?

2. In what ways do the Hindu beliefs support the caste system? What does the Nepali Dor B. Bista mean by "fatalistic hierarchy"?

3. To what extent might the concept of maya affect attitudes toward the person, history, and development?

4. Assess the legacy of Gandhi in the global community during the last fifty years. What were the sources of his spirituality?

5

Peace Without God

Buddha

"IN WHAT ways is Buddhism important for you?" I ventured cautiously.

A Japanese Buddhist businessman and I were seat companions on a flight from Osaka to Hong Kong. After a discussion on the fortunes of international business enterprise, our conversation drifted toward faith and religion in the global community.

In a flash this gentle man responded, "My relationship with my ancestors; you see I want to be on good terms with them. That is why I love Buddhism."

The conversation was a glimpse into the diversity popular Buddhism embraces. Ancestors were completely marginal to the concerns of Gautama Buddha. Yet as the movement developed, ancestral veneration was absorbed into the folk practices of devotees. Some ancestral heroes became folk divinities. Buddhism has developed astonishing flexibility. It has become a most complex phenomenon. For this reason our exploration must be cursory!

A Missionary Movement

Buddhism has a missionary impulse like both Islam and Christianity. These three religions teach that they possess universal truth to share with people everywhere. They each invite people to join their respective communities of belief and practice. The Buddhist missionary movement began about 2,500 years ago, half a millennium before Christianity and over a millennium before Islam. By its very nature, Buddhism thinks globally.

Religions such as Hinduism or the African traditions would never seek adherents from a people of a different religious system. They were national or tribal religions, not universal faiths. This is true of all tribal or national religions. However, modern mobility has thrust such nonmissionary faiths into a world of diverse peoples and nations. Consequently in modern times, even national or tribal faiths sometimes seek to interpret their beliefs to others, but not as missionary movements. (An aberration are cults such as Hare Krishna.)

However, Buddhism, Christianity, and Islam have always been missionary religions. Later we shall explore the reasons for the missionary vision in Islam and Christianity. Now we give particular attention to the central concern of the worldwide Buddhist missionary movement—escape from suffering.

We also explore dimensions of Buddhism that are especially pertinent to the modern global village. These include the paradox of compassion for others and salvation for one's self, history and progress, nature and science, peace and nonviolence, ego-negation and tolerance, intercommunal peace and personal peace, global mission and approaches to pluralism, Buddhist nationalism and global community, ethics for the monks and others, the family, the *sangha* (monastic order), and internationalization. We describe these various themes as a threefold cluster of issues within the three refuges of Buddhism. These are the refuges: I take refuge in the Buddha. I take refuge in the *dharma* (doctrine). I take refuge in the sangha (monastic order).

First, however, we consider the story of Buddha as well as a brief description of the Buddhist worldview.

Siddhartha Gautama Buddha

Siddhartha Gautama, who later became the Buddha, was born in the sixth century B.C. in the town of Kapilavastu on the border between India and Nepal. He was a Hindu prince of the kshatriya caste. For his first twenty-nine years, he enjoyed the opulent lifestyle of a privileged prince. Then he became depressed with the suffering and the transience of life.

One night he quietly left his wife and young son while they slept to become a solitary ascetic seeking enlightenment concerning the cause of suffering. Recall the manner in which traditional Hinduism idealizes the one who leaves home to seek *mukti* (enlightenment). In this solitary quest, Gautama was functioning in a manner consistent with the spirituality of his culture. In Buddhism, Gautama's act of leaving his family and earthly involvements is idealized as the "great renunciation."

Six years later Gautama became enlightened while meditating under a Bodhi tree (the tree of knowledge). Buddhists refer to this enlightened person as *arahat*. He was now the Buddha, the enlightened one who had achieved an insight into reality which was universal for all people.

Buddha communicated the insights of his enlightenment in his first sermon at the Benares Deer Park, preaching to five ascetics. They became his first disciples, thus forming the first Buddhist sangha or monastic order. His Deer Park sermon had four points that have become known as the Four Noble Truths, the essence of Buddhism:

- Suffering is the universal experience of humankind.
- The desire to exist is the cause of suffering.
- Suffering ceases when desire ceases.
- The path that leads to the cessation of suffering is eightfold: Right belief. Right aspiration. Right speech. Right conduct. Right means of livelihood. Right endeavor. Right mindfulness. Right meditation.

The reality of suffering, the cause of suffering, the cessation of suffering, the path which leads to the cessation of suffering—this four-dimensional truth is the core of Buddhist enlightenment.

Buddha was a philosopher and psychologist rather than a religionist. Concerning the gods, he was an agnostic. If the gods do exist, they are higher forms of incarnations than people. In any event the gods and spirits are irrelevant for salvation, which is escape from personal existence into emptiness.

Buddha never objected if lay people sought the help of their gods for personal needs. However, he did not encourage such practices. For the monks the worship of any divinity was beneath consideration. After all, the goal of the person should be escape from all temporal attractions. The gods might be helpful for the earthly needs of those lay persons who are still entangled in the temporal world, but no God or gods could be of any help in achieving salvation. That is the sole responsibility of the person. Buddha was a humanist.

After Buddha's death his teachings were collected. Eventually they became scripture for the Buddhist devotees. Written in Pali, these scriptures are known as the *Tripitaka* (Three Baskets).

The Person and Suffering

Buddhist philosophy is the conviction that the desire to exist is the cause of all suffering. Salvation in Buddhism is escape from suffering. Therefore the goal of Buddhist psychology is to enable the person to cease existing as an individual. This release from personal existence is the only way the person can escape from suffering.

The person functions as an entity because the desire to be a person brings the various strands of personhood together. It is desire to exist, rather than soul, that is the core of personal existence. Although the person is *anatta* (without soul), the desire to exist maintains the person in a state of *anicca* (impermanent continually changing existence).

The entities which comprise a person are five qualities known as *skhandhas*. These changing impermanent strands which are attracted by the desire to exist are described as *Rupa*, the physical manifestations of personal existence; *Vedana*, feeling; *Sanna*, recognition; *Sankhara*, the process of forming ideas through comparison and evaluation; *Vinnana*, the capacity for personal reflection.[1] The personal desire to exist provides the cohesion which holds these impermanent and changing characteristics of the person together.

As long as the desire to exist persists, even death will provide no relief. The clusters of skandhas which comprise the person will be reborn again and again until such a time as the person releases the desire for continued existence. When that happens, the person returns to the universal sea of peace just as drops of water from the ocean wave return to and are absorbed into the universal ocean. The peace which comes from absorption into the universal is nirvana; the meaning of nirvana is emptiness.

Nirvana literally means extinction. However, there is no English equivalent; emptiness might best communicate nirvana. Yet that is also inadequate, for how can one become empty of personhood that is a transient illusion, nothingness.

The person who grasps at existence is like a drop of ocean water which remains a cohesive entity and cannot be absorbed into the ocean of peace. Through the processes of rebirth he is tossed like a droplet of ocean spray, as it were, again and again into the air above the ocean waves. As long as she persists in the desire to exist, the person suffers. The desire to exist assures that the tragedy of individual existence will go on and on and on through the cycles of rebirth.

Both Hinduism and Buddhism struggle with the meaningless cycle of being and nonbeing in which all nature participates. Both systems believe that each person is caught in the tragic cycle of life and death. The Hindu notion is that only the soul appears again and again as the cycles go on. This cycle means the soul is "reincarnated." In contrast, in Buddhism it is the cohesive cluster of five impermanent skandhas which is "reborn." For the Buddhist any individual rebirth in another life after death must represent the cohesion of the whole person, not just her soul.

Buddhist expressions of compassion for people are consistent with this recognition of the essential integrity of the whole person. The doctrine of rebirth is a recognition of the whole personhood; however, the ultimate goal of rebirths is the eventual cessation of personal existence.

Buddhism invites people to take the three refuges from the suffering they experience. Our exploration will reflect on each of the three refuges, giving special attention to relationships between these refuges and realities of modern global community.

The First Refuge: The Buddha

Buddhist philosophy reflects on the meaning of the first refuge of Buddhism: "I take refuge in the Buddha." Our exploration will reveal that the Theravada and Mahayana branches of Buddhism each places different emphases on taking refuge in the Buddha.

Compassion and Salvation

This first refuge is the quest and realization of enlightenment which enables the person to acquire nirvana. Buddha was the pathfinder who has shown the way to the enlightenment which each person must discover for himself. Yet there is a paradox within the soul of Buddhism.

On the one hand, the whole quest for enlightenment is individualistic and self-centered. The purpose of the quest for enlightenment is to break free from the phenomenon of personal suffering. For Buddha that quest meant leaving his young family in the great renunciation. Even his family responsibilities could not stand in the way of his personal quest for enlightenment. The person must seek salvation for himself. At first blush the philosophy seems selfish.

The other dimension of the paradox is that once Buddha acquired enlightenment, he decided to commit himself to helping others acquire this same gift. The whole missionary movement in Buddhism is grounded in compassion for those who suffer because of their entrapment on the endless wheel of rebirth.

In later years this missionary commitment to helping others achieve enlightenment developed into the notion that divinities or ancestral heroes can also provide help. Thus Mahayana (Greater Vehicle) Buddhism was born which accents the "help" side of the paradox. Theravada (The Way of the Elders) Buddhism accents the "on your own" side of the paradox. There is tension within the paradox.

Mahayana Buddhism is enthralled by the merit which *arahats* (people who have acquired release from the cycle of rebirth through enlightenment known as *bodhi*) accumulate by attempting to help others acquire bodhi which can lead to arahat also. Buddha is the example. The Mahayana believe that after he achieved enlightenment he could have chosen to enter the state of nirvana. However, he did not do so. The reason was his compassion for others who were still locked onto the cycle of rebirth.

The Mahayana believe that whenever arahats follow the example of Buddha and postpone nirvana, they accumulate merit they can then share with others. This merit assists people in their state of being now and enables the faithful in their quest for nirvana.

Compassionate divinities also accumulate merit. The *bodhisattvas* are such divine beings who have accumulated huge stores of merit which they bestow on their devotees. Thus in Mahayana Buddhism, as in the Hindu Bhagavad-Gita, the worship of a divinity of one's choice can assist one in the quest for release from the cycles of rebirth in Buddhism or reincarnation in Hinduism. In most Buddhist societies, Buddha, who believed there is no help available from any god, is paradoxically worshiped as the supreme Lord Buddha. His devotees believe Buddha can help them because his compassion has created huge stores of merit.

In Mahayana Buddhist societies, devotion to Buddha, bodhisattvas, or other divinities and spirits might be intense. Devotees may attempt to continually utter a divine phrase, such as *Om mane padme hum!* In most non-Buddhist cultures, this would be considered irrational or even lunacy. Yet for one who seeks the assistance of extraordinary power to break free from the meaningless cycles of

rebirth, the continual repetition of divinity phrases is consistent
with that worldview.

In some societies, devotees attempt to acquire merit through the
practice of *dana*. This is the investment of one's wealth in Buddhist
shrines. In both Thailand and Burma, devotees over the centuries
have invested great wealth in building golden shrines known as stupas, all in an effort to attract sufficient grace to enable the devotee to
cease from the cycles of rebirth. Wealth invested in these shrines
contributes to impoverishment of some Buddhist societies by si-
phoning resources away from enterprises which would contribute
to temporal human and economic development.

From the perspectives of persons committed to wholistic human
development, such practices seem a wrong diversion of resources,
wealth, and energy. Some people ask whether it would not be far
better to invest energy and resources in ministries of compassion, in
efforts which improve the quality of human life. Buddha himself
was not impressed with religious ritual or shrines. His development
of the sangha, with its teaching mission, reveals concern for the
plight of people who have not experienced the enlightenment leading to escape from suffering. Thus expression of compassion for humankind is present in early Buddhism.

The paradox which gave rise to the Theravada and Mahayana
branches of Buddhism also affects the Buddhist approach to compassionate service among people. Compassion poses several problems. There is the danger that one's emotions may become entangled in the plight of the unfortunate. For this reason it is wise to express compassion toward humanity as a whole and avoid excessive
involvement with a particular person. Emotional entanglement with
one who is suffering is contrary to the disciplines needed if one is
seeking personal escape from suffering.

Another danger of compassion is the possibility of encouraging
dependency within the suffering person. Especially in Theravada
Buddhism, dependency is contrary to fostering personal responsibility, which the quest for arahat requires. Orthodox Buddhist philosophy and psychology is grounded in individualistic humanism.
There is no help for enlightenment from any divinity.

There is also the danger that by alleviating apparent physical suffering, people will be detracted from the essence of the cause of suffering, which is wrong desire. Any ministry to physical suffering
only touches the symptoms of suffering. Far more important than a
bandage over symptoms of suffering is dealing with the wrong

mental attitudes which nurture suffering.

The qualities of quiescence in the face of suffering often provide Buddhist people with incredible fortitude in times of suffering. For example, we are amazed by the fortitude of Buddhists within Indochina and Southeast Asia during the Vietnam War and the subsequent Kampuchean atrocities.

An ancient text from the *Dhammapada* says it well.

> If a man speaks or acts with a pure thought, happiness follows him, like a shadow that never leaves him. "He abused me, he beat me, he defeated me, he robbed me"—in those who harbor such thoughts hatred will never cease—in those who do not harbor such thoughts hatred will cease. For hatred does not cease by hatred at any time; hatred ceases by love, this is an old rule.[2]

Even though the core of Buddhism is responsibility for one's own release from suffering, compassion for others is also affirmed. But caution! Avoid becoming entangled. Buddha himself is the example of a quality of compassion which enables one to remain free from the entanglements of suffering. Again the *Dhammapada*— "Even for great benefit to another, let no man imperil his own benefit."[3]

History and Progress

Buddhism, like Hinduism, teaches that human existence is entrapped in a meaningless cycle. History has no purpose. History does not move, except in great cycles which have no ultimate destiny or goal. Consequently Buddhist societies have never developed serious research or writing on history. Only in medieval Japanese Buddhism have some philosophers encouraged an interest in history as a process energized by small cycles. Cultural, human, or economic development are strange concepts in traditional Buddhist cultures which view all existence as a meaningless cycle. These cultures perceive that seeking refuge in the Buddha has no relationship to history or mundane human enterprise.

The existence of the person within history is sustained through the wrongful desire to maintain permanent personhood rather than to accept the impermanent, understanding that personhood is a transient illusion. Freedom from self is found in accepting the reality of *anatta*, "no self." Therefore, the goal of the individual persons who comprise the wheels of history should be the cessation of existence. Escape from the wheel of history and the illusion of permanent existence enables the person to become absorbed into the universal.

Buddhism is in dramatic contrast to the Christian or Muslim
faiths, which believe that the presence of the person is significant
both within and beyond history. These faiths believe that the choices
of the person do make a real difference within real history. Christianity and Islam invite the person into serious and constructive involvement within society and amidst human history. Buddhism
finds such concepts of real personal significance within a human
history of meaning and purpose incomprehensible.

The Buddhist temple of Boro Bubur in south central Java in Indonesia communicates the themes of peace acquired through contemplation rather than through serious engagement within history and
the experiences of life. This massive stone marvel was built in the
eighth century. Each step is steep and high (some about two feet)
leading up to the stupa at the pinnacle of the temple. This is to slow
one's ascent as a reminder that it is wise to move through life slowly and contemplatively.

The temple is in tiers. The lowest tier consists of thousands of intricate carvings in rock of human activities. However, all these delicate
and delightful sculptures are covered by a stone facade! Only one little peep of several feet of exposed sculpture is visible, probably so the
tourist will appreciate the grandeur of the sculpturing enterprise.

"Why," I asked my guide, "are these thousands of stone sculptures obscured forever by the stone facade?"

"Because the sculptures portray human life," my Buddhist infor-
mant explained.

In a flash I recalled the Rembrandt Museum in Amsterdam, with
its majestic European renaissance paintings of human experience,
depicting the wide range of majesty and pathos. I imagined that the
obscured sculptures in Boro Bubur would also portray the mystery
and marvel of human experience. I felt cheated. I could not absorb
the wonder of these stone sculptures that agile hands had engraved
during many decades of tedious chiseling. They showed the glory
and pain of the human story, yet their mysteries were hidden behind
a bland stone facade.

"Why can't we see sculptures of human experience?" I persisted.

With practiced English, our guide became almost elegant: "The
goal of each Buddhist is to avoid any attraction for human life. Even
the beauty of a mother nursing her baby must hold no attraction.
The stone facade over these sculptures is a reminder that we must
become blind to all of life's experiences. For us Buddhists it is as

though there are no such things as life experiences. And that is the way of peace."

The engravers had invested their lives cutting those intricate stone sculptures. After years of effort, their work was covered by bland stone. What a statement on the futility of human life and enterprise!

*Messiah
Complex?*

However, at a higher level of the ziggurat there are visible sculptures of the legendary life of the Buddha. These include legends surrounding his birth. The wild animals became peaceable, with even the lions and snakes laying aside their violence for the way of peace. The stone carvings include a legend of a deer who jumped into a fire as a sacrifice at the time of Buddha's birth. However, the deer was given the gift of new life as a reward for this sacrificial act of self-giving.

"People should take a lesson from the deer and give themselves in sacrificial compassion for others. The deer story reminds us that the reward for compassion may be rebirth in a higher form of life or nirvana where the cycles of rebirth are ended forever. That is true peace," explained our Buddhist friend.

The upper levels of the ziggurat include bell-shaped stupas. The first rows have diamond-shaped windows. The stupas on the highest circle have square windows. The climactic stupa, which is the pinnacle of the ziggurat, has no windows; its circular structure is solid stone with no opening.

These stupas portray the progression toward nirvana. The lower level stupas with diamond-shaped windows indicate rebirth. The higher level stupas with rectangular windows symbolize movement upward toward the experience of bodhi which leads to a cessation of rebirths. Finally the windowless pinnacle is a symbol of nirvana where rebirth shall be no more. That pinnacle stupa without windows is a reminder of eternal emptiness, the goal of Buddhist devotees.

The ziggurat of Boro Budur is a revelation of the essence of the Buddhist worldview. The Buddhist ideal invites the person to seek an enlightenment which leads away from a serious engagement with the experiences of life and history.

Progress in Buddhism is understood to be a cyclical movement toward the cessation of the desire for personal existence. That is nirvana, the experience of emptiness. The enlightened person begins the experience of emptiness and disengagement even before death. That is the ideal toward which Buddhism invites the person. Wholistic human development or secular progress are incomprehensible within a Buddhist perspective.

Nature and Science

Goals such as economic progress, human development, or scientific breakthroughs are in dissonance with the primal vision of Buddhism. Unless a Buddhist culture has been influenced by modern secular ideals, a society nurtured by Buddhism will consider strange indeed secular human progress or the use of technology to dominate and exploit the earth.

However, this does not suggest that traditional Buddhist societies never ravage the earth. A quiescent spirit can nurture retreat from the difficult responsibilities required for care of the earth. A culture which has a laissez-faire attitude toward nature is not necessarily the best for either nature or society. It might be that building a dam across a river to control floods is necessary to save both human lives and precious soil (though of course destroying dams to save salmon, as has been at least discussed in the U.S. Pacific Northwest, might need to be considered in other cases). However, in some circumstances, Buddhist cultures have been exemplary in the care of the earth. The terraces of Sri Lanka are among the agricultural marvels of the world.

Modernity invites Buddhist peoples to participate in an anti-supernatural worldview which is nurtured by naturalistic scientific methodology. Although traditional Buddhist societies have not been inclined to develop scientific-technological cultures, Buddhist philosophy is comfortable with a worldview which believes that natural laws function independently of any creator. A recurrent theme in contemporary Buddhist scholarship is the notion that there is convergence of Buddhist doctrine with naturalistic scientific perspectives.

Of course, legends did develop within later Buddhism which describe Buddha's miracles. Yet the original accounts are without miracle content. In fact, miracles are incompatible with Buddha's philosophy. Therefore Buddhism has no problem embracing a scientific orientation which denies the possibility of a God or gods who intervene within nature or who sustain nature. Buddhist philosophy affirms a naturalistic view of the universe.[4]

The Second Refuge: The *Dharma*

The Four Noble Truths and the middle path to which these truths point is the second refuge: "I take refuge in the dharma." We have already mentioned the Four Noble Truths, but some further amplification will be helpful.

The First Noble Truth is the reality of suffering which is experienced in every stage of life. Birth, aging, and death all reveal the transience of life. Anguish is the common human experience.

b The Second Noble Truth is that suffering comes from desire. Enlightenment for Buddha was the recognition that *tanha* (thirst or desire) for existence is the root cause of all human suffering.

> The desire for what belongs to the unreal self generates suffering, for it is impermanent, changeable, perishable, and that, in the object of desire, causes disappointment, disillusionment, and other forms of suffering to him who desires. Desire in itself is not evil. It is desire to affirm the lower self, to live in it, cling to it, identify one's self with it, instead of with the Universal self, that is evil.[5]

c The Third Noble Truth is the abandonment of tanha. In this Buddha is exemplary. The enlightenment which dawned on him at the Bodhi tree freed him from desire for pleasure or existence. He was convinced he would experience rebirth no more, for he was completely freed from any desire for existence.

living rightly

d The Fourth Noble Truth is the Eightfold Path mentioned already. The path includes right belief, right aspiration, right speech, right conduct, right means of livelihood, right endeavor, right mindfulness, right meditation. The Eightfold Path reveals that the renunciation of tanha is not the abandonment of all desire. It is wrong desire which Buddhism teaches against. Buddhism is a middle path which avoids the extreme asceticism of Hinduism or the hedonism of some expressions of primal mystery cults.

Our exploration of the Four Noble Truths of dharma reveals a quest for the middle way. Gautama Buddha avoided both hedonism and asceticism. As a young prince, he could drink from the well of hedonism. Then for several years he lived as an ascetic. Neither of these paths brought enlightenment.

"I take refuge in the dharma" is therefore an affirmation of a middle way between extremes. The way of the dharma leads one into the path of right desire, not the cessation of all desire nor the acclamation of all desire. The way of the dharma is the middle path of right desire. We shall now explore some of the practical implications of that middle path within the local and global village.

Peace and Nonviolence

One quality especially noteworthy in Buddhist societies is the prohibition against destroying life. This theme is rooted in the ancient Hindu tradition of *ahimsa* (the sacredness of all life). Buddhism, as a reform movement growing out of Hinduism, preserved and developed this ancient value which Hinduism as a whole has largely neglected. It is the same theme Gandhi developed in his commitment to nonviolence.

Buddhists are appalled by the confrontation and violence of many cultures. In Western culture there is so much polarization—between management and labor, parents and children, even the various branches of government and the various political parties. This polarization and confrontational spirit breeds violence. Western societies have led the world into a series of catastrophic wars during the twentieth century. Some tribal societies also nurture confrontation and violence. Shinto Japan has always been a society tinged by violence.

It is therefore not surprising that there are Buddhist sages who believe Buddhism has a gift to offer the nations—the gift of harmonious relationships among peoples. As one small step toward a more harmonious global community, these sages invite people to consider the Buddhist gift of nonviolent respect for life which is ahimsa.

Recently several friends and I enjoyed an evening in conversation with Buddhist monks who comprise a Theravada sangha in Washington, D.C. An itinerant monk from Sri Lanka led the dialogue. This wise sage was in his nineties and a bit deaf. So we shouted and also wrote our questions and comments.

"I don't know!" he laughed with disarming joviality over some of our questions. "In any event, right attitudes and mindfulness are more important that the knowledge we possess!"

Yet one thing he did know. Violence is wrong. He became passionate as he described his reading of the Bible and the violence described in the Old Testament. "Parts of the Old Testament are horrible!" he exclaimed. "I have read the entire Bible through several times. There is much that is good, but also much we Buddhists cannot accept, especially the violence of the Old Testament."

Buddhism, like other communities offering peace, often falls short of its ideals. For many decades Buddhist nations of Southeast Asia have been embroiled in endemic warfare. Whole societies have been decimated by the wars of Vietnam, Cambodia, Laos, and Burma. Nearby Sri Lanka has been boiling for many years with interethnic violence which Hindu and Buddhist loyalties have inflamed. Violence is no stranger to Buddhist societies.

External powers and ideologies have fanned the flames of violence in too many Buddhist societies. Yet in these settings of horrendous tragedy, Buddhist spirituality has been mostly incapable of bringing a resolution to the crises of violence. There has been Buddhist opposition to violence, often expressed in self-immolations by setting oneself on fire as a protest against war or injustice. Yet these sorts of protests have not been sufficient to turn governments and societies toward a more wholesome and reconciling spirit.

Ego-Negation and Tolerance

The endemic violence in the Buddhist heartland countries might be more of an indictment on human nature than on Buddhism as such. The violence might also be a commentary on the primary Buddhist emphasis on seeking inner tranquillity rather than investing energy in developing communal or intercommunal peace. Even amidst genocidal wars in Southeast Asia, Buddhist devotees have revealed the capability of suffering in peace. That is after all the quality of peace that the devoted Buddhist seeks.

Yet what about enthusiastic involvement in the social and political processes as an influence for righteousness, justice, and peace? That is not the path chosen by Siddhartha Gautama the Buddha. Buddhist philosophy invites the person to an enlightenment which is emptiness. This is an invitation to the loss of ego identity.

The quest for emptiness inclines the person and society in directions other than social transformation in the quest for justice. How can one who is seeking to loose his ego identity also struggle for the cause of justice? Is it possible to take human dignity seriously if we deny the person a self?

The Dutch theologian Hans Küng writes,

> We observe that in any society, ego-weakness or even ego-negation bring in their wake uncritical assimilation to prevailing trends, an attitude of opportunistic compromise, a tolerance of everything, and a lack of resistance to injustice and oppression.[6]

In modern Western societies it is fashionable to celebrate the tolerant attitude of Buddhism toward diversity. It is important to recognize, however, that foundational to the Buddhist spirit of tolerance is the quest for loss of ego identity.

In Buddhism there is no comprehension of the ego affirmation of Christian experience, which is anchored in the conviction that the Creator encounters the person. In Buddhist philosophy prayer or any form of communication between God and the person is incomprehensible. Rather Buddhism idealizes forms of meditation which dismantle the self and break free from engagement with the world.[7]

In modern times a tolerance based on negating the ego can become disastrous, for there is no psychological or spiritual basis on which to critique anything. In previous centuries, when Buddhist societies were mostly insulated from the global community, easygoing tolerance may have seemed wholesome. Today that is no longer true. We grieve that some beautiful Buddhist societies are acquiescing to the destructive greed of global economics, sexual hedonism, or the uninhibited exploitation of the earth through uncritical acceptance of technology. A society which tolerates everything the global community offers is heading for disaster.

Intercommunity Peace

However, there are some Buddhists who seek another way. They believe that Buddhism has a mission of encouraging international and intercommunity peace. Such efforts seem to be related to worldview paradigm shifts within Buddhism which modern societies invite.

A breakfast with Tibetan Buddhists revealed that kind of paradigm transformation. We were hosting representatives of the government in exile of the Dalai Lama. He is the head of the Tibetan branch of Buddhism; it is believed that he is the incarnation of divinity. The Marxist revolution in Tibet forced the Dalai Lama into exile in India in 1959. The violence and dislocations which the revolution created for his people has encouraged the Dalai Lama to develop a Buddhist philosophy of interpersonal and intercommunity peace.

Although the intent of our breakfast meeting was to discuss the manner in which a minority community can develop survival skills in a pluralistic society, our conversation quickly drifted into the issues of peace and war, violence and nonviolence.

Our guests raised the observation gently. "Christianized Western societies have initiated global wars. Why is that so?" *Western initiated*

I commented, "There is often a tension between what a society does and the essence of faith. Jesus was nonviolent. He chose not to be- *war* come a military leader, although his admirers offered him political and military power. He rejected this path, choosing rather to accept suffering and death at the hands of his enemies. His life demonstrates that suffering love is stronger than hate. He broke the cycle of violence by accepting the violence of his enemies and forgiving them."

Our guests were astonished. "That is wonderful!" they exclaimed.

"It is important that some Christians explain this dimension of Christian faith to the Dalai Lama. He is interested in this, for he wants to do all he can to encourage global peace."

"How is he doing that?" we inquired.

"The Dalai Lama has a simple plan which is in harmony with the whole life and teaching of Buddha.

"And what is this plan?" we persisted.

"Act toward your enemy in the way which will make him happy!" they stated simply.

"That is a surprising plan," we exclaimed.

Then they reminded us, "However, the plan can only work if people are at peace within themselves. People who are angry and hateful cannot receive the Dalai Lama's plan."

We parted hoping to continue the conversation at another time, in the presence of the Dalai Lama himself. Global peace, they indicated, had become the mission of the Dalai Lama. Yet he experienced loneliness in his mission.

ways to peace

The three global faiths of Islam, Christianity, and Buddhism offer peace for all humankind. So does the ideology of Marxism. Muslims offer peace through submission to God—a peace enhanced, established, and extended by political power. Marxists offer a peace that erodes all class distinctions through the universal dictatorship of the laboring classes. Buddhists invite a peace that is escape from the desires and entanglements causing suffering. Christians invite a peace anchored in love that suffers and forgives. These four peacemaking movements have distinctive approaches to extending peace.

C & Buddha

The divergence between Buddhism and Christianity is symbolized in the Buddha and the Christ symbols. The icons of the Buddha usually show him with arms folded. The arms of Buddha communicate a spirit of aloneness in the quest for peace; they suggest that there is no real help from another. Christ on the cross has wounded hands outstretched. These are the active, embracing arms of one who loves and invites his enemies, of one who has chosen the way of suffering. In conversation together we discover that the Buddha and the Christ invite quite different understandings of the way of peace.

3   The Third Refuge: The Sangha

The sangha is the monastic community which give itself to the practice and propagation of Buddhism.

In many Buddhist societies, all males will spend a portion of their

lives in the sangha. Some invest a lifetime in the sangha. In his later
life Buddha admitted women into the sangha, a model which Buddhist communities have not always followed.

Prior to the Marxist revolution in Tibet, all families attempted to
commit one son to a life's vocation in the sangha. A fifth of the people lived in monasteries! It is, however, unusual for a Buddhist society to practice monasticism with that much enthusiasm.

Mission

The missionary interest which the emissaries of the Dalai Lama
described is consistent with the historic missionary commitment of
Buddha himself. After his experience of bodhi (enlightenment), he
began to teach the threefold refuge to a few of his colleagues. As the
movement grew, he and his disciples formed the Buddhist sangha.

This monastic order had two primary functions. First, it was a retreat and teaching community for monks and later for nuns as well.
Second, it was a missionary-sending community.

During the dry seasons when travel was easy, the monks scattered
throughout the region teaching the three refuges of Buddhism. Then
as the monsoon rains commenced, the monks would return to their
base for communal renewal. This rhythm of retreat and going forth
enabled Buddhism to maintain a strong sense of community solidar-
ity and doctrinal unity while expanding rapidly.

Buddha instructed the monks on missionary methodology. The
early expansion of Buddhism was planned and intentional. They
were never to impose Buddhism on anyone. In fact, they were only
to teach the Buddhist way when invited. They were to resist writing
about Buddhism unless requested. Of course, Buddhist missionary
endeavors have not always been that unobtrusive. Nevertheless the
Buddhist missionary ideal is to extend the community without any
compulsion and in the spirit of true voluntarism. The monks were
the missionaries; the sangha was their missionary base.

Buddhist councils were convened to discuss the monks' responses
to the issues they experienced as the community expanded. For example, in India the movement challenged caste by creating a new
community which united people from various caste backgrounds.
The councils reviewed such problems and also planned for the further extension of the movement. The councils which convened in
the earliest phases of the Buddhist movement are similar to modern
Buddhist councils which have provided significant guidance to the
worldwide mission of Buddhism. Most modern Buddhist communi-

ties are now members of the World Fellowship of Buddhists, organized in 1950.

The comments of U Chan Htoon of Burma following the 1950 World Buddhist Conference in Ceylon (Sri Lanka) reveals the nature and significance of modern Buddhist missionary conferences.

> One thing was notable at the Conference, and that was the unanimous belief of all those people present there that Buddhism is the only ideology which can give peace to the world and save it from war and destruction.
>
> What was aimed at the Buddhist conference was not to attempt to convert the followers of other religions of the world into Buddhists. But what we hoped for was this: people may profess any religion they like, but if their moral conduct is such as is in conformity with the principles of Buddha's teachings or in other words, they lead the Buddhist way of life, then there will be everlasting peace in the world.[8]

That kind of missionary commitment was exactly the concern of the team of Buddhist associates of the Dalai Lama who were at the breakfast meeting. Complementing their missionary convictions, those emissaries were also entrusted by the Dalai Lama with political responsibilities. In these Buddhists the political and missionary impulse flowed together comfortably.

Politics

Although Buddha himself was not concerned about political institutions, the Indian emperor Asoka set the stage for a convergence of religious and political order in Buddhism. He came to power in India in 273 B.C., nearly three centuries after Buddha's birth. At the beginning of his reign, he was involved in a brutal war in the region of the Bay of Bengal. Hundreds of thousands of people were killed or dislocated. Buddhist monks helped Asoka understand the evil of his actions.

Asoka embraced Buddhism. In penance he devoted his personal and political power to the strengthening and expansion of Buddhism. He was impressed with Buddhist ethics, especially the prohibition against violence. He attempted to spread the ideals of nonviolence throughout India. With his leadership and encouragement, Buddhist missionaries carried the faith to lands in south Asia and far beyond into Egypt, Syria, Cyrene, and Greece.

After Asoka, Buddhism in India declined. Eventually the movement nearly vanished from the land in which it had been born. Why? The caste structure of Hindu society resisted a Buddhism that was against caste. Furthermore, both Buddhism and Hinduism are enthusiastically syncretistic and tolerant. With typical flexibility, Hinduism simply domesticated, absorbed, and gently smothered Buddhism.

Yet it was Islam which finally broke the back of Buddhism in India. During the twelfth and thirteenth centuries, Muslims strangled Buddhism in India by closing the monasteries. Buddhism cannot survive without monasteries. They are the means through which a person can experience enlightenment and escape into nirvana. Without the sangha, Buddhism must wither and die. This is especially true within the Theravada. By eradicating the sangha, the Muslims crushed Buddhism throughout northern India.

It is noteworthy that in modern times Marxism strangled Buddhism with the same methods used by the Muslims in India seven centuries ago. In Mongolia, Tibet, and China, Marxist governments wounded Buddhist societies by closing all but a few monasteries. In many communities the wound became fatal; atheistic secularism replaced Buddhism.

That happened in Mongolia, which had been one of the world's most enthusiastically Buddhist societies; prior to communism half the men were monks! However, during a 1994 visit to Mongolia, I was informed that the communist regime had closed seven thousand monasteries. Only one remained, as a showpiece in the capitol of Ulan Bataar. Mongolian Buddhism atrophied. Buddhism cannot survive indefinitely when it is robbed of the third refuge, the sangha.[9]

Although the Buddhist movement was smothered in India, it flourished in other societies in the Asian region. The Buddhist missionary ideal is to interact with cultures graciously. In its primal vision, Buddhism offered no critique of culture. Buddhism has not even given attention to family systems, although in China the monastic orientation of Buddhism led to the criticism that Buddhism was against the family. Buddhism has no comment on polyandry, polygyny, monogamy, or the traditional sexual mores of a society. Buddhism as taught and expressed by the early sangha is an invitation to psychological reorientation rather than a campaign to transform culture.

Yet in Asia, Buddhist expansion and political expressions have not always been gracious. Buddhist expansion into China has been marred by occasional violent upheaval. Buddhism fused with the imperial dynasties and nurtured martial arts. In the Buddhist temples of Songshan, I was astounded by powerful sculptures depicting monks performing violent acts. Even today, in fields adjacent to the temples, boys and girls practice these martial aerobics daily.

The Songshan temples are at the foot of the *Chung* (China) or Middle Mountain which in Chinese mythology is the center of the earth; that mountain is also the heartland of the *Chung Kuo* (Middle Kingdom) which is China. These warrior traditions developed as a Buddhist defense of China, the Middle Kingdom, which had embraced Buddhism.

In Japan, Buddhism also became a warrior ideology. In modern times violence between Buddhist and Hindu communities has become endemic in Sri Lanka. In 1992, violent Buddhist oppression of Muslims in Burma sent thousands of refugees across the borders into Bangladesh. When Buddhism has converged with political systems, it has become as inclined to violence for the preservation of the religio-political system as has been true of Islam and Christianity when the political authority and religious institutions become identical.

In the years just before mid-twentieth century, a surprising convergence between Buddhism and political institutions developed in India, the region where Buddhism had first arisen but then it almost vanished. The issue was caste. Mahatma Gandhi was appalled.

This is what happened. Bhimrao Ramji Ambedkar was from the Mahar caste, an untouchable subcaste. His early spirituality was nurtured by the Mahabodi Society, a modern Indian neo-Buddhist renewal movement. In 1954 he formally confessed that he was Buddhist. Bhimrao was the first minister of justice in independent India. To Gandhi's dismay, he opposed the caste system in its entirety; Gandhi wanted caste abuses removed, but not the system. Bhimrao and Gandhi experienced serious conflict on this issue.

Bhimrao was successful in introducing into Indian law many reforms which have significantly transformed Indian society in the decades since independence. He saw to it that even the Indian national flag contains the Buddhist symbol of the wheel. His is hardly the Buddhism of the Buddha, yet Bhimrao represents a modern expression of Buddhism which has undergone a significant paradigm shift in the light of modern realities.[10]

Buddhist societies left to themselves have never created democratic political institutions. As Buddhism spread into a region, the inclination was rather for the sangha to develop supportive alliances with existing political systems. The monks and nuns need support.

The gifts of lay persons are helpful. So is the financial and moral support of government. The sangha has often become quite fused with monarchical systems.

However, when parliamentary democracy is introduced into a region, the sangha has not resisted. The egalitarianism practiced within the sangha seems to nurture democratic political institutions once they are established within a Buddhist society.[11]

Pluralism

In its original vision, Buddhism is not even a religious movement. It is a way of thinking. The sangha is an ethical and a meditative community. Yet in its later development, Buddhism has shown the capability of being transformed into a religious and even political movement, if that is the desire of its adherents. Buddhism has capabilities of absorbing even apparently contradictory religious diversity. As mentioned earlier, within much of folk Buddhism, the Buddha himself has become divine.

Furthermore, within the Mahayana (Greater Vehicle) branch of Buddhism, local ancestors or traditional gods have been received into Buddhism as bodhisattvas. Recall that these are Buddhist savior divinities, who provide merit for their devotees. The bodhisattvas have helped to make folk Buddhism enormously attractive as a missionary movement; wherever Mahayana Buddhism has spread, the local ancestral heroes and local gods are welcomed into the Mahayana Buddhist cluster of bodhisattvas. This development has given missionary Buddhism incredible adaptability.

Buddhist missionaries insist that the threefold refuge of Buddhism, which is the essence of the movement, is unaffected by the religious practices of people. They believe that the psychological, ethical, and community dimensions of Buddhism can function effectively within any religious system.

From a Mahayana perspective, Jesus, Muhammad, Krishna, or Vishnu would be adaptable as bodhisattvas if perceived as saviors by a community becoming Buddhist. For example, in Japan the Shinto divinities have been largely incorporated into Japanese Buddhism. It is no wonder that nationalism and Buddhism often converge, with the two becoming indistinguishable.

The king's palace and temple in the heart of Bangkok, Thailand, reveal the amazing elasticity of Mahayana Buddhism. Huge painted murals surround the temple areas. They portray the activities of divinities. Most of the gods are from Hindu mythology. These depictions of the wars and loves of the gods encompass the most sacred Buddhist shrine in Thailand, the sacral center of the Buddhist monarchy of Thailand. The murals and icons reveal an inclination toward enthusiastic syncretism. There is room for all the gods in these elaborately painted pantheons.

As Buddhism has spread from society to society, various sects have developed. One of the most pervasive sects in Japan is Zen. One characteristic of Zen is that the quest for enlightenment includes excursions into irrationality. The notion is that rational thought is a mental instrument which obstructs salvation because reason provides cohesion to the phenomenon of the person. At times Zen practitioners have found that a sharp sudden whack with a club can also help to induce enlightenment by short-circuiting the reasoning powers of the devotee. It is not necessary to probe the phenomenon of Zen and the other sects further. However, it is noteworthy that the phenomenon of sects within Buddhism demonstrates the enormous cultural flexibility of this global missionary movement.

Buddhism absorbs astonishing internal pluralism. It also functions comfortably alongside other religions. The Buddhist emphasis on the responsibilities of the person affirms freedom of choice. Buddhism and pluralism are thus quite compatible.

Let us summarize three ways in which Buddhism responds to pluralism, that is, to people or communities who are not Buddhist.

a The first stance is welcoming people who voluntarily want to become Buddhists.

b A second stance is sharing the doctrine in such a manner that people can receive the Buddhist attitudes and practice within the framework of their own religious system.

c A third stance, in which Mahayana Buddhism is especially adept, is incorporating local divinities into the Buddhist system of bodhisattvas.

In brief, Buddhists welcome people into Buddhism, encourage non-Buddhists to absorb helpful insights from Buddhist philosophy, and welcome alien beliefs into Buddhism.

In spite of Buddhist broad-mindedness for pluralism, some Buddhist societies are appalled at any notion of conversion from Buddhism to another faith. We have discerned two basic reasons for this.

a First, the inclusive worldview of Buddhist societies insists that one can remain a Buddhist and at the same time participate in the religious practices of another faith system.

Second, the conviction pervades Buddhist culture that the enlight- b enment of Buddha is universal truth.

We now explore a further inhibition against movement away from Buddhism into an alternative faith system.

Buddhist Nations

Buddhism has frequently developed full integration with the nations in which the sangha has found a home. As noted earlier, the sangha needs support; monks and nuns are dependent on society for sustenance.

The sangha dependency on society encourages the inclination to welcome fusion with national political systems. Spiro Melford has done an excellent case study of the phenomenon of the integration of Buddhism and nation in Burma.[12] In countries such as Thailand, Burma, Cambodia, Mongolia, or Tibet, Buddhism fused with national culture and political life. These nations developed into ontocratic Buddhist societies, wherein the sacred and the political became one. In four of these countries, Marxist governments have attempted to break the back of these ontocratic Buddhist national systems.

When there is fusion of the political order and the sangha, of the nation and Buddhism, it is difficult for alternative faith communities to gain a foothold in the mainstream national culture. The resistance to alternative communities is not that the political system denies the right of people to choose or live their own faith. Rather it is the deep conviction that nationality and Buddhism are one. People perceive that conversion to another faith is a denial of their nationality. Conversion from Buddhism may be considered treason, like renouncing one's citizenship.

Earlier we have noted that some religions such as Shintoism or Hinduism are national religious systems. National religions are not missionary faiths; they do not have a universal mission; they are the faiths of a particular society or nation. However, a universal religion can also become a national faith wherein nation and religion become indistinguishable. Buddhism has frequently merged so completely with nation that the two are inseparable.

The merger of religion and nation has occurred occasionally within the other two universal faiths, Islam and Christianity. For example, the Greek nation and the Greek Orthodox Church are almost synonymous. Somali Muslims say that Islam flows in the veins of every Somali; Islam and the Somali nation could not be separated. Are not the universal faiths of Buddhism, Islam, and Christianity compromised when they become indistinguishable from a particular nation?

On one hand, the compromise, coming when a missionary faith is fused with a nation, is often revealed through the missionary faith becoming an instrument for imperial expansion of the nation. Political imperialism and missionary work are equated.

On the other hand, the compromise might appear in the faith becoming ingrown and ethnocentric or nation-centered, with no concern for sending missionaries to other nations or ethnic communities.

How, then, can a universal faith such as Buddhism maintain a global ethos in settings where it has become fully identified with a particular nation or nations?

Within the former kingdom of Siam, Buddhism and the nation merged. In modern Thailand that merger of nation and religion persists. In the Thai language, the full name for the capital, Bangkok, reveals a convergence of nation, ethnic identities, religions, gods, communities, and regions within an all-encompassing Buddhist nationalism or ontocracy. Here is the Latin script and a translation:

> *Krungthepmahanahorn Amornrattanakosin Mahintara Ayuthaya Mahadirok Pup Nopparat Rathanani Burirum Udomrajnivej Mahasathan Amornpimarn Ouwatarn Satit akatattiya Wisanu Karmprasit.*
>
> City of the Great Angel or God. Angel Who Will Not Die or Does Not Deteriorate. Diamond. Indra God Who Does Not Die. Invincible and Cannot Be Defeated. The Great. The Earth. World, Earth, the Cycle of Life, Death or Rebirth (Eternal Suffering). Nine Precious Stones: Diamond, Ruby, Emerald, Topaz, Garnet, Sapphire, Pearl, Zircon, Gem. Throne of an Eternal Angel. Angel Reincarnating into the Earth. Indra. King of the Land. Narai or Rama of Hinduism. Owner of all Treasures.[13]

Thai friends have given me other names for Bangkok as well. The Great City. The Residence of the Emerald Buddha. The Impregnable City. The Grand Capital of the World. The Happy City.

The full name for Bangkok is a revelation of ontocratic nationalism. All the themes of national and religious identity converge in the tiny, mysterious emerald Buddha seated on his elevated throne in the soul of the temples and mansions of the king's palace.

Bangkok is the residence of the emerald Buddha! This residency encompasses and absorbs the whole nation and all religions and all gods. In fact, the city of the emerald Buddha's residence is the Grand Capital of the World! At each change of season, the king of Thailand ascends the high throne of the emerald Buddha and reverently changes the Buddha's attire. In this act of ministry for the elegant emerald statuette, the king expresses the ontocratic bonding between king, the gods, religions, city, peoples, nation, global community, and Buddha. All are one.

The canopy of the emerald Buddha is large enough to encompass all within his shade. Buddhist national ontocracy nurtures that kind of pluralism. Yet what if some do not desire the Buddha's shade?

Ethics

The sangha is a missionary society; it is also the community in which Buddhist ethics are preserved. Recall that the Buddhist seeks a middle path between asceticism and hedonism. The sangha is the community which most perfectly demonstrates that middle path. Yet we will quickly discover that even the moderate middle path of Buddhist ethics is so demanding that there is no expectation that lay persons can ever achieve the ideal. Only those who take refuge in the sangha can achieve the moral ideal.

There are ten basic ethical commitments and personal disciplines which may be summarized thus:

1. Refrain from destroying life.
2. Do not take what is not given.
3. Abstain from sexual aberrations.
4. Do not lie or deceive.
5. Eat moderately and not after noon.
6. Do not look on at dancing, singing, or dramatic spectacles.
8. Do not affect the use of garlands, scents, unguents, or ornaments.
9. Do not use high or broad beds.
10. Do not accept gold or silver.[14]

Buddha taught that all Buddhists should comply with the first five precepts. The last five are practiced by the monks and nuns within the monastery which is the sangha. It is only in the sangha that the full Buddhist ethical ideals are achievable. All faithful Buddhists should live by the ideals of chastity, fidelity, truthfulness, moderation, and respect for life. Yet in Buddhist societies it is expected that there will be a significant divergence between the ethical principles of the sangha and the general society.

On a visit to a country which is officially and pervasively Buddhist, I was surprised by what appeared to be considerable sexual permissiveness. Public health experts confided alarm that in some towns a high percentage of the young adults are AIDS carriers. News reports indicated that a fourth of the military recruits are HIV-positive. The core cause of the epidemic is prostitution.[15] I was told that the permissiveness in this society is not just a modern development; it has always been so. Why?

Buddhist societies are afflicted with the same ethical dualism which permeates some Christianized societies, where lay people perceive that Christian ethics are only applicable to a monastic lifestyle. In such circumstances lay Christians might be grateful that some people choose a lifestyle of chastity or even celibacy in monasteries, but see no relevance for any such commitments for ordinary Christians. There is occasionally a severe divergence between the mores of society as a whole and the ideals upheld by monastic orders.

However, it is significant that Jesus never established or encouraged the formation of monastic communities. But that is not so with the founder of Buddhism. Buddha established the sangha because he never expected that lay people would be capable of practicing the ethical ideal. The ethics of Jesus are to be practiced in the world by all believers. The expectation is that Buddhist ethical ideals are only possible within the monastic order.

Islam also resists the ethical dualism of Buddhism. Muhammad, the prophet of Islam, never conceived of a monastic order; he believed the ethics of Islam were practical. All Muslims are expected to submit to Islamic ethics. Islam resists any notions of ethical divergence between religious specialists and lay persons.

Buddhist ethics are tiered; only monks and nuns are capable of the ethics of the sangha. The tiered ziggurat at Boro Bubur in central Java reveals the stages of enlightenment and portrays tiered ethics. At the lower levels, the stone icons depict normal human activities; recall that these icons are covered by the stone facade. These lay activities are irrelevant to the quest for salvation. It is only at the higher tiers that the icons become visible, and these describe the high ethical activities of Buddha as he sought enlightenment. Higher yet there are no icons, for this is the region in which the self discovers true emptiness.

The laity function within the ethical realms of the lower levels of the ziggurat. Only monks can function in the higher levels. Monasticism is the only way to live out the Buddhist ideal. There is therefore "a basic tension between 'authentic' monastic existence and 'unauthentic' lay existence."[16]

Only a few are capable of acquiring enlightenment and the ethical ideal. The ethics of the sangha are for those few. As for the rest of society, they will have to await another incarnation.

Family

a male bias

There was debate within the primal Buddhist community on the place of women in the movement. In time Buddha did admit women into the sangha as nuns. However, the broad consensus in Buddhism is that women should invest their lives in nurturing the family.

The great renunciation is a male vocation, hardly a vocation for females. Even today most Theravada Buddhist communities perceive that no woman is capable of enlightenment.[17] That will have to await another incarnation as a man. The quest for enlightenment has always been mostly a male enterprise, and even for them few are capable of acquiring ultimate release from the wheel of rebirth.

Siddhartha Gautama left his wife and infant son, Rahula, to seek enlightenment. He left quietly at night, without even a farewell. His quest for truth superseded his commitment to his family or his responsibilities in society. His son, Rahula, grew up without a father, and his wife became a woman without a husband, for Siddhartha had decided on the great renunciation. To seek enlightenment he turned his back on his parents, wife, son, the princely wealth and pleasures which his family enjoyed, and his responsibilities in society. His father was overwhelmed with grief.

none higher than Buddha

The monastic sangha in Buddhist societies nurtures these ideals of renunciation. Within the soul of Buddhism, there is a critique of any ultimate loyalty other than a commitment to acquiring personal release (arahat) from the wheel of rebirth through the experience of enlightenment (bodhi). Ideally family and all other commitments and responsibilities are secondary to the quest for personal enlightenment.

As Buddhism spread through China, the monks were occasionally accused of being against the family. For those who value the enduring integrity of the family, the idealization of Buddha's great renunciation seemed a dangerous idea indeed. Buddhism has sometimes collided with the Chinese Confucian ideals of political, social, and family order and responsibility.

Imagine the tension between a Buddhist missionary monk and a Confucian academic holding a discussion in the imperial court of China. The Buddhist sage is teaching that the ideal goal of personhood is the great renunciation; the Confucian scholar argues that the integrity of the political system and family institutions will assure happiness for everybody.

It is not surprising that the Buddhist experience in China occasionally included violent opposition by Confucian society. The profound sense of socio-political-ethical responsibility in Confucianism and the Buddhist invitation to renunciation and retreat into the sangha are quite different perspectives indeed.

An International Community

The sangha which Buddha himself organized has in all its diversities always been a significant vehicle for Buddhist missionary endeavor. These monastic orders are centers of Buddhist reflection and teaching, which in Buddhist societies provide encouragement generation after generation for people to abide within the three refuges of Buddhism. The sangha are also missionary centers in societies where Buddhism is not yet accepted. In recent decades, a number of Buddhist world conferences have planned to open new Buddhist missionary centers in non-Buddhist societies, especially in Western countries.

The up-front motive for this modern emphasis on expanding the presence of the sangha in non-Buddhist societies is peace. The Buddhist commitment to peace emphasizes the inner qualities that make for peace and the avoidance of suffering. A central motive in the expansion of the sangha is the common Buddhist conviction that the sangha is the only context in which the enlightened life can be sustained. That enlightenment is peace.

Buddhism also emphasizes attitudes toward one's enemy that make for peace. As mentioned earlier, this aspect of Buddhist faith was strongly emphasized by Emperor Asoka over two thousand years ago, as he attempted to forge a peace throughout India which was grounded in Buddhist ethics.

The sangha provides a transnational network of communities of Buddhist faith that are committed to peace for the individual. However, especially in modern times, there are occasional expressions of the Buddhist sangha which have developed an interest in becoming transnational communities of international peace, as described by the emissaries of the Dalai Lama. It might be that interaction between communities such as the World Council of Churches and Buddhist decision-makers has helped to interest some Buddhists with international peace concerns.

Yet these inclinations must not be overstated. The soul of Buddhism is an invitation to personal peace through taking refuge in the Buddha, the dharma, and the sangha. The idealization of the great renunciation with the quest for personal disengagement from suffering does not encourage vigorous involvement in conflicts between peoples and nations.

Global Issues

Our exploration of Buddhism within global community has given special attention to several key concerns. We have observed paradoxes; some are within the soul of primal Buddhism, and others modernity has forced upon Buddhism.

These areas of tension have included—

- the paradox of individual salvation versus compassion for the community of humankind;
- the paradox of a secularizing global village and a worldview which considers history and human progress as distractions from the quest for salvation;
- the paradox of a worldview embracing naturalistic philosophies of science versus a hesitancy to dominate and control the earth.

We have observed other dimensions of modern realities within a Buddhist context: peace and nonviolence, ego emptiness and tolerance, global mission and pluralism, ethics and the family, or Buddhist nations and the international sangha. We have discerned that Buddhism is an actor in the global community with a sense of mission, a commitment of enabling the person to acquire peace.

We also discovered that the survival of the Buddhist community is dependent on the health of the sangha. Governments who wish to destroy Buddhism can strangle the community by destroying the sangha. Buddhism cannot survive without the monks.

We have explored themes within Buddhism which are especially congruent with perspectives or issues within the modern global community. We note several of these themes:

1. Buddhist philosophy is a naturalistic worldview capable of embracing philosophies of science based on naturalism or atheism.

2. Buddhism provides the emotional supports which enable the person to transcend suffering.

3. Buddhism in its essence is tolerant. It is able to accept pluralism and, when true to its convictions, demonstrates a missionary orientation adverse to any forms of coercion or enticement.

4. Buddhism has sometimes moved beyond a focus on personal peace to commitment to interpersonal and intercommunity peace.

5. Buddha affirmed compassion for humankind with the caution that a person not become emotionally involved with the person in need; it is better to have compassion for humankind than toward a particular person.

6. There have been a few times in the history of Buddhism when efforts have been made to transform social institutions such as caste in India. Yet engagement with social structures is more a divergence than an essential quality of Buddhism.

7. In the sangha there is a bias toward democracy; however, the sangha does not characteristically push a society toward democracy.

8. Buddhism is now an international community which might sometime seek serious engagement with modern international global issues.

We have also explored Buddhist perspectives which modern realities forthrightly confront. We note several special challenges:

1. The Buddhist emphasis on ego emptiness and tolerance suggests an uncritical attitude toward evil.

2. The Buddhist assumption that only the sangha can achieve the moral life leaves Buddhist masses in too many societies with inadequate moral foundations.

3. The Buddhist primary emphasis on peace for the individual encourages withdrawal from realistic engagement with community and global issues. The Buddhist philosophy of life has little or no inclination toward transforming social institutions which function in an unwholesome manner.

4. Buddhist philosophy develops an orientation which tends not to take history and the material world seriously.

Some aspects of Buddhism are undergoing special challenges and even paradigm shifts as Buddhist societies seek to function creatively, constructively, and relevantly within modern societies.

The Lotus

The Buddhist worldview emphasizes that one should let life flow naturally like the flowing of a stream which drifts with the terrain, until it finally reaches the sea and is absorbed into the ocean. Acquiescence to the rhythms of living and nature is idealized. Harmony and peace is the experience of the one who has ceased all wrongful desire to maintain the illusion of personhood, who has ceased resisting the meandering stream of life. Such a person is an enlightened one, as beautiful as the lotus flower which blooms amid the mud holes. That is the ideal.

Several years ago, while riding a bus through the manicured farmlands between Pattaya and Bangkok, Thailand, a Siamese woman was describing the wonders of her country.

Suddenly she exclaimed, "There, see, in that mud hole! That is what Buddhism is about."

I looked. There they were. The lovely lotus flowers covering the mud hole with beauty.

For the Buddhist the lotus flower is the symbol of the peace that comes forth from the mud hole of suffering. The person who has become an arahat, has experienced release from the desire for existence, and is free from suffering although living amidst suffering— that person is like the lotus. The lotus remains pure and beautiful even while arising from the mud; it transcends its context.

Reflection

1. Assess the Buddhist approach to pluralism in the light of modern global realities.

2. Reflect on the modern Buddhist commitment to global mission. What are the possibilities of this mission contributing to world peace?

3. There is a paradox in Buddhism between salvation and compassion. Describe ways Buddhists have tried to resolve the paradox.

4. What is the function of the sangha? What are the ethical implications of the sangha for Buddhist societies?

5. Reflect on the Gandhian and Buddhist commitment to ahimsa. What could people of other faith traditions learn from this commitment?

6. Assess the implications of the goal of egonegation for the well-being of the person and community.

6

Ignore the Gods

Confucius and Plato

CONFUCIUS, the philosopher of the Shantung Peninsula of China, and Plato, the philosopher of the Attica Peninsula of Greece, both lived in the fifth century B.C. Yet they were not contemporary. Confucius died during the first half of the century, and Plato was born during the last half.

Vast human communities in both East and West still live in the long shadows of Confucius and Plato. The concerns of these two philosophers, one from Asia and the other from Europe, in some ways anticipate the commitments of Marxism twenty-four centuries later. Confucius, Plato, and Marx converge in their conviction that human well-being depends on right political institutions—religion is an irrelevant nuisance. A later chapter will describe the twentieth-century Marxist political experiment.

Both Confucius and Plato sought to free people from enslavement to the gods of nature, fate, and location. This chapter probes the reasons these philosophers believed the gods do not contribute helpfully in providing the foundations for wholesome community. What are the implications of building community on a philosophical rather than a religious foundation? These are the intriguing issues which set the tone for this chapter.

Chinese Philosophy

The Forbidden City in Beijing is a key to understanding the significant influence Confucianism has had on Chinese society. The City was built early in the fifteenth century; by 1925, twenty-four emperors had ruled from this fortress whose architecture exuded Confucian themes. The massive entrance adjoining the northern boundary of Tiananmen Square is the Heavenly Peace Gate. People crossing a small moat into the first spacious courtyard can choose from five bridges, each representing a Confucian virtue—benevolence, righteousness, rites, intelligence, or fidelity.

Inside the City, the first courtyard leads into the Palace of Supreme Harmony. Beyond that palace is a second, several-hundred meter courtyard leading to an ascent into the Palace of Complete Harmony. Then a third courtyard leads to the highest palace, Preserving Harmony. The emperor lived adjacent to the Hall of Mental Cultivation. The Hall of Heavenly Purity was where the emperor welcomed foreign guests. These palaces form the heart of the City.

Our university student informants were thankful that the era of Confucian examinations is no more. The highest level examinations were offered only every three years. Three hundred of the best students across China qualified; they gathered for the examination in the highest palace, Preserving Harmony. The emperor presided. Those who failed were sometimes so depressed they committed suicide. Those who passed became the counselors to the emperor who helped direct the affairs of government. Lower level examinations determined who was eligible to counsel on provincial or county affairs.

The scholars and the emperors they counseled ran a tight ship. Our eager guides informed us that the vast courts without trees were for security, so ambushes against the authorities would be impossible. And they described the beatings and executions of dissidents in these courtyards. When subjects wished to petition the emperor and his court of scholars, they bowed prostrate beseeching for an audience.

On October 1, 1949, Mao Tse-tung stood on the balcony above the Heavenly Peace Gate entrance to the Forbidden City. He faced tens of thousands of revolutionaries thronging Tiananmen Square and declared the establishment of the immortal Peoples Republic of China, a revolution that would reach from China to the ends of the earth. In this defiant gesture, Mao Tse-tung intended a break with twenty-four centuries of Chinese political thought; the vanguard of the communist proletariat would forever replace the scholars of Confucianism as the determiners of political philosophy.

Soon the communist regime in China had built a new "forbidden city" on the western edge of Tiananmen. When in June 1989 students from across China brought their petitions for change to Tiananmen, they prostrated themselves before the communist "forbidden city," beseeching for an audience. But instead of dialogue, they received bullets. The communist dictatorship of the proletariat could be even more repressive than the authority of the Confucian scholars had become in a previous era.

Tiananmen Square and these two adjacent "forbidden cities" are a dramatic statement of the juxtaposition of Confucian scholarly salvation and the communist revolutionary salvation offered by Mao Tse-tung. A later chapter will explore the utopia offered by communism. This chapter explores ancient themes that have molded China for more than two thousand years.

P'an Ku

First we look at the ancient yet enduring Chinese worldview in which Confucianism was formed. In contrast to Hinduism or Buddhism, the Chinese believe that nature is real and beautiful. Heaven, humanity, history, and nature are all interrelated. The Chinese have a long view of history and an appreciation for nature.

According to the legends, Chinese history goes back two million years, back to when the first archetypal man, P'an Ku, carved out the earth. As is typical of ontocratic worldviews, at the death of this divine man, his remains became the natural features of China, the mountains, wind, clouds, rain, thunder, fields, stars, and metal. The insects on his body are the people. It is thus not surprising that prior to the radical secularism of Marxism, natural phenomena such as earth mounds or the sky were freely venerated as divine.

This land of P'an Ku is the Middle Kingdom, which is the center of an orderly cosmos. This ancient worldview suggests that China is at the center of the global community. Worldviews resist change. It is not surprising that even in modern times it is rare for top Chinese political leaders to travel elsewhere in the world. Why should they venture away from the center of the cosmos? Rather, let the rest of the earth come to China.

Yin-Yang

Chinese culture is influenced by the notion that good and evil always coexist and interrelate. This idea is rooted in the *yin-yang* (female-male) principle which pervades traditional culture. All existence is an expression of the dynamic tension and relationship between these female-male principles.

Just as it is natural for female and male to coexist, so it is also natural for evil and good to interrelate and coexist. In fact, every twenty-four hours the drama of the interaction between good and evil is evident in the rhythm of day and night. Day is good and night evil. A folk saying indicates that is why the cock crows at the beginning of the dawn; he is announcing the return of the good.

There is nothing anyone can do to prevent the rhythm of *yin* and *yang* or day and night. So relax. The ancient sage or sages of Tao (the way of nature) philosophy pushed this concept far indeed. Good and evil shall always coexist. Happily, even in evil times one can always be assured that in time good will reappear.

However, be aware that even the good is interpenetrated with evil, and that which appears to be good to one person may be evil to another. Thus one can never say categorically that this is evil and that is good. Taoist moral ambivalence has left an enduring imprint on China.

That ambivalence informs the attitudes of many Chinese toward the catastrophic suffering of the great leap forward when thirty million people may have died and the horrible upheavals of the cultural revolution. "Mistakes were made, but there has also been much that is good," a variety of Chinese people told us during a 1994 visit. These included those who had suffered most unjustly."

Taoist moral ambivalence also informs Chinese perplexity about U.S. concerns for human rights in China. University officials commented to me, "It is not good to jail dissidents. However, political stability is good. Why can't Americans understand that good and evil must intermingle?"

Wu-Wei

The notion of maintaining a relaxed spirit in the face of adversity or apparent evil is the soul of Tao philosophy. This philosophy is described in the ancient documents known as "The Way of Life of Lao-Tzu." The central theme of Taoism is *wu-wei*. This means: Don't be meddlesome! Through nonaction let things take their course! Don't interfere in the rhythm of good and evil.

> Listen to the counsel of Lao-Tzu:
> Since the world points up beauty as such,
> There is ugliness too.

> If goodness is taken as goodness,
> Wickedness enters as well.

Elsewhere Lao-Tzu observes that even God moves in the spirit of wu-wei.

> God's Way is bound to conquer all
> But not by strife does it proceed.
> Not by words does God get answers;
> He calls them not and all things come.
> Master plans unfold but slowly,
> Like God's wide net enclosing all;
> Its mesh is coarse but none are lost.

The spirit of wu-wei is the way of Tao, which is the way of nature and of God. The one who follows Tao is the one who flows with the natural stream of nature. This is true strength, just as the flowing water is stronger than the stone. Over time the hard stone becomes smaller and at last disappears, overcome by the gentle meandering stream.[1]

Lao-Tzu, winsome philosopher of China's ancient past, would have winced had he met his biblical prophetic contemporaries, who denounced the evil authorities of their day with somewhat less patience than it takes to wait for a stone to erode away in a stream of water.

The Tao art of harmonizing with the life flow of the universe may involve the early morning practice of gentle shadow boxing amidst the tranquil greenery of a grove of trees as the eastern sky begins to lighten. Whenever I am in Hong Kong, I love an early morning jog on a grass-covered hill just off Waterloo Road. As I jog I feel like an elephant thundering along amidst a herd of gentle gazelles; scores of shadow boxers are inviting their bodies and spirits to absorb the tranquillity of a new day dawning. Some of them carry a bird in a cage, and the bird may chirp in accompaniment with the gentle movements of its human escort.

The commitment to Tao is personal. It is not a community but individual enterprise. Governments and societies should avoid interfering with the whims of the individual. The strong emphasis on the individual in Taoism has left an enduring impact on Chinese culture. "Save face" is a Chinese axiom.

In popular culture, Tao became a source of empowerment. It merged with folk magic known as *qigong*. Like the *mana* of the Melanesian islanders of the south Pacific, *qi* is the impersonal energy which provides the dynamic potency to the universe. Qi can be manipulated for the well-being of the person or for the destruction of enemies.

Yet qigong is not that harmless. In the past two millennia, this expression of the Taoist worldview has become occult. This may be an aberration of Tao but is nevertheless very real. The personal empowerment offered by qigong is especially attractive to people who feel their lot is hopeless. In desperation they may reach for the potentially destructive empowerment offered by occult expressions of qigong.

The Emperor and the Cosmos

The laissez-faire approach of the Taoists to reality was too gentle for the Confucian philosophers. They sought a much more active and political approach to human problems. The well-being of the political order was the center of their interest. This conviction that a healthy political order is essential for wholesome society is rooted in the worldview that China is the center of the cosmos.

The traditional Chinese theory of history is that the qualities of the Chinese emperor affect the quality of the cosmos. Bad emperors create disequilibrium in China and the cosmos. The whole global community is affected adversely by bad Chinese emperors. The rule of good emperors is characterized by harmony in Chinese society, nature, and the whole world. Heaven has determined that this be so.

Chinese history was written to demonstrate this cosmic fact. If an emperor's rule was characterized by social upheaval, international convulsions, or natural disasters, he was obviously not a good man. If there was tranquillity, then he was a good person. This philosophy of history influenced the way the official records were written. Accounts had to demonstrate the axiom that good rulers create well-being in the cosmos; the historians doctored the data to establish the point.

The notion that there is harmony in the cosmos when the political leaders are good might have informed political developments in 1976. After the deaths that year of both Chou En-lai and Mao Tse-tung, the nation and government decidedly discredited the "Gang of Four" who had been intimately involved in the center of power. The disastrous upheaval of the Cultural Revolution and natural disasters, such as the catastrophic Tangshan earthquake of August 1976, suggested that something was wrong at the center of power during the later years of Mao's life. Any leader whose rule is accompanied by such disasters should be suspect.

Government and Well-being

The mission of Confucius, and those who carried on his efforts after he was gone, was to develop a political philosophy which could assure that emperors and the political processes would function in a good manner. This was consistent with the worldview that a righteous political order in China assures the well-being of the cosmos.

The basic teachings of Confucius, the political philosopher, are recorded in the *Analects* (*Lun Yu*), a collection of sayings of Confucius as well as his disciples and colleagues. Three other major works also contain Confucian philosophy—*The Great Learning* (*Ta Hsueh*), *The Doctrine of the Mean* (*Chung Yung*), and the *Book of Mencius*.

The emphasis of these volumes reveals a worldview and value system committed to social proprieties and belief in an intimate relationship between person, society, and cosmological order. Good government is the key to cosmological harmony, because the people will imitate their rulers. The example of the rulers is far more important than the laws they pass.

Who gives the emperor the authority to govern? The ancient traditions said heredity and heaven. The Confucian philosophers debated the issue of authority for a government. While philosophers such as Mo Tzu believed that heaven gives the emperor and government authority to rule, Confucius himself radically desacralized government. He stripped government of any claim to divine right rule. Instead he anchored the right of government to rule in morality. He believed that the will of heaven as well as the functioning of nature were moral order. The emperor had to be a moral person, a virtuous ruler, or he would lose the mandate of heaven.

Neither divine right nor heredity are the final word; virtue is the criterion to judge the legitimacy of government. The people the emperor governed should be capable of assessing whether their rulers were virtuous. In this Confucius was over two thousand years ahead of the European Enlightenment! To enable the subjects to express themselves effectively on matters of such importance, Confucius campaigned to provide universal formal education for all who were capable of study.

Confucius enjoyed questions and discussions concerning religious matters, but, like some of his Greek contemporary philosophers, he was not persuaded that spirits and divinities actually existed. He opposed any religious practices which inhibited the integrity of the political process or were dehumanizing in any way. He insisted on divorcing ethics and politics from religion. He was a secular man indeed!

Li

The ethical path is the way of the ancestors, known as *li*. Confucius believed that cosmic harmony depended on the commitment of the people to live in harmony with the li of their ancestors. In Taoism the way of nature is emphasized; in Confucianism it is the way of the ancestors which is center stage.

The Confucian notion is that in the golden age of the ancestors there was perfect cosmic harmony. This is because the attitudes and actions of the ancestors were right. The li of the ancestors demonstrates right relationships in every dimension of society—between ruler and subjects—between father and son, between husband and wife, between oldest son and younger sons, between elders and juniors.

The commitment to li has provided Chinese society with enormous stability and durability. Even when Chinese people move to lands far from their motherland, for many of them li continues to be their primary ethical gyroscope.

At a meeting with Chinese immigrants to the United States, I asked, "What is your greatest concern about living in this country?"

"That our children will lose touch with the way of our foreparents," was their instant reply. "American culture seems to have little depth. We hope our children will not become too Americanized. We want them always to appreciate the values of our Chinese culture."

In response to that concern, Chinese communities in diaspora often arrange classes on Chinese languages and Confucian values for their offspring. They instruct their children in the Chinese way of life. Yet there are difficulties. Confucianism is a national rather than a global ethic. There are no Confucian disciples traversing the globe attempting to encourage non-Chinese people to accept the Confucian way of life. Only Chinese people can follow the way of li.

A national ethic such as li also creates difficulties for minorities in China. Whose ancestors are the ideal model? Neither Confucianism nor Mao's brand of communism have nurtured a healthy affirmation of the diversities that respect for ethnic integrity demands.

However, Confucian values have provided a strong and self-assured identity for multitudes of modern Chinese wherever they may reside in the global village. These values preserve their strong sense of community identity and ethnic pride.

Shu

What are these treasured Confucian values? The kernel is *shu* (fellow feeling or reciprocity). The essence of shu is summarized in that universally celebrated Confucian statement, "What you do not want done to yourself, do not do to others."[2]

Notice a similarity between this Confucian moral kernel and the so-called golden rule of Christian faith, which affirms, "Do to others as you would have them do to you."[3] The Christian commitment is active. The Confucian commitment seems more quiescent. These commitments would be affirmed in most societies.

For Confucius shu was jovial and practical idealism. He believed society should function with compassion for the poor. Good government should provide opportunities to enjoy life for everyone. Loyalty and respect for the family is the foundation of all other human relationships. The whole ethical system is infused with themes of filial piety. However, a family-first ethic is inclined to nurture nepotism and corruption!

Shu is a happy responsibility. For Confucius these duties of right relationships were a joyful enterprise which included song and celebration. However, for some of his fellow philosophers that was not the case. For them duty was a somber enterprise; song was never appropriate!

The Higher Type of Human

Confucianism is optimistic about human nature. The intention of the whole political system is to enable people to live virtuously and happily. The truly virtuous person is the higher type of human (chun-tzu, meaning a prince or superior person).

That is what Confucianism is about—the ordering of society so the higher type of person emerges. This superior person is righteous, altruistic (jen), and an example of social proprieties (li). The key to the whole enterprise of creating the higher type of person is the virtue of the emperor and the manner in which he governs.

The ancient sage declares, "If there were a true king upon the throne of China, unquestionably Manhood-at-its-best would prevail in one generation."[4]

This is indeed the gospel of political salvation! It is a distant echo of the nineteenth-century vision of the ideal communist man who would be created through communist political and educational formation. Yet there is also a great difference in the two movements. In dramatic contrast to Marxism, Confucianism abhors coercion. Being a good example, rather than laws and coercion, is the essence of good government.

Modernity

Today a fifth of the world's people reside in China. The Confucian ideals still significantly influence this most populous nation on earth and also many of the 100 million Chinese in diaspora. The Confucian culture is a web which binds these amazing people together. How should Confucianism be assessed in the light of modernity in the global community? We make several observations.

First, the traditional Chinese ontocratic worldview was not significantly touched by Confucianism. The masses still believed that nature was divine. Consequently they continued to be vigorous worshipers of various expressions of nature, such as mounds of earth they perceived to be the female counterpart to the divine male heaven.

Only much later, when the Chinese people began to encounter the rigorous monotheism of Islam and the biblical gospel, did a genuine break with the worldview that nature is divine commence among some Chinese people. This break was necessary for Chinese society to embrace at a worldview level the assumptions of modern scientific methodology. The worldview of modern science is not compatible with notions that the gods and nature are one.

At midcentury the Marxist revolution ruthlessly expanded the break with the ontocratic worldview which Christianity and Islam had begun. It did this through a sometimes violent revolution grounded in a radical atheistic secularism.

Second, the fixation on li provides tremendous resistance to change. Early in the Confucian movement, the focus on li began to become a rigid doctrine and discipline.

Scholars took up the mantle of studying and applying li. The primary function of the higher educational system was the study of li in the form of the classics. It became the responsibility of the scholars to counsel government and society on the right way to do things, and that right way was always the way of the ancestors of antiquity.

The conservation of enduring values is the great advantage of this system. Yet the worldview has no "theology" of history on the move. Progress in Confucianism is movement toward retrieval of an ideal which has been in the past. There is no inclination toward cultural change in an unfolding future.

How can Confucian society adapt when the realities of global community require change? Examples of the issues are the attitudes toward children or womanhood. In the ancient traditions, a duty was to marry and have many children. Modern ecological and demographic reality demands a change in that value. In relation to womanhood, the Confucian ideal is strongly oriented toward the male. Yet in the modern global community many societies insist on male and female equality. Certainly the qualities of human relationships which li reveals will always be relevant. However, the scholasticism, rigidities, nepotism of a family centered focus, and orientation toward the past of classical Confucianism are less than helpful.

The Marxist revolution attempted to break the link between modern society and classical Confucianism. Even filial piety was critiqued as inspiring corruption. Consequently the filial piety which has graced Chinese culture for millennia is under severe stress.

"My grandparents love me, but I do not like them," bluntly expounded a Beijing university student to my wife and me during a stroll through Tiananmen Square. "I seldom visit them even though they are near my residence. I do not need them."

In any society a break between generations is tragic; in a traditionally Confucian society it is especially distressing. Imagine the pain of any parents or grandparents whose progeny have spurned them, but especially of those who have always believed that the essential quality of human life is filial piety.

However, although the modern Peoples Republic of China attempted to break with the rigidities of classical Confucianism, enduring qualities of this ancient Chinese sage will always influence Chinese society.

Recently my host in a breakfast meeting in Singapore commented, "We in Singapore value the principles of Confucian ethics. We feel those values are contributing to our prosperity and stability."

Singapore is a beautiful city. The modern buildings are state-of-the-art architecture. It has almost no unemployment or slums. Although it is a dynamic industrial city, air pollution is rigidly controlled. The hedonism of modern Western cultures is prohibited. The business atmosphere vibrates prosperity.

Although Singapore is a Christianizing city, my host affirmed that the Christian leaders in this postmodern technological global city desire to preserve the enduring virtues of the sage from the Shantung Peninsula who lived some 2,500 years ago.

A Singaporean taxi driver surprised my wife and me by asking in his street English, "You flush toilet today? One hundred dollars fine if not you flush toilet."

He continued, "Singapore good city. No problems here because government make so many good rules, like must always flush toilet. Follow good rules wise government make, then all things good.

That why Singapore so nice. But don't forget—do rules always."

Later a Singaporean businessman picked up the same theme, "We have no unemployment or homeless people because government and society work together cooperatively."

Recall the teachings of Confucius on the relationship between a virtuous government and the well-being of the people. Both the taxi driver and the businessperson were describing a government which they perceived as being virtuous, and they were pleased with the results—a prosperous people!

Nevertheless, a political ethic grounded in Confucianism can only survive if the majority are ethnic Chinese. That was the point a Singaporean businessperson made to me during an elaborate Chinese New Year's dinner. He said, "It would be catastrophic for Singapore if the Chinese became the minority. Our system can only work when Chinese with Confucian values are in control."

As we enter the twenty-first century, the global community will be increasingly challenged by the dynamism of traditionally Confucian societies who have managed to drink from the fountains of secularization while at the same time maintaining a healthy commitment to the enduring graces of shu (fellow feeling and reciprocity). The qualities of self-discipline, integrity, hard work, and loyalty which characterize Confucian ethics are a good preparation for over a billion people intent on exercising their rightful role in the global community.

However, modernity has put Confucian political philosophy to a severe test, including Mao Tse-Tung's Chinese version of communist political salvation. The role and political philosophy of China is undergoing an astonishing metamorphosis. A five-thousand-year turning point in Chinese political culture and worldview commenced in 1971, when U.S. secretary of state Henry Kissinger visited Beijing. That event ushered China into the community of nations.

For five thousand years the Chinese self-perception had been that the Chinese nation was the center of the cosmos. Then in the nineteenth century, a great humiliation commenced as Western powers trampled on this proud people and culture. The communist revolution sought to reinstate China as the primal nation among the nations. Mao's revolution would bring salvation to the whole world. However, the cultural revolution created shambles of that dream. In two decades of the communist revolution, China was in the throes of a profound identity crisis.

Then came Kissinger's visit. He helped open the door for the

People's Republic of China to assume a seat in the United Nations Security Council as one of five permanent members. China is now recognized as an equal among equals; it is respected as one of the five great powers with the authority to veto decisions of the Council.

China is neither the center of the cosmos nor the downtrodden pariah. Surely this must be a five-thousand-year watershed development. China is undergoing an unprecedented worldview paradigm shift. Chinese intellectuals are propelled into a quest for a fresh philosophical perception on the meaning and place of China in the global community. These are times of incredible intellectual ferment in China.

There is urgent need for a fresh philosophy of nationhood and government which provides the spiritual and intellectual framework for authentic Chinese participation as an equal partner in a global community of nations. The ancient sages such as Confucius never struggled with those sorts of issues; they assumed China was the center of the cosmos. Modern global realities do not sustain that assumption. These are the issues: What is the role of China as one among equals in a pluralistic community of nations? What kind of political philosophy can equip China for nurturing the well-being of her people, including her ethnic minorities, and for authentic participation in the global village?

Plato's Problem

We turn now to another people in another continent whose quest for universal truth also led them to challenge the authority of the gods. These were the philosophers of the Greek Peninsula of Attica.

The sages who converged at the Aegean port city of Athens were not the only philosophers of the Mediterranean region. Around the sixth century B.C., other schools also flourished in locations such as Italy or Mesopotamia.

Yet it is the Athenian experience which has most affected Western culture. An exploration of that development is necessary for some understanding of the religious and ideological tapestry of modern Western societies.

The Athenian Greeks were strategically located to experience religious pluralism. The thriving commercial centers of Greece were the meeting places of the peoples of the entire Mediterranean region. Each people group contributed their own pantheon of divinities.

The gods embodied expressions of natural or human phenomena

—Poseidon, the sea god; Demeter, the goddess of fertility; or Aphrodite, the goddess of love. Some were linked to the cycles of nature. In the mystery cults, the worshipers identified with the experiences of the dying and resurrecting gods whose annual death and coming back to life caused the cycles of winter cold and death and summer warmth and life. The Greek pantheon of gods enlarged and adapted to accommodate the divinities of other peoples of the region.

The Gods Also Sin

The gods were not characteristically righteous. The stories of the exploits of the ancient divinities of Greece described by Homer in the *Iliad* and *Odyssey* are not flattering from a moral perspective. No caring father or mother would desire their children to follow the moral example of the gods. It was not uncommon for sexual license to be included in the acts of worshiping the Greek gods. Especially among the philosophers, the immorality of the gods encouraged skepticism concerning their validity.

Recall that Confucius also attempted to drive a wedge between religion and morality. Neither he nor the Greek philosophers perceived that the gods were of any help in encouraging moral order. Recall the words of Xenophanes in the preface: "Homer and Hesiod have ascribed to the gods all things that among men are a shame and a reproach—theft and adultery and deceiving one another." [5]

The skepticism of the Confucian and the Greek philosophers concerning the gods is strangely modern. We have observed that modern anthropological and psychological research has demonstrated that people are indeed inclined to worship divinities who are in their own likeness. Sigmund Freud was so impressed with the evidence that he dismissed all belief in a god or gods as purely need-inspired illusion.[6] Many of the Greek philosophers experienced similar skepticism.

Yet the philosophers as well as modern humankind discover that the gods are not easily dismissed. Even if they are the creations of the human mind, as Freud suggests, their power over people is real, formidable, and binding.[7]

The philosophers sought for the one universal principle which was the key to understanding all reality. Was the universal principle fire? Perhaps air? Maybe very small particles in constant movement (atoms)? Exploring the various dimensions of that quest for the one unitary principle is not necessary here. Our intention is to focus briefly on the stream in that quest for the unitary principle which has most significantly affected Western culture—Platonism.

Godless Government Might be Good

Plato was a disciple of the Socrates whose "know thyself" has been taught to Western high school students for many centuries. Socrates sought to comprehend the truth through the process of questioning and discussion. He was dismayed by the irrelevance of the gods to the quest for the moral good.

Yet from the perspective of the political powers, reverence for the gods was necessary to preserve political stability. The gods maintained the political and social order, immoral as they might be. Athenian leaders feared that the ideas of Socrates, which were infiltrating the minds of the young people, threatened the stability of the state.

Consequently Socrates was sentenced to death by drinking hemlock. Although he had opportunities to escape, he refused to do so for that, it seemed to him, would be a moral digression. He believed that the virtuous person must be ready to accept the consequences of his actions.

Plato and Aristotle carried forward the quest for the universal truth which so characterized Socrates. Yet by questioning the authority or even existence of the gods, the philosophers were indeed challenging the sacred basis for the existence of all social institutions including government. That was a revolutionary idea in a global community in which all societies perceived that the integrity of social and political institutions were based on their connections with divinity.

Typically governments everywhere were ontocracies—that is, divine power and political authority merged. In societies such as Egypt, the head of state was a god. To drive a wedge between the gods and the political order seemed a dangerous experiment. Yet that is exactly what Platonism attempted. So did Confucianism.

Seeking Universal Truth

If the political order does not need the sanction of the gods, from whence then does it acquire sanction? Plato struggled with that question. His *Republic* is a political philosophy which is an attempted response. Both Confucius and Plato believed that political institutions which had been stripped of their sacred or divine nature needed the counsel of the philosophers to function properly. The philosophers were responsible for helping to replace the gods as the guardians of the state and social institutions. Plato taught that the philosophers were needed to guide the state because it was they who had developed the intuitive skills to perceive the truth.

And what is the truth? The ideal universal good. The principle which unites the whole universe is the ideal good. The particular expressions of material visible forms should be expressions of the ideal. The ideal can be perceived through intuition.

Plato referred to this gift of intuition as the *logos* (word) which is present in everyone. However, some people are more apt than others in perceiving the logos. Through discussion the notions of intuitive truth can be processed, tested, confirmed, and understood. This is the work of philosophers—to perceive the ideal and counsel on how to apply that ideal.

By challenging the stranglehold which the gods of nature had over social institutions and the natural processes, the philosophers freed the mind for an analytical study of the forms present in the material world. Aristotle was especially effective in carrying on that quest. His observation and category approach to the study of the material earth is the forerunner of modern scientific methodology. The descriptions of his engines still fascinate students of physics. Aristotle defined the skills of right thinking. His methodology for logical reasoning is still a standard inclusion in courses on right reasoning and logic in multitudes of universities in the modern global village.

The intellectual breakthrough of these philosophers of the Acropolis is astonishing and revolutionary. Their insights, if pursued to a conclusion, would free nature and social institutions from the power of the gods. The particular forms of the material world could now be investigated without so much as a nod of respect in the direction of the gods of nature whom the myths had portrayed as the powers which determined natural phenomena. Enterprising minds could make other engines, just as Aristotle had done. The accountability of the state could shift away from the gods who didn't seem to care all that much about human well-being anyway. New reference points for political authority could be developed—the will of the people or the counsel of the philosophers.

The Gods Won't Die

Although these breakthrough philosophical ideas were present and persisted into the coming centuries, not much really happened in society as a whole. Just as the philosopher Confucius could not break the power of the deities of China, so also the philosophers of the Acropolis had almost no evident effect on the religious practices or worldview of the people of the marketplaces of Athens. The philosophers seemed incapable of really touching the masses. The gods did not die or go away.

Vigorous polytheism persisted. The worldview of the people as a whole continued unchanged. For the masses the activities of the deities and natural phenomena were one. The power of the gods and the authority of government merged. Aristotle's engines were interesting, but they were never applied to practical human experience in a manner conducive to human progress. The engines and the gods were an unnatural mix.

Paul + the
Greek G
Just over four centuries after Plato, a Jewish Christian apostle arrived in Athens and walked in the Athenian market. The account states that "he was greatly distressed to see that the city was full of idols."[8] This Jewish Christian teacher was Paul. Just as Socrates, Plato, and Aristotle had done many centuries earlier, Paul climbed the Acropolis and met with the philosophers.

Although the philosophers derided his message with laughter, three centuries after that meeting, the idols of Athens were no more. Even the Parthenon for Athena, the goddess of wisdom, which overlooks the Acropolis, had been transformed into a Christian church. What was the difference between Paul's message and Plato's?

The differences are explored in the next chapter, which introduces biblical faith. They derive from the experience of a people whose history began many centuries before any of the Greek philosophers were on the world scene. This people lived at the crossroads of the continents, namely Israel. They were historians rather than philosophers. They believed in only one universal, righteous, personal, Creator God who reveals himself in history. That is why they were historians.

They engaged in recounting their history rather than in philosophical speculation. This people spoke of repentance rather than enlightenment. They understood repentance to mean turning away from gods created by people and turning toward the one and only God who has created people. They believed that God had chosen them to be a light to all nations in the global community. The next several chapters explore the history and mission of this people.

At this point it is helpful to observe that, metaphorically speaking, there were shackles around the feet of the philosophers of the Acropolis. These shackles prevented them from effectively communicating to the masses their gospel of freedom from the deities.

The first shackle was that the philosophers had no awareness of purpose or movement in history. History and human society were going nowhere. The historical perspective of the philosophers was not much different from that of the polytheists. Both struggled with the question of the ultimate meaning of human existence.

It is noteworthy, however, that the same impetus which led the Greek philosophers to observe nature accurately also propelled a quest for accurate historical observation. Herodotus, a contemporary of Socrates, is the father of Western historiography. His passion for objectivity has inspired similar commitment in the souls of many modern historians. Yet what is the direction of history? What purpose does the study of history serve? What is the meaning of it all?

A second shackle was the elite and impersonal nature of Platonic 2 philosophy. The ideal good was static. It was a principle, not personal. Thus the person is really on her own. She must develop the skills of intuitive insight. What if she does not possess those skills? Or if she does possess those skills, what if she desires to worship and relate to a god? The very nature of Platonism guaranteed that it would always remain the conversation of the elite and never move the masses.

A third shackle was the inability of the Platonic stream in philoso- 3 phy to embrace the material world with enthusiasm. The ideal good was a principle other than the material. That which we see is only a shadow of the real which is the ideal good. Applied to the person, the body is then second-rate compared to the spirit in the person.

Thus the philosophical quest entices one away from a celebration of the material dimensions of life. In the rather earthy societies of the Mediterranean region, there was not widespread enthusiasm for philosophies which did not celebrate the wonder and goodness of the body and the material aspects of existence.

A Home for Philosophy

For more than five hundred years the philosophies of Athens had been bereft of a spiritual home. The polytheistic, mythical, and onto-cratic worldview was incompatible with the orientation of the philosophers. It is, therefore, not surprising that some theologians in the early Christian movement embraced Greek philosophy enthusiastically. These fathers of the church found in philosophy a natural ally in their abhorrence of polytheism and in their basic affirmation of the order and rationality of nature. Over time it was the church which provided a home for the intellectual breakthrough known as Greek philosophy.

Christian theologian Clement of Alexandria described aspects of the attraction well when he exclaimed that although philosophy had some useless "weeds," it nevertheless was a "schoolmaster" preparing people for Christ. He believed that the ideal good of philosophy was a preparation for the God of the biblical Scriptures.[9]

It might even be that the original Platonic notion of the universal ideal good was influenced by the people of Israel, who were the harbingers of biblical monotheism. In the fifth century A.D., North African philosopher and theologian Augustine commented on Plato's travels in the Mediterranean region in his quest to learn what he could from other peoples about the nature of truth.[10] Those travels would have provided opportunity to interact with biblical monotheism.

However, the accommodation between church and philosophy was not completely comfortable. The writings of the early church fathers reveal vigorous debate and interaction with the philosophers. Some insisted that there could be no alliance between "Jerusalem and Athens."[11] The tensions between biblical faith and Greek philosophy are significant.

- The Bible describes the material creation as very good. The philosophers had a low view of the material universe.
- The philosophers had difficulty perceiving that history has any real significance. Biblical faith views history as real and meaningful.
- Biblical faith is permeated with hope and movement forward. The philosophers were inclined towards a cyclical or nonprogressive view of history.
- Plato and his colleagues reflected on the ideal good as a universal principle. Biblical faith invites encounter with the personal righteous Creator of the universe.
- The philosophers were sanguine about human reasoning discovering the truth. Biblical faith is persuaded that God reveals truth primarily through his revelation acts in history.

For many centuries the church and Greek philosophy were locked in dialogue and accommodations; that dialogue persists.

Nevertheless, it was the church as well as Islam which nurtured the wisdom of the philosophers of Athens century after century. In the course of time, the church deposited that wisdom in the care of those who helped to form the movement known as the European Enlightenment of the seventeenth and eighteenth centuries. It is therefore not surprising that there are striking parallels between the philosophies of Descartes and Socrates, between Rousseau or Marx and Plato. This anticipates a later chapter.

Confucius, Plato, and Marx

It is surprising that Confucius and Plato had such similar perceptions concerning the relationship of the gods to the political and moral order. Although the early Confucian philosophers and those of the Acropolis were contemporary, six thousand miles of land separated them. Their thought developed in radically different cultures, that of China and Greece. Surely they never had the opportunity for cross-fertilization of ideas.

Yet both the Confucian and Platonic philosophical streams agreed—the gods are not helpful in nurturing a humane moral and social order. They were convinced that religion does not necessarily create good people. In fact, the gods seemed to influence society toward immorality. Thus both systems consciously turned away from the gods. Nevertheless, neither philosophy was capable of turning the people away from the gods! Only a few heeded the counsel of the philosophers.

Both Confucianism and Platonism struggled with the questions of where moral and political authority can be found. Both movements celebrated the qualities of a virtue which is intuitively understood, although Confucianism also put great stock in the way of the ancestors in defining the nature of virtue. They both insisted that virtue is benevolence in action.

Both Platonism and Confucianism believed that the political order needs to take the counsel of the philosophers. The philosophers give right guidance to the political and social institutions. From whence do the philosophers gain their wisdom? In Confucianism the wisdom of the ancients, li, is right. In Platonism the key wisdom comes from the universal ideal good which is intuitively perceived and provides right guidance. Both systems moved into rigidity. The li of Confucianism reveals only one right way. The ideal good of Platonism is also unbending. There is only one right form and function of government.

There are parallels between these philosophical movements of about twenty-five hundred years ago and twentieth-century Marxism. A later chapter will probe the issues more deeply. For now it is sufficient to note that in Marxism there are also the rigid and unbending laws of dialectical materialism, which remind one of the rigidities of the ideal good and the li. In Marxism there is the communist party, which informs the government on right policies. This is a modern form of the philosophers of Platonism and Confucianism who were to instruct the government on right behavior.

Communism, like these ancient philosophies, believes strongly in the essential goodness of humanity and the need for a right political and educational system to release and enable the flourishing of goodness. In Platonism and Confucianism the test of goodness is action; in communism also *praxis* (action) rather than theory is the essence of the good. Communism agrees with these ancient philosophies that the gods do not have a positive influence in developing wholesome local and global community. These philosophies of Greece and China are agnostic or indifferent to a god or the gods. Communism denies their existence. They all agree that social relationships and political institutions must develop independently of any influence from the gods.

The three philosophies are convinced that they have insights which can benefit the whole world. For Confucius the development of a harmonious political order in China will bring harmony to all people—in fact, to the whole cosmos. For Plato anyone anywhere with intuitive gifts can perceive glimpses of the universal ideal good. For Marxism the classless society brought about through the revolution led by the workers of the world will bring utopia to the entire global community. Each system has a plan which can bless the whole world.

It is also noteworthy that the "isms" which these ideologies have spawned throughout the centuries have tended to take on the power of the very divinities which the philosophers had tried to unseat. An absolute philosophy or ideology can become as demonic as any of the ancient gods.

Did the Confucian sages ever dream of that possibility when Mencius, the trusted disciple of Confucius, traveled from noble court to court in ostentatious wealth?

Mencius justified his opulence by declaring, "The worth of the scholar is greater than that of any ruler!"[12]

Alas! The gods had returned in the robes of a philosopher!

Reflection

1. Why did Platonic and Confucian philosophers attempt to separate the power of the gods from both political authority and morality?

2. Consider reasons for the persistence of the gods (of the ontocratic worldview) in spite of the philosophical objections.

3. What is the source of truth in Platonism? In Confucianism?

4. In what ways does the Chinese view of the relationship between the cosmos and China affect the role of China in the global community?

7

Yahweh Against the Gods

The Bible

BIBLICAL FAITH is a watershed in our reflection on global gods. In the Bible we meet the God who is against all other gods. Through the prophet Moses, we learn that his name is Yahweh (I was, I am, I will be). He is the covenant God who acts in history.

Revelation as in-history-event was the crux of dialogue during a evening of conversation between Muslims and Christians in the Albanian mosque in Philadelphia.

A Muslim who was a doctoral candidate in Islamics at Temple University ventured, "This is the difference between our communities. Muslims believe in general revelation and Christians believe in specific revelation. Our scriptures embody that divergence; the Bible is primarily a history book, whereas the Qur'an is a statement of theistic principles and guidelines for living."

A Muslim colleague elaborated, "But we Muslims cannot accept historical events as revelation."

A Hindu, Buddhist, Sikh, Taoist, Shintoist, Platonist, Confucianist, Jain, or Zoroastrian would raise the same objection as my Muslim friends. History is peripheral to the truths these philosophies and religions expound.

For example, if historical criticism were to demonstrate that drama of Krishna and Arjuna of the Hindu Bhagavad Gita never occurred, that finding would not in the least affect the validity of the Gita. The battle account within the Gita has no essential relevance to the religious and philosophical perspectives the Gita describes. The account as historical event has no relationship to the philosophy of life the drama communicates.

Not so with biblical faith! The Bible is, in fact, the only Scripture whose essence is history.

Some world religions do have writings which they value highly which are comprised of historical or legendary material. The *Hadith* in Islam, the *Mahabharata* in Hinduism, or *Nihon Shoki* in Shintoism are examples. Yet these are never considered the sacred soul of the scriptures of a people; the historical is always of less significance than the most scared scriptures of a religion.

The Bible is a dramatic exception. This is because the biblical perception is that Yahweh, the Creator of the universe, reveals himself to people by what he does.

What does Yahweh do within our history?

The Bible describes Yahweh as the one who was, is, and will be the righteous personal Creator God. He meets people in personal encounter. Yahweh, Creator of the universe, invites people into a covenant relationship with himself. He is the covenant God; Yahweh commands his covenant people to worship only him.

Biblical faith is convinced that Yahweh reveals himself through his acts of creation and his acts in history. The creation event needs no book to describe it. That revelation event is self-evident. Let the scientists probe its mysteries and wonders. However, history is lost unless it is recorded in memory or writing. For over one thousand years, biblical writers accepted the responsibility of recording and interpreting the surprising acts of Yahweh in history. The Bible is their record of these revelation events.

The biblical writers were surprised to discover that Yahweh acts in history for the purpose of forming a people who live in a covenant relationship with him. The Bible is the written account of events which the biblical writers believed to be the acts of Yahweh in history as he worked toward the goal of forming a covenant people. The Bible is also their interpretation of those events.

The writers believed that recording these events and their interpretations was not a purely academic or philosophical exercise. Occasionally biblical writers confessed that these Scriptures were inspired by Yahweh himself; they believed they were carried along by the Spirit of God as they wrote.

The discussion in much of this chapter and the following chapter is based especially on the first portion of the Bible known by Christians as the Old Testament (Old Covenant). Chapter nine is based especially on the New Testament, which is the second part of the Bible. However, in this chapter we also survey the broad sweep of the biblical worldview as developed within the Old and New Testaments.

Biblical faith views both creation and history as the arenas in which God's self-disclosure takes place. These perspectives on creation and history are the foundations for the Jewish and Christian understanding of the global village and participation in it. It is necessary to know something of the Christian view of creation and history to comprehend the nature and function of the church as a global community. This chapter will explore these two themes, creation and history.

The First Theme: Creation

The first sentence in the Bible announces, "In the beginning God created the heavens and the earth" (Gen. 1:1).

It is not surprising that biblical faith never refers to the earth or universe as "nature." The term nature suggests a self-forming and a self-sustaining universe. The biblical term is "creation." This is because Yahweh creates *and* sustains the heavens and the earth.

Biblical faith has no sympathy with atheistic notions that the earth and life came into existence through the impersonal impulse of natural laws. The biblical worldview is also completely different from that of deism—the notion that the universe is an autonomous entity which ticks away on its own, propelled by natural laws which function independently of the sustaining care of the Creator. The Bible announces God as both Creator and sustainer of the whole universe.

The two opening chapters of the Bible, Genesis 1 and 2, set the tone for the whole Bible in describing the earth as good. Creation is orderly and understandable. It progresses in step-by-step development, beginning with the formation of the heavens and the earth and culminating in the creation of humankind.

The woman and man are creatures—created with the other mammals. Humankind is created from the dust of the earth. They are biological creatures like the cows or monkeys. Yet people are more than biological creatures, for they are unique, created in the image of God who he breathes into them the breath of his very own life.

The man and woman are commanded to subdue the earth, to till and trim the garden. They are to care for the earth, use the good earth for their well-being. Even the animals receive their names from humans. The earth and all creation are good, until man and woman are created. Then it becomes very good! Humankind is expected to cooperate with God in making the good creation become very good.

Yahweh Versus the Gods

The Bible reveals Yahweh as "other" than the universe he has created. Biblical theologians refer to the otherness of God as *transcendence*. The Creator God who is other than the earth is nevertheless actively and creatively present. Theologians refer to God's presence as *immanence*.

This worldview is a dramatic revolution when compared to all the other religions of the Middle East at the time when the biblical Scriptures were being recorded. The Bible describes the encounter. It is a theological and worldview battle between the ontocratic beliefs of the surrounding societies and the faith view of the people who believed they had been called into a covenant with Yahweh. (Later we shall explore in more depth the origin of these covenant people and the basis of the covenant.)

The battle was acute in Canaan, the region known as Palestine today, as these people who were in covenant with Yahweh began to settle this region which was inhabited by peoples who practiced the traditional religions of the ancient Middle East. The conflict is described in the Bible (especially in the historical narratives of Joshua, Judges, 1 and 2 Samuel, 1 and 2 Kings, and 1 and 2 Chronicles). The era of conflict persisted for many centuries but was especially intense from about 1400 to 1000 B.C. Later we shall comment more on the experience of occupying Canaan. At this point we observe only one dimension of that occupation—the conflict between the biblical view of creation and the local perceptions of nature.

Religion of the Prom Land? "Chop down the trees on the peak of every green hill," commanded the prophets from time to time. The Canaanites interpreted the groves on the hilltops in a way which totally contradicted biblical faith. These people believed that divinity and nature were fused into oneness. Like the ancient Chinese mentioned in the previous chapter and multitudes of other ancient peoples, the Canaanites believed the earth and sky were divine. The hills represented fertility where earth and sky met.

The divine sky watered the divine earth, and in this divine interaction fertility was created. The green trees on the hills, with their roots in the divine earth and their branches stretching into the divine sky, bonded sky and earth, enabling the consummation of fertility.

Human sexual activity in the groves on top of the pregnant hills helped to seal the divine fertility bond between sky and earth.[1]

"No! No!" cried the prophets. "Yahweh is the Creator of both heaven and earth. Fertility cults or sacrifices to the gods of nature are anathema. Do not worship any aspect of heaven and earth. These are not divine. Only Yahweh is God. So do not worship the fertility gods in the groves on the high hills."

Secular Development

The collision between biblical faith and groves of sacred trees has a strangely modern twang about it. The story of the church in mission in ontocratic cultures through the centuries as well as in modern times has also often included a confrontation with nature gods and spirits, culminating in cutting down groves in which these gods and spirits were worshiped.

I observed that conflict among the Zanaki people of Tanzania among whom I grew up.

story on G vs prince. + powers

One day Itini, the first Zanaki Christian, was confronted by tribal elders who accused him of not honoring the traditional nature gods. He had begun to fell a tree he needed for a rafter in his new house. The tree was part of a grove where the nature gods lived. The spirit experts threatened death by cursing if he did not desist.

To the alarm of the Western missionaries, Itini determined that the gauntlet had been cast. There was no alternative except to chop down a portion of the grove of trees in which the nature gods lived. Just as in biblical times when the prophets commanded chopping down the groves where the nature gods were venerated, so Itini and a colleague shouldered axes and cleared a portion of the grove as a sign that only Yahweh is God.

They cut down only the number of trees needed for the house Itini was building. To have cut more trees than needed would have been presumptuous and unduly confrontational. Yet by cutting a portion of the sacred grove, the point had been made that Yahweh the Creator is sovereign over nature spirits.

In a few days the spiritual elite of the society came with their paraphernalia, including bells and gourds, to curse Itini and his family to death. They had already dug his grave. Yet he did not die. From that day in that society, a crack began in the power system of the nature gods and spirits.

Indeed the modern Christian missionary movement, in continuity with the biblical story, has been a powerful force in divesting nature of divine aura. These biblical perspectives have now percolated into cultures everywhere. These views affirm the appropriateness of subduing the earth without fear of retribution from any gods.

However, Japan is an example of a modern industrial society in which the ontocratic worldview persists in the form of Shintoism. This patriotic religion perceives of the Japanese islands as a precious dimension of divinity. For this reason Shinto sacrifices to the gods are sometimes offered in preparation for building a highway.

Biblical faith would abrogate the practice of offering sacrifices in worship or veneration of the divine earth prior to building a highway. However, the Bible does call for reverent development of the earth in a manner which blesses both creation and humanity. People should plant at least one tree for every tree they chop down!

story?

Recently I met with a Dyak chief in the jungles of West Kalimantan in Indonesia. Only a decade before he and his village had become Christian.

"What have you received from the Christian gospel?" I asked this Dyak gentleman with an impressive gray-reddish goatee.

He stroked his beard, then said, "We aren't afraid of the birds anymore. We just let them squawk and go ahead with our work. It is easier being a chief now. We pray, plan, and work, paying no attention to the birds."

What a revolution! The gospel in this setting had quickly robbed the birds of their stranglehold on these people. For many centuries the Dyak had believed that the birds were omens of the spirits of nature. Experts interpreted their calls and guided the villages in sacrificial rituals calculated to pacify the nature spirits. Often the rice planting or harvesting had to be neglected because of ominous communications from the birds. Now in an instant, the bondage of many centuries had been broken.

This chief, it occurred to me, was becoming a secular person. That thought anticipates later chapters which review the emergence of secularism in the global village. Yet it will be helpful to recognize that this exploration assumes that there is a difference between a secular commitment and secularism. A biblically-based secular perspective enables one joyfully and without fear to cooperate with God in developing and caring for the good earth, using it for human well-being. (Latin *saecularis* means coming once in an age. It refers to the temporal dimensions of life.) Secularism is an ideology of material and human development which does not perceive of any need for responsibility to Yahweh the Creator.

Biblical faith opposes secularism but encourages secular commitments. The material is good and real; biblical faith believes that the
material creation is not a deflection from reality as the Hindus or
Buddhists suggest or less good than spirit as the Greek philosophers
taught. God's first commands to humankind were secular. Have
children, subdue the earth (develop the earth and make it better), till
the ground, trim the garden, name the animals. Develop the good
earth in a wholesome way.

When a people hear the biblical story and receive that faith into
their own experience, nature is stripped of any aura of divine power. Thus it is that biblical faith is a powerful and effective force for
secularization. The process of secularization includes taking away
from nature any participation in divinity.

Later we shall discover that biblical faith also opposes any notions
that the political-social powers are divine. Biblical faith is uncompromising in its insistence that neither governments, social institutions, nor creation in any of their varied expressions are divine. Only
Yahweh is God.[2]

An intriguing riddle in the phenomenology of religion is that neither Confucius nor Plato were able to break the power of the divinities over their people. The previous chapter explores that phenomenon. Through the tools of philosophy and political theory, both
Confucius and Plato hoped to free people from the tyranny of the
gods. Yet in time Confucius himself was considered divine by the
Chinese masses. In Greece, polytheism and mystery religions continued to lure the masses, despite the persistent skepticism of a
whole train of philosophers.

Yet the secularization which the sages of Greece and China were
unable to accomplish over two millennia ago happened to that Dyak
chief and his village in months of their hearing the Christian gospel.
This has been the case wherever the Christian faith takes root.

Biblical faith has been more effective than philosophy in exploding the ontocratic worldview because it is rooted in a response to
Yahweh's acts in history rather than in philosophical speculation.
Even a child can be instructed by the account of Adam and Eve in
the garden and can grasp the secular implications:

- God created the earth, but the earth isn't a god.
- God wanted Eve and Adam to enjoy the good earth that
  he created for them.
- God told Adam and Eve to cultivate their garden.

Plato's speculation about the *logos* was more difficult to comprehend, but not more profound or revolutionary than the biblical accounts!

During the first centuries of the Christian era, the life and witness of the church in the Mediterranean region finally overthrew the nature gods. This was something five centuries of philosophical development had not accomplished. In China, the nineteenth- and twentieth-century Christian missionary movement was the forerunner of the radical secularization imposed on the country by the Marxist revolution. It is not coincidental that key leaders in that revolution were trained in Christian schools. The Christian faith firmly plants seeds for secularization by proclaiming that only Yahweh is God, that no other powers or phenomena are divine.

The Seedbed of Science

The biblical view of creation and humankind's relationship to creation is the seedbed of the worldview which has nurtured modern scientific technology. The biblical perceptions which have laid the foundation for a secular technological worldview include the following convictions:

1. Creation is good, orderly, and understandable.
2. Humankind can think God's thoughts after him and through observation and study comprehend the intricacies and laws of creation.
3. Humankind is to help make the earth become "very good" through working to develop the gifts of creation for the well-being of people and creation as a whole.
4. Creation is not divinity.

The pioneers who developed the foundations for the modern scientific revolution were undergirded by these foundational biblical themes.[3] It is not surprising that the modern technological revolution began in a region of the world which had been Christianized for over one thousand years.

A conversation in the Garden Hotel in Singapore with an official in the Ministry of Foreign Affairs illustrates these themes.

"Why," I asked, "has the Christian community in Singapore increased from 10 percent to 22 percent of the population during the 1980s?"

My host replied forthrightly, "Singaporeans are seeking a faith which is free of superstition and provides a worldview which nurtures human development and scientific technology. We believe that a biblical worldview provides that kind of orientation."

Of course, throughout the centuries of the Christian era there has often been resistance from the church to some of the notions put forward by the scientific community. Probably every high school student knows the account of the church's dismay with Galileo (d.1642), who agreed with Copernicus that the earth circled the sun rather than the sun circling the earth. The church objected because the theologians believed that the earth must be the center of the universe and the solar system. Furthermore, Galileo's observations conflicted with Aristotle, whom the church accepted as final authority in all such matters.

In spite of the opposition of the church authorities, Galileo's persistent urge to observe and discover the workings of the universe was grounded in a biblical theological worldview; he was not an astrologer who ascribed to the stars and planets uncanny or occult powers. He was a scientist who believed that the Creator of the universe applauded the efforts of humankind to understand the wonders of the universe.

The scientific revolution has brought incredible blessing to humankind. I was born and grew up in East Africa. My boyhood African friends and I are still living. Many times quinine saved my life from being snuffed out by malaria. Quinine comes from the bark of a tree indigenous to the Congo Valley. Modern science developed that gift from the quinine tree in a manner which has saved millions of lives, including mine.

My mother dispensed modern medicines daily from our back porch stoop to other mothers with crying, sick children. It was not uncommon for mothers coming to that stoop to report that they had given birth to half a dozen children and all had died. They hoped that their new babies would live; that is why they came to my mother for help. Soon the church brought a dispensary into the community, and modern health education began to spread through the land.

I remember the advent of a microscope in that clinic. It enabled technicians to examine drops of urine or blood to determine the parasitic source of disease. Today infant mortality rates are much lower. Even smallpox has been totally eradicated from my childhood community and, in fact, from the entire earth.

The church has nurtured the scientific technological worldview and has also enthusiastically helped to spread to the ends of the earth the good news of a better life through the application of science. The modern phenomenal expansion of church ministries into hundreds of thousands of communities around the world is a significant facilitator for introducing the wonders of science to underdeveloped communities throughout the world.

Wrong Choices

Nevertheless, biblical faith warns humankind to be aware of the tragedy of missing the way. We discover in the biblical account that the first human couple turned away from God. They decided to use all the fruit of the garden for themselves, even the fruit from the tree of knowledge of good and evil which God had forbidden. The account says that they disobeyed God because they hoped to become like God. Their selfishness, arrogance, and independent spirit created the fall from good into evil.

Even the good earth suffered the consequences. (Later we explore other dimensions of evil, but here we comment on the consequences of human evil for the good earth.) The earth is cursed because of the selfishness of humankind. Surely the zenith of this wickedness of cursing the good earth is the nuclear bomb, which if ever unleashed would curse the whole wonderful earth which God has prepared for people to live in and enjoy. Are the scientists correct in claiming that this earth has been in formation for a billion years? In one hour humankind may reduce the whole planet to oblivion. Indeed the earth is cursed by the evil of humanity.

The litany of evil which people do against the good earth is endless. Not all the evil is a recent development attributable to modern technology. Witness the deserts in northern Somalia. The northern plateau of this northeastern African country is a well-watered area of pleasant climate and rolling hills. Yet it is desert. The undulating hills are denuded; only rocks and stones are visible. Overgrazing by goats has ruined the land. The whole earth groans because of the wide-spread exploitative misuse of God's good gifts.

Nevertheless, in modern times the misuse of technology has become especially diabolical. That very technology which holds so much promise for good has become, in the hands of greedy or thoughtless people, a demon more fearsome then the nature gods of a pre-Christian era.

For example, a 1988 issue of *Newsweek* carries this headline: "The Global Poison Trade. How Toxic Waste Is Dumped on the Third World." [4] The article describes how some third world countries desperate for cash sometimes feel compelled to accept toxic wastes from Western countries in exchange for urgently needed hard currency. What a wickedness that is! Nations too poor to share in the blessings of technology become the waste dumps for those nations who enjoy technology.

Care for the wilderness he loved was on the mind of an aged Australian sage at an outdoor barbecue in Fennel Bay just north of Sydney.

"What is the greatest concern for Australians these days?" I inquired.

"Ecology! Ecology!" he responded in staccato.

"Who is responding to that concern? Is the church helping or are other groups such as the Muslim community helping?"

"The church! Irrelevant! Irrelevant! Irrelevant!" he exclaimed.

If the Australian sage is right, then something has gone seriously awry. If communities who profess faith in the Creator God, are not caring for the good earth, then they have abandoned their responsibility as believers.

Renewing the Earth

Biblical faith recognizes a sad tension between Yahweh's covenant command to humankind to "subdue" the earth in a manner which enables the earth to become "very good" and human rebellion and sinfulness which makes the good earth experience a "curse." The biblical drama, however, does not let the curse of distorted human relations with creation go unchallenged. Yahweh calls people to repent, to make a U-turn, to turn away from the selfish and greedy exploitation of creation. Yahweh invites people into a right relationship with him, a relationship which empowers people to relate to creation in a manner which blesses the earth and renews it.

Jubilee is a biblical theme we shall notice occasionally in our exploration of biblical faith. This celebration theme develops from the creation narrative, in which Yahweh is described as resting on the seventh day after completing his work of Creation. Therefore humans are also invited to rest from their work and enjoy the good gifts of their labor.

The Bible describes the joy of resting from work one day a week. Everyone is to take an annual vacation and to save a tenth of their yearly income for the vacation bash. People are also to provide rest for the earth. Farmers should let their fields rest once every seventh year. People should avoid exploiting the earth and should not squeeze all possible profit from the land. For example, the olive trees should be harvested but not beaten until every single olive has been gleaned. The land, animals, trees, and people are to enjoy the rest and celebration of Jubilee.

That faith community, who planted the conceptual seeds in European cultures that created the scientific technological worldview, needs to speak a word of conscience and responsibility in these modern times. Jesus is the central figure in that faith community known as the church. In his life and ministry, Jesus revealed a redemptive relationship with creation. He lived in the spirit of Jubilee.

sm

For example, the Christian Scriptures describe Jesus in compassion and prayer accomplishing the extraordinary act of breaking five loaves of bread and two fishes and feeding a hungry congregation of five thousand men plus women and children. Then he ordered his companions to gather all the crumbs so no food would be wasted; they collected twelve baskets of food fragments. This and other extraordinary events are signs in the Christian faith of Yahweh's invitation to humankind to live both in mastery over and harmony with creation. Jesus exerted mastery over creation, but he never abused the gifts of creation. He saved even the crumbs.

The Christian Scriptures explain that through the mission of Jesus "the creation itself will be liberated from its bondage to decay and brought into the glorious freedom of the children of God."[5] Jesus related to creation in a manner which blessed the good earth.

The Christian faith teaches that through the empowerment of the Spirit of Jesus, the church should also live in a redemptive relationship with creation, that is, be a blessing to creation. Jesus both demonstrates and invites people into the kind of renewed relationship with the earth which actually does redeem the earth from the curse of exploitation. People who faithfully obey Jesus relate to creation in a way that removes the curse which the earth has experienced because of humankind's evil.

The Bible exclaims that all creation shouts for joy as it responds to the gentle, renewing, and creative touch of the people who walk in the way of Jesus. Yahweh commissions that new community to be a light to the nations. Yahweh calls that community to reveal that the curse against creation is gone through their quality relationships with one another and with creation.[6]

Wrap-up

This discussion of God as Creator has described some of the revolutionary and universal significance of the opening phrase of the Bible: "In the beginning God created the heavens and the earth."[7] We have seen how that biblical perception explodes the primal ontocratic nature myths which fused divinity and nature in the emergence of the earth and in the ongoing processes of nature. One cannot exaggerate the significance of this biblical worldview breakthrough: God is other than creation!

"G is" + stands above creation

The biblical prophets persisted in the conviction that God is other than creation even though this belief was against all other ancient worldviews. They faced relentless pressure for syncretism and compromise. Faithfully they protested tendencies which would compromise God's transcendence. That commitment is symbolized in their plea to their fellow country persons, "Don't offer sacrifices in the groves on the high hills! The heavens and the earth are not divine in any way. Nothing in all creation is divine or can represent God. Only Yahweh is God."

We have discovered that the groves of trees atop the hills of Canaan were the symbols of the ontocratic worldview. These trees united the divine earth and heavens. The ontocratic systems strangled the human spirit; they became mechanisms which entrapped human societies in the meaningless cycles of nature. The ontocratic religious systems often literally required human sacrifices. This was true in Canaan and around the globe. It was true in ancient times and in modern times as well.

In a later chapter we shall reflect on the crucifixion of Jesus of Nazareth on a tree (cross) on a hill called Golgotha just outside Jerusalem. Christians perceive in the crucifixion of Jesus the ultimate critique of the ontocratic powers of nature. The Messiah is crucified on a tree on a hill. He is sacrificed on a tree which ontocratic systems considered to be sacred, yes, actually divine. Yet the sacred tree on a hill is unmasked in his crucifixion as an instrument of death. However, in his resurrection from the dead, he has broken the stranglehold of the ontocratic powers; they could not destroy him.

It is for that reason that the Dyak chief could exclaim, "We are not afraid of the birds anymore!"

The Second Theme: History

The Bible is not a scientific treatise, but the biblical writers believed that Creation, as an act of God, reveals God. Biblical faith affirms that a second manner in which Yahweh reveals himself is through his acts in history and the faithful interpretation of those acts through his witnesses.

The biblical writers believed they had a mission—the faithful recording and interpretation of the acts of Yahweh in history. In the Bible, revelation moves from the particular historical event to the universal truth. It is not the other way around. The particular informs the universal; the universal perceptions are not the criteria of truth.

B faith is
historical

This is to say that biblical faith is not based on philosophy. Rather, biblical faith is historical. For this reason, in contrast to the other chapters in this book, the descriptions of biblical faith which we are now investigating will consist mostly of a review of several worldview blockbuster events in history. The exploration will reveal that the biblical worldview comes from the faith response of a people to what they believe Yahweh has done in history.

The Christian belief in the bodily resurrection of the dead is an example of a faith based on historical rather than philosophical conviction. However, in Judaism, which is also a biblical faith, there is little thought given to the resurrection of the dead. Why the difference between Judaism and Christianity in this matter? The answer helps unlock the differences between faith responding to events and religion based on philosophy.

Jewish &
Christ
view of
the resurn
sn

A brief description of the Bible will reveal the reason for the difference in the Jewish and Christian perceptions of the resurrection of the dead. As noted earlier, the Bible is divided into two parts. Christians call the first part the Old Testament, and the second part the New Testament. The former was recorded before Christ, and the latter after Christ. The Jewish people refer to the Old Testament as the *Tanach*. That is their Bible, for Judaism does not accept the New Testament as their Scripture. However, both Christians and Jews accept the Tanach or Hebrew Scriptures as the primal foundation of their faiths.

The Old Testament or Tanach is not clear about life after death. There is little said on the issue. Therefore, consistent with the Old Testament, modern Judaism gives little or no attention to the question of life after death. Why does the Tanach show so little concern about the state of the person after death? The reason is that this would be speculation; it would smack of philosophical conjecture. Yahweh's acts in history during the whole era of the development of the Tanach revealed little concerning the life-after-death question. Therefore in both the Old Testament and Judaism the issue is not important.

In lively contrast to the Old Testament, the bodily resurrection of the person is a central theme in New Testament faith. Why? Because witnesses whom Christians believe are reliable have reported that Jesus rose from the dead.

Christians believe that the resurrection of Jesus is a definitive God-act in history which unlocks the mystery of human destiny. The risen Jesus promises that we will all rise too at the climactic conclusion of history. So Christian faith rests in the confident hope of a bodily resurrection at the conclusion of history. This conviction is not the consequence of speculative or philosophical reflection. It is rather a faith response to a dramatic God-act in history, the resurrection of Jesus Christ.

From a Christian perspective, the implications for global community are astounding. The biblical conviction is that each God-act reveals universal reality. The event reveals universal truth. Thus Christians believe that the resurrection of this one man, Jesus, reveals the intention of Yahweh for the whole human community, for all of the earth's approximately six billion people, and for all of those billions who have already died.

From the perspective of philosophical speculation, the Christian hope is crazy. It fits no philosophical or religious categories. Isolated from the resurrection of Jesus, any notion of a bodily resurrection of the dead is nonsense. Yet because of the resurrection of Jesus, Christians hope for a future resurrection.

Joyful Community *Created by a call to repent*

The acts of Yahweh in history focus in one direction—the calling together of a new community of people who live in a right and joyous relationship with the Creator. Christians believe that from the beginning of history into these modern times, God has always been *Repent-* calling people to make a U-turn away from egoism and loyalty to *ance* false gods in order to become his people.

The invitation to turn toward Yahweh began already in the primal garden of Eden right after the first human parents, Adam and Eve, turned away from God because of their desire to live in self-centered independence. Immediately, the very day they rebelled, God appeared in the garden seeking the couple.

"Adam, where are you?" cried God. *adam where are you*

"Over here hiding behind a bush," whimpered Adam.[8]

The Bible describes Yahweh consistently, throughout the ages, patiently persisting in the call, "Adam, where are you?"

Yahweh persists because he loves people. After all, God created them in his very own image. They are his daughters and sons, living persons who partake of God's very own immortality. Yahweh calls people because his sons and daughters experience their greatest joy, fulfillment, and human potential only as they live in a right covenant relationship with Yahweh, with one another, and with creation. The Bible also describes Yahweh as one who enjoys fellowship with people.

Yet each person's response to God's call is completely voluntary.

The joy of fellowship between God and people who respond to him is a voluntary relationship. Yahweh never coerces. /

The total drama of biblical revelation leads Christian believers to the conviction that in God himself there is harmonious personal community. *Trinity* is a theological term used by Christians to convey the concept of God in community.

Remembering that biblical theology attempts to avoid philosophical speculation, it is important to recognize that the term Trinity is an attempt by Christians to express various ways they believe God has revealed himself in history and Creation. God has revealed himself as Creator or Father. Then in Jesus he has revealed himself as with us in human form, as Savior, as the Son who identifies fully with our human situation. He has also revealed himself as the Spirit who is always present. Thus it is that God's acts in history reveal him as Creator or Father, Savior or Son, present or Holy Spirit. This is why Christians speak of God as Trinity—Father, Son, and Holy Spirit.

The term Trinity also suggests that God enjoys communion in himself. That kind of statement does suggest theological speculation! Yet not necessarily so. God's acts in history, and especially in Jesus of Nazareth, have led to the conviction that "God is love."[9] One cannot love alone; love requires communion, relationship. Therefore Christian theology functions in the conviction that in God himself there is loving communion and fellowship.

Just as Yahweh finds fulfillment and joy in communion and fellowship, so people created in God's own image also experience their fullest humanity only when they also share in the loving communion which God experiences in himself. The whole thrust of biblical faith is God's patient, persistent invitation to people; "Come to me, all you who are weary and burdened, and I will give you rest."[10] The Christian gospel invites people to love one another with the same love God experiences in himself.[11] That kind of quality community is peace. Christians believe this peace has surprising implications for global community.

Broken Community

The peace which flows from wholesome relationships between God, the person, community, and creation is sabotaged by human greed and self-centeredness. In biblical faith the demons and spirits, and even the devil himself, encourage brokenness in human community. But they do not have ultimate power to introduce evil into the human experience. Nevertheless these evil powers who are other than humanity are very real. They are the evil spirits and demons and even angels who are in rebellion against God.

They do all they can to bring evil into human experience by influ- encing people to make evil choices. These powers also have the capacity to magnify the evil which we do, to give evil a momentum and power larger than human control.[12] Yet the evil spirit powers are not the center of the drama of evil. Biblical faith insists that the primary generator of evil is in the person. It is personal rebellion against the good which is the root of evil, not the devil.

Neither does biblical faith consider the lack of enlightenment to be the root of evil as Platonism, Buddhism, or Hinduism teach. In contrast to these philosophies, which believe that evil comes from ignorance, the Bible places the finger of blame on wrong choice. Evil enters community because people choose evil, not because of malevolent spirits and demons, genetic deficiency, adverse environment, or ignorance.

The Bible asserts that the human will is the centerpoint of battle between good and evil in the person and in the global community. The will is the turning point between good and evil. In the Bible free human choice is center stage. Therefore, "choose you this day for yourselves whom you will serve," Joshua, leader of Yahweh's people, commanded.[13]

Evil in biblical faith is the human arrogance and self-centeredness which creates broken relationships between God and the person, between people, between people and creation, and in the human being's own personhood. The root of all evil, of all broken relationships, is the personal and collective decision to turn away from God; it is the decision of humankind to celebrate and applaud egocentricity.

The parents of all humanity, Adam and Eve, used the precious gift of free will to turn away from God to live in a self-centered manner. Immediately the consequences of their egoism and greed began to adversely affect all their relationships.

In our exploration of creation, we discovered that human selfishness curses creation. We also discover that evil distorts all other aspects of human experience. This includes the precious intimacy of marriage and the relationship with our Creator. Adam and Eve were ashamed in each other's presence and God's presence. The account in the third chapter of Genesis in the Bible is dramatic and pathetic. They sewed leaves together to cover their shame, and they began the game of projecting blame elsewhere for personal failure.

Biblical faith supports the perceptions of the psychological disciplines, which see that in societies everywhere people compensate for feelings of guilt by the devices of cultural camouflage or the projection of guilt onto others. These two ways of coping with guilt merit comment.

Camouflage involves hiding the inner feelings of guilt by appearing nice on the outside and acting superior to others. Both individuals and whole cultural systems function in this manner. Societies often arrogantly consider themselves better than others. In recent centuries some Western peoples have camouflaged their guilt with the proud and impenetrable leaves of supposed cultural superiority and a civilizing mandate. This is to say that they equated technological superiority with goodness; less technically advanced societies have been caricatured as not as "good."

Projection is placing blame or guilt on another. Often an animal or even a human is sacrificed as a scapegoat for the sins of the people. The guilt of the person or people is projected onto the one sacrificed. People feel ashamed because they know they fall short of the good. In their shame individuals and societies project onto others the blame for personal failure. That is called the psycho-projection of guilt.

The primal parents not only experienced strains in their marriage relationship. In their family strife, they also sowed the seeds of sorrow and bitterness. Jealous Cain killed his brother Abel. The psychoanalyst Sigmund Freud spoke of the primal murder deep in the subconsciousness of the human species. He perceived the son murdering his father. Here it is, the primal murder, although the biblical account describes the older brother killing his younger brother. Murder had made its home in the first human family.

This Eve and Adam family is the parent family to all the tribes, languages, and races of humankind. The Bible affirms the obvious— all of us, all cultures and societies, all language groups and races and civilizations, are tainted by this primal brokenness. In various ways all people partake in the death of wholesome relationships which the first family experienced as they turned away from God.

A remarkable feature of biblical literature is its realism in describing the human situation as we actually experience it. Except for Jesus, all major biblical characters are portrayed as flawed. All have missed the way of righteousness in one way or another.

Abraham, the spiritual father of all who walk in the way of biblical faith, is described as a doubter and a deceiver who would have led others to believe Sarah was not his wife. He deceived his hosts so they would not kill him to marry her because she was so beautiful.

Moses, who led the people of the covenant from slavery in Egypt, lost his temper in a most disgraceful manner, committing murder.

King David, a man after Yahweh's own heart, was guilty of adultery, then the murder of the woman's husband.

The apostle Peter was a coward. The apostle Paul had a tragic break in relations with Barnabas, his closest Christian companion and friend.

Biblical writers have no illusions about human nature.

An ancient biblical account of the Tower of Babel dramatizes the distortion and alienation in human experience.[14] The people of earth gathered in the region of Mesopotamia to build a great tower which would reach up to heaven. It was an arrogant act. In displeasure God brought confusion on them by providing them with different languages. Consequently linguistic misunderstandings forced the abandonment of the project, and the peoples, now divided by language differences, scattered throughout the earth.

A Call and a Promise

It is in this kind of world, divided by nations and languages that are hostile to one another, that the Creator determines to form a new God-centered nation who will be a blessed presence among all the nations. It is in a milieu of strife, hostility, and universal distortions of authentic wholesome community that God sets about the exuberant business of calling people to return to him, so they may experience life and true wholeness in a renewed God-centered community.

However, the Bible always assumes that the God-centered community is an alternative community among other communities. Even at the climax of history, when the God-centered community has extended throughout the earth, it is people from every tribe and nation and language who comprise the community of Yahweh. It is a universal community in communities.

This is the nature of biblical pluralism—a voluntary community of faith among other communities. Although the vision is for the new community to be a blessing to all nations and offer healing to all peoples, there is no anticipation that everyone will decide to turn from self-centered alienation and toward God. The biblical vision is of the God-centered community consisting of people from every tribe, language, and nation existing and ministering as a community in and among every tribe, language, and nation. This is the biblical hope.

However, later we will explore other approaches to pluralism which developed in the Old Testament. After their exodus from

Egypt, the people of the covenant eventually entered Canaan and settled there. Bloody and sometimes genocidal wars accompanied the
occupation of the land. The theological basis for a genocidal or repressive approach to the problem of pluralism is a moot issue in modern
times (the next chapter will describe those themes in biblical history).

Nevertheless, at its core biblical history is the drama of Yahweh
calling people to make the U-turn toward their loving Creator Father. He forms these people who repent into a new community who
live in a right and joyous relationship with Yahweh, who enjoy
wholesome relationships with one another, and who bless the earth
through their presence and work. The Bible describes this relationship as a covenant; it is a covenant which bonds God, people, and
the earth together in a relationship of well-being.

The drama began about four millennia ago with Abraham and
Sarah, a Mesopotamian couple. Their kindred worshiped the nature
divinities of the region. Quite unexpectedly the Lord surprised
Abraham with this call and promise.

> Leave your country, your people, and your father's household
> and go to the land I will show you.
> I will make you into a great nation
> and I will bless you;
> I will make your name great,
> and you will be a blessing.
> I will bless those who bless you,
> and whoever curses you I will curse;
> and all peoples on earth
> will be blessed through you.[15]

Abraham and Sarah obeyed this call. The Jewish people view Abraham and Sarah as the father and mother of their peoplehood. Christians and Muslims also consider Abraham as the spiritual father of
their respective faith communities. This is to say that half of the modern global community claim Abraham as their spiritual father and the
harbinger of their faith. What is this faith? What did obedience to this
call mean for Abraham and Sarah? Four dimensions follow.

First, the call involved an incredible promise: all nations will be
blessed through their obedience. (However, God does warn that
those who reject his blessing will reap the consequences of that rejection; they will be cursed.)

In all other religious systems in the Middle East, the blessing of divinity empowered the person or community to dominate others. This is true of religious systems everywhere. The gods empower their favorite people to oppress and exploit others.

This call, however, turns those concepts on their head. God's blessing on Abraham and Sarah and their true spiritual descendants will be such that in being blessed they will also be a blessing. The power to exploit others is not included in the blessing. Rather, they and their descendants are commissioned to be a community who minister grace among all nations.

Second, the call involved leaving their family and traditions. This family had deep spiritual, cultural, economic, and kinship roots in Mesopotamia. They were called to leave all of that. Why? Because their people were not oriented toward God the author of human well-being. God called Abraham to embark on a pilgrimage of cultural transformation, a commitment to leaving the dehumanizing patterns of an enduring, ancient, traditional heritage to become a God-centered people committed to humanizing their traditions.

Abraham and Sarah were Semites; the traditional religion of the Semites of Mesopotamia was polytheistic and included the worship of the moon god, Sin. Women married Sin and through temple prostitution bore children to this god. Jewish rabbinic tradition asserts that these Semites sacrificed offerings of children to their gods. The tradition says that God called Abraham to leave these people who sacrificed children for the imagined well-being of society.[16]

Surely one core criterion of the good which Abraham sought was the salvation and care of the children. His pilgrimage away from a culture that allegedly sacrificed children in the interest of society, is a statement all cultures might consider. The cultural, social, and spiritual health of a people is revealed in the way they nurture the well-being of their children, those born as well as those in the womb.

Abraham and Sarah and all their true spiritual descendants are on a journey which requires a critical assessment of culture and tradition in the light of human well-being. The people on this faith pilgrimage seek to leave those cultural expressions which dehumanize and to create new forms which encourage the growth of the person. The call of God to Abraham was and should continue to be a powerful impetus for cultural change for his spiritual descendants.

Third, God gave Abraham no army to acquire the land he had promised. The only weapon he could use to occupy the land was obedience to the call of God. It was God who would provide the land. God did this by giving Abraham the goodwill of the people living in the land.

However, that goodwill was not automatic. Abraham lived in a manner which helped to cultivate goodwill—such as purchasing land for a burial plot rather than receiving the plot as a gift. Because the people knew that Abraham was a blessing among them, they gladly made room for his family in the land.

In the Old Testament the people of the covenant frequently used violence to acquire or protect their claim to land. Even Abraham used violence to defend himself against invading bandits on one occasion. Yet the alternative theme of nonviolence is never completely forgotten in the Old Testament narrative. Sometimes it is only a whisper, yet the ideal of nonviolence is present. This theme is anchored in a confident trust that God will provide for his people.

God's intention was to provide the land for Abraham in a manner which redeemed Abraham from needing to resort to the instruments of violence. Later Abraham's son Isaac discovered this truth in the anvil of experience. The account describes the Palestinian ruler Abimelech demanding that Isaac move elsewhere, because Isaac had become too powerful. It appears that Isaac was powerful enough to destroy Abimelech, and he could have justified such an action by recalling the promise of God that the land was God's gift to Abraham and his posterity forever. Yet in faith Isaac chose to move rather than violently defend his place in the land.

So Isaac moved to Gerar. Imagine his dismay, however, to discover further difficulties in the new location. He opened and cleaned a well which his father Abraham had dug many years earlier. However, the native inhabitants forced his herdsmen away from the well which Abraham had dug. This happened twice. They dug new wells, only to have them confiscated. Only after digging the third well were the locals content to leave Isaac in peace. "Now the Lord has given us room in the land and we will flourish!" exclaims Isaac gratefully.[17]

Fourth, the fulfillment of the promise of God depended completely on God's faithfulness. The most painful trial for Sarah and Abraham was that they had no child. How could God fulfill his promise that their seed would multiply like the stars in the sky if they had no offspring? They agonized over this for several decades until, alas, Sarah was past childbearing age. So Sarah and Abraham agreed that Abraham would sleep with Sarah's maid, Hagar. A son, Ishmael, was born.

Yet when God appeared after the birth of Ishmael, he promised to bless Ishmael, but reaffirmed the promise that Sarah would give birth to the son of promise. God didn't need help in fulfilling his promise; what God desired was only trust and obedience.

At last Sarah gave birth to Isaac, whom the Jewish people consider their spiritual and genealogical connection with Abraham and Sarah. Muslims consider Ishmael their spiritual link with Abraham. This divergence projects firmly into Middle East realities even today, with perplexing implications for intercommunity harmony in the region. (This anticipates the next chapter.)

We have reviewed the call and promise of God to Abraham and Sarah rather carefully because they are the foundation for a biblical understanding of the function and qualities of the people who live in faithful obedience to God amidst the nations. We summarize several noteworthy themes in the Abraham and Sarah story which have special relevance for a people living among other peoples:

1. They were committed to cultural change in the direction of humanization.

2. They were called to be a voluntary community of blessing to all the nations.

3. They trusted God rather than relying on the instruments of force or violence to acquire the resources, such as land, which were needed for livelihood.

4. They lived in obedience to God with the confidence that he would fulfill his promises.

In brief—the survival of Abraham and Sarah and their peoplehood was dependent on God's faithfulness and their obedient trust in him. Covenant is the biblical term for this relationship. To what extent have these covenant qualities informed the manner in which believers in the God of Abraham and Sarah relate to global community issues, such as peace and war, pluralism, cultural change, or human freedom?

The promise of God is a long-term drama. The promise is both present- and future-oriented. God promised Abraham and Sarah a son in the present and guaranteed that in time their offspring would be as numerous as the stars and the sand of the seashore. Faith in the promise compels futuristic thinking. The God-centered community lives with purpose and promise.

The promise of God explodes the cyclical or past orientation of all other religious systems. It is not fixated on the past. Nor is it caught in the meaningless cycle of creation, preservation, destruction, and death which is the perspective of all religious systems which see nature and history as one. The promise of God to his covenant people gives history meaning; it is not trapped in the cycle of nature or the inertia of the past.

Beginning with Sarah and Abraham, the Bible describes a two-thousand-year-drama of God calling and forming this new nation. It is a new people who live among the nations as a light to the global community, yes, an invitation to all the peoples of the earth to turn toward God and participate in the new covenant community.

A Free People

A high point in the drama occurred in Egypt, where the descendants of Abraham and Sarah were enslaved by Pharaoh. Several centuries before the enslavement their grandson Jacob, also known as Israel, moved to Egypt with all his descendants because of a severe famine in Canaan. Ever since that time the descendants of Abraham, Isaac, and Jacob (Israel) are often called Israel. The term means "Let Yahweh rule." Israel refers to a people in covenant with Yahweh, a people who accept the rule of Yahweh over their lives.

(In the next chapter we shall explore the formation of the modern state of Israel and attempt to discern whether there are differences between this modern state and the biblical covenant which brought into being the first people known as Israel.)

The formation of this covenant people, who were the descendants of Abraham, is anchored in their deliverance from slavery in Egypt. Yahweh called two Israelites, Moses and his brother Aaron, to lead their people from slavery into freedom. However, Pharaoh the king only scoffed and repressed the people even more severely. Yahweh intervened by devastating Egypt with ten horrible plagues in relentless sequence. The last plague, the death of the firstborn in every homestead across the land, broke the will of Pharaoh. The Egyptians begged the Israelites to leave their country. In an astonishing act of divine retribution, Pharaoh and his hosts were drowned in the Red Sea trying to pursue the escaping people. This deliverance is the fundamental root experience for Israel; it is the source of their primal vision and identity as a people.

Israel's root experience of deliverance from enslavement has ignited the hope of millions of other oppressed peoples throughout the ages. This is especially true in modern times, as the biblical story expands around the world because of the increasing availability of these Scriptures in the languages of the peoples. In a kernel the account is a statement; it is an affirmation that no political or institutional system has the authority to oppress a people. It is a declaration of fundamental human rights, proclaimed and brought about by Yahweh himself.

The account of the ancient deliverance of Israel from slavery in

Egypt has encouraged leaders of freedom movements in the twentieth century as widely diverse as Mao Tse-Tung, Martin Luther King, Mahatma Gandhi, Jomo Kenyatta, Desmond Tutu, Che Guevara, and Nelson Mandela. Some have been leaders with deep faith in God. Some have led freedom movements which have refrained from using the instruments of violence. Some have been completely secular in orientation. Some have ignored the fact that in this great deliverance the slaves did not gain freedom through violently attacking their masters. Yet regardless of the perspectives of these leaders of modern freedom movements, all have been encouraged by the stern command of Moses to Pharaoh given in the name of the Lord: "Let my people go!"

A New Community

Shortly after the deliverance from Egypt, the people gathered in the desert at Mount Sinai. There Yahweh met the throngs of undisciplined former slaves. He revived the covenant he had made with their parents, Abraham and Sarah.

The covenant included the creation of a tent, a tabernacle, which stood amidst the nomads of Israel whose own homes were tents, as they migrated through the deserts from Egypt to Canaan. In the inner sanctuary of the tabernacle was a box known as the ark of the covenant, and on top of that box was the mercy seat. It was there that the glory of Yahweh was revealed again and again. Yahweh met his peo-ple there, at the mercy seat in the tabernacle.

When God used a moving pillar of cloud in daytime and a pillar of fire at night to indicate that he wanted his people to move to another place, they collapsed their tents and set out on the next stage of their journey through the desert. This tabernacle with the pillar of cloud or fire recaptured again the Abrahamic vision that God calls his nation among the nations to be a nation in pilgrimage. The people of Yahweh must never settle for the status quo. They are a people called to ongoing change, to movement toward the future, to wholesome cultural transformation, to a pilgrimage of hope in obedience to Yahweh.

The Mount Sinai covenant included Ten Commandments.

The preamble proclaims, "I am the Lord your God who brought you out of Egypt, out of the land of slavery."[18]

Then we meet the first three commands:

1. Have no other gods.
2. Do not make idols or worship them.

3. Do not misuse the name of God.

These commands call for exclusive commitment to God.

The last seven commandments confront people in a simple and forceful manner with the requirements of wholesome behavior and attitudes:

4. Rest on the Sabbath.
5. Honor your father and mother.
6. Do not kill.
7. Do not commit adultery.
8. Do not steal.
9. Do not give false testimony.
10. Do not covet.

The fourth command is a delightful surprise, for it requires God's people to rest on the seventh day. In other words, don't work so hard that you can't enjoy life.[19]

Over the centuries, this somewhat secular covenant eroded the significance of religious ritual for the people of the covenant, while accenting right and just interpersonal relationships. This is surprising. In the previous chapters we have observed the opposite trend in Buddhism and Confucianism.

Of course, religious ritual did develop. The biblical accounts in Leviticus and Numbers describe the development of a complex ritual of animal sacrifices even before leaving Mount Sinai. In the following centuries these rituals became pervasive. Many years later when the newly built temple in Jerusalem was dedicated, both the Old Testament books of Kings and Chronicles describe King Solomon sacrificing so many animals that they could not be counted. Yet the prophets were uneasy, lest the systems of religious ritual usurp that which was most important—a fear of God that resulted in righteousness. Religious rituals were never to be center stage.

Some centuries later the prophet Samuel rebuked the first king of Israel, Saul, for offering animal sacrifices while disobeying the Lord. The prophet's rebuke is sharp and pointed:

> Does the Lord delight in burnt
> offerings and sacrifices
> as much as in obeying the voice
> of the Lord:
> To obey is better than sacrifice,
> and to heed is better than the fat of rams.[20]

Nearly a millennium later, the prophet Hosea stated this same conviction with forthrightness:

> For I desire mercy, not sacrifice,
>   and acknowledgement of God rather
>   than burnt offerings.[21]

Remarkably, the Sinai covenant with Yahweh and with one another was the sole basis of peoplehood. All other ancient peoplehoods were based on ethnicity, language, political coercion, or an ontocracy in which the political order was considered divine. However, this covenant people was dramatically different. Anyone from anywhere was welcome as a full member in the community. Ethnicity and language affinities were not the basis for membership in this new covenant community; participation in Abraham's lineage was not a requirement for incorporation into the covenant. Aliens were to be welcomed! The glue which held the new community together was the covenant.

It is astonishing how open this community was. Nationalities in the covenant community who are specifically noted in the Old Testament represent the rich kaleidoscope of peoples in the region. They included Moabites, Hittites, Gibeonites, Hivites, Perizites, Ammonites, Ishmaelites, or Elamites. This phenomenal development of a nation bonded by voluntary covenant is the forerunner of modern constitutional democracies and nation-states based on constitutional commitments rather than on the bonding of ethnicity or language or culture or coercion.

In modern times we are aghast at the ferocity which interethnic violence can unleash. I was baptized with sorrow recently when entertaining a dinner guest from a nation-state being destroyed by inter-clan violence.

Ahmad, our guest, lamented, "I never dreamed tribalism could come to this. My nation is destroyed. No schools or hospitals or industries or farms are functioning any more. It is only death everywhere."

That same evening our television revealed another region of the world rent by interethnic violence, South Africa. Yet on that evening's news we saw President F. W. de Klerk, Chief Mangosuthu Buthelezi, and Nelson Mandela signing a covenant pledging that they would work for interethnic and interracial peace. They concluded the signing event with prayer, an open recognition that the will of God their Creator is a nation comprising various ethnicities bonded together in a constitutionally defined relationship. They sought to live in peace with one another. The April 1994, South African elections were a vindication of that commitment.

A genius of the biblical faith community is that it was bonded by covenant rather than ethnicity. Ethnicity was still respected. Biblical narrative is peppered with statements such the Ishmaelite or the Hittite or the Cushite. Yet these various ethnicities were bonded in a covenant of nationhood. The biblical account insists that the stranger must be welcomed into the community. Ancient Israel's creation of a covenant community which included and respected various ethnicities is the pioneer of the sort of national ethos which a post-apartheid South Africa seeks.

This new covenant nation was not based on the special privileges guaranteed by a divine-kingly code such as that of the Babylonian Hammurabi. There were to be no privileged classes in this new covenant community; all were loved by God, and all were equally under his judgment. The king and the slave were equally precious to God, and the Lord welcomed all peoples to embrace and become voluntary participants in the covenant community.

The integrity of the person was respected in the covenant community. We recognize that in modern liberal societies there is astonishment at the harshness of the Old Testament laws which demanded an eye for an eye, a tooth for a tooth, and a life for a life. Yet even those laws were a reinforcement of the integrity of the person. The person was created in God's image. Whether she was wealthy or poor, powerful or a slave made no difference. The one who injured another created in God's image had to experience the same form of harm to himself.

The person was infinitely more valuable than property. It was never permissible to harm the person for damage to property. The compensation for theft or damage to property was repayment and fines, never bodily harm. No matter what the offense, a person should never be imprisoned. Circumventing freedom through imprisonment was considered an abhorrent aberration of the freedom and dignity of the person created in God's own image.

Even the lending of money was to reflect respect for the person. Loans could not include interest payments for that would be taking advantage of the poor, and every fifty years all loans were to be forgiven. The economics of the covenant people were intended to protect the dignity and well-being of the poor. The commands of Yahweh required that the covenant community nurture and preserve the dignity of each person, all of whom are created in God's own image.

The Prophets

The prophets of Yahweh were a conscience calling the people and their leaders to serve God faithfully. The biblical prophetic confrontation with any unjust political authority or practice contrasts astonishingly with all other ancient Middle Eastern religions and systems of government.

The prophet Moses challenging the awesome power of Pharaoh sets the stage for all subsequent confrontations between the prophets of Yahweh and political authorities who function unjustly. In ancient Egypt the government was ontocratic, as was true of all other Middle Eastern political systems. Divinity and government merged into one ontocratic union. Pharaoh was a son of the sun god Aton; he was divine, the apex of the power hierarchy. The appropriate worship of the divinities of nature and the state plus the skillful manipulation of magic were used to induce tranquillity and prosperity for the people whom Pharaoh ruled. Yet Moses, a nomadic shepherd, son of Hebrew slaves, confronted the awesome power of Pharaoh only in the name of the Lord.

The divine Pharaoh and all his magicians could not stand against the one true God who is the Creator of all things. The power of Pharaoh was broken, and the Hebrew people were freed from slavery so as to worship and serve God as a free people.

This confrontation doomed the ontocratic view of political authority. The same confrontation happens wherever biblical faith finds a home among a people; the divine absolute powers of the political order are finally broken. Any notions that political authority partakes of divinity are demolished. Even rulers who claim to rule by "divine right" must submit to God's ultimate authority.

In Israel the prophets reminded the kings that they too needed to repent (*shub*), to make the U-turn toward Yahweh. No priest of the divinity Aton in Egypt would ever have dared to challenge the divine Pharaoh, nor would a priest of the divinity Marduk in Mesopotamia have imagined challenging King Hammurabi, the representation of divinity. In Israel it was always different; the true prophets of Yahweh never relented in calling the political leaders to accountability to Yahweh.

"You are the man!" sadly exclaimed the prophet Nathan, as he confronted King David concerning his sin of adultery and murder.

"Then David said to Nathan, 'I have sinned against the Lord.' "[22]

No king or authority is exempt from the need for repentance among the people of God. Repentance is a profound corrective to human rights abuses. No government has the right to abuse the rights of others, for all people are loved by God; all are created in his own image. Yahweh abhors the use of power for personal privilege or the oppression of the poor. Yahweh commands that the king also live in repentance.

A People with Hope

The prophetic movement reached a crescendo during the time when Israel was scattered from Canaan, which they had occupied after their deliverance from Egypt. For some eight centuries, they had thrived in this land God had promised to Abraham and his posterity. They developed a stable political monarchy and erected an elegant temple for the worship of Yahweh in Jerusalem.

For Israel it was an astounding calamity that by 586 B.C. the Assyrians and Babylonian empires had destroyed the political nationhood of the covenant people; even the temple was destroyed. Multitudes were scattered to the surrounding regions far from their homes in Canaan. Hundreds of thousands were forcibly resettled in Babylonia along the banks of the Tigris and Euphrates rivers, far from their homeland's Jordan River. They now had no place or state or temple.

Yet in this tragic circumstance, a cluster of prophets saw that the covenant people were now indeed becoming the light to the nations which was God's appointment for them. Yahweh was doing a new thing among the nations through their faithful witness during dispersal and great suffering.

The prophet Isaiah explains,

> I will also make you a light for the Gentiles [nations]
> that you may bring my salvation
> to the ends of the earth.
> This is what the Lord says—
> the Redeemer and Holy One of Israel—
> to him who was despised and abhorred . . . ,
> Kings will see you and rise up
> princes will see and bow down
> because of the Lord, who is faithful,
> the Holy One of Israel, who has chosen you.[23]

The theme of promise and hope permeates biblical faith. This faith vision was already present when Adam and Eve turned away from God at the beginning of human history. On that sad day God made a promise. A son born to the woman would someday deal a death blow to evil, although the son would also suffer in the battle against evil. The prophetic promise was succinct.

> He will crush your head,
> and you will strike his heel.[24]

The "you" in this statement is the serpent, who is a representation of the devil, the one who attempts to seduce humanity into evil. This promise of a son who will deal a death blow to evil is a theme which persists throughout the Old Testament. Later prophets clarified that he would come through the genealogical line of King David, whose father was Jesse. The prophets proclaim that this son will carry forward the ministry of God's covenant people among the nations. He is also called Messiah, the anointed one.

Christians believe that Jesus is the promised Son, the Messiah. The Greek term for Messiah is *christos*. This is why in English Christians refer to Jesus also as Christ. Chapter nine explores the Christian conviction that Jesus of Nazareth is the Messiah whom God had promised. The exploration includes discussion of the ways the life of Jesus contributes to peace and reconciliation in the global community. In anticipation of that chapter, it is helpful to reflect on the vision and hope of the prophet Isaiah for a universal peace which would accompany the rule of this son.

> They will neither hurt nor destroy
> on all my holy mountain
> for the earth will be full of the
> knowledge of the Lord
> as the waters cover the sea.

> In that day the Root of Jesse will stand as a banner for the peoples; the nations will rally to him and his place of rest will be glorious.[25]

The Bible and Global Issues

This chapter has explored the biblical view of creation and history. Some of the themes are especially relevant to the realities of global community.

1. Biblical faith announces that the earth and all creation are creat-

ed good and that humans have the responsibility to care for the good earth. Humans are commanded to work cooperatively with God to develop the earth into a better environment.

2. The faith nurtures a worldview which encourages scientific inquiry and technological development. This includes the convictions that the earth is good; that humans, who are capable of thinking God's thoughts, can and should investigate the laws of creation; that the universe is other than divinity; that humankind should use and develop the earth for the well-being of humanity and in a manner which blesses the earth; that the good earth can become very good through human enterprise cooperating creatively with God.

3. Biblical faith insists that the universe is open—that is to say, that God who created the universe also sustains the universe. The core of biblical faith is the conviction that God reveals himself through his acts in creation and history. However, in chapter 11 we shall discover that modern enlightenment culture has become skeptical concerning the biblical theistic worldview. This is a fundamental tension between a modern naturalistic worldview and a biblical worldview.

Some modern Christian theologians, such as Hans Küng, attempt to resolve the tension by reinterpreting the biblical accounts in a way that frees them from any notions of miracles.[26] Küng seeks to communicate Christian faith in a manner credible in modern culture. Such reinterpretations are a major paradigm shift for Christians.

Can the church survive such a revolution in belief? Is it possible for a community of Christians to remain faithful if they do not believe in the possibility of the Creator's marvelous acts of revelation in history or creation? For example, is a church still authentically biblical without a belief in the bodily resurrection of Jesus Christ? Or has such a church made a fatal peace pact with the prevailing culture?

Most Christians observe that God is conservative in revealing his power through the extraordinary. This is to say that God's acts in human experience are most often experienced in the normal routines of life. For example, a hungry family praying for food might experience an answer to that prayer through the generosity of a neighbor. Although there are biblical and modern accounts of the extraordinary multiplication food for the hungry, that is quite unusual indeed. God usually feeds the hungry through the generosity of people.

In biblical as well as modern times, there seem to be parameters within which extraordinary events occur. God seems to have chosen to respect those parameters. For example, there are many accounts of lame people being made whole. Yet I have not heard of any account, either in the Bible or in our modern era, of a person without a leg having a new leg created through prayer for miraculous leg-making. Christians observe that it seems that the Creator himself has chosen to restrain himself from intervening in some of the fundamental laws which give the universe cohesion and predictability.

Interestingly a faith such as Buddhism has no tension with a naturalistic philosophy. Recall that on its own Buddhism would not provide the worldview which undergirds the technological exploitation of the earth. However, Buddhism is at peace with a naturalistic worldview. Buddhism does not experience the sharp tension which exists between biblical faith and modern naturalistic philosophies.

4. The Bible proclaims that the person is created in God's own image and that male and female are equally the image of God. Therefore the person is eternally significant. All economic, political, and cultural systems should function in a manner which preserves and nurtures the integrity and dignity of the person. All people, including the most severely disadvantaged, are equally created in God's image and need to be respected and honored.

In the Old Testament imprisonment was never considered an acceptable method of punishment for any crime, for that would limit the freedom of the person created in God's image. People could be ostracized from society, but never imprisoned. How would a modern society apply that conviction! *Habeas corpus* regulations in societies influenced by the Judeo-Christian tradition are a modern expression of respect for the right to freedom of the person who has been accused of a crime.

The Old Testament is saturated with a conviction that there can be no comparison between the value of the person and that of property or wealth. The person should never receive bodily punishment for crimes against property—fine the offender, but don't afflict his body. However, a person should receive corporal affliction for injury of another person—an eye for an eye.

5. The Bible insists that the person is responsible for the choices he makes. Evil enters human community through wrong choices. Evil permeates humanity; the Bible portrays evil as human attitudes and actions which dishonor God, dehumanize people, and exploit creation.

These Scriptures describe the joy of people who choose the way of righteousness in covenant obedience to Yahweh. God confronts people calling them to repentance and righteous living. The righteousness of God is universally good, inviting all people to a life of peace, love, and joy.

6. Biblical faith communicates that the earth is very good, and history is the arena of God's redemptive action. Therefore both creation and history are real; they are not a sideshow or illusion. People need to function with responsibility in the real and meaningful realm of creation and history. They should enjoy creation and celebrate with joy the acts of God in history and his presence in their lives and community.

7. The Bible insists that no authority except God is ultimate. Therefore all people, including the powerful, are called to repent and submit to his authority. Only Yahweh is god. No political system or ideology has ultimate authority. Justice, righteousness, and concern for the poor are required of those in power. God is far more concerned about justice than religious ritual.

In the Bible the king and all authorities must also be accountable. They should function righteously and for the well-being of the people. In time this accountability seed planted in the Middle East became a tree known in modern times as democracy. It seems that wherever the Bible has entered into a culture, in due course democratic ideals begin to take root.

8. In its ideal expressions, Old Testament pluralism invites voluntary participation in the covenant community and affirms the reality of diversities of communities. The covenant community is comprised of diverse peoples; it is not based on ethnicity. This ancient nation is a significant pioneer of modern efforts to create multiethnic pluralistic nations bonded by a constitution rather than by a common origin. (However, the next chapter will also explore biblical approaches to the problem of pluralism which led to genocide against those who were not participants in the covenant community.)

9. The Bible encourages a pilgrimage of faithful people who should transform their cultures for the good. The essence of biblical faith invites movement forward in the direction of humanization, with particular concern for those who are weak or vulnerable, such as the elderly, lame, poor, and the children. This is one reason why cultures which have been exposed to biblical faith usually undergo significant change.

In the Bible there is an assurance that the commitment to the kinds of transformations which are for human well-being are not in vain, for God himself calls people to live in hope. He is present and actively involved with people in enabling changes which contribute to the humanization of culture and society.

10. The core Abraham and Moses accounts reveal the covenant

community forming nonviolently and noncoercively. This is often submerged and sometimes hardly detectable in the Old Testament, yet it is a gentle but persistent theme which becomes explicitly evident in the life and teachings of the Messiah. This anticipates chapter nine.

11. We observe that societies nurtured by biblical faith often develop distortions of the core of vision of that faith. For example, the biblical command to "subdue" the earth is in the context of "care" for the earth. Yet Christianized societies have often chosen to neglect the command to subdue the earth in a caring way and have instead opted for the path of exploitation.

In a similar way, the biblical theme of covenant peoplehood has often been interpreted by societies who have been formed by biblical faith as an affirmation of the right of the covenant people to dominate and destroy other peoples. This destructiveness has sometimes been expressed in genocide; it is often expressed in cultural arrogance. Furthermore God-fearing people might equate their covenant people- hood with genealogical descent and ethnic bonding. These are distortions of the core biblical vision that the covenant people are to be open to aliens and a blessing to the nations.

Another prevalent distortion is the notion that human beings have no obligation to work for justice because it is solely God's responsibility to bring about righteousness and peace throughout the earth.

Inclinations toward such distortions are recorded, debated, and critiqued in the biblical text itself; they are not only a modern phenomenon.

Reflection
1. What was the significance of the conflict between biblical theism and the prevailing ontocratic worldview of Middle Eastern societies during the early centuries of Israel's formation?

2. Consider the relationship between the biblical view of creation and the worldview of scientific technology.

3. From a biblical perspective, in what ways does humanity cause creation to "groan" or experience "curse"?

4. Consider this statement: Biblical faith is historical rather than philosophical.

5. What are the implications of the Abraham and Moses events for cultural transformation and freedom movements?

6. Why did the people of the covenant live with hope?

8

The God of Abraham

Israel

ALL NIGHT DEPTH BOMBS sent booming vibrations throughout our ship. It was March 1947. We were anchored just off the port of Haifa, Palestine.

Our troop ship, the *Marine Carp*, now converted into a postwar passenger carrier, was filled with Jewish people seeking entrance into Palestine. All day British gunboats circled our ship, ready to shoot any who tried to swim ashore. The nighttime depth bombs would kill any who swam in the darkness.

My father was a Christian pastor and enjoyed many hours of discussion with Jewish passengers on that ship. On one occasion he and a Jewish gentleman wept together as they explored the meaning of the promises of God through Abraham and their confirmation through the prophets. My father and the Jewish acquaintance bonded in friendship. Both had a quaint first name—Jonas!

A year later Israelis and Palestinians locked in combat following the May 14, 1948, inaugural of the state of Israel. Egypt, Lebanon, Iraq, Syria, and Transjordan (Jordan) joined in battle allied with the Palestinians against the Israelis. That war defined the boundaries of Israel as recognized by the United Nations armistice agreements. (Yet many Israelis were convinced that these boundaries were incomplete for they were not congruent with those of biblical Israel.)

Other wars followed—1956 with Egypt; the 1967 Six-Day War in which Israel occupied Syria's Golan Heights, Jordan's West Bank including Jerusalem, the Gaza, and Egypt's Sinai Peninsula; the 1973 Yom Kippur War with Egypt and Syria, which led to an oil embargo; the 1982 military occupation of southern Lebanon. Endemic violence has been a sad aspect of life in Israel.

Yet for Israel negotiating any land for peace has been exceedingly stressful. The May 1994 transfer of Gaza and Jericho to Palestinian self-rule after twenty-seven years of Israeli occupation involved tremendous political commitment and persistence. There are theological as well as security reasons for these difficulties. This chapter is especially concerned with the theological dimensions of the peace process.

The emergence of this Israeli peoplehood in the Middle East within the bonding of a modern nation-state in 1948 is one of the great surprises of the twentieth century. This region—the land bridge between Asia, Europe, and Africa—is critically important for the whole world. The well-being of humankind is affected by the relationships between Israel and her neighbors.

The 1973 oil embargo by enemies of Israel against friends of Israel reminded the whole earth of how intricately interrelated is the global community and how the volatility of the Middle East can and does affect us all. Israel is at the center of the drama. Even the tragedy of the August 1990 Iraqi invasion of Kuwait was perceived by many in the region as authentically linked with the issue of Israel.

On a visit to Israel and Jordan in September 1990, at the commencement of the embargo against Iraq, I experienced little love for Saddam Hussein among the Palestinians with whom we conversed. Yet he was their hero. Why? Because in the summer of 1990 Hussein was the only credible counterbalance to Israeli power. Many Palestinians hoped that a victorious Iraq would invest the revenues from the oil fields of Kuwait in the cause of liberating the Palestinians from Israel. It is not surprising that those who experience Israel as the regional oppressor felt hope for their liberation evaporating as the one hundred thousand sorties of the Desert Storm bombardment pulverized Iraq's military, communications, and industrial infrastructure. The increase in Islamic militancy is one consequence of that loss of hope.

The Covenant

Officially the state of Israel is an Orthodox Jewish nation. Although many modern Jewish citizens of Israel are secular or even atheistic, the orientation of this state is Orthodox Judaism.

There are similarities between Judaism and Christianity. These include a common understanding of God, humanity, and the universe. For this reason these two expressions of faith and peoplehood are often linked as the Judeo-Christian tradition. The spiritual mooring of Israel is the *Torah*—the first five books of the Tanach, which are Genesis, Exodus, Leviticus, Numbers, Deuteronomy. The previous chapter also described Christian roots which draw spiritual nourishment from the Torah and the Tanach (Old Testament).

For Christians, Jesus is the glasses through which they view the Torah and the Tanach. The previous chapter noted that the Christian church is a people who believe that Jesus is the Son or Messiah whom the Old Testament prophets anticipated. Therefore, Christians interpret all Scriptures, including the Tanach, in the light of the one whom they believe is the ultimate truth, Jesus of Nazareth.

On the other hand, the Jewish people as a whole have never believed that Jesus is the promised Messiah. Thus they interpret the Tanach in the light of their own history and worldview. There are, therefore, significant differences between Judaism and Christianity in their interpretations of these ancient Scriptures. These divergencies do inform their respective understandings of their peoplehood in fundamental ways.

The intention of this chapter is to focus on the Jewish experience as it relates to global community. The profile of their primal story as recorded in the Tanach has been described in the previous chapter. Now our exploration looks at that story anew, with particular concern for the manner in which these biblical events inform the worldview of modern Israel and her relationships with her Arab neighbors.

Abraham and Sarah

Abraham and Sarah are the beginning point. Recall God's call to Abraham and Sarah. He commanded Abraham to leave his father's household in Haran and "go to the land I will show you."[1] The couple obeyed God. He led them into the region of present-day Israel, and after the family had walked through the land, God appeared to Abraham and promised, "To your offspring, I will give this land."[2]

Sometime later Abraham and his nephew Lot needed to part ways because their respective herds of cattle had become so large they could not graze together. Abraham permitted Lot to seek out the best land in the valley. Immediately after that generosity God renewed the land promise to Abraham with these words:

Lift up your eyes from where you are and look north and south, east and west. All the land that you see I will give to you and your offspring forever. I will make your offspring like the dust of the earth, so that if anyone could count the dust, then your offspring could be counted. Go, walk through the length and breadth of the land, for I am giving it to you.[3]

Muslims, Christians, and Jews, all of whom may be aware of this promise, ponder, Who are these descendants of Abraham to whom God has promised the land? The Muslims claim spiritual descent from Abraham through his oldest son, Ishmael. Arabs may even claim direct genealogical descent through Ishmael.

Christians also ponder. Does God's promise to Abraham refer to the Jewish people, to Arabs and Jews, or to all who claim to adhere to the faith of Abraham? That would include Jews, Christians, and Muslims. In that case the promise of land for his descendants is an assurance that God will always provide a place for all who believe in God, who are scattered throughout the nations.

For Orthodox Jewish people the promise is focused and clear. The land refers to Palestine. It is their land, promised by God. They point out that the promise was reaffirmed and clarified to Isaac, the son of Abraham and Sarah with this assurance: "I will make your descendants as numerous as the stars in the heaven and will give them all these lands, and through your offspring all nations on earth will be blessed."[4]

There are some Jewish people whose view of Scripture does not give much credence to such prophesies or ancient promises. Yet for pragmatic or identity reasons, they may still strongly support the right of Israel to exist in Palestine as a state. They point out that history dictates that the location of the Jewish state must be Palestine, because for millennia that is where the Jewish people lived.

The biblical account explains that the promise of God to Abraham and Isaac is the reason their descendants occupied Canaan (modern Palestine) beginning about the sixteenth century B.C. Regardless of how one views Scripture or the promise, the reality is that the biblical account of God's promise to a man called Abraham and his spouse, Sarah, who lived about 4,000 years ago has contributed significantly to the creation of the modern state of Israel in Palestine. The mid-twentieth-century developments in the Middle East lie within the long shadow of the Sarah and Abraham story.

On the eve of the October 30, 1991, commencement of Madrid peace talks between Israel and her Arab neighbors, Israeli prime minister Yitzhak Shamir commented that for thousands of years Israel has had a right to the land of Palestine. He was referring to the Abraham account. Then he added that perhaps the Arabs also believe that they have a right to the land.

On what basis do both Arab and Jewish people claim the land of Palestine? The claim goes much deeper than rights because of occupancy. The roots of the conflict which Shamir was referring to derive from a struggle in the home of Abraham.

Ishmael and Isaac

The ancient biblical story is tumultuous. When God called Abraham, he promised both land and descendants. The couple waited ten years for God to fulfill his promise of progeny. The previous chapter described a discouraged Sarah asking Abraham to sleep with Hagar, Sarah's maid, hoping that the maid would conceive a son for the barren couple. Abraham agreed. A son was born to Hagar and Abraham. He was Ishmael. Even before his birth, jealousy invaded the home. On one occasion Hagar fled into the desert to escape the vindictiveness of Sarah.

God promised Hagar, "I will so increase your descendants that they will be too numerous to count."[5] Several years later God made a similar promise to Abraham concerning Ishmael with these words: "As for Ishmael, I have heard you; I will surely bless him; I will make him fruitful and will greatly increase his numbers."[6] Later God reaffirmed, "I will make the son of the maidservant into a nation also, because he is your offspring." [7] We also read that God was with Ishmael.[8]

These promises tucked away in obscure antiquity may seem insignificant to modern scholars of religion. Yet they are core issues in the modern Middle Eastern context. For people who have been schooled to believe that every word of Scripture is inscribed in heaven and can never be modified, such statements are exceedingly important and affect the formation of entire worldview systems.

Even in Muslim centers of learning far from the Middle East confrontation, there is an "aha" of appreciation when these passages are examined. This is perceived as evidence that both the biblical and Qur'anic accounts agree that Ishmael is blessed. Muslim scholars insist that it has to be so, for in all Semitic traditions the eldest son receives the blessing. Muslim theologians would see the blessing of God on Ishmael extending into the present. Islam and the Arab nation are thereby blessed.

This brief excursion into Islam anticipates a later chapter. Nevertheless, at this point it is important to recognize how intertwined the whole Abrahamic tradition is with the self-perception and people-hood identity of Islam and Judaism, not to mention Christianity.

Although Ishmael is a son of Abraham, God still insisted to the amazed Abraham that Sarah would also bear a son. Prior to the birth of Sarah's son, the account describes intense anxiety in Abraham's home concerning the issue of covenant and blessing. Abraham and Sarah had waited twenty-five years for the promised son. There seemed to be no possibility that the ninety-year-old Sarah would ever give birth. Ishmael was now a teenager.

Amidst this spiritual turmoil Abraham pleaded, "If only Ishmael might live under your blessing!"[9] The Lord enthusiastically agreed to bless Ishmael. "But my covenant I will establish with Isaac," insisted the Lord. Yet this promised Isaac was not yet born and Sarah was turning ninety![10]

When the son was finally born, it is no wonder they called him Isaac, which means laughter. Throughout the centuries people have always laughed as they heard the story of the incredulous Sarah giving birth to a son at age ninety.

In the biblical Genesis account, Ishmael is blessed indeed. Yet the covenant promise is with Isaac, whose conception by the ninety-year-old Sarah is an astonishing event. Just as Isaac's birth is the fulfillment of promise, so God will establish his covenant of blessing with the nations through Isaac and his descendants.

Nevertheless, the promise is always a gift that cannot be grasped but only received. God communicated this truth by commanding Abraham to sacrifice Isaac on an altar on the mount where the temple of God was later built and where the Mosque of Omar in Jerusalem stands today. Abraham obeyed. But just before he killed his son, God intervened, commanding Abraham to substitute a ram for his son. Thus Abraham learned anew that the promise of God could not be seized, it could only be gratefully received. It is God's gift.

At that time God promised Abraham,

> I swear by myself, declares the Lord, that because you have done this and have not withheld your son, your only son, I will surely bless you and make your descendants as numerous as the stars in the sky and as the sand on the seashore. Your descendants will take possession of the cities of their enemies, and through your offspring all nations on earth will be blessed, because you have obeyed me.[11]

Freedom and Land

About four thousand years ago the drama of the land began to unfold. Abraham, his son Isaac, and his grandson Jacob were completely dependent on the hospitality of the peoples of ancient Canaan to have any place in the land. The previous chapter describes how difficult this was for Isaac because his neighbors pushed his herdsmen away from the wells either he or his father Abraham had dug. Yet in due course, God provided a place in the land for these covenant people by giving them favor among the inhabitants of the land.

Recall that the same theme of God himself defending his covenant people is central to the drama of deliverance from slavery in Egypt. It is important to remember that the peoplehood of Israel was decisively formed in the event of this deliverance. This is their core "root experience" creating "abiding astonishment."[12]

Every year since that event some 3,500 years ago, the Hebrew families gather in their homes on Passover night to remember and celebrate that great deliverance through the mighty hand of God. They reenact the meal which Hebrew families shared together the night of their deliverance from slavery. This simple commemorative meal consists of a Passover lamb and unleavened bread.

The lamb is a reminder that, on the night of their deliverance, each Hebrew family slew a one-year-old lamb and daubed their door frames with the blood. That night, as the families gathered to eat the roasted lamb, the angel of the Lord passed through all the land. The angel avoided every home marked by blood on the door frame. But he entered all other homes and slew the firstborn of cattle and humans throughout the land.

In anguish Pharaoh and the whole country sent the enslaved Hebrews from Egypt. Their exodus that night was so unexpected that they did not have time to leaven their bread. The yeastless bread eaten by Jewish people today during Passover is a reminder of the haste with which the people left Egypt on the night of their deliverance.

This people of the covenant can never forget their miraculous deliverance from slavery. They can never forget the renewal of the covenant in the desert at Mount Sinai shortly after their departure from Egypt. These events of deliverance and Sinai are described in the previous chapter; it is not necessary to reiterate here.

Yet it is important to recognize that the whole development of the Torah is grounded in three fundamentally significant events which have formed this covenant peoplehood:

1. the call of Abraham and Sarah and the birth of Isaac,

2. the deliverance from slavery in Egypt,

3. the covenant at Mount Sinai.

The core commitment and confession of the Torah which pulls together the central meaning of these acts of God is the *Shema*.

> Hear, O Israel:
> The Lord our God,
> The Lord is one.
> Love the Lord your God
> with all your heart
> and with all your soul
> and with all your strength.[13]

Righteousness and Generosity

Faithful Jewish people recite the Shema many times daily. It is the soul of their faith and covenant peoplehood. The Ten Commandments which form the heart of the ethical system of this peoplehood are firmly grounded in the Shema. Righteous living is a loving response to the one whom they believe to be the only true God, the one who has called them to become his covenant people.

A commitment to the well-being of the neighbor is central to their whole ethical system. These people, who had experienced being foreigners in a strange land, who knew the heartbreak of slavery, were to be considerate of the stranger and alien in their midst. They were never to forget that God had delivered them from slavery. In gratitude and joy they were to treat the stranger, slave, orphan, widow, and poor with kindness and generosity. They were to receive and accept the alien as one of their own. They were to live with the same generosity toward others that they had experienced from God.

Jubilee and Joviality

The year of Jubilee pulled together into a social institution these themes of joy and generosity. Although the year of Jubilee came only once every two generations, the generosity of Jubilee was to penetrate every aspect of community living, day by day and year by year. This celebration theme develops from the creation narrative, in which Yahweh is described as resting on the seventh day after completing his work of Creation. We are also invited to pause and enjoy the good gifts of our labor.

Each Sabbath has always been a mini-Jubilee. Even today, as they have for several thousand years, on Sabbath eve families gather for the lighting of the Sabbath candles and a meal. The Sabbath is a day of rest, a day to enjoy the good gifts of life. The faithful participate in synagogue worship. Then when the Sabbath is over, Jewish communities participate in festivities. In Israel the streets of the cities fill with joyful people. The mood is festive. Laughter, dancing, song, and fraternity fill the streets of West Jerusalem and all the Jewish cities and towns of Israel.

Everyone in biblical times was to take an annual vacation and save a tenth of their yearly income for the vacation bash. During the annual seven-day Feast of Tabernacles after harvesttime, each family was to join the whole nation in a central location to enjoy the bounty of God with feasting, celebration, and recounting the story of the mighty acts of God. They lived in shelters made of tree boughs during this festive national outing. They were also commanded to give generously to those who were poor to strangers so that no one would miss out in the celebrations.

People were also to provide rest for the earth. Farmers should let their fields rest once very seventh year. People should avoid exploiting the earth and not squeeze all the profit possible from the land. For example, the olive trees should be harvested, but not beaten until every olive has been gleaned. The land, animals, trees, and the people were to enjoy the rest and celebration of Jubilee.

The purpose of labor was not greedy gain or the uninhibited acquisition of wealth. Rather the purpose of work was to develop and receive from the good earth the gifts needed for human well-being. Regular times of rest enabled perspective—rejoice in the fruit of your labor; live generously; take gentle care of the good earth, remembering that it also needs rest.

God's intention was that these themes of generous and joyful participation in his bounty break forth in a crescendo of joy in the year of Jubilee. That event was to happen after every cluster of seven weeks of years, that is every fifty years. The year was to be inaugurated by the blowing of trumpets. At that moment all Hebrew slaves were to be set free. All debts were to be forgiven. Any land which one might have purchased was to be returned to the original owner. Jubilee was to be an equalizing revolution which helped to level the disparities of wealth and position which had occurred during the previous half-century.

In all these encouragements to live joyfully and generously, there was the foundational recognition, "Remember that you were slaves in Egypt!"[14] Therefore the prophet Moses commanded, "Be joyful at your Feast—you, your sons and daughters, your menservants and maidservants, and the Levites, the aliens, the fatherless and the widows who live in your towns!"[15]

Can these themes be practiced in a nation—the themes of generosity, of ministry on behalf of the oppressed? Even Israel in biblical times experienced a failure of will in practicing the institution of Jubilee. It was a wonderful plan but perhaps never really implemented.

Yet the intention of Jubilee did exert significant influence on the society. The prophets reminded the people who enjoyed political and economic power to consider the plight of the poor and the alien. In the word of the prophet Amos,

> You trample the poor
>   and force him to give you grain.
> Therefore, although you have built stone
>   mansions,
>   you will not live in them;
> though you have planted lush vineyards,
> you will not drink their wine.
> For I know how many are your offenses
>   and how great your sins.
> You oppress the righteous and take bribes
>   and you deprive the poor of justice in
>   the courts.[16]

These biblical Jubilee themes have significantly influenced many modern societies. In most modern nations employees rest from their employment a minimum of one day in seven. There are now systems of graduated income tax which tax the wealthy proportionately more than the poor. Inheritance laws in many modern societies attempt to level wealth somewhat by preventing all the wealth in a family from accumulating from generation to generation. Bankruptcy laws permit those hopelessly in debt to receive a dispensation from their creditors.

The United Nations partners with many nations in providing humanitarian support to refugees around the earth. Slavery is now universally prohibited. Nations with adequate food share with the hungry. Many of these humanitarian commitments within modern societies have their roots in the Jubilee themes of compassion for the dispossessed and poor.

Even though Israel may never have fully implemented the social institutions of Jubilee, the Jubilee ideals have always been a con-

science in Jewish society. Furthermore, they have become an ideal
for many other societies as well, which have been influenced by the
Judeo-Christian tradition.

The Covenant and War

Recipe for
Holy war

Just as Israel lacked the will to fully implement Jubilee, so they
also had a failure of nerve in fully relying on God's promise concerning military defense. After the miraculous deliverance from
Egypt and the Sinai covenant, these descendants of Abraham and
Sarah began a pilgrimage across the desert toward Canaan (Palestine), the land which God had promised for the children of Abraham
and Isaac. The journey took them forty years!

On the journey across the desert, God instructed them how to conduct battle after they became a settled people in Canaan. The priests
were to lead off with trumpets and choirs praising the Lord. Anyone
recently married or engaged to be married, anyone who had recently bought a house or a field was to go home to enjoy the acquisition,
for it would be tragic if a person died before enjoying these gifts of
God. Anyone fearful was to return home. After all, the Lord would
fight for his people. They were not to take a census of men of military age, lest they trust in the number of their soldiers rather than in
the Lord. They did not need a great army and had no reason to fear
the chariots and horses of any enemy.

The Scriptures assured Israel that in all likelihood the enemy
would already be destroyed even before the army arrived on the
battlefield. Going into battle was to resemble more a songfest than
war. Before the battles for the land began, God promised,

> I will send my terror ahead of you and throw into confusion
> every nation you encounter. I will make all your enemies turn
> their backs and run. I will send the hornet ahead of you to
> drive the Hivites, Canaanites, and Hittites out of your way.[17]

The manner in which they overthrew Jericho, the first major city
across the Jordan River, is an echo of this promise of God. They
marched around the walls of the city for seven days. On the seventh
day they circled the city seven times, singing as they went. On the
seventh circle, they shouted and the walls collapsed. Then they destroyed and plundered the city.

Yet as they became settled in the land, and as their political institutions developed, militarization became a serious temptation.

Could a people in the center of Middle East international pressure survive without an army or military alliances? Was trust in God alone sufficient to preserve their nation?

One of the most perplexing enigmas of biblical faith is the paradox of the people of Israel, called by God to be a blessing to all nations, using violence to secure a place and survive as a nation among nations in the Middle East. In biblical times, whether it was God who fought the battles or Israel or both, the occupation of Canaan by these descendants of Abraham and Sarah was horrendously violent.

The wars highlighted a negative side of God's promise to Abraham. In addition to the promise that all nations would be blessed by Abraham's descendants, there was also the stern warning: "Whoever curses you, I will curse!" [18] The invading people of Israel believed that all who stood in their way or who opposed them were cursed. When judged by the Ten Commandments, biblical accounts describe the inhabitants of Canaan as exceedingly wicked and fit for extermination. The inhabitants of whole cities, such as Jericho, were obliterated.

Israel believed God had promised this land to them; they were the descendants of Abraham to whom God had promised the land along the banks of the Jordan River. Thus those whom they found already in the land were really there without divine mandate, unless they became members of the covenant community. Indeed significant numbers of the Canaanite people did unite with the community of the covenant. Yet for centuries the battles raged with the indigenous inhabitants of Canaan as Israel occupied the land and subdued or eradicated entire societies.

Between 1400 and 1000 B.C., Israel became a settled people along banks of the Jordan and the Sea of Galilee extending through Canaan to the Mediterranean Sea. As their nation developed, the nature of the battles shifted to colossal engagements with other nations and empires in the region who confronted Israel mercilessly. Israel developed a powerful army. King David disobeyed God by taking a census which showed that he had 1,300,000 men capable of battle. King Solomon had 1,400 chariots and 12,000 horses. Israel was a people who prepared for war and knew warfare.

Occasionally God intervened in a manner which reminded Israel of their deliverance from Egypt many centuries earlier. An example is the time King Jehoshaphat was confronted with the massive armies of Moab and Ammon, who were preparing for battle against Jerusalem. The whole city gathered before the Lord God seeking counsel. Then God spoke through the prophet Jahaziel. He proclaimed, "Listen, King Jehoshaphat and all who live in Judah and Jerusalem! This is what the Lord says to you: 'Do not be afraid or discouraged because of this vast army. The battle is not yours, but God's.' "[19]

God commanded them to sing as they advanced against the enemy. Obeying God's command, Jehoshaphat and his army went into battle with the priests leading the way and with trumpeters and choirs praising God. They sang as they marched,

> Give thanks to the Lord,
> for his love endures forever![20]

The enemy army self-destructed when the soldiers from these several nations turned against one another. By the time Israel's army arrived at the battlefront, the enemy were all dead bodies. It took Jehoshaphat and his army three days to gather the loot. When they returned to Jerusalem, the multitudes gathered at the temple for a praise service before the Lord.

Contemp.
Holy war

A brief diversion into modern confrontations with several repressive regimes is enlightening. The dramatic challenges of unarmed people against the military might of communist Eastern Europe and the Soviet Union is a modern example of the manner in which the people of the covenant in biblical times sometimes confronted enemies. Hundreds of thousands of peaceful demonstrators in the Soviet Union brought to naught the August 1991 coup which attempted to enforce continuation of the communist regime. The same kind of essentially nonviolent confrontation overthrew the Marcos regime in the Philippines and exposed the futility of apartheid in South Africa. Such events remind us of the biblical confidence that God himself fights for the oppressed.

In an era of horrendous weapons for killing people, many within the global village are learning the futility of war and violence. A more potent weapon for authentic confrontation is the exuberance of an unarmed people movement, confidence in God, prayer, persistence, and the voice of conscience such as that of Pope John Paul II in his alliance with the workers movement in Poland against the excesses of Soviet power. Of course, this sort of confrontation is not always immediately effective. It took years before the system in Poland began to crack. And the 1989 Tiananmen Square massacre in China significantly delayed the movement toward a more humane society in that country.

The Covenant and the State

The prophets had always been skeptical about the nation-state. The prophet Samuel, who did finally anoint Israel's first king, resisted the idea of a king in every way he could. He finally bowed to popular demand. Samuel believed that the development of the state would deflect Israel from her mission in the world to be a covenant people among the peoples.

The nation was incongruous with being God's people. It might be a pragmatic necessity, but it was not God's highest plan for his people. To develop political and military institutions like those of the surrounding nations was a compromise of the ideals of covenant peoplehood.

In the previous chapter we discovered that by 586 B.C. this four-and-a-half-century experiment of being the people of God *and* a nation-state ended when the Babylonians overwhelmed Jerusalem, the capital city of the Southern Kingdom, Judah. The Northern Kingdom, Israel, had collapsed under Assyrian pressure 135 years earlier. The magnificent temple which had been dedicated by King Solomon in 960 B.C. was razed.

Although some of the covenant people were permitted to remain in their homeland, most were forcefully scattered to foreign lands. Many were taken to Babylon. This was a time for weeping. In their great sorrow, some of their prophets helped the people catch a fresh vision of what it means to be the people of God. Temple and monarchy were not essential to being the covenant people who blessed the nations.

The prophet Isaiah wrote in those tragic times,

"I will praise you, O Lord.
  Although you were angry with me,
your anger has turned away
  and you have comforted me.
Surely God is my salvation;
  I will trust and not be afraid.
The Lord, the Lord, is my strength
    and my song;
  he has become my salvation."
With joy you will draw water
  from the wells of salvation.
In that day you will say:
  "Give thanks to the Lord, call on his name;

make known among the nations
    what he has done,
and proclaim that his name is exalted."[21]

All these ancient issues of the relationship between nation-state and the meaning of being God's covenant peoplehood converge in the modern state of Israel. The issues of being God's covenant people among the nations are as persistent today as three thousand years ago.

Some nations and peoples may not be acquainted with the biblical story and consequently do not really comprehend the nature of the issues as they affect world community and Israel's self-perception. Others may wish Israel would cease to consider herself a covenant people. Nevertheless, the fact remains that the perceptions concerning the meaning of God's covenant with Abraham have been and continue to be powerfully relevant to the creation and continuation of the state of Israel and to Jewish people everywhere.

Judaism

The principle characteristics of modern Judaism were significantly formed during the exile in the sixth and fifth century B.C. and then the gradual return of some Jewish people to the homeland of their parents in Palestine. Prior to the exile, the people of Israel are best characterized as a faith people in pilgrimage and discovery. After the exile they had become a clearly defined religious community.

Exile and Renewal

The trauma of exile, with the concurrent crisis of identity, made the community less open to others than before. Ethnicity rather than covenant increasingly defined peoplehood. They received the name Jews during this era, and Judaism as a religious system developed to define and nurture their religious identity. The exile into Babylon refined and redefined their perceptions of the covenant. The same dynamics have been in process over the centuries since the exile. A brief review of that process is necessary.

The synagogue developed during the Jewish exile into Babylon in the sixth century B.C. In the absence of the temple or any central locus for worship, the scattered Israelites built worship centers where they could convene every Sabbath day for the reading of the Torah, singing, homily, and fellowship. This development is the forerunner for the weekly church service as experienced by millions of Christians worldwide today and the Friday assembly in the mosque for Muslims. For the Jewish people the synagogue has been vital in nurturing faith and continued identity as a peoplehood throughout the many centuries of their dispersal among the nations.

The exile also nurtured a much greater interest in Scripture. The Torah, history, poetry, and writings of the prophets became the spiritual food which nurtured faith, hope, and identity during this crisis period. The collecting and organizing of their Scriptures became an urgent need during the exile and during the revival of faith which they experienced in the postexilic period. During the culmination of this era of renewal, their priest and leader Ezra gave special attention to the role of Scripture in the life of the people. Ezra is called the second Moses.

After their seventy years in exile, the benevolent Persian king Cyrus enabled many of the Jewish people to return to Palestine, where they rebuilt the temple. Imagine the incredible difficulties of a people who have been in an alien land for seventy years, now returning to the land of their parents and attempting to reestablish community with those Jewish people who had never left the land. It was an awesome feat—forging a common peoplehood out of such diversity, carving out homesteads and a living from the ruins of the past, and rebuilding the temple. The effort was exhausting, and spiritual malaise sapped the energies of the Jewish communities in Palestine.

A century after the rebuilding of the temple, renewal came under the leadership of Ezra and Nehemiah, who journeyed from exile in Mesopotamia to join the Jewish community in Palestine. They came with a mission: the rebuilding of the walls of Jerusalem and the renewal of faith and covenant. It was a dramatic and awesome mission, culminating in a renewal of covenant which has placed a definitive imprint on the Jewish people to this day.

The post-exilic renewal which took place under the leadership of Ezra and Nehemiah focused on the return to place (Jerusalem and the temple) as well as a commitment to obedience to the law of God, the Torah. Never again did this community compromise with idol worship. They were convinced that their flirtation with the worship of false gods had invited the anger of God on them, leading to the dispersal of their nation.

Israel also believed that their forefathers had been exceedingly careless in obeying the revealed laws of God. They believed they had intermingled indiscriminately with aliens, even intermarrying with them. The people longed for renewal, for a deep cleansing of their sin which had grieved God.

Some time after Ezra and Nehemiah had returned to Jerusalem, they convened a seven-day convocation. It was the traditional Feast of Tabernacles, which had been neglected for many years. For seven unforgettable days Ezra read the law of God to the people. The assembly wept in repentance and joy as they heard the law of God. They renewed this covenant to never again depart from his way.[22]

How could the people preserve the fruit of this remarkable renewal? How could they be confident that they were really in obedience to the law of God? For example, the law commands them to avoid work on the seventh day. Yet what is work? How far may one walk on the Sabbath before one becomes guilty of violating the law? These kinds of questions troubled a people who believed that the terrible tragedies of their exile had been God's vengeance on them for neglecting his laws. Those questions pushed Judaism toward increasing fixation on right codes of conduct.

The struggle for faithfulness was not all marked with sobriety. Joy permeated their Scriptures. During the annual festivals, they renewed community, remembered and celebrated the goodness of God, and rejoiced. In the midst of the traumas of the exile and post-exilic period, the annual festivals were renewed and invigorated.

In the first month of their lunar year, which begins in March or April, there was the week-long Feast of Unleavened Bread with the Passover. Then they enjoyed the Feast of Weeks which culminated in Pentecost, a time to celebrate the first fruit of the harvest.

Three feasts adorned the seventh month—the Feast of Trumpets or Rosh Hashanah, which is the feast of New Year; Yom Kippur or the Day of Atonement; and finally a seven-day harvest home festival, the Feast of Tabernacles.

Throughout the centuries and in these modern times, the annual Jewish festivals, respected in their homes and communities around the earth, have nurtured their global peoplehood as they have celebrated the goodness and faithfulness of God revealed in creation and their history.

During the centuries which followed the renewal of covenant under Ezra and Nehemiah, the Jewish religious teachers (rabbis) worked energetically to clarify the meaning of the Torah and its application in everyday living. For the next eight centuries, that process developed, culminating in the Talmud; its development is described later.

Not only the Torah and other Scriptures influenced the development of Judaism in this postexilic period. Other systems of thought, especially Persian and Greek religions and philosophies, were also influencing the Jews. The religion of Zoroastrianism among the Persians may have contributed to a growing appreciation for angels and the last judgment at the end of the age. The Pharisees championed these ideas. Hellenistic philosophy from Greek centers such as Alexandria also influenced Judaism toward rationalism. The Sadducees drank from these wells. Groups formed in Judaism reflecting different responses to alien influences.

Although the Jewish people drank from the diverse cultural and philosophical streams of the peoples with whom they interacted, they did not become syncretistic. All these new streams were judged and evaluated and assimilated in the overall and foundational commitment to the one true God and the Torah which God had revealed through the prophet Moses. All alien ideologies and practices were absorbed and honed in the framework of their uncompromising commitment to God and their covenant with him.

A Scattered People

This commitment to being God's covenant people created occasional crises between the Jewish people and the surrounding peoples and nation-states. We cannot detail the whole story, but several of these tragedies have been especially significant in defining Jewish self-perceptions concerning their place in the global community.

A horrible event occurred in the second century B.C. The Syrian Antiochus Epiphanes determined fully to absorb all Jewish people into a homogeneous Syrian empire. He placed an image of the deity Zeus in the temple and offered swine as sacrifices. The swine is considered an unclean animal by Jewish people. All Jews throughout Palestine were commanded to offer similar sacrifices of swine to Zeus in their home communities. The Jews were forbidden to keep the Sabbath, own any Scriptures, or practice circumcision. Death was the punishment for disobedience.

In revulsion and outrage, the people rallied around Mattathias and his son Judas Maccabeus. They rebelled massively against their oppressors. In 165 B.C. they gained freedom from Syrian rule.

Two centuries later it was the Romans who ignited a Jewish conflagration in Palestine. For a century the Romans had ruled Palestine; gradually they developed policies which indicated less and less respect for Jewish religious commitments. Revolt erupted throughout the area in 69 A.D. Amidst unbelievable bravery and carnage, both the temple and Jerusalem were razed. The brave Jewish defenders of Jerusalem never surrendered. All were killed. Hundreds of thousands of Jews scattered to other lands.

Roots of anti-semitism →

Southeast of Jerusalem, Jewish defenders fortified themselves on the mount known as Masada. For several years they resisted the Roman siege. When the Romans finally overwhelmed the fortress, they discovered that all 960 defenders were dead. They had committed mass suicide rather than surrender their freedom to the Romans. To this day Israel reflects with pride and determination on the "spirit of Masada." Jewish people vow that never again will a Masada be their plight; they will defend themselves against all who would seek to determine their destiny.

Masada and the destruction of the temple have become events for Israel almost as formative as the deliverance from Egypt. Shortly we shall describe the development of the Talmud and modern Zionism; these developments are rooted in this first century A.D. calamity. This experience is a root reason for the theological and political turmoil in modern Israel as the nation struggles to find the way with her surrounding Arab neighbors and the Palestinians.

Sixty years after the destruction of the Jewish temple, the Roman Hadrian determined to build a temple to Jupiter on the ruins of the old temple. Again there was a conflagration. Palestine was ruined, depopulated. All Jewish people were deported from Jerusalem and the name of the city changed to Aelia Capitolina. The temple to Jupiter was built on the temple site. Jewish people could return to the old temple foundation wall once a year on the anniversary of its destruction to lean against the wall and weep. Hence the name, Wailing Wall.

Even in Babylon and Egypt, to which many of the Jews fled, they occasionally experienced persecution. In the first century, genocide exploded against Egypt's one million Jews. In the third century in Babylonia, Zoroastrian Persians forbade Jews from lighting their Sabbath candles. The Jewish people could not submit to a prohibition of a practice so precious in their faith. The result: riots and massacres.

In later centuries, similar tragedy followed the Jewish migrations to Europe. The Constantinization of Christianity mentioned in earlier chapters led to a terrible distortion of Jewish-Christian relations throughout Western Christendom. The Constantinization of the church meant that in time there was little or no room for religious pluralism in Europe.

It was expected that everyone in a Christian nation should belong to the church. Alternative faiths such as Judaism were severely circumscribed. The Jewish communities were severely harassed. Gentile Christians accused the Jews of responsibility for the crucifixion of Jesus. These attitudes toward Jews have planted in the soul of Judaism a profound suspicion of the intentions of Christianity.[23]

The distortions of Jewish Christian relations have been expressed in dreadful ways. The European Crusades beginning in the eleventh century triggered backlash massacres of Jews in Germany and elsewhere. In the following decades, a number of European countries issued orders of expulsion for Jews. By 1492 Spain, which had once been a significant center of Jewish culture, learning, and enterprise, expelled all Jews. In other areas of so-called Christian Europe, Jews were confined to ghettos encircled with high walls. In some countries they had to wear a distinctive Jew badge whenever they ventured out of the ghetto. The pain of this rejection lives on and on.

Several years ago I joined in a Sabbath morning conversation between Jews and Christians in the synagogue adjoining the University of Nairobi in Kenya. The conversation drifted to the experience of the Jewish people in European Christendom. A young Jewish businessman was explaining the awful pain of this rejection and persecution. Suddenly he began weeping. We waited somberly until he regained some composure.

Then he took a piece of unleavened bread such as is used in the sacred Passover meal and said, "In some communities the Gentile Christians took our Jewish babies, slaughtered them, then forced us to mix the blood of our own babies in the flour used to bake the sacred Passover bread."

Most of us joined in weeping with him.

The Holocaust commenced on the night of November 9, 1938. That infamous night is remembered as Kristallnacht, the "night of broken glass." Throughout that night gangs hurled projectiles through the glass windows of Jewish synagogues, shops, businesses, and homes. In forty-eight hours in Germany and Austria, thirty thousand Jews were sent to the gas chambers at Dachau and elsewhere. Two hundred synagogues and 7,500 Jewish businesses were destroyed. That was only the beginning.

During the next seven years, seven million Jewish people perished in the Holocaust. That event, as no other, mobilized Jews around the world to commit themselves to the formation of the state of Israel.

The Talmud and Peoplehood

How can a people, scattered throughout the nations of the earth for two millennia, a people with a kaleidoscope of cultures and languages, come together in Palestine during the mid-twentieth century and discover that they are indeed still one people?

What has nurtured this family of faith over the centuries; what is the basis of their cohesiveness? The Torah and their Scriptures? Yes, that is a significant unifying reality. The synagogue and their annual festivals? Yes, the weekly gathering for worship on the Sabbath and their annual festivals have provided cohesiveness and identity for these scattered people. A common faith and Scripture, common worship patterns and festivals—all these have helped to nurture and preserve Jewish peoplehood scattered among the nations.

Yet superseding all of these is the Talmud.

the Talmud

> Its six major parts and sixty-three volumes have been as meat and drink to the tragic Jews who fled from east to west and back again during the long ordeal of the Middle Ages. Its physical bulk has had—and this constitutes a rather exceptional circumstance—no little relation to its spiritual inexhaustibility. It has served as a rampart of moral resistance that rose higher and stood firmer than the brick and stone of the ghetto walls that Europe raised to hem the Jew in. Though condemned as magic and as devil's lore, burned in the market places by angry civil authorities, or torn apart page by page and thrown on the waters, the Talmud always survived to feed the souls of a persecuted people determined to live by its regulations or have no further part in life. Others might laugh at what was contained in it, but to the Jew it was the wisdom which is of God.[24]

The spiritual perspectives which produced the Talmud were present in embryo in the renewal of faith and peoplehood kindled by Ezra and Nehemiah during the fifth century B.C. At that time the people renewed their covenant with the Lord and committed themselves to obey the law of God as revealed in the Torah.

Yet they experienced difficulty in faithfully obeying the instructions of the Mosaic Torah, for times had changed considerably in the millennium since Moses had led their nomadic ancestors through the deserts of Sinai. This felt need for current interpretations and applications of the Torah was the fertile spiritual soil which nourished the four centuries of effort which culminated in the completion of the Talmud.

Rabbinic oral and written traditions and sermons which comprise the Talmud were developing long before the actual written compilations began. The event which catalyzed the vision and the effort was the destruction of the temple in 70 A.D. At that time a rabbi, Johanan bin Zakkai, escaped from the conflagration in Jerusalem and settled in the little town of Jabneh by the Mediterranean Sea.

With astounding foresight, Rabbi Zakkai focused energy in two directions. First, he gathered around him a renewed council who could function in place of the defunct Sanhedrin which had governed Judaism for many centuries. For nearly four centuries this reconstituted council guided Judaism. Second, he and the scholars around him began the incredible task of collecting, recording, organizing, and codifying traditions and opinions concerning the Torah which had been handed down through the centuries.

The traditions were *Halakah*; the opinions of the rabbis were *Midrash*. After the razing of Jerusalem under Hadrian, the whole school at Jabneh moved into Galilee, where several centers developed to continue this effort. These scholars worked intensely, often needing to move to new locations because of violence and upheaval. Generation after generation they labored; for 150 years they worked. Finally their voluminous effort was completed; it is called the *Mishnah* (Repetition).

Yet this was only the first part of talmudic writing. As the Galilean effort came to a conclusion, the Babylonian scholars received the baton, and proceeded also recording the *Haggadah* (the oral teachings of the rabbis). These traditions were interlaced with anecdotal and historical wisdom. For another two hundred years, these Babylonian scholars labored. Like their Judean and Galilean predecessors they often needed to move secretly to new locations to avoid anti-Jewish rabble or other forms of civil violence and upheaval. This two-century effort culminated in the completion of the *Gemara*.

The Babylonian Gemara and the Judean-Galilean Mishnah together comprise the Talmud. This enormous effort reveals the awesome commitment of Jewish people to live in full obedience to the laws of God which are revealed in the Torah. The Talmud is a fence around the Torah, which minutely defines right conduct so that there may be no transgression of the laws of God.

Heroic Jewish scholars invested at least 350 years developing this monumental volume. Scores and scores of scholars invested entire lifetimes in this effort. As one generation passed from the scene, another generation received the baton and pressed on. These scholars worked with urgency.

They believed that their work would help the Jewish people survive as the covenant people of God among the nations of their dispersion. Their people were deprived of a place. The Promised Land was theirs no more. The temple was obliterated; only an idolatrous pagan image stood where the temple had once been. Scattered and persecuted, the very survival of Jewish peoplehood was in question.

Israel had a mission to the nations. They were called by their covenant God to be a light to the nations, and a blessing among all the peoples. This mission could only be accomplished as they lived in obedience to the laws of God. The Talmud which these scholars wrote over a period of three and a half centuries defined the peoplehood and mission of Israel in the global community. The Talmud was life-giving and life-sustaining nourishment for a suffering people in diaspora and in mission among the nations.

Promise and Hope

Why should these people remain faithful to the Torah, when the cost of obedience to the covenant so often involved suffering, displacement, and death? The answer is hope. Hope in the promise of God has always helped to nourish and sustain their faithfulness.

Recall again God's promise to Abraham that "all peoples on earth will be blessed because of you!"[25]

In various ways this promise was affirmed again and again through the prophets of God. They spoke and wrote of a Son who would come some day; he would be Messiah, the anointed one of God. During the exile and postexilic period, the messianic hope reached a crescendo.

The prophet Isaiah eulogizes that hope.

> The Spirit of the Lord will rest on him—
>   the Spirit of wisdom and of understanding,
>   the Spirit of counsel and of power,
>   the Spirit of knowledge and of the fear of the Lord—
> and he will delight in the fear of the Lord.
>
> He will not judge by what he sees with his eyes,
>   or decide by what he hears with his ears;
> but with righteousness he will judge the needy,
>   with justice he will give decisions for the poor of the earth.
> He will strike the earth with the rod of his mouth;
>   with the breath of his lips he will slay the wicked.
> Righteousness will be his belt
>   and faithfulness the sash around his waist.[26]

Christians and Muslims believe that Jesus of Nazareth is the fulfillment of the messianic promises. Judaism as a religious system
does not accept that Jesus is the Messiah. Herein is the great divide
between Judaism and Christianity, as well as a divide between Islam
and Judaism.

Jesus was Jewish, and all of his early disciples were Jewish. During his ministry many Jews were persuaded that he was the
Messiah. During the first formative years of the church, nearly all
the members were Jewish, and with the exception of two books, the
whole New Testament was written by Jewish people. It is clear that
many Jewish people did believe in Jesus as Messiah.

Yet Judaism as a religious community never accepted Jesus as
Messiah. The fundamental reason is that he never established a viable, politically identifiable kingdom. His ministry did nothing to encourage the urgent felt need of the Jewish people to form a nation
under God which would be independent of Rome which ruled Palestine at the time of Jesus. Their vision was that the Messiah would
establish a worldwide Pax Israel, somewhat like Rome, which by the
time of Christ had established the Pax Romana.

From the perspective of many Jews who chafed under Roman imperialism, the formation of the church as a community committed to
the kingdom of God seemed to be an irrelevant and insignificant
substitute for the urgent need for political independence from
Rome. Even from the distance of two thousand years, the objections
of Judaism to Jesus as Messiah are as clear and crisp today as they
were in first-century Palestine: the Messiah will free Israel from oppression and will bring peace to the earth. Peace has not yet come.
Therefore, Jesus cannot be the Messiah.

Yet the messianic hope has sustained Jews throughout the centuries of persecution and diaspora. That hope undergirded their commitment to the Talmud. Just as Ezra and Nehemiah over 2,400 years
ago assured the people that God would fulfill his promise to them
as they submitted to his law, so talmudic Judaism has sought to
obey God faithfully so that he would indeed fulfill his promise of
Messiah.

The State of Israel

Although Jewish orthodoxy hopes for a personal Messiah, other
Jews speak of the time when the Jewish nation will bless the earth
through being a people of peace. Still others speak of a worldwide
messianic age. That people of blessing is Israel. The hope for Messi-

ah nurtures this peoplehood whose patriarch, Jacob, was named Israel by the Lord their God.

Zionism and Palestine

Hope for the Messiah is a core theme undergirding the commitment to form the state of Israel in Palestine. For centuries Orthodox Judaism had lived in the hope that when the Messiah appears he would lead the Jewish people back to Palestine and establish their nation, a nation which would bless the world with peace. That peace would bring to consummation God's intentions for history. Century after century they waited, but the Messiah did not appear.

The periodic persecution of these people in diaspora gave many Jews an intense longing for a homeland in Palestine, even before the Messiah came. They had waited long enough! Israel needed a theology of action. It is therefore not surprising that a century ago Zionism emerged as an invitation to prepare the world for the Messiah's coming by taking action. Zionism proclaimed the hope that the Messiah would return *after* Israel had taken the faith step of establishing their nationhood in Palestine.

Arthur Hertzberg of the World Jewish Congress writes concerning Zionism that the "deepest undercurrent is the conviction that the Zionist state is the transforming event of Jewish history and that it is, at the very least, a preamble to the end of days, in this world."[27]

In 1896 Theodor Herzl published *The Jewish State*. This was a watershed. The seeds of Zionism had been planted in fertile Jewish soil. In 1947, just over half a century later, the United Nations took action recognizing the right of Israel to form a nation-state in Palestine. Israel was formed in a convulsion of violence which displaced hundreds of thousands of Palestinians.

What of the Messiah? The hope for the Messiah lives on. The Orthodox Jews who form the official religion of Israel plead for faithfulness to the Talmud, for defense of the Israeli peoplehood and nationhood. These commitments are a preparation for the Messiah. They live in hope.

Of course, not all Jews are Orthodox. There are also the Reformed and Conservative Jewish communities. Reformed Judaism is a significant movement in North American Jewry. For these Jews the formation of the state of Israel may be justified for pragmatic reasons; it is necessary to assure the survival of this peoplehood. Conservative Jewry has broken free from talmudic restrictions and mostly anticipates that the Messiah is an era of peace. They hope that the state

of Israel will contribute to the establishment of that peace. That is
Israel's mission to the nations.

Yet peace has not come to Israel or the earth. Israel's survival has
depended on armed might. In the wake of Israel's fortieth anniversary, violence in the West Bank and Gaza increased as the Palestinian *Intifada* (the shaking off) gained momentum. It was tragic and
ironic that a state birthed by a people who had suffered so much had
become the oppressor of others. Thousands of Palestinian children
had been maimed through beatings, homes had been demolished,
death had become a regular occurrence.

Biblical Israel was to be an open society. All others were welcomed into the covenant community. The ideal was a community
not bonded by ethnicity but covenant. And the peoples came.
Indeed modern Israel is remarkably elastic in absorbing Jewish pluralism; when in Israel recently I was told by Jewish leaders that over
130 Jewish nationalities have already immigrated to Israel.

However, modern Israel has experienced difficulty absorbing
peoples whose ancestors are not Jewish. Palestinian Arabs who have
lived in the land more than one thousand years cannot become full
citizens of the Jewish state. Israeli Supreme Court decisions question
whether it is possible for a Jew who believes that Jesus of Nazareth
is the Messiah to become a citizen. Israel as a state and pluralism in
Palestine are in collision.

The Israeli approach to pluralism is similar to that in all other
countries in the Middle East. The dominant religious community
defines the rights and privileges of the minority communities. In
this region of the world, a secular state in which religion and the political institutions are separate is a most difficult aspiration. At its
best the Israeli form of pluralism and that of other states in the region is a benevolent consideration of the interests of the minorities.
Yet any pluralism which does not accept all communities as equal
participants in every aspect of national life has in itself the seeds of
potential abuse.

In Lebanon, on the northern borders of Israel, a political system
which recognized Christian dominance worked fairly well. That is
the perspective of Lebanese Christians; Muslims would perceive
otherwise. Then the demographic balance between Muslims and
Christians tilted in favor of the Muslims. That happened during the
1970s, and the consequences of the need to rearrange power in the
light of changing demographic realities have been catastrophic.

Israel has also studied demographic trends in her nationhood with anxiety. However, as the 1980s came to closure, massive Jewish immigration from the former Soviet Union commenced. The hundreds of thousands of new Israeli settlers from the former Soviet Union assured Jewish demographic dominance well into the twenty-first century.

Painful Peacemaking

A generation after the creation of Israel, the nation had become tragically divided in spirit. The 1967 war and the subsequent expansion of Israeli control over Jerusalem, Gaza, the Golan Heights, and the West Bank created a severe impasse in the soul of Israel.

Different theologies collided. Israel could not remain true to her calling to live justly and continue forcibly and violently occupying the lands acquired through conquest. Even leaving conscience aside, the community of nations would not tolerate Israel sinking deeper and deeper into the quicksand of fascist-style atrocities against the Arab peoples. Yet to surrender the occupied lands threatened to eradicate God's ancient guarantee of land and security for Israel; some of Israel's Arab neighbors vowed the destruction of Israel.

In that crisis two significant spiritual and faith themes competed in this tiny nation hugging the shores of the eastern Mediterranean. Both themes derived from biblical roots. One theme drew from the vulnerable patriarchs, Abraham and Sarah, Isaac and Jacob (Israel), receiving the land as a gift of God's grace, sharing the land with others.

That vision worried about the potential for evil in any state and the potential evils of excessive reliance on military power. The vision opposed expansion of Jewish settlements in occupied territories and policies of oppression against Palestinians. This theme championed the biblical insistence that all people are created in God's image and are therefore worthy of respect and justice. Proponents called on decision makers to take the risks necessary for peace and justice.

The second theme insisted that the land belongs only to the Jewish people. These Jews believed that occupation of the land by Israel was central to God's promise to Abraham. All other people were guests in the land. The rights of the outsiders needed to be respected as long as they cooperated with those to whom the land belonged. The formation and continuation of the state of Israel was by divine mandate. Eventually the boundaries of modern Israel had to approximate those of biblical Israel after they had occupied all the land God had promised to Abraham.

These descriptions are caricatures. Yet they reveal the dialogue. At the center of the conversation are these questions: What does the call and promise of God to Abraham mean for the people of Israel who are his descendants through Isaac? What is the role and mission of Israel among the nations?

The next two chapters explore Christian and Muslim perspectives as well. The faith perspectives of the Christian church, the Muslim *ummah*, and Israel have confounded this region of the world with pathos and tragedy and hope. The theological issues are always there; everyone realizes that faith perspectives are either the rock on which the peace must be established or the boulder on which all peace efforts will fragment. The faith questions which confront the spiritual progeny of Abraham in the Middle East are whimsically similar to the question Abraham himself wrestled with all his life—how does God accomplish his promise of blessing to his people and to all nations?

These faith issues were a core consideration during the 1978 Camp David peace discussions. For nearly two weeks, President Jimmy Carter of the United States (a Christian), President Anwar Sadat of Egypt (a Muslim), and Prime Minister Menachem Begin of Israel (of the Jewish faith) dialogued about peace in the very lands the nomadic herdsman Abraham traversed. Middle Easterners have told me that only an American president who was a man of faith could have given leadership to that peace process, for it is only through faith that one can enter with empathy into the underlying issues which divide and unite this region.

All three of these leaders were men of faith. Their first joint action, as the thirteen days of marathon negotiations commenced, was a call for prayer for peace to the global community of Muslims, Jews, and Christians. Carter describes using his personal Bible in some of his conversations with Begin concerning the issues of land and peace. At one point when the negotiations were at an impasse, Sadat held forth a vision of Jews, Christians, and Muslims meeting someday at Mount Sinai as a sign of the consummation of a regional peace process.

Implicit in their discussions was an awareness of the significance of the Abraham faith pilgrimage for the Middle East today.[28] In the years subsequent to the Camp David accords, others have persistently believed that peace is the will of the God of Abraham for the peoples of the Middle East. Clusters of Muslims, Christians, and Jews have patiently worked and prayed for peace. Yet the obstacles to peace have been overwhelming. Peace requires an awesome paradigm shift in the worldview of both Arabs and Israelis. Peace requires contrition, forgiveness, and vulnerability.

Thirteen years after Camp David, on the eve of the 1991 Madrid

conference for Middle East peace, a British Broadcasting Corpora-
tion World Service newscaster said it well: Many of the participants
coming to the conference believed that only divine intervention
could bring peace among the nations meeting in the Middle East
Peace Conference.

The rightful place of Israel among the nations was the core of the
national debate and agony as Israel faced the Arab nations on October 30, 1991, in Madrid. What a frightful event! For the first time in
forty-three years, Israel met the official representatives of her neighboring Arab nations. The issues of land for peace are in the soul of
both Israeli and Arab self-understanding, an understanding informed by several thousand years of history.

The self-understanding of the participants at the astonishing commencement of the 1991 Middle East Peace Conference was also informed by their respective scriptures—the Qur'an of the Muslims,
the Tanach of the Jews, the New Testament of the Christians. It was
indeed a meeting of the genealogical and spiritual descendants of
Abraham. Hindus, Buddhists, and Confucianists were not present,
although the whole global community is affected by the tensions in
the region. It was a gathering of representatives of nations and peoples whose heritage has been the family of Abraham: Jews, Muslims,
and Christians.

Nearly two years later, on September 13, 1993, the whole world
paused in wonder. The world witnessed another peacemaking event
on the White House lawn in Washington, D.C., an event which terri-
fied multitudes of Israelis and Arabs. There the prime minister of Israel, Yitzhak Rabin, and the leader of the Palestine Liberation Organization, Yasir Arafat, signed an accord as a first step toward peace in
Palestine/Israel. The two thousand people representing the global
community of nations who gathered on the White House lawn for the
event realized that this was only the beginning of a long and difficult
journey toward a secure peace. They hoped and prayed that the God
of Abraham would prosper this act of courage, faith, and hope.

For many years, even in Israel's malaise, unexpected and specific
grassroots efforts for reconciliation and justice have emerged among
some Jewish, Muslim, and Christian people. Some of the accounts are
amazing and heroic. In modest ways these brave and persistent peacemakers have salted Israelis and Palestinians with a more reconciling
spirit. These peacemakers have nurtured the kinds of risk-taking commitments to peace that the September, 1993, accords demanded.

We note some of these communities of reconciliation. During the last quarter of the twentieth century, a surprising development in Israel has been the emergence of the messianic communities. These Jewish fellowships in Israel and among Jews worldwide believe that Jesus of Nazareth is the Messiah.

In Israel itself, a few of these messianic congregations include Arab Palestinian Christians. Some people hope that the reconciliation between Jews and Arabs taking place in these congregations or between Arab and Jewish congregations is a sign in the Middle East of the possibility of a new way. They hope that these modest expressions of peace between Arabs and Jews can subvert animosities and plant the seeds of trust necessary for the difficult political processes of peacemaking.

Yet these signs of hope are miniscule. And neither is strife a foreigner to Arab Christians or messianic Jews, nor are these communities immune to the political polarizations in Israel and among the Palestinians. Nevertheless, Jesus does reveal a remarkable approach to reconciliation.

At dinner one evening with a messianic Jewish couple from Israel, we began talking of reconciliation. Soon I noticed that one of them, David, was weeping quietly. Then David spoke, "I have been thinking that probably every family in the region has lost a son in battle during the decades of Israel's existence as a state. I may lose my own son, Joshua."

After a long stillness he continued. "Yet there is hope. The hope is in Jesus. He is the reconciler, because when he was dying on the cross, he cried out, `Father, forgive them!' I believe he can break the cycle of violence by enabling us also to forgive our enemies.

"I hope that we Jewish people who believe that Jesus is the Messiah can reveal that kind of suffering, reconciling love. Yet we fail so often. We also are trapped in the polarizations of our region."

Several years later I had a similar conversation, but this time with a Palestinian Arab from Bethlehem, whose people had suffered catastrophe under Israeli military occupation. It was one of those sad weeks in early 1991, when several Israelis and Palestinians had been killed.

"Do you see any hope for peace between Israel and the Palestinians?" I asked.

"Of course!" he responded energetically.

He continued, "Jewish believers in the Messiah are meeting in Joppa monthly for prayer with Palestinian Arab Christians. I tell you, that is a miracle. It is only a seed of hope. Yet these seeds can become a tree of healing for our whole society."

Such efforts are infinitesimal. They are tiny, hardly observable seeds of hope. Yet they are so radically other than the spirit of the region that people notice and ponder. Is there a better way?

"Middle East Christians are the glue that hold this region together," exclaimed King Hussein of Jordan in a conversation on October 16, 1986, with Professor Raymond Bakke, director of International Urban Associates, Chicago.

Perhaps the king was reaching for the possibility of a better way when he surprised Bakke with that comment. Of course, the followers of Jesus are not always very good glue; in the Middle East the tragedy of Christian violence in Lebanon has poisoned the society. Yet the ethics and life of Jesus do invite his followers to become communities of reconciliation even in the most hostile environments.

There are other signs of hope as well. Occasionally Muslim, Jewish, secular, as well as Christian people seek opportunities for reconciliation and understanding.

The Peace Now movement in Israel seeks to influence Israeli political processes. This group has been a conscience prodding the government toward surrendering control of occupied territories in exchange for peace. The September 1993, accords were a small step in that direction. They have favored direct negotiations with the Palestine Liberation Organization, a goal finally realized as the post-Madrid peace process progressed. Peace Now has perceived of the peace accord with Egypt as a first step in a process toward peace with all Israel's neighbors.

The Rapprochement Group in Beit Sahour, near Bethlehem, is a community seeking reconciliation. They are a tiny cluster who seek to provide opportunities for conversations between Palestinian and Jewish people. These conversations are often electric with tension, yet they persist in the hope of finding a better way. The Beit Sahour group occasionally convene joint Jewish and Arab vigils for peace. They participate in festivals and joviality together. Slowly seeds of trust are planted. These are little-noticed efforts. Yet political peace must have these kinds of grassroots support. Otherwise peace would be an illusion.

The world was grateful that the 1978 Camp David conversations led to a peace accord between Israel and Egypt. Thirteen years later, broad-based conversations began in the Madrid Middle East Peace Conference. Quite unobtrusively the Norwegian government nurtured trust by hosting informal conversations between representatives of the Palestine Liberation Organization and Israel. Finally in September 1993, the PLO and Israel signed accords in Washington. Were these beginnings authentic steps toward peace? The obstacles nurture despair.

Yet there are those Jewish, Christian, and Muslim believers who have always lived with the conviction that the God of Abraham is the God of hope.

Israel and the Nations

The conclusion of chapter 7 summarized ways in which the biblical Scriptures speak to modern global issues. This chapter has explored ways in which the modern Jewish community, and especially the state of Israel, reflect on and express those biblical Scriptures known as the Tanach. In addition to the themes described in the previous chapter, we have explored several new themes which are important for global community.

1. Abraham is the spiritual father of both the Muslim and Jewish community. In fact, many Arabs and most Jews consider themselves to be Abraham's genealogical descendants as well. The division between Ishmael and Isaac in the home of Abraham some four thousand years ago is projected right into the modern Palestinian-Israeli conflict. The conflict has global significance for in various ways all nations are affected—witness the 1973 oil embargo.

2. Land has been a key issue. God promised this land to Abraham and his descendants forever. Does that promise extend to the descendants of both sons of Abraham, Ishmael and Isaac? How should the land be acquired? Should the community of promise receive the land through the generosity of those already living in the land as was true of Abraham, Isaac, and Jacob? Or may those seeking the Promised Land acquire it through violence, as Joshua did when Israel first occupied the land several thousand years ago?

Palestinians insist that it is not right for the Jewish immigrants to equate the Palestinians with the polytheistic Canaanites of Joshua's time; after all the Palestinians also fear the God of Abraham.

3. Israel lives in the memory of Masada and the Holocaust. All of world Jewry insists, "Never again!" Consequently during the first decades of nationhood, Israeli insecurities invited increasing repression. It was sadly evident that a people who were once violently oppressed and had come to Israel to escape such tragedy had also become oppressors.

4. The Palestinians and Israelis are global communities. For Jews everywhere the survival of the state of Israel is vital to their security as a peoplehood. Prosperous Jewish people in other lands often send generous donations to Israel. In some circumstances they influence political processes in their nations of citizenship, encouraging expressions of support for Israel. This is especially so of the Jewish community in the United States.

Most Palestinians likewise enjoy global connections with Arab communities, be they Christian or Muslim. They are capable of marshalling enormous support, as evidence in the 1973 oil embargo. Palestinian-Israeli conflict has affected political systems globally and sometimes has eroded the peace in regions elsewhere.

5. Israel as God's covenant peoplehood is called to be a blessing to the nations. For many years the security patrols in Israel and in the occupied territories as well as the belligerent spirit between Israel and some of her neighbors indicated that the nations bordering Israel had often not experienced Israel as a blessing. Is there a fundamental conflict between the exigencies of statehood and the calling to be a covenant people of blessing?

The prophets of ancient Israel were not pleased with the development of the state as expressed in the emergence of monarchies. Modern Israel struggles with the same tensions. Is it really possible to merge the institution of statehood with the invitation of God to become a people of blessing to all peoples? Yet the ideals which Israel at its best embody are a blessing.

6. The Jubilee theme in Israel is one expression of a blessed vision: celebrating one's work, forgiving the debts of others, releasing all captives, providing for the needs of the alien. These themes which have blossomed from the spirit of ancient Israel have significantly influenced modern societies.

These Jubilee influences include the principles of one day of rest out of seven, paid vacations, pension plans, bankruptcy laws which let the person burdened with debt go free, abolition of slavery, parole for the imprisoned, asylum for refugees, tax systems which redistribute the wealth of a society, and citizenship which is open to all people.

Reflection

1. Consider this comment: Israel and her neighbors live in the memory of God's promises to Abraham concerning Ishmael and Isaac.

2. What are the potential areas of tension between statehood and being God's covenant people?

3. Account for Israel's continued identity as a people among the nations.

4. In what ways did the Constantinization of Western Christianity distort Jewish Christian relations?

5. The peoplehood of Israel commenced about four thousand years ago. During all these millennia, in what ways has Israel been a blessing to the nations?

6. Consider ways in which the Jubilee themes have percolated into the laws and practices of your society.

7. Consider the different theological perspectives that have influenced Israel's stance toward Jerusalem and the peoples of the occupied territories in the aftermath of the 1967 war.

9

The Wounded God

Messiah

Rejoice greatly, O Daughter of Zion!
Shout, daughter of Jerusalem!
See, your king comes to you,
righteous and having salvation,
gentle and riding on a donkey,
on a colt, the foal of a donkey.
I will take away the chariots from Ephraim
and the war-horses from Jerusalem,
and the battle bow will be broken.
He will proclaim peace to the nations.
His rule will extend from sea to sea
and from the River to the ends of the earth.[1]

THESE are the words of the prophet Zechariah recorded toward the close of the Old Testament era.

Jesus of Nazareth

Five centuries later, Jesus of Nazareth rode into Jerusalem on a donkey. The throngs broke into jubilant praise singing.

Hosanna to the Son of David!
Blessed is he who comes in the name of the Lord!
Hosanna in the highest![2]

246

Children waved palm branches, and the crowds placed their garments on the street in front of the donkey as a welcome for Jesus. The religious and political leaders were chagrined, but Jesus declared that if the children stopped praising, the stones would sing.

How many in the festive parade knew of Zechariah's prophetic vision that the donkey rider into Jerusalem would be the Messiah whom the prophets had foretold since the time of Adam, the king whose reign would stretch unto the ends of the earth, the one who would break the battle bow and proclaim peace to the nations? Perhaps many in the crowd were unaware of these Scriptures, but the religious authorities knew Zechariah's prophecy and had no doubt what Jesus meant by riding that donkey. They were furious.

Who was this Jesus of whom the crowds sang? He was born into the home of Joseph and Mary of Nazareth. The biblical account describes his birth. While still a virgin his mother, Mary, became pregnant through the power of the Spirit of God. This was a sign that the son whom she would bear would be the Holy One of God. Just before Jesus' birth, Mary and Joseph needed to travel one hundred miles south to Bethlehem for a Roman census.

Jesus was born in a cattle shed in Bethlehem, for there was no room for them in the inn. A manger was his bed. Angels announced his birth to astonished shepherds on a nearby hill that night.

Shortly after his birth, the family had to flee to Egypt as refugees to escape the threats against his life by the jealous king, Herod, who had learned that the king of the Jews had been born in Bethlehem. Sometime later, after returning to Palestine from Egypt, the family settled in the town of Nazareth, where Joseph worked as a carpenter and stonecutter. Presumably that was the young adult vocation for Jesus as well. His public ministry began when he was thirty years of age and lasted three years.[3]

With "signs and wonders," Jesus announced the advent of the kingdom of God. Then at the climax of his ministry, he proclaimed his authority by riding into Jerusalem on a donkey. As if to reinforce the reality of his kingship, Jesus went into the temple and astonished both his admirers and detractors by chasing out the merchants with a whip. In the confusion of scattering change, animals, and doves, he proclaimed that the house of God should be a place of prayer, not a den of thieves.[4]

The religious authorities were livid. In hours their governing council had plotted to have Jesus executed. After a farce of a trial, he was condemned to die by being nailed to a cross. Many accusations against Jesus had bombarded the court that day. He was finally condemned to death by crucifixion on a cross because of the charge that he claimed to be the Son of God. The charge was true. He *had* claimed to be the Son of God. The Jewish theologians considered that claim blasphemous and worthy of death.

He was crucified between two thieves, each also hung from a cross. Jesus died in mockery and ignominy, a crucified king.[5] His disciples were shocked and depressed. The throngs, who had sung his hosannas several days before, experienced Jesus of Nazareth as just another of life's big disappointments.

Jesus was probably crucified on Friday and that evening buried in a tomb hewed from a rock on the outskirts of Jerusalem. The authorities placed a guard by the tomb, and sealed it. Then we read,

> After the Sabbath, at dawn on the first day of the week,
> Mary Magdalene and the other Mary went to look at the tomb.
> There was a violent earthquake, for an angel of the Lord
> came down from heaven and, going to the tomb, rolled back
> the stone, and sat on it. His appearance was like lightning,
> and his clothes were white as snow. The guards were so afraid
> of him that they shook and became like dead men.
> The angel said to the women, "Do not be afraid, for I know
> that you are looking for Jesus, who was crucified. He is not
> here; he has risen, just as he said. Come and see the place
> where he lay. Then go quickly and tell his disciples. He has
> risen from the dead and is going ahead of you into Galilee.
> There you will see him. Now I have told you.[6]

The biblical accounts describe Jesus as appearing to his disciples over the next forty days at least eleven times in various and usually surprising circumstances. Descriptions of these appearances are recorded in writings attributed to persons intimately acquainted with Jesus or closely involved in the developing Christian community. The writers include Matthew, Mark, Luke, John, Peter, and Paul. At the conclusion of these appearances, the record says, his followers witnessed Jesus' ascent into heaven.

Jesus' last words to his amazed disciples were a commission to take the gospel into all the earth, inviting people from every people to become his disciples.[7] Gospel means good news. For Christians gospel means the good news of Jesus. Christians believe that all dimensions of Jesus are good news, including his life, ministry, teachings, crucifixion, and resurrection.

The First Believers *beginning of th ch*

For ten days after Jesus' last appearance, 120 of his disciples waited in prayer in an upper room in the city of Jerusalem. They waited in obedience to Jesus who had promised to give them a gift—the Spirit of God himself, who is sometimes also called the Holy Spirit or the Spirit of Jesus. On Pentecost, the Jewish feast celebrating the first fruit of the harvest, the Holy Spirit came upon the disciples like tongues of fire and with the sound of a rushing mighty wind.

People from throughout the city ran to the place where the disciples were to hear and see what was going on. The disciple Peter stood and began to preach. The people were "exceedingly amazed," for through the extraordinary power of the Holy Spirit each person was hearing the good news in his own native tongue. At the conclusion of the sermon, Peter urged the people with many words to make the U-turn away from sin and commit themselves to Messiah (Christ).* By evening three thousand people had believed and were baptized with water as a sign of their commitment to Jesus Christ and inclusion in the church. That was the birthday of the church![8]

Recall that several thousand years earlier people scattered because of language confusion when God was displeased by their arrogant banding together to build the Tower of Babel. After Babel, God called Sarah and Abraham and promised to bless all nations through the new nation he would form from their descendants. We have explored how this promise began to be fulfilled through the presence of the people of the covenant among the nations.

However, Christians believe that God had an even greater vision. They believe that at Pentecost, on the birthday of the church, God's promise to Abraham to bless all the nations through his descendants began to be fulfilled in a much larger and special way. The three thousand who were baptized at Pentecost were diverse. Sixteen communities, peoples, regions, or towns are mentioned. Yet something extraordinary happened. The account describes each one hearing the good news of Jesus in her own native tongue. Although their languages were different, all were united in hearing the gospel. They were baptized, becoming members of the new family of God.

Christos (Christ) is Greek for the Hebrew title *Messiah,* which means "the anointed one," usually "king." The Hebrew practice was to anoint kings and priests with oil as a sign of being set apart by God for special responsibility.

The divisions of Babel began to be healed at Pentecost in a new and remarkable way when these believers in Jesus began to worship together, to eat together, and even to share their goods with each other. Already at Pentecost this new community among the nations was beginning to bring healing and reconciliation between hostile peoples. Later even Jews and Gentiles began to worship and eat together. Earlier that kind of fraternity had been unthinkable.

As the church spread, the astonishing love between Jews and Gentiles amazed those who were not yet part of the fellowship of those who believed in Jesus Christ. Onlookers in the urbane Syrian metropolis of Antioch nicknamed this new community "Christians."[9] Citizens of Antioch observed that only Jesus Christ could create the unity which bonded these Jews and Gentiles; Africans, Asians, and Europeans; slaves and free people, men and women. The church didn't object to the nickname!

The New Testament Account

The church throughout the centuries has been grateful that during Jesus' lifetime one or several of his disciples seems to have kept notes of sermons and events in the life of Jesus. Scholars refer to these accounts as *Quelle*, which means "source." Shortly after his death and resurrection, Christian believers began a more systematic writing process which resulted in the four accounts of the life of Jesus which are included in the New Testament. They are Matthew, Mark, Luke, and John. The early church welcomed these written accounts early in its missionary and teaching ministry.

Legendary anecdotes did develop and several books of these materials circulated. Some of these non-biblical writings are called apocryphal. Some extra-biblical documents fantasize about the miraculous powers of Jesus. The consensus of the church was that these materials should be excluded from the core of the New Testament canon (list) of universally accepted Scripture. The church as a whole decided to include in the New Testament only those Scriptures recorded by apostles or apostolic persons who had a close association with the disciples of Jesus.

The church needed a trustworthy description of the life and teachings of Jesus so believers could teach and proclaim the gospel with confidence. The leaders of the church did not want legendary material to creep in, thereby driving a wedge between the real Jesus of Nazareth and the Jesus who was proclaimed by the church. The early church was concerned that the Jesus proclaimed by the church be the Jesus of history. This concern and commitment is well stated by one of the four writers, the medical doctor Luke, who was the apostle Paul's faithful companion.

> Therefore, since I myself have carefully investigated everything from the beginning, it seemed good also to me to write an orderly account for you, most excellent Theophilus, so that you may know the certainty of the things you have been taught.[10]

One task of contemporary New Testament scholarship is determining how successful the authors were in providing an authentic and reliable account of Jesus of Nazareth. At least some modern scholarship is inclined toward increasing confidence in the trustworthiness of these accounts.

Of course, all the New Testament writers described Jesus from the perspective of persons who believed that he is indeed the Messiah promised by God. Event and the faith response of the writers interact within the gospel accounts. For example, the biblical writers believed the resurrection of Jesus actually happened, and they were transformed by that conviction. In dramatic contrast, the guards at the tomb of Jesus and their supervisors were horrified at the thought of the resurrection. They announced that disciples of Jesus had stolen his body from the tomb. The same event—yet we observe radically opposite responses. Within the gospels event invites faith and faith interprets event. Event and faith embrace. Together they become theology.

Thus New Testament history is rather different than would be a history of the United States Civil War. Although the writers of Civil War history will have personal perspectives and biases, the event of the war does not elicit the kind of rejection or acceptance response the resurrection of Jesus does. No one debates whether the Civil War occurred. A history of the Civil War, while instructive, does not confront the reader with faith choices and ultimate questions about human destiny. For that reason Civil War history is quite different than the event-faith accounts concerning Jesus in the New Testament.

In addition to the four gospel accounts of Jesus, the New Testament includes apostolic letters written to the young churches, and a history of the early church, the book of Acts. These writings give further glimpses into Jesus' life and corroboration for the accounts recorded in the Gospels. These various descriptions of Jesus undergird the faithful church in its witness around the world. The church proclaims Jesus of its Scriptures with confidence, and invites people to faith in him.[11]

The biblical narrative includes multiple names for Jesus, each an indication of a dimension of his ministry and personhood. We shall consider only two names: Emmanuel and Son of Adam.

Immanuel

Immanuel is one of the names angels ascribed to Jesus during the circumstances surrounding his conception and birth. The "*El*" in Immanuel is the universal Semitic name for the Creator God. It is the root word for *Allah*, the ancient Arabic term for the Creator, and the name for God used by Islam. In the Hebrew, Immanuel means "God with us."

Students of religious phenomena are aware of the tendency of a people to project onto divinity their own values. Recall from the first chapter the discussion on the research of anthropologists, who demonstrate that our perceptions of the gods or God are colored by our cultural biases. We discovered that this observation is not only a modern insight; even the Greeks of antiquity pondered that the Ethiopians worship black gods and the Greeks white ones. Many modern scholars demonstrate that our perceptions of divinity are inventions of the mind and therefore illusion.

Interestingly, these views of the divinities are similar to that of the Bible. The Old Testament prophets ridiculed divinities which were the creation of the imagination of humankind. They mused on the folly of cutting down a tree, carving it, decorating it, then worshiping that which is the creation of one's own mind and hands. Biblical faith would agree with these scholars that the gods which are the creations of the human mind are false.[12]

This is not to suggest that these gods are without power. They are powerful and influential and entrap whole societies in their stranglehold. They may be benevolent; often they are evil or amoral. However, in biblical faith none of these gods are worthy of human allegiance. Only the Creator of the universe, only the one who has created humanity in his own image, is worthy of worship.

Yet how are people to be confident that their worship of the one true Creator God is not contaminated by their cultural relativisms?

The Christian response is Jesus, who is Immanuel. Christians believe that the life and teachings of Jesus as Immanuel clarifies in a surprising and disturbing way the true nature of God. Christians believe that Jesus corrects the illusions concerning God, because he is the full revelation of God. According to Christians, Jesus is the clear, definitive, and specific expression in history of the self-disclosure of God, the Creator of the universe.

Jesus was a disturbing presence within his Jewish culture. That is also true wherever a people invite him to be present. A people or person who believes in Jesus will never be the same again. He is disturbingly relevant to every community, yet so altogether "other" at the same time. Christians believe Jesus as Immanuel is always the disturbing stranger yet connects profoundly with the person's true humanity.

If, as the church claims, Jesus is Immanuel, what do we then learn of God through the life and ministry of this man? Jesus of Nazareth inaugurated his public ministry in a Jewish synagogue in his home town of Nazareth by reading from the prophet Isaiah,

> The Spirit of the Lord is on me,
>   because he has anointed me
>   to preach good news to the poor.
> He has sent me to proclaim freedom for
>   the prisoners
>   and recovery of sight for the blind,
> to release the oppressed
>   to proclaim the year of the Lord's favor.[13]

Then with the congregation gazing expectantly at him, he announced, "Today this Scripture is fulfilled in your hearing."[14]

The life, ministry, and teaching of Jesus was consistent with that announcement. He healed the sick and lame. Twice he raised a dead person to life as a sign that God has power over death. He commanded demons and spirits who had become residents in people to leave the persons they tormented. The demons obeyed Jesus.

On two occasions Jesus fed several thousand hungry people through the extraordinary act of multiplying the scant loaves of bread and fishes another had given him. On each occasion after the meal, he arranged for his disciples to gather all the crumbs in baskets. Nothing was wasted. He cared for all the good gifts of creation. He demonstrated lordship over creation through extraordinary acts consistent with his ministry of compassion for humankind.

Jesus forgave sinners. He blessed the children. He confronted the political and religious powers, calling people to repent and enter God's kingdom.

Jesus invited people to observe his life closely. He assured his disciples they would discover that "anyone who has seen me has seen the Father."[15] Indeed the Christian conviction is that the only one and true God, the Creator of everything in heaven and earth and throughout the universe, has chosen to fully and definitively reveal himself in Jesus of Nazareth. We read, "For God was pleased to have all his fullness dwell in him."[16]

Son of God is another name for Jesus which conveys the conviction that God has revealed himself in the Messiah. Before his birth, an angel told the mother of Jesus, the virgin Mary, "He will be great and will be called the Son of the Most High."[17]

Both Immanuel and Son of God convey the Christian conviction that in Jesus of Nazareth we meet the God of all Creation.

Son of Adam

Luke, the medical doctor-historian, concludes his seventy-five-generation genealogy of Jesus thus: "The son of Adam, the son of God."[18]

King David of Israel is nestled somewhere around the middle of that chain of names, which goes all the way back to the first parent of all humanity, Adam, whose spouse was Eve. Luke is making a significant point through that genealogy. He is demonstrating that Jesus of Nazareth was fully human. His ancestry begins with Adam and Eve, as is true of all people. His genealogy extends to Adam through the family line of King David, the first king of Israel to reign in Jerusalem. Through these genealogies Luke is demonstrating that Jesus is not an angel or demigod but a person.

Early in the Christian era, a theology known as *Docetism* developed. This was the notion that Jesus was only God, that his humanness was only an illusion. This is a Christian heresy.

Biblical Christianity believes that Jesus was fully human, yet fully righteous. Christians believe that he is the "new Adam," the man who is the kind of person we should be. His life is therefore completely relevant to everyday human experience. Sincere Christians yearn to be Christlike in everyday life.

Jesus astonished people with the clarity and forcefulness of his ethics. A core cluster of his ethical teachings are called the Sermon on the Mount.[19] The sermon is brief, readable in ten minutes. Self-giving, suffering, compassionate love is the soul of his approach to ethics. He functioned in a manner which ran counter to well-established institutional systems, religious rituals, or cultural practices inimical to human well-being. He lived and taught integrity—let your yes be yes and your no, no. He called for sexual chastity, not only in action, but in spirit and within one's thoughts. He urged simplicity and discouraged the accumulation of wealth; his followers should live generously. Christians shall do good even to their enemies, whom they should love!

The early church believed that these ethical commitments, like those of the Ten Commandments, are a good news way of living in communities everywhere.

Although Jesus functioned with an authority which astonished people, he also revealed humility and vulnerability. At dinner the evening of his arrest and crucifixion, his team of twelve disciples were arguing concerning who was the greatest. This attitude of self-aggrandizement was totally contrary to the whole spirit of the kingdom of God which Jesus lived and proclaimed. In sadness Jesus arose from the table. Taking a basin of water and a towel, he washed the feet of his disciples, one by one. In washing their feet, he was inviting them to repent of their arrogance and serve one another.[20]

The Surprise *the Crucifixion & res.*

The ultimate act of self-giving love is the cross. In Jesus the Christian faith sees God's suffering love for humankind revealed.

In all other religious systems, people believe that God is invulnerable. Neither God nor the gods ever suffer for us. Divinity is too great or too impersonal or too far away or too indifferent. God does not suffer for people. That is the unquestioned assumption of all other religions and philosophical systems.[21]

Nevertheless, in Jesus crucified, humanity is confronted with a dramatic revolution in our understanding of God. The surprise of the Christian gospel is simply this: God has chosen to suffer because of humankind's sin and rebellion.

With hands outstretched, nailed to the cross, in complete vulnerability, Jesus looked at the arrogant soldiers and menacing crowd, then cried out, "Father, forgive them, for they do not know what they are doing!"[22]

Outstretched arms, while vulnerable, are also for embracing. They are the sign of active invitation to come, to be reconciled, to be healed by the love of God. This is the good news, the gospel, which the church proclaims. God so loved the global community that he sent his Son to bring healing to persons and to the nations. "God is love."[23]

An intriguing phenomenon in the anthropology of religion is animal or human sacrifices. French anthropologist Ren, Girard has demonstrated that the inclination to offer sacrifices is universal in the religions of humankind. Girard has shown that sacrifices are especially pertinent in times of hostility. At such times the antagonists select the best animal or human available and vent their anger on this innocent victim. The surrogate victim must also be approved by God or the gods. Sometimes the sacrifice is a lovely virgin girl; the sacrifice must be the best, so excellent that it partakes of "otherness."[24]

The perfect sacrificial victim does not take vengeance. By absorbing the hostility of the protagonists without vengeance, the dying sacrifice breaks the cycle of violence.

The New Testament proclaims that the crucifixion of Christ does break the cycle of violence and hostility. Christians believe he is both Son of God and Son of man, the best that humanity and God could offer. He is the innocent one. In his sacrificial death, he absorbs the hostility of enemies without vengeance and thereby makes peace between enemies.[25]

Recall the Hindu and Buddhist objection to notions of forgiveness. The law of karma is unbreakable. The deeds one does determines one's destiny. Forgiveness for the wrong one does would break the power of the law of karma and create moral chaos. One must accept the consequences of one's actions; the moral and social order must be maintained.

The New Testament agrees that the wages of sin must be paid. Yet the biblical writers proclaim that Jesus took the place of all sinners; therefore the sinner is forgiven and free. Jesus was crucified as an evildoer on a cross which was considered a cursed death for only the vilest people. Yet he was sinless. He voluntarily took the place of sinful humankind on that cross, the just dying for the unjust.[26]

Therefore each person and all humanity are invited to accept forgiveness. Yet the moral order is not sabotaged. Forgiveness is most costly; Jesus took our place in the courtroom. In gratitude for Jesus' suffering self-giving, believers will seek to walk in righteousness.

Christians believe that through the life, crucifixion, and resurrection of Jesus Christ a cosmic transformation has happened within global community. Through this decisive act of love, God has made it possible for all people to experience the forgiveness of their sin and cleansing of their guilt. God and humankind are reconciled. There are thus new possibilities for humankind. These possibilities include the defeat of the powers of evil, the healing of the curse which creation has experienced through humanities' exploitation of the good earth, reconciliation between enemies, and the resurrection of the dead.

Through the Jesus event, the fellowship which God experiences in himself is given as a gift of grace to humankind. This fellowship is received with joy as a gift of God's grace by the new covenant community, the church, whose members live among the nations. Of course, love among Christians is always experienced and expressed imperfectly, for believers in Christ are always only disciples learning to love one another.

The Church

The church in its New Testament meaning is not a building or a place. Rather, it is a people who gather in the name of Jesus. Jesus declared, "For where two or three come together in my name, there am I with them."[27]

Most churches meet at least weekly. The meeting includes such things as prayer, fellowship, worship, singing, reading Scripture, discussion, teaching, preaching, communion, and perhaps probing some issue or planning for the ministries of the church.

Preaching is proclaiming of the word of God with authority. Preaching is a sign that God confronts and calls people to turn away from self-centered living to a God-centered commitment. Christians believe that as they gather and hear the word preached, the Spirit of Jesus is present to reveal their sin, encourage confession and repentance, assure them of forgiveness, and empower them to live in love, joy, and peace. Preaching and worship help build the faith of Christians.

After the church has gathered, it scatters into the surrounding community for work, play, service, and living in the neighborhood. Hopefully the members of the church express the spirit and attitudes of Christ in their responsibilities in the community. Then, perhaps a week later, the church gathers again for fellowship and worship in the name of Jesus. This is the church: the people who gather in Jesus' name and scatter for work and ministry.

Christians believe that the faithful church is empowered by the Spirit of Christ, who enables them to love and serve others joyfully. The communion (mass, eucharist, or Lord's table) is a sign of that empowerment. Most Christian congregations share in the communion service regularly. The communion involves sharing and eating bread together as well as drinking wine together as a congregation.

The communion practice was established by Jesus Christ at that last supper when he washed the feet of his disciples. As he shared the bread and the cup, he explained that these represented his body and his blood through which the new covenant community is created. The communion is a regular renewal of faith; it is remembrance of the root experience in the formation of the church—the crucifixion and resurrection of Jesus Christ. It is a commitment to Jesus Christ through whose death and resurrection sin is forgiven and believers become members of the new community, which Christians often refer to as "the family of God."[28]

Family is a central theme in the church community, for believers in Christ are known as sisters and brothers, and there is neither male nor female in Christ. Both are equal, although roles may differ, particularly in sensitivity to local cultural norms or differing interpretations of some of the scriptural passages describing differing roles in the New Testament church. These Scriptures describe brothers and sisters as "members of the household of God."[29]

The Family and Singleness

The conviction that the church itself is a family of siblings in which Christ is the leader is the basis on which the church builds its understanding of singleness, marriage, and children.

Singleness is a high vocation. The person finds completeness and salvation through faith in Christ and membership in the church family. Marriage and children add nothing to one's personal completion. In fact, the devout single person may focus on the kingdom of God more clearly than those distracted by marriage.

Although many interpreters understand Scripture to expect that the husband functions as the head of the home, the New Testament is careful to insist that this function be exercised in the spirit of ministry to the needs of one's spouse and family, just as Christ ministers to the needs of the church. Headship does not suggest the notion of ruling over one's spouse, but rather of self-giving, sacrificial love on behalf of the spouse. The marriage covenant is binding as long as both partners shall live.

The Christian ideal prohibits polygyny or divorce, for in marriage the spouses become "one flesh." God himself unites them and no person has the authority to dissolve that union.[30]

Marriage is a sign of God's love and covenant with the church. Just as Christ loves and redeems the church, and the church responds in joy and commitment to Christ, so the husband should love his wife, and she should honor and respect him. The covenant bonding between spouses is precious and must be nurtured and preserved.

Children are a blessing from God but have no relationship to the validity of the marriage. They are a precious gift and eternally significant. The church abhors abortion or acts which abuse or discredit the importance of the little ones. Children are to honor their parents, and parents are to respect their children.

A significant ministry of the church is to encourage a spirit in fathers which turns their hearts toward their children. The generation gap is thereby creative rather than explosive.

Nevertheless, in contrast to a faith such as Confucianism, filial piety is not the ultimate virtue. In Christian faith the ultimate commitment of the person should be the kingdom of God. It thus can happen that the call of God can bring tension into family relationships. Even Jesus experienced tension with his family, who sometimes did not understand or appreciate his mission.

The Christian understanding of singleness and the family is anchored in the conviction that authentic, joyous personhood can develop most completely only within enduring and secure covenant relationships. The church and the family are twin expressions of God-centered covenant community.[31] A significant contribution of the faithful church to global community has always been the vitality, joy, and stability of faithful Christian families and single people who live in chastity.

The Church and Culture

The early church struggled with the problem of cultural identity. The very first Christians were Jewish. Although they came from different national backgrounds, they practiced the Jewish traditions which had been nurtured by the Old Testament for many centuries. It was a rich culture and enjoyed a precious ethical heritage.

Soon, however, non-Jewish Gentiles from surrounding communities began to believe in Jesus Christ. They began worshiping with the Jewish believers or, as in Antioch, began to form congregations who were mostly or even completely Gentile. Gentiles did not subscribe to many Jewish customs, especially their usual diet and dress styles. Jewish males were all circumcised, a practice Gentiles considered anathema.

The issues became so intense that a conference was convened in Jerusalem to determine directions. Should the church be a monocultural community informed significantly by Judaism and the Old Testament? Or should it be a multicultural community? The decision of the Jerusalem conference is remarkable. The apostolic leaders decided that the only criterion for inclusion in the Christian community is commitment to Jesus Christ as Lord and his ethical teachings such as sexual chastity. Other cultural practices, such as dress or circumcision, were irrelevant to the essence of Christian faith.[32]

This decision was risky and astonishing. How could the church maintain cohesion and unity when such diversity was assumed and encouraged? To this day that is one of the great marvels of the church. It is a community enjoying astonishing diversity, yet at the core there is unity in the common commitment to Jesus Christ as Lord.

One of the most significant contributors to this diversity is the persistent effort of the church to translate its Scriptures into the languages of people everywhere. Within several years of the Pentecost birthday of the church, Christians began writing letters, accounts, and theological and ethical teachings. In time, some of these books were accepted as Scripture and collected into what is now known as the New Testament. These documents were recorded in the Greek language, the most commonly spoken tongue in the Middle East region at the time of Christ. By the second century, Christians were translating the Bible into Syriac and Latin, then three of the languages of Egypt, then Geez in Ethiopia. Today portions of the Bible have been translated and published in more than two thousand languages. Parts of the Bible are available in the languages of over 98 percent of the earth's people.

There is a significant theological reason for this energetic effort by Christians to translate the Bible into the languages of peoples. Theologians speak of Jesus as being the incarnation of God. God is revealed in a person within a particular culture. The church translates its Scriptures so that Jesus can become incarnate and present within the idiom and cultures of peoples everywhere. When a people receive the Bible in their own language, that in itself contributes powerfully to cultural diversity within the worldwide Christian family.

Different Christian Communities

A consequence of diversity in the church has been the emergence of Christian denominations. There are basically three main families of denominations. The oldest family includes the Orthodox churches, some of whom trace their founding to the apostolic period, the era immediately after Christ. This church family is largely rooted in lands within the regions of Palestine and beyond where the church first began. In other areas, churches have been planted by missionaries from those first churches.

Many of the ancient Orthodox churches have experienced centuries of pressure from Islam or other religious and ideological systems such as Hinduism and Zoroastrianism. In much of the twentieth century, Marxism was a severe pressure point for some Orthodox churches. Prayer, spirituality, and patient suffering are qualities which often characterize these ancient churches.

Over the centuries, the Orthodox churches have taken deep root in their respective cultures. They are often known by their national or peoplehood qualities, such as Syrian Orthodox, Ethiopian Orthodox, or Russian Orthodox. Sometimes there is no separation between national identity and Orthodox church adherence. For example, there is a solid assumption in Greece that all Greek citizens are also members of the Greek Orthodox Church. In this case national and church identity are the same.

A second family of churches is Catholic. At the Council of Chalcedon in 451, the seeds were planted for division between the Eastern Orthodox and the Catholic churches. Over half a millennium later, in 1054, the division became complete. Happily in recent years conversations have begun between the Catholic Church and the Orthodox churches in the hope of a healing of the wounds of division. Church union is not the goal, but mutual respect and fellowship is the hope.

The Catholic Church is a truly universal communion of Christian congregations. It is the largest Christian family, with about a billion adherents. This church traces its origins to the apostolic witness of Peter, one of the disciples closest to Jesus. The Roman Catholic pope, head of this church, claims to be the spiritual descendant of Peter. Under the leadership of the pope, the Catholic Church enjoys remarkable spiritual unity, even though through its vigorous missionary commitment it has become rooted in all but a handful of nations.

The Protestant churches form the third main expression of the Christian family. The roots of the Protestant movement are in sixteenth-century Europe, where leaders such as Martin Luther, Ulrich Zwingli, and Conrad Grebel believed and taught that the Catholic Church was departing from New Testament faith. Consequently a tragic and sometimes violent schism occurred between the Catholic Church and these emerging fellowships, which "protested" what they believed to be departures from biblical faith.

The Protestant movement has been marked by the multiplication of denominations, or different faith families. The Anabaptist stream of the sixteenth-century Protestant Reformation had a keen missions commitment, but in time severe persecution softened their missionary passion. It was not until well into the seventeenth century that Protestant Pietists began to cultivate a missionary vision. Especially in the nineteenth and twentieth centuries, Protestant missions have led to the formation of Protestant churches around the world. Many modern Protestant denominations have no connection with Europe but were formed in societies far different from Europe.

Each of these major groupings and subgroupings in the Christian family contribute to a kaleidoscope of diversity which is rich and exuberant. Within all this diversity, the worldwide church, whenever it is faithful to its calling, experiences a special unity because of the universal Christian commitment to Jesus Christ.

Sometimes the church fails horribly and becomes divisive and even violent. Sinfulness is no stranger to the church. However, the New Testament witness concerning the way of Jesus Christ is clear. Divisiveness and hostility among Christians is not the will of God. In those circumstances, God calls the church to repentance and reconciliation.

The Church and the State

How should the church relate to the state, the political order, or social institutions? This question has perplexed Christians throughout the Christian era, and the answers vary greatly.

One reason for different perspectives on church-state relations is that the prominence of the church in the nations of our world is different. In societies such as Greece or Poland, national and church identity converge; most citizens profess to be Christians in these countries. In such nations the state and church experience an intimate relationship. In other nations, such as Cambodia or Australia, the church has always been a minority community quite to the edge of society. The role of the church in the history and life of a nation affects the relationship between church and state.

There has been historical development in the understandings of church-state relationships. In the first three centuries of church history, Christians were often a persecuted minority. The reason for the persecution had to do with a clash in loyalties.

Recall the ancient notion that the state is ontocratic, that is to say, that the gods and political powers merge. This same notion was prevalent in the Roman Empire during the first centuries of the Christian era. It was also a prevalent notion in other national systems, such as south India, where thriving churches were planted. Christians and Jews, however, believed that there is only one ultimate authority, God. They believed that no state or emperor is in any sense divine. For this reason the Christians and Jews refused to bow before the Roman emperor or offer sacrifices in his honor.

The rapidly growing church insisted that only Jesus Christ is

Lord, not the emperor. Consequently during the first three centuries of Christian experience, thousands were martyred for their faith. They were burned at the stake, thrown into the jaws of lions, beheaded, tortured, or drowned. The persecution also touched the church in societies beyond the Roman Empire.

In spite of such persecution, the church continued growing rapidly. Eventually the Roman government made peace with the church, and the persecution ceased. Nevertheless, it is a fact of church history that in one location or another the church seems to experience periodic persecution. Every generation has had its accounts of persecution in some place in the global community. Even today there are places the church is being persecuted.

A significant reason for this occasional tension between the political and social institutions and the church is the Christian conviction that only Jesus Christ is Lord. Biblical faith insists that only God is worthy of total loyalty; he is the ultimate authority. This is not to say that Christians are not loyal to the state or social institutions. They *are* loyal—unless! When the demands of social or political powers seem counter to the Spirit of Christ, faithful Christians often find themselves in conflict with those powers.

Warfare is one issue with which the church has always struggled. The teaching and example of Jesus reveals that the kingdom of God is never established through the instruments of violence or coercion. How, then, should the church relate to the state in time of war?

The Hindu Arjuna also struggled with the moral dilemma of war in the Bhagavad-Gita. Recall the dialogue between Arjuna and Krishna, who is an incarnation (*avatar*) of Vishnu, the god of moral order. Arjuna was assured that when the way of one's caste demands war, that is the moral act. To flinch and avoid the conflict would be wrong, even if one is killing kinspeople. This is a Hindu solution. Is it also a New Testament resolution to the issue of violence in a lawless world?

For the first three centuries of church history, the Christian consensus concerning war was clear and quite different indeed from the counsel in the Bhagavad-Gita. For the most part the believers in Jesus refused to participate in the military or warfare. They believed their loyalty to the kingdom of God transcended the expectations of nation or empire which might be contrary to the way of Jesus.

However, in the fourth century, the marriage of church and empire which commenced during and after Constantine made that position difficult. This was especially true when Constantine sent whole military battalions through rivers, baptizing all the soldiers. Later church theologians such as Augustine developed notions of just wars in which Christians could and should fight. Yet not all Christians agreed with such ideas.

In modern times the nuclear arms race sharpened these issues critically for thoughtful Christians. An example of this kind of theological reflection is a letter by U.S. Catholic bishops in 1983 to all Catholic congregations in the United States. This statement, "A Pastoral Letter on War and Peace," called on Christians to witness against nuclear arms and suggested that believers consider desisting from work or involvement in the nuclear arms industry.

That statement illustrates the nature of the dialogue in the global church as it considers the conflict between the kingdom of God, which is committed to suffering love, and the claims of the modern nation. The New Testament recognizes with respect and appreciation the existence of the state and acknowledges that the state needs to use the sword to maintain its integrity and civil order.[33]

At the same time, the New Testament demonstrates that the ethical core of the kingdom of God is suffering, redemptive love. God's kingdom brings together a new transnational community from every tribe and nation which is bonded together with the love of God. The tension between the requirements of the state and those of the kingdom of God become particularly agonizing when warfare between nations brings members of the Christian covenant family into violent conflict with one another through their participation in opposing armies.

Throughout Christian history there have been persons and communities of Christian faith who have refused participation in warfare. These disciples of Jesus challenge the authority of the state to require people to fight and kill. Sometimes governments have developed alternative service options for those who are conscientious objectors to war.

In modern times, most Christians believe that the church is not called by God to control the mechanisms of political power. One reason for this conviction is that modern pluralistic societies are rarely ready to tolerate political control by any faith community. Yet this modern reality is not really contrary to the perception of the New Testament. The centerpoint for this conviction is Jesus himself, who avoided using political mechanisms to achieve his objectives. Jesus encouraged voluntarism; he respected personal freedom and choice.

At the height of his ministry, while in the north of the country in

Galilee, Jesus was offered kingship and presumably an army by some of his enthusiastic followers. He refused the offer.[34] Instead he set his face to go south to Jerusalem. Several times on that steady journey southward, he told his disciples that in Jerusalem he would be betrayed and crucified. Jesus turned his back on the temptation to establish the kingdom of God through the mechanisms of political or military power. He faithfully chose instead the suffering way of the cross to bring about the rule of God.

Throughout history it is evident that whenever the church yields to the temptation to grasp and use the instruments of political and military power to preserve or advance its interests, the consequences are distortion of the gospel and corruption of the church.

We have alluded to military implications of the Constantinization of the Western church; there were also political consequences. In the year 313 Constantine legalized Christianity in the Roman Empire. Thereafter a process began which brought about a political marriage between the church and the empire. Most modern Christian theologians believe that this comfortable merger of state and church interests gradually distorted the gospel and the church in Western culture.

There are other examples throughout history of such distortions. It seems that the integrity and ministry of the church are best expressed when the church functions as a conscience in society rather than as a political power. Referring to the church, Jesus put it succinctly, "They are not of the world even as I am not of it."[35]

Christians believe that it is right and wise for the state to hear the witness of the church and to be advised by the conscience of the church. They also believe it is best for societies to be open to receiving the compassion ministries of the church on behalf of the poor or dispossessed. However, even in circumstances where a state system or a society is adversarial to the Christian community, the faithful church will still seek to be a blessing among peoples in that local setting.

The church does not need to enjoy the favor of the authorities to function as a community of grace and blessing. Persecution does not prevent the church from contributing in at least some ways to the well-being of a society, even if only through prayer and the character of its people. The faithful church seeks opportunities to bless society, even though the forms of ministry will differ considerably in an open society which encourages the ministries of the church versus one which attempts to limit or hinder the church.

The Church and Pluralism

In modern times the church has contributed significantly to the development of secular government. This is to say that the church as a community within and among communities seeks to encourage the evolution of government structures which affirm and encourage pluralism. However, historically the church has often opposed secular government, as in Europe's Middle Ages. This was a consequence of the Constantinization of Western Christianity and an aberration from the primal vision of the New Testament.

Even in the contemporary global village, there are dramatic exceptions. The violence in Northern Ireland and Lebanon has been an example where a fusion between church and political order made authentic pluralism impossible. The consequence has been a sociopolitical explosion. Likewise in some Orthodox Christian societies, there is continuing resistance to pluralism.

Yet the general thrust of Christian conscience in modern times reveals the church seeking to encourage the development of secular government structures which protect the freedom of conscience and religious practice for everyone. In most modern societies the church urges governments to function in a manner which encourages pluralism.

Government structures which support human rights, including the right to affiliate with diverse religious associations, are consistent with biblical and especially New Testament faith, which describes the covenant people as a community among and within other communities. That is also consistent with the biblical conviction that God has given everyone the freedom of choice, including the choice of faith. The state should affirm pluralism but also receive counsel from those communities of faith who sustain a society's ethical and spiritual moorings.

The Church and Mission

Recall that God's call to Abraham and Sarah four millennia ago included the promise that his descendants would be a blessing to all nations. They would be a people among the peoples. Christians believe that Jesus calls the church to become an authentic fulfillment of that promise of God to Abraham.

The mission of the church proceeds from the nature of God as revealed in the Bible. Mission is anchored in the conviction that God loved the global community so much that he sent his one and only Son, so that all people can be saved from evil and death and the global community can experience healing. Mission is the response of believers to the conviction that God is love. That conviction is the soul of authentic Christian mission.

In the New Testament the church is often called the "body of ~~Sm~~ Christ." This means that the church is called to express the same ministries of compassion to humankind that characterized Jesus Christ.

Jesus prayed; the church is also called to prayer.

Jesus healed the sick; the church likewise ministers healing, often through the development of hospitals or through the dedicated service of medical people.

Jesus loved the children; the church also cares for the orphans and seeks to nurture and encourage the children.

Jesus forgave sinners; the church also ministers grace and forgiveness in the name of Christ to those oppressed by feelings of guilt.

Jesus fed the hungry; the church is called to serve a hungry world with food and the means for viable development.

Jesus confronted the political and religious powers who exploited the poor; the church is also to be a witness and conscience to the powers, calling them to accountability when their policies and structures are inimical to justice.

The church is called to serve the global community with the same compassionate spirit in which Jesus served.

I shall never forget the day I stood in Mother Teresa's orphanage ~~Story~~ in Calcutta. Peter Kuzmic, a Yugoslavian, accompanied me. Mother Teresa's ethnic roots are also in the former Yugoslavia, since she was born in an Albanian home in Skopje.

We saw babies who had been gathered from garbage pails along the streets only the night before. These were dying children whose mothers' breasts had no more milk. Rather than see her infant expire in her arms while trying to suckle nourishment from her dry breasts, a mother would simply lay the dying baby in the garbage pail.

The nuns, like angels of compassion, searched those filthy pails night after night seeking dying babies. Their mission was to rescue these infants and nurse them to health. Youngsters who were recovering reached out to us to be held and loved.

As we left the orphanage, Peter asked, "Do you know what Mother Teresa said when she was interviewed by Yugoslavian national television after she received the 1979 Nobel Peace Prize?"

"I have no idea," I replied.

Peter continued, "The interviewer asked Mother Teresa, 'Why do you do it?' With a face caressed with joy she responded, 'Because Jesus loves me.' " In Calcutta that day we had witnessed the church revealing the compassion of Christ in surroundings of grief and death. This was an expression of ministry which the New Testament refers to as the church being the body of Christ.

Jesus commissioned his disciples to be his witnesses throughout the global community, until every society has heard the gospel. He commanded them to make disciples of all peoples. His vision was for the church to become a genuinely global community of blessing within and among all tribes, nations, languages, and races.

The early church took that commission seriously. In the first century of the Christian era, churches had been formed in many communities across northern Africa, westward across the southern regions of Europe extending into Spain, and eastward in Mesopotamia, Persia, and even India. In concert with those early beginnings, modern times have seen churches multiplying as new congregations are being formed in society after society.

It is now difficult to identify any nation in which there is no church. At a global Christian consultation on world evangelism in Amsterdam in 1985, representatives were present from 183 nations, which at that time was the most comprehensive representation from states ever convened for any purpose.

Throughout the centuries, there has been a positive response in many regions of the global community to the invitation of the church to the peoples to believe in Christ. As the church approached the conclusion of the second millennium of the Christian era, a third of the earth's approximately six billion people were professing Christians. This meant that the Christian community had become the largest and most widespread faith community in the global village.

The New Testament explains that the call of God to the church is to be present and minister among all peoples of every race, language, culture, religion, and ideology. The church is to function throughout the world in such a way that the nations are indeed blessed and healed. The church in mission also invites people to make the U-turn away from egocentricity and the divinities of culture. It invites people to commit themselves to Jesus Christ as the Lord and Savior of their lives. It invites people to become members of the Christ-centered family, the church.

Although most Christians are grateful for the global growth of the church, it is nevertheless a central commitment of the faithful church in mission to serve the needs of humankind regardless of the response of people to the presence and ministry of the church. The church's commitment to compassionate ministry should not be defined by whether a person or a people are seemingly open to the Christian faith. The church is called to love and serve even the ene- ⊆ ᘯ mies who would wish to destroy the church. The church is called to be a blessing to all peoples regardless of their commitments.

The church has often distorted its mission. Occasionally the church has cooperated with imperial regimes and sought assistance from an empire for the extension of the church. This was often the sad experience among the Indian peoples of South, Central, and North America, where church expansion and imperial expansion were fused, often with horrible consequences for Indian culture and peoplehood. Any partnership between the church and political or economic imperialism is a fundamental distortion of the soul of Christian mission.

A more subtle distortion is cultural arrogance. Often the church in mission functions with the assumption that those peoples among whom it ministers will receive the culture of the missioning church. Particularly in modern times, the missionary movement has often been a significant vehicle for spreading Western culture around the globe. This is because the wealth of the West has enabled these churches to extend their mission presence into distant societies and among cultures very alien to the West.

Akin to the issue of cultural arrogance is triumphalism. In some settings the church in mission becomes fixated on success, as if growth and evident effectiveness were the criteria for authentic mission. Triumphalism is alien to the spirit of Jesus who washed the feet of his disciples and experienced the ignominy of crucifixion.

The Church and the Poor

Jesus taught more about the dangers of wealth and possessions than any other matter. Although he could participate in feasting in the homes of the wealthy, again and again he called on his disciples to share their possessions generously with the poor. On one occasion he commanded a rich young man to sell all that he had and give to the poor. Just as Christ voluntarily became poor to serve people, so those who follow Christ are to become poor for the sake of others.

The church throughout the ages has often neglected these fundamental teachings and example of Jesus. The church, like other human institutions, has sometimes become the exploiter of the poor. In some societies it has acquired lands and turned the peasant peoples into serfs who serve the whims of the clergy of the church. In the

West, Christian theologians have sometimes developed theologies of capitalism which justify the uninhibited accumulation of wealth. A critical reason for the attractiveness of Marxist ideology during much of the twentieth century was as a reaction against the fusion of church with economic systems which exploit the poor.

SM

Yet wherever the church lives in obedience to the life and teachings of Jesus, it has always been an exception to those powers and institutions who exploit the poor. In many regions of the world today, the local and global church is perceived as a community of hope for the poor. In the slums of Chicago, in the rural hamlets of peasant potato farmers of the high Andes of Peru, among the orphans and homeless children of Nairobi, among the impoverished drug addicts of Hong Kong, or the victims of the catastrophic 1991 floods in China, the church is present, sharing and identifying with the poor as a community of hope. In multitudes of communities there are those financially prosperous Christians who do share sacrificially and generously for the well-being of the poor.

As a global community, the modern church is remarkably well positioned for ministry among the poor and for help in times of catastrophe. In modern times, when a cataclysm occurs, the church usually responds with compassion and assistance.

For example, immediately after the Gulf War of 1991, trucks loaded with medicines given in the name of Christ rolled across the Jordan-Iraqi borders. Christians representing the global church made connections with fellow believers in Iraq, enabling local and global churches to partner in assisting the wounded and dying.

About the same time in my own community, as was true in many other communities, church relief agencies invited Christians to provide blankets for Kurdish refugees. The need was announced in Sunday morning worship services. Christians voluntarily shopped the stores throughout our community for blankets, personally paying for the blankets they purchased. One clerk told my wife she could not understand the run on blankets throughout our community. Large department stores were sold out. Within days of the Kurdish refugee crisis, planeloads of blankets were landing in Turkey and Iran. These were a sign of Christian compassion in a time of terrible catastrophe.

Other agencies are also involved in providing help in times of such cataclysm. The church is not the only agency of compassion. Yet it is a remarkable community, with unique worldwide relationships with fellow communities of faith which enable the church to function with resiliency and presence again and again when cataclysm strikes our global village.

Assistance for the poor in times of cataclysm is important. Equally significant is long-term commitment to sharing resources in a manner which enables authentic community development to occur among the world's poor. The variety of global networks of Christian congregations provide remarkably effective channels for community-to-community resource sharing. Not only is the networking for resource sharing important, but the local congregation or parish in itself often functions as a community of hope and empowerment which releases energy for authentic local community development.

The various expressions of development among the poor may include involvements as diverse as planting trees for erosion and desert control in eastern Africa, creating low-rent housing for low-income people in North American cities, or introducing wheat as a dry season crop in Bangladesh, thereby enabling that hungry nation to become a two-crop region. The local congregation in fellowship with the regional and global family of faith becomes, in hundreds of thousands of settings, a community of hope, empowerment, and uplift for the poor.

The Church and Reconciliation

Whenever this global community functions in faithfulness to the New Testament vision, it can become a truly significant community for global reconciliation and peace. Exploitation of the earth or fellow humans, hostility, violence, and injustice are completely contrary to the Spirit of Christ. The church is called to express the Spirit of Christ among the nations, and in this way the church hopes to help the nations experience "healing."[36]

Often the faithful church is called to stand between hostile communities. By absorbing the violence as Christ absorbed the hostility on the cross, the church becomes a suffering, reconciling presence.

Sometimes Christians are involved in extraordinary acts of reconciliation, as in the wars that devastated regions of the former Yugoslavia following the collapse of communism. Christian reconcilers crossed battle lines sharing food, clothing, and medicines with those the combatants labeled the enemy. Some forcibly conscripted soldiers refused to shoot. In heroic grassroots efforts, reconcilers worked for peace, forgiving those who had killed family and friends. In Bosnian Mostar, a new and exuberant congregation emerged amidst the war, a church where people from Muslim, Orthodox, Catholic, Serb, and Croatian backgrounds met one another in peace in the name of Christ the reconciler.

Jesus used the analogy of salt and light to describe the church as a healing and reconciling presence among the nations. In communities broken by strife and violence, the faithful church seeks to be a people who through their life and witness demonstrate their conviction that God is most fully known in the vulnerability of a baby in Bethlehem and a refugee child in Egypt, in the compassion of the man from Nazareth, in the suffering of that man on a cross between two thieves on a hill called Calvary (Golgotha) just outside Jerusalem, in his forgiveness of those who crucified him.

During the twentieth century, the church has become an authentic universal community uniquely positioned to work for global peace. It is, therefore, hardly a coincidence that twice in the first four decades of the formation of the United Nations, the head of the Catholic church was invited to address that global assembly of nations. Why?

Is it not that the representatives of the global community of nations perceive the worldwide church to be a sign showing the way toward the international fraternity for which the United Nations strives?

The Person and the Eschaton

The vision of the faithful church moves beyond the present to the future (*eschaton*). Christian faith anticipates that the Messiah will return again and consummate the kingdom of God eternally. This promise gives the church courage and hope. Although the ministries of the church are never adequate in the context of total global need, the church nevertheless functions in anticipation that in God's own time the kingdom of God will be completed and fulfilled. The faithful church is the community in which the kingdom of God is already beginning in the midst of the nations and peoples of earth. The church is called to reveal hope for the present and future.

Story

We experienced that hope one dark night in the shantytown of Khayelitsha, on the outskirts of Cape Town, South Africa. We were invited into the home of the Norawanas for a prayer meeting. These Xhosa Bantu were a people displaced within their own land. The South African Group Areas Act (1950) had provided a legal basis for removing tens of thousands of Xhosa from their homelands. Thousands were dumped into this township to begin life anew. Often the removals were in winter; children died of pneumonia. Khayelitsha was the sad face of apartheid. It was the fruit of bitter injustice.

Yet here we were in Khayelitsha enjoying a prayer meeting. Singing broke forth. Pastor Norawana began to dance mightily, as with exuberant hope and joy he led this small congregation of dispossessed Xhosa in hymns of praise. The crowded Norawana living room rocked with joy as they sang, "Look, he is coming. Just around the corner. Jesus is coming!"

Apartheid had not broken the spirit of these people; they were already free. Such confident, jubilant hope in God would someday doom apartheid.

Several months later Nelson Mandela, head of the African National Congress, was freed after twenty-seven years of imprisonment. His release hastened the momentum toward political restructuring for a post-apartheid South Africa. For black South Africans, the waiting in hope had been long and painful. Yet faith does not despair; Africans sometimes liken persistent hope to a turtle. When the beatings come, the turtle retreats into its shell and waits; when the beating stops, the turtle begins its journey anew, confident that it will surely sometime arrive at its destination.

Christian hope also extends beyond this life. Christians believe there will be a bodily resurrection of the dead at the eschaton, the concluding climax of history when Jesus Christ returns to earth in power to establish the kingdom of God forever. The conviction of the church is that God is actively drawing all history, all people, all communities, all creation toward that final glorious climax in the future.

Christians believe that the person is centrally significant in this drama, for each person will experience a bodily resurrection at the eschaton. At that day God will bring about the consummation of his new creation, the fulfillment of the kingdom of God in which righteousness and peace triumphs over evil forever.

Christians also believe that the eschaton is judgment day. Just as the kingdom of God has already begun, so also judgment is also already present. Our self-centered living creates a harvest of judgment now. At the eschaton the judgment, which we already observe among us, will be consummated.

Christians believe that our present life is eternally significant; it is important to invest life wisely. Each person's present existence and choices do make a real difference. The hope of the eschaton is a beacon inviting the person to turn toward Christ who empowers joyful, generous living and away from the selfishness which erodes full personhood. The Christian hope is an invitation to turn away from paths that invite judgment.

The Christian hope in the bodily resurrection of the dead dramatically impacts the manner in which the faithful church views the significance of the person in the present. The promise of the resurrection reveals that each person is eternally significant, as a whole person. Therefore the church needs to minister to the whole person in the present as well as preparing the person for eternity. The body, soul, mind, spirit—all the dimensions of the person—need healing and wholeness. The church believes that each person, each of the approximately six billion persons who inhabit the global community, is precious to God now and eternally.

The Church and Global Issues

Both Israel and the church are nurtured by the same Scriptures which the Jewish people call the Tanach and Christians refer to as the Old Testament. Chapter seven describes ways these Scriptures have nurtured the Jewish and Christian communities of faith. We also discovered that the ideals and worldview of these Scriptures have become significant outside the Jewish or Christian communities.

These ideals have helped form some universal modern attitudes and approaches to global community issues. These realities are as diverse as pluralism, ecology, the person (both male and female), property, technology, development, children, human rights, economics, the nation-state, democracy, cultural change, work, enjoyment and meaning of life, joviality and vacations, generosity, and religion. The church considers itself to be in basic continuity with themes such as those in chapter seven and also with the Jubilee themes described in chapter eight.

The present chapter has picked up additional themes significant for the global village. This chapter has explored the Christian conviction that Jesus is the Messiah; the exploration has included the church, which was created following his crucifixion and resurrection. The confession of faith in Jesus as Messiah is the foundation of the faithful church and defines the manner in which the church relates to global issues, as summarized here:

1. The Old Testament belief that the person is of great value created in God's own image receives enormous reinforcement in the resurrection of Jesus Christ. That resurrection is also a promise that God's intention and invitation is for every person to enjoy full bodily resurrection life eternally. The person is infinitely precious. There is a sense of urgency—all are invited to believe, to repent, to turn toward Christ, in whom there is life.

2. The freedom and dignity of the person must be respected. Volunteerism rather than compulsion should characterize healthy societies. Thus pluralism will be the normal experience of societies. Although the church confesses that only Jesus Christ is Lord, that confession should be voluntary. In the New Testament, we discover the church seeking to invite people into faith but respecting the right of the person to alternative loyalties.

3. The church believes that the life, death, and resurrection of Jesus Christ is a gift of grace which brings healing and wholeness to the person. Forgiveness, a free conscience, righteousness, reconciliation, love, joy, peace, purpose, community, the meaning of life, and a right and joyous relationship with the Creator—all are offered the person through the life and ministry of Christ. The gospel refers to this gift as abundant life.

4. Although the church attempts to be salt and light in society encouraging that which is good, the church is compromised in its mission when it acquires the mechanisms of political, military, or economic power. It is called to serve rather than control, to influence ᵴ ⫪ rather than demand, to confront rather than coerce. It is preferable to recognize the separate functions of the church and state.

There are limitations when a church does not control the mechanisms of political power. Society often moves in directions contrary to the convictions of the church. For this reason some Christians and church communities argue that political control is justified. Throughout Christian history there were numerous times when the church did control the political order in particular settings.

Yet the stance of political control is quite different from that taken by Jesus. In contrast, Islam, which we shall explore in the next chapter, does have a political and economic plan.

5. The church should be more concerned about justice and righteousness than religious ritual. Jesus' act of cleansing the temple, while he in anger defied the use of the place of worship for profitable religiosity, is a model of confrontation with exploitative religious activity which faithful Christians take seriously.

6. The church considers singleness, with sexual chastity, as a high vocation. Marriage is a covenant of loving commitment in which God himself joins the husband and wife in an indissoluble monogamous union as long as both shall live. Children are a blessing but not essential to the success of a marriage. The covenant of marriage is a sign of Christ's love for the church; that is to say, the husband is called to love his wife in sacrificial concern for her well-being.

7. The church is a universal community present as at least a significant minority in all but a few nations. At its best the faithful church is an authentic transnational fellowship bonding the peoples of the global community in a special unity which transcends national and cultural differences. That unity is based on a common commitment to Jesus Christ and his teachings which form the basis of a universal Christian understanding of righteousness.

ana stds   8. The ethics of Jesus are perceived by many as impractical. For example, how can one organize a society or a nation on the basis of love for one's enemy or selling one's goods and giving one's wealth to the poor? The perceived impracticality of New Testament ethics has often led Christian communities into retreat from serious involvement with the issues of global community.

Nevertheless, Christian communities which do take the life and teachings of Jesus seriously become truly alternative communities in any local, national, or global community. Just one example—Christians who practice the teachings and example of Jesus in relationship to wealth and possessions will share generously and sacrificially with the poor. Prosperous Christians will choose to lower their standard of living so as to share more generously with those who are impoverished. It is this spirit of generosity and concern for the poor which propels the modern global church into becoming a remarkable international community of compassion.

9. The church celebrates pluralism within this global family. In fact, the encouragement of cultural pluralism is one source of denominational variety in the church. The unity of the global church does not negate the need for the church to take deep root in local culture. The translation of portions of the Bible into some 2,000 languages has given a boost to the ability of the church to take deep root in local culture.

10. The church experiences tension between its local cultural roots and its universal commitments. At no time does this tension become more intense than in times of war. The nation goes to war, yet the church is a universal community bonded in love even for enemies.

Most expressions of the modern global church have found the paradox of love for the enemy and war against the enemy almost impossible to resolve. Just-war theories have been developed to enable the Christian to decide when a war is justified. Yet the teachings of Jesus and his example of suffering at the hands of his enemies in his crucifixion invite the way of suffering love for enemies.

11. In some situations the church has been an effective communi-

ty for reconciliation between antagonistic communities or nations. Certainly that is a calling of the church—to help break the cycle of violence and retribution through suffering love. That is the ministry of Christ crucified, who reveals in his suffering and death that God himself enters into human violence and hate. God then brings reconciliation and healing through forgiveness rather than vengeance.

12. The church is called to serve people with compassion. Jesus announced that in his life and ministry the kingdom of God was and is at hand. This is the kingdom in which there is authentic ministry on behalf of the poor, the blind, the oppressed, the prisoner. The church is called to be the body of Christ, ministering in our wounded, suffering global community in the same spirit and compassion Jesus of Nazareth revealed.

13. The church is called to good stewardship of God's good earth. Jesus wasted nothing, not even the crumbs of bread and fish after miraculously feeding multitudes.

14. The church invites hope. Christians believe that the resurrection of Christ is the assurance that in God's own time and way evil and death will be overcome by righteousness and abundant life. They believe that the kingdom of God has been inaugurated in Jesus Christ. They believe his resurrection is the guarantee that Jesus is Lord and that at the climax of history he will establish the kingdom of God forever in a new creation in which righteousness and peace will prevail. That hope inspires Christian persistence, confidence, and patience.

15. Finally, prayer is essential to the Christian way. The church has a vocation of prayer for the well-being of the global community and for all people. The church is keenly aware of the pervasiveness of evil. Righteousness will never prevail through human effort alone. It is God who brings about his kingdom. Through prayer, believers partner with God in this enterprise of introducing the signs of abundant life throughout the global village. Jesus taught his followers to pray, "Your kingdom come, your will be done on earth as it is in heaven."[37]

These statements represent the ideal vision of the New Testament church. However, the church, like all other communities, participates in the evil and dehumanization which pervades much of our global village experience. Christians also participate in cursing the good earth through the destructive use of God's Creation. In the wars of the twentieth century, Christians have often fought and killed with the same vengeance as others. Often the church has sought control of political power and used that power for its own advantage at the expense of the rights of others. Christians believe that everyone participates in sinfulness.

Nevertheless, the intention of this exploration of different religions and ideologies is to probe the primal vision and norms of each faith system. While we comment on some distortions of that vision, the commitment of this study is to investigate the source. For the Christian faith, we have explored the root experience of the church who is Jesus of Nazareth.

Reflection

1. In what ways does the Christian hope of the resurrection of the dead and the second coming of Christ affect the church's view of mission? Of history? Of the significance of the person?

2. What is there about the nature of the church that occasionally creates tension between the church and political or economic institutions?

3. Comment on this statement: The church is an authentic global community.

4. What does the New Testament mean when it refers to the church as bringing healing to the nations?

5. Describe the Christian view of singleness and family and the place of Christ in the family relationships.

6. Consider this statement: The church should affirm cultural relativism but not moral relativism.

10

Allah Without Associates

Islam

M Y DEAR BROTHER, please submit to Islam," an aged
Muslim sheikh pleaded with tears as he embraced me.
"Submission to God is peace."
The sheikh's invitation is in harmony with the mission of the
global Muslim *ummah* (community). As mentioned before, Islam,
like Christianity and Buddhism, is a missionary faith.

Submission to Allah
The cornerstone of Muslim witness is the conviction that there is
one God only who is the Creator and sustainer of the universe. God
has no associates. He alone is sovereign. That is the witness of one-
sixth of the earth's people who are Muslims.

Muslims exert astonishing influence in global community. They
have a mission—the expansion of peace into all regions of the earth.
That peace comes from submission to the will of the one and only
God who has no associates. That is Islam.

Origins
Muhammad, the prophet of Islam, was born in the year of the elephant (A.D. 570). That is the year the Christianized empire of Abys-
sinia (Ethiopia) attacked Mecca in Arabia using elephants. Traditional
lore describes the birds hurtling pebbles on the advancing Ethiopians.

Thus the birds helped save Mecca and the family of Muhammad from destruction.

This drama of sixth-century Arabian interaction with Christianized Ethiopia is an open window revealing the influences which helped to form Muhammad. Muslim beliefs and practices have not developed in a monotheistic vacuum. Sixth and seventh-century Arabians intermingled with Jewish and Christian communities and had some awareness of their biblical traditions. Christian and Jewish communities on the Arabian periphery and within Arabia itself exuded the aura of civilized peoplehood.

The surrounding Christianizing peoples had a book of God in their own languages. The Egyptian Christians had translations of the Bible in three dialects two centuries before Muhammad. The Ethiopians also had their own translation of the Bible. So did the Syrians. For six centuries the Greeks had both the Old and New Testaments. Yet the Arabs had no book of God in their own tongue.

No wonder so many of the Arab clans were considered barbarian by the civilized peoples of the region who possessed a book of God in their own languages. Muslims refer to the period in Arabia before Muhammad as *jahiliyah*, meaning the era of ignorance. The polytheistic Arabian clans with their perennial skirmishes were not a unified peoplehood. Sensitive Arabians trapped in jahiliyah yearned for inclusion in a peoplehood who were united and formed by a book of God.

Throughout the centuries Muslims have marveled that the merciful God did not ignore the plight of the barbarian Arabians living in jahiliyah. Miraculously God revealed Islam to these ignorant people. He revealed the Qur'an to Muhammad who could not read or write. Muhammad, the seal of all prophets, had been only an orphan of Mecca in Arabia; the Qur'an, the final book of God, is an Arabic Qur'an revealed in the language of those very people whom the world had once ignored.

In the inscrutable mercy and sovereignty of God, the orphan becomes prophet, the Arabic book of God becomes the final revelation, and the new peoplehood of God arising from among the jahiliyah of Arabia become the harbingers of the Islamic *ummah*, a light for all peoples. Those who were once considered barbarians have become the first participants in the new community of peace who submit to the will of God which is Islam.

The Hanif and Abraham

Muhammad's fellow Arabians were mostly jahiliya, who were enthusiastic polytheists. Yet most Arabians also believed in one Creator God who was above all other gods. A few worshiped only this Creator God; they stood within Abraham's tradition. These monotheists were known as hanifs.

The religious tradition of Muhammad's family was at least a vague expression of the monotheistic faith of Abraham. His father's name was Abdullah, which means the servant of Allah. As noted in the previous chapter, according to the Hebrew biblical texts, Abraham had spoken of God as El some twenty-five centuries earlier. Some students of Semitic languages perceive that the Ilah or Allah of Islam is the Arabian equivalent of the creator God, El, of biblical Hebrew.

Some of Muhammad's relatives were hanifs. They objected to the excesses of polytheism. They were inclined to worship Allah. The hanifs were intrigued by the oral traditions concerning Abraham and Ishmael. The etchings of the story, as passed down through the traditions or as recorded in the Qur'an, fascinate.

Abraham was prepared to offer his oldest son, Ishmael, as a sacrifice to God. The angel of God intervened and saved the lad by providing an animal for a sacrifice. Thereafter Abraham and Ishmael together cleansed the sacred *Ka'bsah* and rebuilt the house of God in Mecca.

The Ka'bah is the House of God in which there is a sacred black stone, in the heart of Mecca. Prior to Muhammad, many Arabian clans brought their idols to the Ka'bah. Muhammad transformed this center of Arabian polytheism into a sacred sign of God's transcendence and sovereignty.

Muslims believe that Abraham and Ishmael likewise had cleansed the Ka'bah from polytheistic worship many centuries earlier. They also prayed that God would provide an apostle for their descendants who would be one of them. Muhammad is that prophet and apostle! His spiritual and genealogical family descends from Abraham and Ishmael, who had established the true worship of God in the island of the Arabs many centuries previously. It is no wonder that Muslims believe Islam is the faith of Abraham.

The Prophet and the Qur'an

The prophet of Islam was a Meccan merchant who traveled widely. He was a reflective person and often went to a cave about three miles from center city Mecca for prayer and reflection. It was in this cave in the year A.D. 610, toward the end of the Arabian lunar month of Ramadan, that the revelation of the Qur'an began. Muhammad described the advent of revelation as a great light, which he later identified as the angel Gabriel.

The bright messenger commanded,

> Proclaim!
> In the name of thy Lord and Cherisher
> Who created—
> Created man out of a mere clot
> of congealed blood.[1]

The forty-year-old Muhammad did not know what to make of this event. Soon he received another revelation, then another and another. His wife, Khadija, was a steadfast encourager. She assured him that these revelations were from God and he should proclaim the message to his fellow country persons. Muhammad followed her counsel and for twelve years preached in polytheistic Mecca.

Muhammad condemned the idolatry. Even the sacred Ka'bah was a pantheon for hundreds of Arabian deities. He called for a more just society. God cared for the orphans and widows and so should society. Only a few heeded his preaching; most ignored him; some persecuted him and his followers. He was often discouraged. Yet in times of depression he was sustained by the memory that God had rescued him from abandonment in his orphan childhood.

The Qur'an proclaims,

> Did he not find thee
>   An orphan and give thee shelter?
> And he found thee wandering
>   And he gave thee guidance.
> And he found thee in need
>   And made thee independent.
> Therefore, treat not the orphan
>   with harshness
> Nor repulse the petitioner
>   Of the bounty
> Of thy Lord—
>   Rehearse and proclaim.[2]

A decade after he had begun preaching in Mecca, Muhammad ex-

perienced deep despair. Several hundred of his followers had immigrated to Ethiopia to escape the persecution in Mecca. His wife and
supporter, Khadija, died. His uncle Abu Talib also died. He had been
Muhammad's guardian as an orphan. The Meccans respected his
uncle, who had used his stature among his townsmen to protect
Muhammad from those who wished him harm. Now that Abu Talib
had died, Muhammad's own life seemed in danger.

The Miraj and Jerusalem

It was during his time of discouragement that Muhammad received
extraordinary affirmation in what Muslims describe as the *miraj*, or ascent into heaven. According to the traditions, in a mysterious instant
he was whisked to Jerusalem, a city of great significance to both Jews
and Christians. From the Dome of the Rock in central Jerusalem, he
was taken into the seventh heaven on the winged horse, Buraq.

Muslim tradition describes the miraj as an encouragement to Muhammad to continue his prophetic call. It sealed the significance of his
ministry in the context of the biblical prophets; he ascended to heav-
en from the very rock on which the temple of God had once stood.

The miraj also guaranteed collision between Jewish and Islamic
peoplehood. Popular belief identifies a niche in the Dome of the
Rock as the spot where the foot of the horse rested when it descend-
ed from heaven with Muhammad. The miraj sealed Jerusalem as the
third most sacred city for Muslims, with Mecca and Medina being
the other sacred centers. Today the Dome of the Rock Mosque
stands over that sacred rock from which the miraj commenced. This
rock is also the place where Solomon's splendid temple once stood.
The niche of Buraq the horse and the Wailing Wall, which is the
foundation of the ancient Jewish temple, are at the same rock.

This is also the rock where Jews and Muslims remember a special
event. The Jewish people believe that this rock is where Abraham
was prepared to offer Isaac as a sacrifice, until God intervened by
providing a ram as a substitute. Muslims believe this is the place
where Abraham was prepared to offer Ishmael as a sacrifice, until
God intervened with an alternative sacrifice. Therefore, for both
communities this rock is the place where their respective peoplehoods were redeemed through the intervention of God.

In modern times, this collision between Jewish and Muslim perspectives has become especially vexing. Jerusalem and the Rock are sacred
both to Islam and Judaism. The whole international community has
been implicated as nations have struggled to decide whether they

should place their embassies accredited to Israel in Jerusalem, or respect the profound Muslim objections to any hint of recognition of a right for Israel to extend political control over Jerusalem and the Rock. The miraj might have been an encouragement to Muhammad; however, it does complicate a resolution of the Jewish-Muslim struggle for control of Jerusalem.

The Problem of Suffering

The encouragement which Muhammad received from the miraj changed nothing in Mecca. This Arabian commercial and religious center created an agonizing theological crisis for Muhammad. The problem was this: surely the God of all creation is sovereign and all-powerful. Therefore, why does the faithful apostle of God suffer? The persecution and rejection which he experienced often pressed him into self doubt and discouragement.

Muhammad's personal struggle with the meaning of suffering in the overall plan of God is also a universal question. Recall the quest of Buddha seeking an answer to the riddle of suffering. His search led him to the conviction that divinity was irrelevant to the human condition. But Muhammad believed God had selected him as a prophet; the notion that God is indifferent to the human condition was not an acceptable option for him.

Yet why did the God whom he served not rescue him from his plight in Mecca? The question moved beyond only the problem of personal suffering. It probed the very nature of divine providence, power, and intention. How *does* God reveal and establish his will? How does a community of faithful believers come into existence? How is that community of faith sustained and protected in a world which forgets and ignores the will of God?

Muslims believe it was providential that at this time of distress emissaries from Medina began to meet with Muhammad requesting that he come to their city as prophet and statesman. Factional strife was devastating their city. They sought Muhammad's leadership.

The Flight from Suffering

Then the *hijrah* (flight) occurred. This immigration of Muhammad's Meccan followers 250 miles north to Medina commenced in July, 622 A.D. By mid-September Muhammad joined the immigrants; the journey took about 9 days. Muslims calculate their era as beginning on July 16, 622; that is the first day of the lunar year in which the hijrah commenced. The hijrah is the Muslim root experience.

The Islamic era does not begin with the birth of Muhammad, the beginning of revelation, or his death. It is the hijrah which marks the beginning of the Islamic era. This is an event of decisive theological significance. The hijrah provides Muslims with a solution to the riddle of unjust suffering; God rescues the prophet from his enemies.

This hijrah also conclusively demonstrates the authenticity of Muhammad's prophethood. How does the hijrah affirm his prophethood? It does so by providing him the opportunity to establish the Islamic ummah, the community of peace which submits to the will of God. At Medina, Muhammad received the instruments of political, economic, and military power. With these empowerments he was able to establish the community of peace.

As long as Muhammad was in Mecca, he was only a largely ignored prophet. He could not establish a coherent community of peace. In Medina all of that changed. He was now both prophet and statesman, both preacher and general, both teacher and judge. In Medina Muhammad established peace through political power. The flight from powerlessness in Mecca to political empowerment in Medina is a demonstration that he is indeed an apostle of God.

Recall that Siddhartha Gautama Buddha also had a flight. That flight is known as the "great renunciation." He left his wife and son as well as his political responsibilities to seek personal peace through escape from suffering. Buddha sought a personal peace through inner enlightenment. His personal peace involved a radical disengagement from family and political involvement. Buddha invited a peace which is found in retreat from political responsibilities; that is a radically different perspective on peace than that of the prophet-statesman Muhammad in Medina.

Jesus also invited people to the way of peace. Yet he chose to confront rather than disengage from the political systems. That confrontation led to his crucifixion and death.

It is noteworthy that the hijrah of Muhammad is the opposite of the way of the cross which Jesus chose. Six centuries before the hijrah, Jesus had also struggled with the question: How is the kingdom of God established? At the height of his popularity in Galilee in the northern regions of Palestine, his admirers invited him to become their king. We assume that a Zealot army would have been at his command. Yet Jesus rejected this offer.

Instead Jesus turned his face toward Jerusalem, telling his followers that he would be betrayed and crucified in that city. Rather than use the instruments of political and military power to establish peace, Jesus chose the suffering way of the cross.

Thus we see the Islamic understanding of the nature of the kingdom of God and the manner in which the community of peace is established and preserved. They are the opposite of the gospel understanding. The way of the hijrah and the way of the cross are fundamentally different foundations on which the respective communities, ummah and church, are established. The emigration of Muhammad from suffering in Mecca to political triumph in Medina and the journey of Jesus from triumph in Galilee to crucifixion and death in Jerusalem are movements in opposite directions.

Islam perceives that suffering for truth is an aberration. In Christian faith suffering for righteousness is redemptive. These different perceptions of the efficacy of suffering converge in the Messiah, Jesus. Both Muslims and Christians agree that the Messiah is Jesus. Islam, however, denies his crucifixion. The denial is consistent with Islamic theology: If God is sovereign, then he would not let the Messiah suffer the ignominy of the cross.

The difference between the cross and the hijrah has specific and practical implications for Christians and Muslims. For the faithful church, the way of obedience to Christ is a life of suffering, redemptive love, even toward one's enemies. For the faithful ummah, the way of faithfulness is to strive for Islam by all means necessary.

Striving for Islam is *jihad*. Although this word conjures up holy war for many, that is really the last acceptable defense which Muslims may use. Foremost, jihad means internal striving for faithfulness within oneself. Jihad also encourages defending the faith through the pen and mouth, an approach Christians and Jews also use!

The Creation of the Ummah

The hijrah enabled Muhammad to establish the ummah (community) of believers who submitted to the law of God. The manner in which this first Muslim community functioned and the characteristics of its lifestyle is considered normative for all orthodox Islamic communities around the world. Faithful Muslims everywhere desire that their communities conform to the ideal model developed in Medina under their prophet's leadership.

As the Islamic ummah under the leadership of Muhammad gained control of Medinan affairs, the relationships of the various alternate groups such as Jews or idol worshipers were defined and regulated. The laws and practices of the town were brought under the authority of the ummah. People suspected of treason against the ummah were punished. Several hundred Jews were slain in Medina for presumably attempting to usurp the power of the ummah. Yet all who cooperated with the ummah were well treated. The rights of alternative faith communities were protected.   *use of violence*

Even in this nascent stage, Muhammad insisted that there should be "no compulsion in religion."[3] Although violence to protect the faith might be necessary and right, there has developed consensus among some modern Islamic scholars that violence to extend the faith is not consistent with the true spirit of Islam.[4] They argue that violence is only justifiable as a last resort when protecting the ummah. We observe, however, that both in its early history and in modern times the ummah has not always followed that counsel.

The ummah has a mission among the nations. That mission includes extending the rule of the ummah to the ends of the earth. The regions which are ruled by the ummah are the *dar al-salaam* (region of peace). The regions not yet under the control of the dar al-salaam are the *dar al-harb* (region of war). Thus the whole global community participates in two communities—the region of peace or the region of war.

The fundamental mission of the ummah is to extend the region of peace throughout the global village. Muhammad himself demonstrated this Muslim missionary commitment. After the rule of the ummah was established in Medina, war developed between Mecca and the ummah. The battles extended to other groups in Arabia who also opposed the ummah. The ummah focused economic, political, and military pressure against groups who opposed it. All communities in Arabia were invited to accept the rule of the ummah. Within a decade of the hijrah, not only had Mecca come under the rule of the ummah, but all of Arabia was likewise under the rule of the Muslim nation. Arabia was incorporated within the dar al-salaam.

The ummah grew as people accepted the invitation to believe in the faith of Islam. The dar al-salaam enlarged through political and juridical expansion. All the people groups in Arabia did not become members of the ummah just because Muslims had extended their rule over them, thereby incorporating them into the dar al-salaam. Inclusion in the dar al-salaam meant that the ummah had control of political and military authority; inclusion did not mean that people had confessed faith in Allah. Muslims encouraged people within the dar al-salaam to submit to Islam. But ideally, at least, they avoided coercing conversions.

Pillars of Belief and Practice

The ummah extends *daawah* (invitation) to all peoples to submit to the beliefs and practices of Islam. The profile of the belief and practice of the Muslim congregation who gather for prayers in the community mosque is simple and easily communicated. Muslims agree that there are five pillars of belief:

- Believe in one God only.
- Believe in the prophets of God.
- Believe in the books of God.
- Believe in angels.
- Believe in the final judgment.
- Some Muslims add belief in predestination as a sixth pillar.

There are also five pillars of duty or practice:

- Make the confession of faith: there is no God but Allah and Muhammad is the apostle of Allah.
- Pray five times daily facing Mecca.
- Fast during the month of Ramadan.
- Give alms to the poor.
- Take the pilgrimage to Mecca if possible.
- (Some Muslims add jihad as a sixth pillar of duty. Jihad requires a Muslim to defend Islam however necessary.)

Elaboration on these pillars of faith and practice is not necessary, except to recognize that these commitments are the primary glue which binds the world Muslim community together. All development of Islamic theology and practice subsequent to Muhammad has been only an explanation and a development of these foundational pillars.

How do these pillars of belief and duty guide the Muslim contribution to the global community? That question sets the tone for the exploration of Islam in the remainder of this chapter. Several pillars of belief or duty are especially pertinent to the themes of this exploration, and a brief elaboration follows. We shall highlight the fast, the pilgrimage, the prayers, the prophets, and the books.

Two of the annual Muslim festivals relate directly to pillars of duty: the fast and the pilgrimage. These festival pillars are especially pertinent to Islam as a global community.

The fast during the month of Ramadan is a remembrance of God's gift of revelation. The Qur'an invites,

Has not the time arrived
For the Believers that
Their hearts in all humility
Should engage in the remembrance
Of God and of the Truth
Which has been revealed.[5]

The month-long daytime fast from early dawn to sunset unites the worldwide Muslim community in remembrance of the gift of revelation. Believers also perceive of the fast as a form of identification with the poor. The gift of revelation is a mercy to humankind; the Muslim believer should also show mercy to the hungry and the poor.

Every night the fast is broken with feasting. Then there is the grand conclusion of the fast with three days of festivity, when the first sliver of the crescent new moon appears at the end of the month of Ramadan. The feasting reminds Muslims that the night of revelation is more excellent than ten thousand other nights.

The Qur'an exclaims,

We have indeed revealed this (Message)
In the Night of Power;
And what will explain
To thee what the Night
Of Power is?
The Night of Power
Is better than
A thousand months.[6]

Another significant festival pillar is **the annual *hajj (pilgrimage)*** to Mecca during the month of Dhu-al-Hijjah. This festival also unites the entire ummah. The event is a bonding experience for the pilgrims as well as for every Muslim homestead and hamlet. Muslim communities everywhere commemorate the pilgrimage with the sacrifice of an animal. The sacrifice is a reminder of the Islamic tradition that Ishmael was saved from death when an animal was miraculously provided as a substitutionary sacrifice.[7] The identification of Islam with Abraham and Ishmael are central themes in the pilgrimage; recall that Muslims believe Abraham and Ishmael worshiped together at the Ka'bah.

The identification of the ummah with the origins of human history is also a theme within the hajj. Muslims believe that the Ka'bah is the place from whence human community on earth commenced, and Adam was the first Muslim. The Ka'bah was Adam's first home. For Muslims the pilgrimage to the Ka'bah is a visual demonstration of and a commitment to the primal faith of humankind which is the true religion of Islam.

All pilgrims dress alike in white sheets—the rich and poor, those of high status and beggars stand equal before God. Yet when the pilgrims return home they have a new name: *Hajji* for the men and *Hajjia* for the women. The hajjis and hajjias recount the stories of their pilgrimage among their kin and friends. As the boys and girls listen, they determine that someday they too will be pilgrims to Mecca, and will pray at the Ka'bah.

Faithful Muslims everywhere participate in **the prayers** five times a day facing the Ka'bah. The right worship of God requires bowing with their faces to the ground. Often a faithful Muslim will have a carbuncle on her forehead, which comes through kneeling so often with her face on the ground. The bowing in prayer is a sign of her commitment to submit to the guidance of God, a guidance which is the same as that revealed to Adam, Abraham, and Muhammad, and all the other prophets of God.

Bowing in prayer facing the Ka'bah is a sign that the will of God does not change. Ritual prayer or *salah* unites the believer with all those faithful worshipers throughout the ages who have submitted to the unchanging will of God. The daily prayer is a powerful ritual providing unity, not only with the faithful of the past, but with all contemporary Muslims living in communities around the earth.

Salah can take place anywhere, yet many prefer the mosque, where the believers stand in rows and bow in unison, all together, the young and old, the rich and poor, the powerful and the powerless, bowing before God, all facing the niche in the mosque which indicates the direction of the Ka'bah and Mecca. (Men and women are always separated in prayer and worship.) The prayer is always in Arabic, as is the recitation and reading of scripture. The language of worship itself bonds the believers in the local meeting with all those millions of other believers in distant places.

The prayer which Muslims recite during salah is the *Fatiha*, or opening. This is the first chapter in the Qur'an; it is the perfect prayer that summarizes the essence of all prayer.

An English interpretation of the prayer follows:

> In the name of God,
> Most Gracious,

Most Merciful
Praise be to God,
The Cherisher and Sustainer
   of the worlds;
Most Gracious, Most Merciful;
   Master of the Day of Judgment.
Thee do we worship,
   And Thine aid we seek.
Show us the straight way,
The Way of those on whom
   Thou has bestowed Thy Grace,
Those whose (portion)
   Is not wrath,
And who go not astray.[8]

God's guidance is a precious gift. He reveals his guidance through **the prophets**. There have been many prophets throughout history; the Qur'an identifies twenty biblical personalities as prophets. The Qur'an names twenty-five prophets; the traditions state that there have been as many as 124,000 prophets throughout the ages.

However, the very first prophet was Adam. He was the first to receive guidance from God. Sadly the descendants of the first human parents soon began to forget God's good guidance. The role of the prophets, then, is not to bring a new word of revelation, but rather to retrieve again and again the primal guidance so quickly forgotten by human frailty and negligence.

In several specific instances, God has revealed his guidance through written scripture. **The books** of God are revealed through the mediation of angels. Prophets who receive scripture are known as *rasuls* or apostles. There have been only five rasuls—Abraham, Moses, David, Jesus the Messiah, and Muhammad. The book which the prophet Abraham received is lost. However, other books of revelation remain available, including the *Taurat* (Torah) of the prophet Moses, the *Zabur* (Psalms) of the prophet David, the *Injil* (Gospel) of the prophet Jesus the Messiah, and the Qur'an (Recitation) of the prophet Muhammad.

Muslims believe the Qur'an is the final revelation of God and summarizes all former revelations. It is the criterion of all truth, for it is in perfect harmony with all the former revelations of God.

Although all Muslims must believe in books of revelation which they recognize as Torah, Psalms, and Gospel, these books of scripture are not contained in the Qur'an as scriptural entities. The Qur'an alludes occasionally to accounts from these other scriptures and declares that God will never permit his revelation to be corrupted. Surprisingly the Qur'an commands Muslims to go to those who had the previous scriptures to receive clarification on the meaning of obscure Qur'anic passages.

We read, "If thou wert in doubt as to what we have revealed unto thee, then ask those who have been reading the Book from before thee."[9] Nevertheless, most Muslims never read any portions of the Bible; only the scholars are aware that the Bible contains the Taurat, Zabur, and Injil which the Qur'an refers to as revealed books. However, Muslims often debate the authenticity of these biblical scriptures.

Muslims, Christians, and Jews

The Jewish community, the church, and the Muslim ummah are confident that they are the faith heirs of Abraham. All three communities believe that there is only one God, one humanity, one morality. Yet each of these communities has a different truth center.

Islam is grounded in the belief that the Qur'an is the criterion for all truth. It sifts believers from those who do not believe. Only unbelievers reject the Qur'an when they hear it read.

Christian faith is founded on the conviction that Jesus the Messiah is the criterion of truth. Christians confess that Jesus is Lord and therefore interpret the biblical Scriptures from that perspective. They also evaluate the Qur'an in the light of Jesus.

The soul of Judaism is the belief that the Torah is the center point of truth.

Dialogue between Jews, Christians, and Muslims is helpful in providing better understandings of these different perspectives. Yet the experience of theologians who participate in dialogue demonstrate that these differences are fundamental.

For several decades I have regularly participated in dialogue between Christians and Muslims, often in a mosque or church setting. In dialogue we discover that there are convergencies. For example, both agree that Jesus is the Messiah. Yet within these convergencies, there are painful divergencies. For example, Muslims deny the crucifixion of Jesus; yet Christ crucified is the core of the Christian gospel. Such divergencies are not academic; they are the core of faith and the foundations of the respective faith communities.

Foundational theological commitments do affect the intercommunity relations between Muslims and Christians, sometimes with tragic consequences. On the other hand, in multitudes of communities Muslims, Christians, and Jews live together in harmony. Their faith divergencies do not prevent fairly relaxed relationships. However, it is sad that often an understanding develops which bases inter-community peace on avoidance of any conversations about faith.

When on a visit to the Middle East, I asked a Jordanian Christian business person to describe the quality of Christian-Muslim relations in his country.

"Positively excellent!" he responded expansively. "We talk about all matters of mutual concern in a harmonious spirit. Yet when any matter of faith enters the conversation, we simply turn our backs on each other and walk away."

There is an awareness among the participants in Muslim-Christian-Jewish dialogue that ultimately the Qur'an, Jesus, or the Torah lead us in quite different directions. These three faith streams whose spiritual legacy is Abraham comprise half the world's population. They meet and intermingle throughout the global community. This is the core issue that unites and divides these faith communities: What does it mean to be a people in covenant with God and in mission in our world?

Islam and Culture

The vision of Islam is clear—the people who comprise the ummah must submit to the will of God as revealed in the Qur'an. That submission is peace. Islam, like Judaism, has inspired enormous energy in clarifying and defining the will of God. The Qur'an is at the very center of the community. It is an Arabic Qur'an, revealed over a period of a couple decades to Muhammad the prophet of Islam.

Muslims believe that the Qur'an is the perfect copy of the eternal word of God; it is the earthly replica of the heavenly Mother of Books. The Muslim view of revelation is exact and verbatim. The angel Gabriel taught Muhammad the exact words in the heavenly book, word by word, and line by line. As he recited these scriptures to his followers, they in turn memorized them, or wrote them on surfaces such as "scraps of parchment and leather, tablets of stone, ribs of palm branches, camels' shoulder-blades and ribs, pieces of boards and the breasts of men."[10]

Shortly after Muhammad's death in 632, his companions began compiling the Qur'an. During the reign of Othman, who was the third caliph, they completed the compilation in a form similar to the Qur'an today. Muslims believe the Arabic Qur'an as we have it today is the exact replica of the eternal heavenly tablet.

The Muslim view of revelation is challenged by modern global culture which has been formed by the European Enlightenment (chapter 11). The Enlightenment worldview insists that all claims to truth must be based on evidence and that the scriptures of any religion should be studied in the light of the historical and cultural context in which those scriptures developed. These approaches to the study of scripture are known as the historical-critical method.

For many years biblical scholars have been enriching the Christian understanding of their Scriptures through this approach to biblical study. This is not to suggest, however, that the historical-critical method has never been a problem to Christians. For example, many Christians are disturbed when the historical-critical method assumes that extraordinary events are impossible.

However, the objection of Muslims to the historical-critical approach to the Qur'an is consistent and deep. The issue is this: How can the Qur'an be studied from a historical-critical perspective if it has come directly from God? It is a revelation which transcends and supersedes history and human culture.

An illustration of the problem alluded to above—the Qur'an denies that Jesus was crucified. Yet there is much biblical and some extra-biblical evidence that he was crucified. However, if the Qur'an is the direct dictated word for word revelation from God, there is no way to debate the issue of the crucifixion of Jesus. Any contrary historical evidence is just an illusion.

Inviting Muslims to view the Qur'an from a historical-critical perspective is encouraging Islam to undergo a major paradigm shift. The consistent resistance of Muslim scholars globally to any such considerations suggests that the ummah suspects that the Islamic faith could not survive such a paradigm shift. Islam is grounded in the conviction that the Qur'an came from God. Computer analysis of the wonder of the rhythm of its divine poetry is appropriate, but assessing the Qur'an from a historical or cultural perspective is irreverent and irrelevant. It cannot be done.

The Qur'an is in Arabic. Translated, it ceases to be the exact recitation of the word of God as revealed by the angel Gabriel. Although in recent years there have been some translations of the Qur'an, none of these is Qur'an. They are only interpretations of the Qur'an, for the original recitation was in Arabic. It is for this reason that learning sufficient Arabic to recite portions of the Qur'an will always accompany the Islamization of a people.

It is not surprising that Arabian cultural influences seem to accompany Islam. That notion is reinforced by the location of the Ka'bah in Arabia, the heartland of the Arabian culture. Both the annual pilgrimages and the direction of the daily prayers turn toward the Arabian center. For a person looking at Islam from outside the faith system, these nudges toward an Arabian cultural orientation may either encourage or discourage interest in Islam. It depends on what a person is seeking.

However, in recent years there has been sharp resistance to Islamization in some areas in Africa and Asia. Resistance to Islam is often triggered when it appears to a group that Islamization will tug their culture toward Arabization. To my knowledge all African Muslim theologians and scholars are calling for the de-Africanization of Islam so that the African expressions of the ummah may become more truly Islamic. In contrast, African Christian theologians call for the Africanization of Christianity. In an age when much of the global village is becoming self-consciously ethnic, a universal faith which seems to undermine ethnic culture and identity can create resistance.

The societies of southern Sudan have resisted Islamization from northern Muslims with catastrophic consequences. Southern resistance has invited endemic war and occasional genocide. During the first half of the 1990s, southern Sudan had become an example of the way not to extend dar al-salaam over a people. The southern peoples as a whole just do not want Muslim hegemony over their cultures and social institutions. Consequently hundreds of thousands have died.

The issues of faith versus culture run very deep in Islam. The word *Islam* means "submission." The word *Muslim* means "a person who has submitted to Allah." Muslims believe that Islam is the way of submission to the will of God; in that submission a person finds peace. The revealed will of God specifically informs every area of human culture. Muslim scholars therefore speak of Islamic culture.

In reality there are many Muslim cultures. There is considerable diversity within the worldwide Islamic ummah. The Muslim Somalis of northeastern Africa describe this phenomenon with a proverb: "Custom is more powerful than religion." However, although there is considerable cultural diversity in the worldwide Muslim ummah, the theologians lament that diversity. The ideal goal of Islam is the formation of one universal Muslim culture.

The Way of the Prophet

The theologians believe that one universal Muslim culture is a reasonable expectation when all Muslims truly conform with the teachings of the Qur'an. That is the goal of all faithful Muslims. Yet they need assistance in defining how these teachings apply in practical life.

The *Shari'ah* (law or path) provides that guidance. Recall that Judaism developed the Talmud to define the meaning of the Torah for everyday living. The sources and composition of the Talmud and the Shari'ah are rather different. Yet both the Jewish and Muslim community desired to obey God's will fully. The quest for obedience to God inspired the development of the Talmud within Judaism and the Shari'ah within the Muslim ummah.

Shari'ah is really an authentic expression of the way of the prophet Muhammad. After all, he knew better than any of his contemporaries the true meaning and application of the Qur'an. It is thus not surprising that very early on Muslims developed a concern for patterning their lives on the ideal model of the prophet Muhammad, who they believe was the seal of all prophets. To follow Muhammad's example, Muslims learn as much as possible about the *sunna* (the *example* of the prophet Muhammad). The oral and written hadith (the tradition concerning the prophet) help them in their quest.

During the first two centuries following the prophet Muhammad's death, Muslim scholars began developing the comprehensive system of guidance known as Shari'ah. The Qur'an is at the center of the whole system, but the traditions of the prophet of Islam which are known as the hadiths are also a significant source of Shari'ah authority. The hadiths are based on the anecdotes concerning the way in which Muhammad conducted himself. They describe the precious sunna of the prophet.

Traditions and legends concerning Muhammad multiplied after his death. It was a huge task for the Muslim scholars of the third Islamic century to search out the authentic reports of Muhammad's sunna. They needed to ferret out traditions to determine which ones were authentic transmissions of the sunna. In the third century of the Muslim era, two authoritative works were compiled, one by Muslim and the other by al-Bukhari. The latter has gained particular prominence within the worldwide Muslim community.

The collection by al-Bukhari consist of 7,300 traditions, each attested for authenticity through the reliability of the *isnad* (chain) of witnesses through which it had been handed down. The isnad of evidence for each tradition is recorded. For example: "It was told us by Abdullah ibn Yusuf who said, it was told us by al-Laith, who had it from Yazid, who had it from Abdu'l-Khair who had it from Uqba ibn Amir—he said. . . . "[11]

Together all these hadiths form a composite portrait of the sunna of Muhammad; they define the personality traits and practices which faithful Muslims desire to emulate. No other major religion has developed such a focused interest in the personality of its founder. Although Buddhism, Confucianism, and Christianity each are named after their respective founders, none of these religions has developed such a fascination with the founder's personality as is found in Islam.

However, Muslims resent being called Muhammadans, for they rightfully point out that they do not divinize Muhammad. Yet through the universal Muslim desire to emulate the sunna of Muhammad, the personality of the seal of the prophets influences the thought and practice of faithful Muslims quite significantly. Thus, with some qualifications to be sure, one can speak nevertheless of a Muslim personality.

Consensus and Change

As the hadiths were being formalized, the Shari'ah system was also developing. During the second and third centuries of the Muslim era, scholars working from within different regions or perspectives of the ummah wrote four principal systems of Shari'ah: Hanafi, Maliki, Shafi'i, and Hanbali. Each of these systems of law was based on three sources of authority—Qur'an, sunna, and *ijma'* (consensus). Differences between the Shari'ah systems were to some extent determined by the different weight the scholars gave to these three sources of authority.

Ijma' needs further comment. For the first two or three centuries of the Muslim era, the process of ijma' was dynamic and developmental. However, as the consensus of the *ulama* (experts) was recorded into the various systems of Shari'ah law, the developmental process ceased. Thereafter any attempts to modify or reinterpret Shari'ah came under censure as innovation. Muslim conviction is that the function of the ulama was only clarification of the will of God. Once that process of clarification was completed and the decisions recorded, the duty of all Muslims was now self-evident—obey the Shari'ah. Don't change the Shari'ah! That would be *bidah!*

Islam has always prohibited bidah, or innovation. This is consistent with the Islamic worldview which believes that Islam is not a new religion, but rather a retrieval and elaboration of the original faith of Adam. Thus even Muhammad, the seal of the prophets, has brought nothing new. There can be no innovation in religion; bidah is prohibited.

The Islamic view of bidah in a world of change foments debate and tension within the worldwide ummah. Often the politicians and modernists join hands calling for reinterpretation and change, while the theologians insist that change cannot be Islamic. In recent years the tensions between modernity and the theologians has in some circumstances become explosive. The Muslim scholar Falzur Rahman has identified the crisis in the soul of the Muslim ummah in modern times in this way: How does a theology of no change cope in a world of change?[12]

Nevertheless, Muslim theologians believe that the most perfect expression of Islam is that of the prophet and his companions. The Shari'ah helps define that ideal community. A hadith says it well: "The best generation is mine (i.e., of my Companions), the next best the following one and the next one the succeeding one. . . ."[13]

Thus it is that the faithful Muslim community seeks to replicate the faith and practice of Muhammad and his companions in the modern context. That is a difficult calling!

The Shi'ah

The difficulties of knowing the way of faithfulness are especially evident in the contrasting approaches to authority developed by the Shi'ah and Sunni Muslim communities. These differences within the primal Muslim community were exacerbated when civil war broke out as Ali ibn-abi-Talib, the son-in-law of Muhammad, became the fourth caliph. He was assassinated.

The worldwide Muslim community still lives in the shadow of that war and assassination, for ever since this conflict Muslims have divided into the Shi'ite and Sunni communities. Today the Shi'ite Muslims comprise about a tenth of the worldwide Muslim community.

Authority is the issue dividing Shi'ah and Sunni Muslims. Sunni approaches to authority have been described. The Shi'ah believe that spiritual authority is incarnated in the imam, the genealogical descendant of Ali, who was married to the prophet's daughter. Over the centuries various Shi'ah groups have developed, usually over disputes as to which son of the imam should become the next imam.

The dominant Shi'ite community in Iran is the Ithna Ashariyah, or Twelvers. They believe that the line of spiritual authority vanished after the twelfth imam. The true imam is now hidden, and only indications of this spiritual authority are evident through the ministry of the ayatollahs. Someday, it is believed, the hidden imam will reappear in an imam who may establish the dar al-salaam throughout the earth.

There had been hope by some Iranian Shi'ah Muslims that Ayatollah Khomeini might have been the incarnation of the imam. His failure to extend his version of the dar al-salaam significantly beyond Iran suggests that the Ithna Ashariyah hope for the reincarnation of the imam has not yet been fulfilled. However, his disciples have not despaired; they seek to export Ayatollah Khomeini's version of the dar al-salaam everywhere.

The martyrdom of Ali, and later his son al-Husayn at Karbala, contributes a suffering theme in Shi'ah Islam. This martyr legacy within Shi'ah Islam sometimes opens doors for Shi'ah Muslims and Christians to meet with some degree of understanding on the suffering and crucifixion of Jesus. Every year on the tenth of Muharram, Shi'ah Muslims throughout the world participate in passion plays commemorating al-Husayn's martyrdom. Worshipers sometimes flay themselves in an attempt to identify with his suffering. These themes of suffering and even martyrdom for righteousness sake are cultivated by Shi'ah Islam.

The Mystics and Their Way

Sufism is the mystical stream especially prevalent within the Sunni ummah. Sunni Islam emphasizes submission to the will of God, although God himself is the hidden one, the unknown and unknowable one. In its quest to experience God, sufism strains at the leash of orthodox constraints. As in Shi'ah Islam, sufism also has its martyr history. The martyrdom of al-Hallaj in the third century of the Muslim era has inspired many sufi devotees. Al-Hallaj believed that a person could experience unity with God.

The sufi quest for unity with God moved through the ummah like a slow burning grass fire. Today a high percentage of the Sunni Muslims are involved in some form of sufism. These sufis form communities who rally around the spiritual efficacy of a saint, either living or dead. Through the saint disciples learn the inner mystery of the *tariqah*-orders, which is the way of knowing God.

In some tariqah-orders, the way to become absorbed into divinity includes the use of euphoria enhancing techniques such as drugs and the constant repetition of the name of God.[14] This is known as *dhikr*. For a number of years, our family lived across the street from a mosque in which a sufi congregation gathered every Thursday night. The dhikr chant continued late into the evening. The rhythm of the dhikr was consoling. Yet the use of drugs which accommodated these mystical events became addictive for many of the young men. These practices debilitated the well-being of our neighborhood.

Often the sufi saints are local persons. They therefore provide powerful cohesion and identity to the local Muslim community. For example, at Kudus in central Java, Muslim companions awed me with astonishing descriptions of miracles wrought by their saint of Java. They described how the walls of the mosque at the shrine were built by angels overnight from a pile of bricks imported from Egypt! Even after his death, people believe they are blessed and empowered through prayers offered at his tomb.

Many poor Javanese Muslims will never have the opportunity to visit Mecca. They cannot even read or hear God's word for their Arabic is too poor. Yet they can touch the mystery of God through pilgrimages to the tomb of their own Javanese saint, which adjoins the mosque. And they come, hundreds of thousands annually on pilgrimages to Kudus. Although they may never visit Mecca, the blessing of God is present among them through their own saint.

In regions of the earth where violence is endemic, the sufi communities often function as islands of peace. Of course, sufi communities can also become involved in violence. Nevertheless, as alternative communities to the mainstream of orthodox Islam, these communities sometimes function as signs of the dar al-salaam.

These communities within the Muslim ummah have often provided the missionary impetus for Islam. They function as training centers equipping disciples to strive faithfully in the way of Islam. Usually the sufi missionary disciples in any particular tariqah are bonded together in a covenant. Each tariqah-order has its own covenant symbols and rituals.

The relationship between orthodox Islam and sufism is not always cozy. Nevertheless, sufism can be a bridge between Muslims and other communities. Some of the sufi practices and beliefs concerning absorption into divinity might have commonality with Hinduism and Buddhism. In Ethiopia for many centuries, Orthodox Christians, animists, and Muslims have joined in pilgrimages to the graves of some of the great Muslim saints, seeking the blessing of God together. This is one reason why the mainstream ummah worry about sufism. It opens the door for syncretism with other religions.

A Witness to the Nations

Muslims refer to Islam as the religion of the mean, *din al-wasat*. It is not given to the excessive asceticism of Christian monasticism, nor the impracticality of Christian ethics, nor the legalism of Judaism, nor the hedonism of paganism. The Islamic community was birthed and nurtured in Arabia, the nation which exists amid the nations. In the same way the ummah is the middle community of faith and peace which stands between the nations, offering practical and achievable moral and religious guidance.

> Thus have we made of you
> An *ummat* (community) justly balanced,
> That ye might be witnesses
> over the nations.[15]

Muslim teachers affirm that the ummah supersedes Israel as the community called by God to be a light to the nations. The Qur'an recognizes that at one time God preferred Israel "to all others." [16] Yet now through the emergence of the Muslim ummah God is fulfilling his call and promise to Abraham to be an imam (spiritual leader) to the nations. It is through the Muslims, who are the spiritual progeny of Abraham's firstborn son Ishmael, that God's promise to Abraham is fulfilled. Abdullah Yusuf Ali comments, "The arguments about the favor to Israel is (*sic*) thus beautifully rounded off, and we now proceed to the argument in favor of the Arabs as succeeding to the spiritual inheritance of Abraham."[17]

The Muslim witness is grounded in the conviction that Islam is the middle faith; it is also the primal and final faith. It is the primal faith, for Islam was the faith of Adam, the father of all humanity. Every people group have had a prophet or prophets calling people to the primal and universal religion of Adam. For this reason, every child is born a Muslim. Only the parents or society educate a child away from Islam. The natural inclination of humankind is the faith of Islam. We read that Islam is the "standard religion" which is according "to the pattern on which he has made mankind."[18]

Adam, Abraham, and Muhammad each enjoyed a similar mission, the establishment of the true worship of God at the Ka'bah. The religion of the primal (Adam), middle (Abraham), and final (Muhammad) is the same. Thus Islam is the primal, middle, and final faith of humankind. There is no change. There cannot be innovation in religion. Muhammad brought nothing new. His prophetic mission was to proclaim the will of God, which is identical with the guidance revealed to Adam and Abraham and all other prophets of God. Muslims in prayer facing the Ka'bah in Mecca are a sign that Islam is the primal, middle, and final religion.

The Region of Peace and the Region of War

We have discovered that the Muslim ummah is engaged in a mission of peace in the global human community. We now explore more intentionally the implications of that mission, with particular attention to the universal issues of survival as a wholesome, viable, global human community. In what ways does Islam address modern global issues? What is the nature of the peace which Islam offers a world in which there is much despair?

The Islamic mission commitment moves on several levels. There is the shahada which is the word of confession and witness: *La Ilaha Illa'llah Muhammadan Rasulu'llah* (There is but one God, Muhammad is the apostle of God). Today Muslims proclaim the shahada faithfully from the minarets of their mosques in hundreds of thousands of communities around the world. *Daawah* is the invitation to faith which the shahada implies. The confession and witness is also an invitation for all who hear to submit to the will of God.

The mission of Islam also includes *dawlah*—the political or governing order of a society. The ummah is incomplete until it controls the mechanisms of political power. Thus, although Muslims may exist as a community of faith in societies or political orders not controlled by Islamic power, these Muslim faith communities are only incomplete islands of Islamic practice until they become full participants in the Islamic dar al-salaam. That requires political control of the society.

In Islam the faith community and the political system should be governed by the same authority. Muhammad is the model for this merger of the two; in Medina he was both prophet and statesman.[19] And the function of the political order is to protect the well-being of the ummah; the state has no other essential function. The Medina experience has become normative for Muslim political expectations.

The Islamist Bernard Lewis says,

> The body politic and the sovereign power within it are ordained by God himself to promote his faith and to maintain and extend his law.[20]

The principal function of government is to enable the individual

Muslim to lead a good Muslim life. This is, in the last analysis, the purpose of the state, for which alone it is established by God, and for which alone statesmen are given authority over others. The worth of the state, and the good and evil deeds of statesmen are measured by the extent to which this purpose is accomplished.[21]

The Islamic conviction that state and religion should be one is not unlike much of the Christian experience during and after the fourth century, when Christian communities within Europe and the Middle East had become Constantinianized. However, the union of church and state is a distortion of the New Testament model, and within Islam the separation of church and state is a distortion of the Medina model. The primal norms of the church and ummah are radically different in their understanding of the relationship between the community of faith and the state system.

The missionary goal of Islam is that the whole earth may some day be blessed by being brought under the benevolent authority of the Islamic dar al-salaam. However, that goal is still far distant. Consequently, until that happens the world is divided into two regions, the region of peace and the region of war. The region of war is known as the *dar al-harb*. This is the region which has not yet come under the rule of Islam.

Kenneth Cragg comments,

> Community may be an inadequate word, . . . but there is hardly a better word available to express the consciousness of "otherness" deep in the Muslim mind and soul, whatever precise political or cultural form is chosen to implement it. *Dar Al-Islam* and *Dar Al-Harb* is a fundamental distinction running through all humanity: the household of submission to God and the household of non-Islam still to be brought into such submission.[22]

The Ummah and Pluralism

A region can become dar al-salaam even though there are few Muslims present. The key is rule and authority. The region of peace is ruled by the ummah, even though Muslims may be a minority community in that society as a whole.

The goal of Islam in mission is to extend daawah (the invitation to believe) and also dawlah (Islamic rule) to all people and societies. The expansion of the dar al-salaam throughout Arabia during the final decade of Muhammad's leadership of the ummah is the model for the expansion of Islam throughout the earth. During that first decade of growth throughout Arabia, Muslims extended the region of Islamic peace through using both daawah and dawlah. Expanding political control and the invitation to believe went together. That is the way Muslim mission proceeds most authentically.

Communities which are not Muslim are protected by the ummah in the dar al-salaam. In a significant number of Middle Eastern societies, Christians, Jews, and Zoroastrians have had over 1,300 years of experience living within the dar al-salaam. The effect has been the development of the millet system. The millet is an identifiable community, although usually not as tightly circumscribed as the Jewish ghettoes had once been in Europe. Each non-Islamic community functions in the confines of its own millet. Each millet is permitted to practice its own faith, but with constraints.

Here are examples of the constraints and privileges of the millets. Religious conversions may take people only in the direction of Islam. A Muslim man may marry a Christian woman, but no Christian man may marry a Muslim. In the traditional millet system, Christians or Jews were not admitted into the military. However, they paid extra taxes for the privileges of military protection. The millets need to seek permission from the Muslim authorities to build a place of worship; in many circumstances patterns have developed which make it difficult to acquire such permissions. The millet system defines the non-Islamic community.

Persons in such protected communities often feel they are not as equal as they would be in a secular state which adheres to the United Nations Declaration of Human Rights. In recent years the Islamic Declaration of Human Rights has highlighted tension points between the United Nations commitments to human rights and the commitments of the Muslim World League. The Islamic declaration emphasizes the rights and integrity of communities. The United Nations highlights the rights of the person.

A critical issue is the right to persuade and be persuaded, to be converted from one faith community to another. Ideally Islam affirms the right of the community to worship freely. It is much more difficult for Muslims to accept the right of the person freely to choose her faith community, unless that choice is toward Islam.

The Ummah and the State

These issues of religious commitment and political power confound the Middle East region (and all other regions of the world as

well) wherever religion and political power converge. In Islam a
genuinely secular state is inconceivable, although the politicians in
some settings have sometimes boldly attempted to develop secular
political institutions, as in the Baath political party in Syria and Iraq.
Nevertheless, religious affiliation and political power are mingled in
the whole Middle East region.

Sometimes these religious political systems work fairly adequately. Tragically there also have been horrendous convulsions—endemic civil war in Lebanon between various Muslim factions and between Muslims and Christians, the Turkish pogrom against Arme-
nian Christians in the late nineteenth and early twentieth centuries,
hostility and violence between Israel and the Arab Christian and
Muslim communities in the region. In the nation of Israel, religious
considerations bring strain into relationships among her own Jewish, Christian, and Muslim citizens.

In another region of the world during the mid-twentieth century,
the Islamic concept of ummah and dar al-salaam confounded Mahatma Gandhi as he strove to bring a united India into independence from England. Chapter four noted that Muslims, Hindus, and
Christians strove together in the nonviolent struggle for independence. However, as freedom from imperial rule came into view, the
Islamic community under the leadership of Muhammad Ali Jinnah
determined to form a separate Muslim state. Gandhi worshiped the
Hindu god Rama. Hindu polytheism horrified Muslims. They could
not participate in a state in which the key leaders practiced idolatry.

Although Muslims appreciated and respected Gandhi's central
role in the independence struggle, their leaders warned against the
dangers of participation in either a secular or a Hindu state. Gandhi's
fasts and appeals for unity availed nothing. Muslims remembered
earlier eras when the ummah had dominated the sub-continent.
They yearned for a return to the dar al-salaam of those times.

Consequently the Indian subcontinent was split in 1947 between
the secular state of India and the Muslim state of Pakistan. Hundreds
of thousands died in the conflagration which ensued. For many
weeks fires of burning hamlets lit the night skies of the Punjab as
Sikhs, Muslims, and Hindus, who had lived together in considerable
amity for many centuries, turned on one another in horrendous fury.
The mayhem was unbelievable; entire train loads of fleeing refugees
were slaughtered. More than ten million people were displaced.

Of course, not all Hindus in Pakistan left, nor did all Muslims in
India leave. Nevertheless, the recreation of the dar al-salaam in the

Indian subcontinent involved a horrible paroxysm of violence and enormous dislocation of peoples. Yet many Muslims are convinced that the cost was justified, for the Muslim ummah functions with most completeness when it exists in the dar al-salaam.

The Ummah and the Secular

The Islamic imperative to combine political and religious power is grounded in Islamic theology. The Islamic *shahada* confesses that God is one—that is *tauhid*. Any divergence from tauhid is *shirk*—that is, being loyal to authorities other than God. Shirk is blasphemy, for God has no associates. Shirk is the ultimate sin. And just as there is one God, so there is also one guidance. That guidance is Islam.

God who is one has revealed one universal guidance for humanity. All areas of existence must submit to his will; no human experience or institution is exempt. It is therefore impossible for the faithful community ever to divide the secular and religious or the political and spiritual. While it is true that some modern Muslim states have attempted to secularize, these attempts are laced with tensions. In all these societies the dialogue between the theologians and the politicians is intense. Sometimes the tension becomes violent.

The theologians know that Muhammad's rule in Medina must be the primal norm for the Islamic state. However, a secular pluralistic state cannot fit that norm. Consequently during the twentieth century the Middle East political reformers who sought to separate the ummah and the political order did not look to Islam for their inspiration. They reached into the pre-Islamic heritage of their societies in Iran, Iraq, Egypt, Syria, Turkey. Yet those experiments have been fraught with difficulties; Iran has experienced a colossal backlash.[23]

Muslims also experience dismay living in secularized Western cultures where nothing appears sacred. These concerns became globally significant following the 1989 publication of Salman Rushdie's *The Satanic Verses*.[24] The global Muslim ummah was in profound dismay, for this fiction seemed to be a veiled yet irreverent portrayal of Muhammad. Some Muslim *ulama* called for Rushdie's death. He went into hiding to escape assassination. Violent riots exploded in many Muslim communities far from Britain where the author resided.

While Muslims perceived Rushdie to be guilty of blasphemy, British authorities proclaimed the inalienable right of free speech. Many faithful Muslims were perplexed, astonished, outraged that Western societies seemed incapable of comprehending the seriousness of blasphemy. Is there nothing sacred in Western culture? Is there no reverence, not even for the prophets through whom God reveals his will? Surely freedom of speech must not include the right to blasphemy! Only God is God! He has no associates!

There are powerful economic, ideological, cultural, and political cross-currents in the modern global community which are contrary to the Muslim ideal. One modern trend is the encroachment of Western culture and hedonism into Muslim societies. These seductive forces invite exuberant and intense Muslim reform movements. In spite of powerful contrary currents, all these reform movements attempt to model their lives according to the example of Muhammad and his companions.

The Ummah and Israel

A vexing modern development has been the creation of the state of Israel in 1948 and Israel's occupation of Jerusalem since the 1967 war. Recall that Jerusalem is the third most sacred city for Muslims. Israel has therefore projected a serious theological crisis into the soul of the Muslim ummah; Israel exists in a region formerly under the control of the dar al-salaam. Yet the Muslim theologians insist that no global opponent can overwhelm the faithful ummah.

From a Muslim perspective, the creation of the state of Israel is far more than a political and real estate crisis. It is a theological crisis, with roots in the hijrah itself, when Muhammad migrated from the ignominy of Mecca to become a successful statesman and general in Medina. Muslim apologists point to the triumphs of Medina as evidence that Muhammad is the faithful prophet of God. That perception is extended to the ummah. Just as the faithful prophet was victorious over his enemies in battle, so God will also preserve the faithful ummah from defeat.

The Qur'an elaborates the theme that God will defend the faithful ummah.

> O ye who believe!
>   When ye meet a force,
> Be firm and call on God
>   In remembrance much and often
> That ye may prosper;
>   And obey God and his Apostle;
> And fall into no disputes,
>   Lest ye lose heart
> And your power depart;

And be patient and persevering;
For God is with those
Who patiently persevere.[25]

These verses emphasize four themes—belief in God, obedience to God and the apostle (Muhammad), perseverance, fearlessness. These basic themes are elaborated further in the Qur'an and the traditions. These teachings would lead Muslims to believe that God will not permit defeat for the faithful ummah. Those who turn their backs in battle when fighting for the ummah will be punished by God, but those who die will be eternally rewarded. Retreat is acceptable only as a tactical move, in preparation for final victory, just as Muhammad retreated from Mecca for a period of time before returning in victory and triumph.

In light of Muhammad's experience in Medina, it is not surprising that Muslim brotherhoods oppose negotiations with the enemies of the ummah. Some would want these enemies to be defeated and treated ruthlessly—unless they show penitence, in which case they should be treated mercifully[26] These Muslim theologians perceive that such understandings are a faithful response to the teachings of the Qur'an and the sunna of the prophet of Islam.

The themes of war and peace described above significantly inform the response of the Muslim ummah to the phenomenon of Israel. It is understandable why Egypt was a pariah among all the Muslim states in the Middle East after the 1978 Camp David peace accords and the later signing of the peace treaty between Israel and Egypt. The nation of Islam, which includes Egypt, should avoid negotiating with the enemies of the ummah.

However, the Palestine Liberation Organization (PLO) always has been a secular organization. The Arab Christian influence in the PLO encouraged a secular orientation in that organization following the 1948 debacle. It is not surprising that the secular nature of the PLO could enable more negotiating flexibility than would be theologically possible for an Islamic organization. Yet in spite of theological objections, all Israel's neighbors desire a more normal relationship; they have recognized that Egypt might after all be a model of possibilities.

Thirteen years after the Camp David accords between Egypt and Israel, other nations in the region seemed persuaded that a negotiated peace might not be the theological and political catastrophe they had feared. On October 30, 1991, cautiously and fearfully Israel and her Arab neighbors met in Madrid for the first time to explore peace.

On September 13, 1993, nearly two years after Madrid, the world pondered in amazement as PLO and Israeli leaders met on the White House lawn in Washington, D.C., to sign an accord for a mutual commitment to work toward peace.

However, many Muslims are persuaded that greater faithfulness to God and his apostle Muhammad would be the most effective response to the expansionist presence of the state of Israel in the region. It is noteworthy that no Muslim Palestinian organizations were involved in the peace accords initialed between Israel and the Palestinians. The secular PLO signed the accords. The inclination of the Islamic groups was to consider negotiations with the enemy at best as an irrelevant sideshow, and at worst as treason.

The presence of Israel in a region of the earth which was once included in the dar al-salaam nurtures a Muslim yearning to live with the same expressions of submission to God's will as practiced by Muhammad and his companions. From Kudus to Timbuktu, from Paris to Medina, a wind is blowing across the Muslim ummah. How did the prophet do it? That is both the question and the essence of resurgent Islam. Submission to Islam is the only way the ummah can again become an indestructible and victorious community.

The Muslim Nation and the Nations

Recall the Qur'anic assertion, "Thus have we made you an *Ummat* justly balanced, that ye might be witnesses over the nations." [27] The ummah today struggles heroically to maintain its credentials as the "justly balanced" community. The nation-state is one of the most intransigent distortions of the ummah.

Occasionally Muslim nations have gone to war against each other. The more than one million fatalities in the Iran-Iraq War sting the conscience of the world Muslim community. External forces are blamed for helping exacerbate that conflict. The weakening and bleeding of Iran and Iraq was in the self-interest of some of the great powers.

The 1991 war the United States and her allies launched against Iraq after the Iraqi invasion of Kuwait was a theological earthquake. How does one comprehend theologically the intrusion of military powers from the dar al-harb in the dar al-salaam? Arabia, the land which had birthed the ummah, sought help from the region of war for protection from a fellow Muslim country! The land of the Ka'bah, toward which all Muslims face in prayer, was protected by the armies of unbelievers. The region of peace accepted help from the region of war! A whirlwind of theological ferment swirled throughout the global ummah in the wake of that war.

Muslims are dismayed by the fracturing of the ummah through national divisions. They recall the first four Muslim leaders after the death of Muhammad and remember them as the "rightly guided caliphs." These four—Abu-Bakr, Umar, Uthman, and Ali—set the tone for an expanding multinational community united by Islam. Caliphate dynasties came and went, often determined by imperial fortunes or personal ambition. Nevertheless, throughout the centuries the institution of the caliphate often provided a symbolic center for the far-flung Sunni ummah. The caliph was a sign that there can be only one Muslim nation.

In modern times, after the disintegration of the Ottoman Empire, the caliphate was abolished in 1922 by Mustafa Kemal Ataturk. The whole nation of Islam was shaken by this event, which abrogated a significant sign of the unity of the ummah among the nations of the global community. Nevertheless, in time other pan-Islamic institutions have arisen which attempt to overcome nationalistic divisions. The World Muslim League is one such institution. A significant function of the League is attempting to enable the ummah to transcend political and national considerations so the worldwide community of Islam really functions as one global ummah.

The transnational commitments of Islam are fully consistent with the primal vision of the emergent ummah in Medina. The Muslims under Muhammad's leadership looked beyond the immediate task of bringing peace between the conflictual clans of Arabia. The nations beyond Arabia were also their concern.

Muhammad and the Muslims were dismayed by the conflicts between the Christianized nations. Some of these conflicts seemed related to theological differences. The Qur'an describes the mission of the ummah as bringing unity and understanding among all believers in God. Modern Muslims often describe the ummah as the moderate middle community whose mission is brotherhood and sisterhood in a world divided by national and religious strife. Christian denominations, Hindu caste, racism, or tribal strife anywhere reveal the need for the Muslim community which unites people from nations, tribes, and races in the submission to God which is Islam.

Nevertheless, Muslims have experienced division, even in the primal community. It is said that Muhammad predicted seventy-three divisions and sects among Muslims. These tendencies began already in the primal community.[28] Violence marred the leadership of even the first four "rightly guided caliphs." Uthman, the third caliph, was murdered. Ali, the fourth caliph, was assassinated. As mentioned earlier, civil war at the time of Ali's death solidified the division of Muslims into Shi'ah and Sunni communities. Strife in the nation of Islam is not just a modern development.

The Ummah and the Family

Marriage and family practices vary widely among Muslims. Nevertheless, the Shari'ah does provide a profile of acceptable and expected family practices.

Islam is opposed to extramarital sex. So as not to entice men sexually, women are veiled in many Muslim societies. In some societies they are not to be seen in public. Covered overhead walkways arch across the narrow streets in the quaint Indian Ocean island town of Lamu, just off the coast of Kenya. These walkways enable Muslim women to visit from house to house without being seen by men on the street. Yet in other Muslim societies women are full members of the work force.

Debate concerning the status of women in Islam creates tension in many Muslim societies. Does the soul of Islam really affirm that women are fully equal to men? Is it right that the daughter gets half as much inheritance as the son when the father is deceased? Is it ever acceptable for a husband to beat his recalcitrant wife? Should the wife be a field or a companion? Is it appropriate for the children to belong to the husband when there is divorce? Just prior to the 1991 Gulf War, scores of Arabian women drove cars through Riyadh as a protest against the roles society had circumscribed for them.

There are Muslim communities which do enjoy stable family relations. Nevertheless, in modern Muslim societies, there is tension between modernity and tradition in the quest for marital stability and women's rights. Reformers lament the instability of family relationships which blight many Muslim societies.

Some reformers plead for a reinterpretation of Shari'ah and the Qur'an. They lament that divorce in the ummah is too easy and that the rights of the woman are not sufficiently considered. They are concerned because the Qur'anic description of woman as a field[29] is interpreted by too many Muslim men as justification to discard a woman, who cannot bear more children, in favor of a younger woman of childbearing age. However, Muslim defenders of traditional practices point out that the track record for women's rights and marital stability in more liberal Christianized societies is often less than ideal.

Although prostitution is prohibited, many societies do accept the Muslim institution of temporary marriage for the traveler who desires a sexual companion when away from home. Divorce is hated by God, yet it is acceptable when necessary. In the temporary marriage arrangement, divorce is institutionalized.

Polygyny is permitted in Islam, provided all wives are treated equally and there are not more than four. Some modernists attempt to reinterpret Islam in favor of monogamy, suggesting that polygyny demeans womanhood and erodes quality family relationships.

Muslims have often confided to me that Islam cannot receive the Christian perception of marriage as a binding one flesh covenant relationship united by God. They tell me that Islam is the practical religion; it does not aspire to the unrealistic Christian ideals of marriage and family life. In Islam marriage is a contract; in biblical faith it is a covenant.

Muslims believe children are a blessing from God. Faithful Muslims could never condone abortions, for human life is precious. Some Muslim societies struggle with the propriety of birth control.

When visiting in remote Bangladeshi villages, I learned that a vigorous debate was raging in the mosques concerning the ethical implications of family planning—this in one of the earth's most densely populated societies, where over 100 million people live in an area smaller than the South Island of New Zealand. In this Muslim society, the babies are received as one of God's most precious blessings. The preachers in the mosques passionately pressed this question: Is it not presumptuous to "plan" these blessings?

The Ummah and the Earth

The marvel of conception and birth reveal the creative power and wonder of God. So does all of creation. The Qur'an describes the wonders of creation as *ayat*—signs which point people toward God. Muslims speak of creation rather than nature. God creates and sustains the earth and the universe, but the creation is not divine.

Islam strongly emphasizes the sovereignty and transcendence of God. Some streams of Muslim theology have significantly accented these dimensions of faith in relationship to creation. In practical terms, this can lead to the conviction that it is presuming on God's sovereignty to expect nature, which he creates and sustains, to function with predictability. Creation is therefore considered capricious. This line of thinking is not conducive to the development of scientific technology. Instead, it encourages fatalism.

Yet at the soul of Islam there is a different spirit. Humans are created to be God's caliph, caretakers of the earth. Islam in its truest essence joins hands with all humanity in modern ecological commitments. Humankind is commanded by God to care for the good earth which God has created. Biblical faith and Islam converge in this commitment.

Nevertheless, in this convergence a significant difference is present. In the Qur'an, God teaches Adam the names of the animals. In the Bible, Adam names the animals. These divergences in the primal accounts of creation may seem insignificant. But they are not, for these differences nurture a full-orbed worldview. In Islam God provides guidance which instructs humankind in every aspect of life. In biblical faith Adam names the animals, while God looks on, perhaps with some amusement, seeing what these people will do.

The accent in Islam is on submission to the will of God. The accent in biblical faith is on human responsibility in a covenant relationship. Through the centuries, as these quite different emphases have influenced cultures and societies, significant divergences have also developed in the manner in which these cultures perceive of a right and ideal relationship between people and the earth.

A development consultation in East Africa several years ago is an example of the different worldviews which seem to emerge from Qur'anic and biblical faith. Muslims and Christians had planned respective consultations on economic development in an arid region in northeastern Africa. The Muslim conference focused primarily on teaching Arabic throughout the region, so all children could actually read the Qur'an. In this way they would have access to God's guidance on right development. The Christian conference had some biblical devotionals, to be sure, but the main input for the conference came from scientifically trained ecology and development experts.

The long-term consequence of the Muslim commitments in this region will be increased religious practices and the Christian commitment will increase secular and development-oriented activity. Muslims might worry that the Christian-secular approach will be irreverent, rely too much on human enterprise, presumptuously ignore or damage the ayat of God in creation. Such worry is not without justification. In time the wells which the churches dug induced more intensive grazing in the areas around the water. The consequence was denuded grasslands and desert for miles around the wells. Respect the ayat of God, implore the Muslims!

The Ummah and Progress

Approaches to development, especially human and cultural development, are informed by a society's understanding of history. Consider these examples.

A Hindu or Buddhist worldview considers history a tragic and meaningless cycle controlled by fate.

An African traditional worldview understands all history to be moving from the present to the past. Both the Chinese and Africans idealized the past.

The ideal good of Greek Platonic philosophy was an unchangeable universal principle which governed the universe and history.

Northern hemisphere polytheists viewed history as a phenomenon trapped in the cycles of death and resurrection of the nature gods.

A biblical worldview sees history moving from the garden of Eden and the tragic human distortions which occurred there to a consummation in the future in a majestic city, the fulfillment of the kingdom of God. Biblical faith is permeated with a sense that history has purpose and destiny and movement.

In the Muslim perspective, Islam is the primal, middle, and final religion, without innovation or change. The Islamic view is that history is suspended between creation and the final judgment. History is neither cyclical nor linear, oriented toward neither past nor future. There is no movement.

These views of history affect people's attitudes toward personal responsibility and the meaning of life.

In prayer five times daily, the community of Islam turns toward the Ka'bah, the primal navel of the earth, where Adam first appeared when sent from paradise for a period of testing for him and his progeny. At the judgment day when history ends, the testing will be over, and all humans will receive their reward, either in the gardens of paradise or in hell. History is a parenthesis between Adam and the judgment.

The geographical expansion of the dar al-salaam does take place in history. In that sense there is movement in history. Yet the mission of Islam is an invitation to conformity in the parameters of the Shari'ah, which is a clarification of the right guidance practiced by Adam, Abraham, Muhammad, and other prophets of God. That guidance does not change; the function of prophets after Adam is just to retrieve or clarify. Muslims facing the Ka'bah in prayer or going to the Ka'bah in pilgrimage are affirming that history is anchored to the faith and practice of Adam.

The Muslim view of history is nurtured by the Islamic doctrine which abhors *bidah* (innovation). That theme has already been explored. The faithful ummah lives with internal tension as the community faces the Ka'bah in submission to the unchangeable guidance of Islam in a world of movement and change.

Global Issues

We have found that the hijrah and Muhammad's subsequent establishment of the original Muslim ummah in Medina is a root experience for Muslims. That event informs Muslim understanding of their mission in the global community. That mission is the extension of the region of peace throughout the earth. We have discerned ways in which the Muslim region of peace relates to the issues of global community and well-being.

Our exploration has surveyed specific ways in which the ummah relates to a variety of issues in modern global community. These include pluralism, the nation-state, authority, cultural diversity, the political order, international relations, peace and war, violence and nonviolence, secularism, cultural development and change, human rights, womanhood, family, children, ecology, economic development, ethics, and the meaning of human history.

We have found the Muslim contribution to all global issues is defined by the core conviction of Islam—God is one and has no associates. This conviction is expressed concretely, practically, culturally in the universally authentic guidance God has revealed as his will.

Yet Muslims live in a global community in which people have countless other loyalties. For this reason the Muslim ummah unapologetically and urgently challenges and invites the global community to submit to the will of God. It is not surprising that in many regions of the earth there is tension between the ummah and other communities. Most Muslims are not worried by that tension; it is to be expected wherever communities are still outside the reign of peace which is the dar al-salaam.

Muslims believe that Islam is the peace which comes from submission to the will of God. The Islamic witness is heard in vast regions of the global community—*La Ilaha Illa'llah Muhammadan Rasulu'llah* (There is but one God, Muhammad is the prophet of God). Daily the Muslim ummah proclaims its witness and invitation to faith, submission, and prayer from the hundreds of thousands of minarets in the hamlets, towns, and cities of our world.

Whether the Muslim communities have come under the jurisdiction of the dar al-salaam or are islands of peace in regions as yet beyond the rule of the region of peace, the faithful worshipers of Allah demonstrate the bonding of this global community in their daily prayers, always facing the Ka'bah in Mecca.

For multitudes of the world's approximately 1,000 million Muslims, the witness and invitation is serious business. They are persuaded that the way of Islam is the only hope for peace.

One evening in a mosque in one of North America's great cities, the elders told me, "We are an island of peace separated by thousands of miles from the support inclusion in the dar al-salaam would provide. Although we are alone, we try to be faithful witnesses in a society which does not respect Islam. Once our neighbors burned this mosque to the ground. We are an island of peace in a violent country.

"We hope and work for the day when this troubled land of America comes under the control of the dar al-salaam. In the meantime we shall live faithfully as a witness and invitation to the way of peace."

Reflection

1. What are the unifying aspects of Islam?

2. In what ways does the notion of an Islamic culture help or hinder the growth of the ummah in modern times?

3. Consider the Islamic view of humankind and history. In what ways might these views affect economic and cultural development?

4. Consider the implications for global community of the Islamic view of dar al-salaam and dar al-harb.

5. Recall that the Temple Mount in Jerusalem figures centrally in the account of the miraj. What are other events for Jews, Muslims, and Christians which make that mount significant? What are the implications for global peace of the conflict between the Jewish and Muslim communities over the issue of control of Jerusalem? What reasonable suggestions do you have for the resolution of the conflict?

6. From an ideal Islamic perspective, how should the ummah relate to the phenomenon of pluralism?

7. What is the mission of the ummah?

11

Freedom from the Gods

The Enlightenment

C OGITO ERGO SUM!" exulted René Descartes as he leaped from his bath, dashing naked into the street to proclaim his sudden intuitive glimpse of reality.[1]

Legendary as this seventeenth-century anecdote might be, Descarte's bathtub insight, "I think, therefore I am," is a philosophical, religious, and intellectual watershed in Western culture. His discovery is similar to that of the Greek Socrates more than two millennia earlier, who had intrigued his disciples with the search to "know thyself."

Yet Descartes was a pioneer in Western thought who set the tone for one of the most formative and far-reaching eras in human intellectual development, that of the seventeenth and eighteenth-century European Enlightenment.

Taproots

The intellectual and spiritual taproots of the Enlightenment are biblical faith and Greek rationalism. For over a thousand years, the Christian church was the dominant institution on the European cultural horizon. By the fourth century of the Christian era, the church was significantly present in many regions of Europe, as far north as England and as far west as Spain.

The church grew, although there was occasional persecution and harassment by the imperial authorities. However, the spread of

Christianity's influence across the European continent proceeded with even greater zest following Constantine's A.D. 313 Edict of Milan, which legalized Christianity in the Roman Empire.

Fourth century Palestinian church historian Eusebius was exuberant. He saw a day coming when the church would have the opportunity to influence the worldview and values of a whole continent and develop a Christian civilization.[2] That did happen. The continent was Europe, inhabited by many peoples whose traditional religions were typically primal polytheism and spirit veneration. For a thousand years and more, the church wooed and sometimes coerced the peoples away from their ontocratic primal religious orientations and into the Christian church.

These were fruitful years for the Christian faith in Europe. The church sowed the intellectual and spiritual seeds of the Christian gospel, which transformed the worldviews and cultures of the European peoples. This transformation gathered momentum as the Bible gained increasing circulation. Well over a century before the Enlightenment commenced as a movement, the Bible was becoming more widely known in European societies because of translations and the introduction of printing.

Recall that in biblical faith God is Creator and sustainer of the universe. This means several things.

> Creation is other than God.
> The earth and universe are good.
> Creation is orderly and understandable.
> Humankind is commanded to care for the good earth.
> People are to develop the earth for the well-being of humankind.

Earlier chapters have explored the dramatic implications of this biblical worldview when compared to other religious systems. These biblical perceptions are the spiritual and intellectual seedbed for a full-orbed scientific and technological culture.

The church also preserved the rationalism of the Greek philosophers and entrusted these insights to its theologians and philosophers. Actually, during the chaos of Europe's Dark Ages, it was scholars living in the protection of the Islamic dar al-salaam which mostly preserved the Greek intellectual treasures for later European consumption. As Europe's spiritual and intellectual climate developed, Greek perceptions were a welcome window into fresh possibilities for European culture.

Recall that chapter five describes some of the attractions between Greek philosophy and the early church. In time both biblical faith and the philosophies of the sages of Greece contributed to the development of European intellectual culture. It was an exceedingly dynamic culture. By the dawn of the sixteenth century, European societies had spawned more than three score universities![3]

In due time the synergy of Greek philosophy interacting with medieval European Christianity created astonishing ferment in European culture of the seventeenth and eighteenth centuries. Twentieth-century scholar A. N. Whitehead comments,

> When we compare this tone of thought in Europe with the attitude of other civilizations when left to themselves, there seems but one source for its origin. It must come from the medieval insistence on the rationality of God, conceived as with the personal energy of Jehovah and with the rationality of a Greek philosopher.[4]

The discussion in chapter six on the Confucian and Greek philosophical experience described the tensions which developed between the Chinese and Greek philosophers and the worldview of popular primal religions. Although the philosophers were skeptical or disbelieving of the gods, they were never able fundamentally to transform the worldview which nurtured polytheism. That worldview believed that the divinities and nature intermingled in oneness. In China, Confucius himself became divinized. In Greece the mystery cults grew in significance even as the philosophers held forth on the Acropolis.

Biblical faith, anchored in history rather than philosophical speculation, finally and decisively broke the power of the primal nature deities in the Greek experience. As the witness of the church extended across Europe, the same phenomenon occurred. Sometimes quickly, more often gradually, people abandoned the notions that the cycles of nature are fused to the deaths and resurrections of divinities. The transformation was often explicit. For example, the sacrificial rites involved in worshiping and entreating the sun just after the winter solstice were replaced by Christmas, a celebration of the birth of Christ.

This transformation was necessary for a scientific and technological worldview to emerge. Although all societies do develop technologies, a worldview which genuinely and enthusiastically fosters a scientific orientation could only develop in a culture which had abandoned the nature deities. A scientific technological worldview cannot thrive in a culture which believes that a nature spirit or divinity will bite if one builds a highway across its terrain. It is no accident that polytheism never provided a spiritual home for the ideas of Greek philosophy. In the European experience, the church discovered and embraced many of the insights of the Greek philosophers. This polytheism could never do.

The biblical understanding of the person, society, and government also nurtured the spirit of the Enlightenment. The church taught that the person is eternally significant, created in God's own image. She can think God's own thoughts. The church believes that the person experiences his greatest fulfillment in the community of faith and truth.

During the apex of Catholic Christianity, it was evident that the church was the only truly international community in Europe. The church was the only community which could unite the peoples of the continent as the imperial power of Rome declined. The Catholic Church had united peoples in the bonds of universal truth; the Enlightenment sought universal truth as well.

The church also nurtured the conviction that the state is not the final authority. Although the notion of the divine right of kings persisted, the church nevertheless believed that the political powers should heed the counsel of the church, for it was the church and not the state which spoke with the authority of Christ. In the tradition of the Old Testament prophets, the church confronted the political authorities when necessary.

The medieval theologians believed the church was the expression on earth of the eternal kingdom of God. The church had a transnational global vision which superseded the state. By the seventeenth century, the worldwide missionary endeavor of the European church had already begun. All of these themes influenced the Enlightenment.

For a thousand years, the church molded European culture. The Enlightenment was the child of this Christianized culture. It thrived on the church's perception of creation, humanity, morality, and society. Yet the Enlightenment is also a reaction against the church. It was a movement whose architects were determined to guide European culture in directions more humanely and globally sensitive than was the church in seventeenth-century Europe.

In previous chapters we have occasionally reflected on the distortions of Western church we have described as Constantinization. The fourth-century Roman Emperor Constantine enabled the church to become a participant in political power. A process commenced of increasingly intimate integration of church and state.

As time passed, the role of the Western church changed from what it had been when the church was a minority community. Instead of conscience in society, the church became the policeman. The church became authoritarian and possessed the power to enforce its will. It developed enormous financial and political power. Too often the church functioned as a self-serving institution which dehumanized people rather than as a community in ministry for others.

Even in realms such as scientific investigation, the church claimed the last word, as demonstrated in the trial of Galileo, a contemporary of Descartes. Galileo's telescopes confirmed for him that the earth and planets revolved around the sun, a notion the church believed theologically erroneous. The church censured Galileo.

The authoritarian power of the church troubled the philosophers of the Enlightenment. Equating the kingdom of God with the church was a fateful theological development. If that was true, then the church was in itself the ultimate transcendent authority. Whenever any institution, including the church, perceives that it is the ultimate authority, then there will be abuse of power.

The church's confrontation with governments was more concerned with maintaining power and privilege than in defending the poor and oppressed. Too often the church's promise of heaven after death became a theological basis for neglecting justice and oppressing the poor. The philosophers sought to free European society from the sometimes dehumanizing stranglehold of the church.

The philosophers were also troubled by the divisiveness which the church had brought into European society on the heels of the Protestant Reformation. At the time of René Descartes's bathtub experience, the Thirty Years' War between Protestant and Catholic princes and regions was devastating central and northern Europe. Both Protestants and Catholics hounded dissidents. Torture and death were awarded those whose heretical views might encourage others in beliefs and practices which lead to hell.

Descartes's "I think, therefore I am" was a declaration of independence from a church system which neglected the needs of the person. The philosophers insisted that through the use of reason, humankind could and should take charge of its own destiny. However, in this quest for a more humanized culture than the established church was creating, the pioneers of the Enlightenment were not alone. In various European societies, Christian reform movements inside and outside the established church had also attempted to bring correctives to the distortions of institutional Christianity.

There were occasional Christian reform movements in the church even prior to the Enlightenment which used the Bible itself to critique church dogma, tradition, and practice. That is why the Roman Catholic priest Martin Luther nailed his Ninety-five Theses on the Castle Church door in Wittenberg, Germany, on October 31, 1517. That act ignited the reform movement which in due course became the Protestant Reformation. Luther was inviting a debate on church dogma and practice based on a biblical critique. Yet as noted above, the Protestant Reformation also became entangled in political loyalties which plunged northern areas of Europe into a tragic paroxysm of violence.

Other reform movements flourished both in established Catholic and Protestant churches and sometimes also outside these state church systems. Noteworthy are the Anabaptists who were prepared to lay down their lives for their conviction that freedom of conscience for every person is the will of God. By insisting on adult baptism, they put the axe to the European state church system, which had developed during and after the era of Constantine.

Their martyrs stung the conscience of Europe, thereby preparing the way for modern commitments to broad-based human rights. They laid the foundations for modern political institutions, which affirm and encourage religious pluralism. These sixteenth-century Anabaptists were trail blazers for many dimensions of cultural and political transformation sought by the Enlightenment a century later.

Reason Replaces Revelation

Nevertheless, as the Enlightenment progressed, it became increasingly adversarial to establishment Christianity and skeptical of biblical faith, if not actually opposed to the biblical worldview. Some of the intellectual pioneers of the Enlightenment made an explicit attempt to free the human mind, not only from what they considered to be the abuses of Christian dogma and practice, but also from the shackles of biblical revelation.

Consequently, reason and empiricism replaced the Bible as the means to truth. John Locke, an Englishman (d. 1704), philosophized that divine law was also natural law which could be discerned through reason alone. French philosopher Voltaire (d. 1778) was appalled at religious persecution and sought to discredit superstitions and beliefs which instigated such horror. He believed that self-evident natural laws were the only reasonable basis on which to construct ethical commitments. Scottish philosopher David Hume (d. 1776) was an agnostic and yet optimistic that the benevolent essence of human nature was an adequate basis for moral behavior.

Intellectual turnings such as these in Western philosophy and culture were the beginning of a colossal shift away from biblical faith. These turnings have also affected global culture in astonishing ways.

The brief profile of the Enlightenment which follows only sketches some of the themes especially apropos to global village—nature, ethics, religion, truth, and the person.

Nature

There was the conviction that creation is orderly and understandable. In the thirteenth century, Roger Bacon was a scientist, philosopher, and theologian whose pioneering work foreshadowed the Enlightenment. Yet Isaac Newton is the towering contemporary scientist of the Enlightenment. Newton, like Bacon, was a theologian who received from biblical faith the worldview which undergirded his scientific methodology. His research led to the conviction that God had established natural laws which direct the harmonious flow of nature. The task of scientific methodology was to investigate these laws and apply this understanding for the benefit of humanity.

As the notion of natural laws began to permeate European culture, the concept of "nature" began to replace "creation." In the Bible the earth and universe are always referred to as creation, which reveals a worldview convinced that God creates and also sustains what he has created. The biblical worldview also demands human accountability to God for the way we relate to creation. However, by referring to creation as nature, the Enlightenment introduced a subtle yet significant shift into Western culture, for it is possible for nature to function independently of God, governed only by natural laws.

If creation is only nature, then there is no need for people to be accountable to the Creator for the manner in which they use nature. For many disciples of the Enlightenment, God himself became largely an irrelevant hypothesis—and then only as a first-cause explanation for the existence of nature. Although the fathers of the Enlightenment would not have predicted these consequences, this cosmic shift in worldview helped to invite the uninhibited technological destruction of nature.

There is now no God to whom humankind is accountable for their destructive exploitation of nature. It is evident that the technological centuries which have followed the Enlightenment have brought dramatic improvements in the quality of human life worldwide. It is also evident that the spirit of unaccountable technological exploitation of nature has already ruined entire regions of this planet.

Ethics

John Locke took the Newtonian theories of the laws of nature and applied them to morality. He was a pioneer. Others such as Voltaire agreed that, just as the natural scientists were discovering the laws of nature, natural laws could also be identified in the realms of the moral good. These philosophers were convinced that revelation is not necessary or helpful in defining morality.

One reason for their disdain of appeals to revelation as a basis for morality was that the philosophers were not impressed by the moral qualities of the established church, which often seemed more committed to greed than morality. The church's critics claimed that it used its presumed access to revelation to oppress rather than humanize people. They argued that reason needed to be the basic foundation of human morality. The same scientific method that unlocked the laws of nature could unlock the "self-evident" laws of morality.

Yet a problem arises. Does nature provide a valid basis for morality? Nature was actually considered divine throughout Europe prior to Christianity. Did those pre-Christian systems nurture a healthy morality? Was it moral to sacrifice a virgin to the sun god after the winter solstice as was the practice among some northern European societies? The fact is that nature knows no ethics.[5]

Evidence of the ambivalent ethical perspective nature provides is what my wife and I felt when we visited Monticello, Virginia, the home of Thomas Jefferson. He was author of the United States Declaration of Independence. Jefferson's pen anchored that declaration in the "Laws of Nature and Nature's God." The evidence at Monticello suggests that Jefferson loved the laws of nature more than the people who were his slaves.

Jefferson created a magnificent estate for himself and his family! He experimented with nature, exploring new possibilities. He imported flowers and trees from distant lands. Experts have restored the trees, flower bed, and vegetable garden arrangements. The vegetables are planted in patterns according to their color configurations; for example, purple, white, and then black eggplants are in symmetrical arrangements. Above his remarkable garden is a glass-enclosed room in which Jefferson sat to read. The estate is an elegant example of what a person working with nature can create.

Near his glass-enclosed reading room above the patterned vegetable garden is a plaque. In small script it reveals that 157 slaves were needed to maintain this estate. The script elaborates that the slaves worked from sunrise to sundown, seven days a week including holidays. When Jefferson died his will decreed freedom for only five of his slaves; the remainder were sold to pay off the debts on the estate. Many of those black families were broken the day of that slave auction.[6]

In this elegant Monticello estate, nature's god seemed to have no qualms about expressing a greater love for the land than for the people who tilled that land.

Jefferson was a deist, a true son of the Enlightenment. The deist perception is that God might have created the world in the distant past but is not presently involved in history or nature. Thus the only reliable cues we possess concerning right and wrong we receive through nature. Although Jefferson confessed that he detested slavery, for him the love of nature and his elegant estate usurped authentic concern for his slaves.

Beautiful Monticello is a sign in the soul of the North American heritage. That sign reveals that nature is not a solid foundation for ethics. We recognize that too often the churches also provided a distorted conscience concerning slavery. Yet Monticello is especially poignant, for this estate was owned and administered by the father of the U.S. Declaration of Independence. Jefferson provided a clear trumpet call for Americans to taste the delicious freedoms which the Enlightenment offered. Yet for Jefferson, when there was a collision between the well-being of his slaves and the care of his flower beds, the flowers took precedence.

Religion

The notion of "religion" began to enter the intellectual furnishings of Western awareness. Prior to the Enlightenment, church and faith were the soul of the culture; this was the way of life. The Enlightenment changed all of that by giving faith and church a label—religion.

The phenomenon of religion can be studied and analyzed scientifically. Some people are religious and others not. A person can opt for religion, ignore it, or oppose the phenomenon. Enlightenment thinkers believed that reason rather than religion needed to be the arbiter of self-evident morality and truth. They were convinced that any reason-based morality is a universal global morality, whereas morality appealing to religion tends to be narrowly defined and applicable in the confines of a sectarian community.

Skepticism of religion and the church was not always benign. Eighteenth-century historian Edward Gibbon described the role of the church in the Roman society in his book *The Rise and Fall of the Roman Empire.*[7] With irony he demonstrated that religions, including Christianity, contributed to the cultural, moral, and political decline of Rome. A contemporary of Gibbon's, Abbe' Raynal, described the glories of a non-Christian Asian culture in *The Philosophical and Political History of the Indies*. These were influential books.[8]

These histories, like all scholarship of the times, claimed to be objective and scientific. These "objective" histories demonstrated that religion in Europe was not necessarily conducive to human happiness and well-being. There was deepening uncertainty that Christianized European culture had a civilizing mission in the world.

The idea that history could be studied scientifically unleashed dynamic historical research and writing. The assumptions of natural science invaded these efforts in historical objectivity. In the natural sciences, the worldview shift from creation to nature ushered in skepticism concerning extraordinary phenomena. There was no room for the extraordinary in a worldview in which self-sustaining natural laws governed the phenomena of nature. Therefore history needed to weed out accounts of extraordinary events. Thus the rewriting of the accounts of world religions dismissed stories of the extraordinary as being legend, fantasy, or superstition.

Before long, the scientific historians were applying the tools of their discipline to the Bible. In the hands of scholars who did not believe in biblical theism, the Christian Scriptures were analyzed with the assumption that the extraordinary does not occur. The universe is a closed and autonomous system with no possibility of acts of God in nature or history.

We have observed that the U.S. philosopher-president Thomas Jefferson embraced a deistic approach to history and nature. Although Jefferson was not a biblical scholar, he rewrote the New Testament accounts of Jesus in accordance with the perspectives of the scientific historiography of the late eighteenth century. He scissored out all references to the extraordinary in the life of Christ. The account ends with a dead Jesus in a tomb, for in Jefferson's worldview, there could be no resurrection of Jesus. Jefferson named his work *New Testament: Philosophy of Jesus.*[9]

Jefferson viewed himself as a good Christian. Yet the title "philosophy" for his rewritten scripture reveals a radical divergence from Christian faith; biblical faith is not a philosophy. Jefferson's approach to the Bible is consistent with the so-called scientific historiography. The assumption is that God never acts in history or creation.

Thomas Jefferson was not an atheist; neither was he a biblical theist. Like Jefferson, many who moved in the worldview of the Enlightenment considered themselves deists. As mentioned above, deists accept God as the most reasonable first cause for the existence of the universe, but his existence has little or no relevance to the processes of history or nature. For the deists, nature and history are like a clock, which once made and wound, runs on and on with no assistance. We are on our own! We alone are responsible for our destiny.

Truth

Universities developed to encourage people to seek the truth. The Latin and French roots of the term *university* suggest the entire realm of knowledge turning toward a center of worth. "Uni-Verse"—all knowledge with a truth center.

It was in third-century Alexandria, Egypt, that the forerunner of the modern university movement occurred. Origen (d. 254 c.) was one of the professors in this school, which attracted students from throughout the Middle East region. They came because no area of inquiry was considered off-limits. This exuberant center for universal enquiry was the Alexandrian Catechetical School.

The Alexandrian school is the forerunner of the liberal arts universities that have accompanied the spread of the church into many regions of the global village. These church-related universities have been founded on the premise that all reality is worthy of study. And there is coherence and plan in all dimensions of knowledge. There is a center toward which all data points, truth in which all reality converges. That center is God. He is the source of all truth, and therefore all reality is touched with meaning and purpose.

The Enlightenment agreed with the church that there is a truth center. However, the Enlightenment placed human reason, not God, in that truth center. By enthroning human reason at the center of the university, the Enlightenment nudged God into the periphery of reality. The consequence is that there is now no truth center.

The university has become a hodgepodge of unrelated accumulation of data; our modern universities demonstrate that human reason alone is incapable of discerning universal truth. Personal or group values and data have usurped the place of a truth center. There is no turning toward a center, for there is no awareness of a center.

what is truth? The loss of a universal center pervades Western culture. A debate in my home community illustrates our confusion. The central city high school staff developed a course on core values for living. The school board, community, and staff became sharply divided about this course. While some argued that there are basic universal human values which such a course should communicate, others were equally adamant that it is nonsense to speak of core values.

"We shall teach values which our own community cherishes," the staff promised. "We shall, for example, teach integrity."

The objectors complained, "You can't do that, for our community has no consensus on values. Integrity is certainly not a core value in our community."

Thus in a society infected by drug abuse, teen-age pregnancies, AIDS, broken homes, theft, murders, unemployment, child abuse, and arson, sages who lead our city high school are incapable of agreeing on any foundation for community values. The best they can do is provide an educational system which provides data. The learning experience must be designed in such a manner that it is bereft of any truth or value center.

The disciplines of the natural sciences are also bereft of a center. For example, a 1991 issue of *Newsweek* described some incredible explorations in astronomy during the decade of the 1980s. One of the perplexing discoveries is that there seems to be pattern in the galaxy systems. One of the patterns is that the galaxy clusters are spaced at 400 million light-year intervals!

The article quotes Edmond Bertschinger of the Massachusetts Institute of Technology asking, " `Why should the process that made galaxies pick out that pattern? It is so beyond our understanding that theorists dismiss them for the time being'—hoping they're an illusion."[10]

Why would some astronomers feel uneasy about this pattern in the universe? Obviously the pattern does not fit into contemporary theories of the universe. The quote from Bertschinger does not elaborate.

Pattern suggests plan. Plan is only possible if there is purpose, if there is a truth center. However, Enlightenment culture has determined that human reason alone shall be enthroned at the centers of learning. Human reason alone is incapable of discovering the ultimate purpose of the universe. Yet evidence of plan in creation would suggest that there is universal truth, a center which gives plan, meaning, and purpose.[11]

However, it is difficult for contemporary Enlightenment culture to digest indications of plan or purpose. "The god of physics gives us what we wish. But he does not tell us what we should wish," observes George Santayana as he describes the plight of Enlightenment culture.[12]

A professor in a secular university may not exclaim, "The purpose of human life is to glorify God and enjoy him forever!" Such a statement might lead to dismissal from the university.

Yet it is considered academic sophistication to state, as an anthropology professor once did in my class, "You are only animals. There is nothing special about being human."

Is there supporting evidence for any of these alternatives? Western society has discovered with surprise that we experience meaninglessness when human reason becomes a global god. Yet the culture persists in a worldview of meaninglessness. It is difficult to receive evidence to the contrary.

Nevertheless, in modern times, in the soul of Enlightenment culture itself, there are indications of a persistent and disturbing nudge to consider the possibility of plan or meaning. Modern people experience that disquieting invitation right in the scientific community.

Modern theories of the universe must accommodate the evidence of both chaos and causality in nature. There is no predictability in chaos, such as in a tornado. Causality is precisely predictable, such as the rotations of the planets around the sun. Yet in the intermingling and complex phenomena of both chaos and causality, we discover overall pattern and organization. These discoveries confound the dominant theories of simple causality which informed the scientific community for the past three hundred years.

Physics and mathematics are also going through major paradigm shifts. Computers demonstrate amazing design and pattern in mathematical formulas; these patterns often converge with similar structures in nature which electron microscopes reveal. The computer and electron microscope are unlocking the astonishing "organized complexity"[13] of the universe.

That organized complexity seems especially and remarkably focused toward the development and sustenance of human life on earth. Human life would be impossible if there were even the slightest divergence in the overall pattern, such as in the amazing complexities required for the formation of the carbon molecule. This is astonishing. It is as though a master architect put the universe together.

It is most astonishing that people are able both to observe and to decipher the pattern. This is true even though the pattern might be mysteriously encoded. An example is the exceedingly complex ladderlike structure of the DNA molecule which is the carrier of genetic imprints. It is amazing that people are able to crack the codes. The pattern is a mystery hidden in codes which are often profoundly complex. Yet some people have the genius to decipher the mind of the architect by cracking those codes. And the codes all hang together, like a crossword puzzle. When one code is cracked, it provides clues as to how to crack other codes.

The evidence points toward a unitary principal or plan in the universe. That plan provides for the intricate complexities and interdependent patterns which enable the existence of human life on earth.[14] But who is the architect?

The Person and Government

The Enlightenment put the person at the center of the universe. Through intellect alone persons could come to an understanding of truth and morality. The function of truth and morality was happiness for the individual. The ingredients needed for the person to experience happiness were natural rights, built into the laws of the universe, just as Newton's laws of physics. They included the right to freedom and to own property.

The sharp accent on individual happiness as the good was in danger of becoming nihilism and anarchy. Jean-Jacques Rousseau was a voice for the counterbalance of the rights of society functioning in harmony with individual rights to produce true happiness. His book *The Social Contract* argued that all individual rights must be social.[15] His vision was of government functioning in a contractual relationship with individuals and society, as all work together to produce the social and cultural conditions in which happiness could thrive. The function of government is to guarantee the rights of the person in society.

For Rousseau government does not acquire legitimacy by divine right, but rather through a social contract with the governed. There is no transcendent authority to which government is accountable. Rational ideas are a more reliable basis for government policy than are our notions of God. Such understandings of government have inspired the evolution of liberal democracies.

Yet in time a fateful difficulty arose. The rational ideas that had replaced God became gods; in the twentieth century, several rational deities have brought hell on earth. "Scientific" truth created ideas and these ideas became ideologies that could not be challenged because they were founded on "scientific" truth. They became the arbiters of political institutions and created a fixation on performing global missions. Nazism and Marxism are examples; so is United States manifest destiny. Respectively, these ideologies were based on the "science" of human racial evolution, the "science" of dialectical materialism, and the "self-evident" truths of nature.

World War II was therefore not a collision of nationalisms. Rather it was an Enlightenment war, a conflict between "scientifically" grounded ideas that had a worldwide political mission. An ideological war is far more dangerous than a conflict between nations![16]

Ironically, and in astonishing contradiction to the value which the Enlightenment placed on the person, the notion of the significance of the person has also contributed to a worldview which can condone the genocidal wars of modern times. In modern societies, which are permeated by the notions of the rights, freedoms, and responsibilities of the person, everyone shares responsibility for the wars which the government of the people administers. This notion can provide a sense of justification for the bombing and destruction of civilian population centers.

Of course, the destruction of civilians has always been a temptation in times of war; in ancient times whole cities were sometimes obliterated. Nevertheless, the twentieth-century phenomenon of specifically targeting cities such as Hamburg or Hiroshima for destruction or sowing the fields of farmers in Laos with cluster bombs seems to be nurtured by a worldview which holds civilians responsible for the acts of their governments.

A Global Philosophy

European governments and societies were influenced by and experimented with the convictions of the Enlightenment. The Enlightenment also has embraced non-European societies. In fact, during the nineteenth and twentieth centuries, the influence of the Enlightenment has extended far beyond Europe. Most cultures around the world have been affected. Societies throughout the global village both embrace and reject the global influence of Enlightenment philosophy.

The American Experiment

We shall especially explore one experiment which sought to embrace the philosophy of the Enlightenment in forming a political system. The experiment we explore occurred in another continent, North America. The United States Declaration of Independence is the epitome of Enlightenment thought:

> We hold these truths to be self-evident, that all men are created equal, that they are endowed by their Creator with certain unalienable Rights, that among these are Life, Liberty and the pursuit of Happiness.
>
> That to secure these rights, Governments are instituted among Men, deriving their just powers from the consent of the governed.
>
> That whenever any Form of Government becomes destructive of these ends, it is the Right of the People to alter or to abolish it, and to institute new Government, laying its foundation on such principles and organizing its powers in such form, as to them shall seem most likely to effect their Safety and Happiness.
>
> (The Declaration of Independence, July 4, 1776)

a new age document ↓

The leaders of the American experiment were proponents of the Enlightenment. That was the foundation of the Constitution which they formed with its Bill of Rights; balance of powers between legislative, judicial, and administrative branches of government; and elections for government officials. These all reveal a worldview which had been informed by the Enlightenment. This is especially true of the separation of church and state which is a significant characteristic of the American way of life.

The Enlightenment championed the inalienable rights of the individual to freedom, property, and the pursuit of happiness. These philosophers of two and three centuries ago were confident that their values based on reason were right, not only for Europeans, but for all humankind. In the American experience, this notion was enthusiastically embraced. The Americans believed the "self-evident" natural right of the individual to "the pursuit of Happiness" is universally valid. The Americans were convinced that they were the pioneers for these rights, and had a "manifest destiny" to spread the good news of individual liberty and freedom throughout the earth.

The boundless space and opportunity which the Western frontiers provided helped to sustain these optimistic notions that the spread of personal freedom around the globe is inevitable. The mission of the United States of America was and is to help that happen.

Even more than two centuries after the Declaration of Independence, a U.S. presidential candidate can woo voters by proclaiming that this nation is the last best hope for humanity.

After the Americans had subdued the continental frontiers, they commenced expending increasing energy on their global manifest destiny. All the wars Americans have engaged in during the twentieth century have been interpreted as protecting or spreading the ideals of freedom and democracy. Even the Vietnam War was interpreted by political leaders as being an extraordinary act of national sacrifice and generosity on behalf of an oppressed people who desired the same freedoms Americans enjoyed.

In the hard political realities experienced in the confrontation with communism, those Enlightenment-inspired freedoms which Americans have sought to defend have occasionally degenerated mostly into the freedom to own property. Too often the right of Americans to own property in other lands has been the freedom most energetically defended. Especially in countries in the Caribbean and Central and South America, there has been frequent U.S. military and political intervention to protect the presumed right of U.S. property and business enterprise to function freely in the region.

Western Hegemony — influence, leadership

The Enlightenment provided a rationale and justification for European and U.S. hegemony in the world during the heyday of nineteenth- and twentieth-century colonialism. However, it also appears that the European colonial governments, who had been most influenced by the principles of freedom championed by the Enlightenment, were the most readily persuaded to retreat from the evils and improprieties of colonialism.

Portugal was never significantly influenced by the Enlightenment. Might this account for the fact that Portugal was the last European power to surrender control over an African colonial empire? On the other hand, Britain, a center of Enlightenment development, eventually accepted the call for freedom for India which Gandhi championed. That was the beginning of the mostly peaceful dismantling of Britain's vast global empire.

Yet the philosophers do not merit all the credit for a commitment to the ideals of freedom and human dignity. Although the church as viewed by the philosophers of the seventeenth and eighteenth centuries often functioned in a manner which seemed inimical to the happiness and fulfillment of the person, it is nevertheless true that the humane ideals which the philosophers cherished are nurtured by biblical Christian faith. The Christian gospel has often inspired and empowered the church to minister with and among oppressed people. That has been true throughout the colonial experience.

For example, I lived in East Africa when African nations were gaining independence from colonial Europe. At that time, 80 percent of the educational systems were operated by the churches. The churches were energizing communities and were encouraging the spread of secular education.

Although the church in mission often seemed to benefit from the presence of European colonial government, it is also true that in many situations the church was the most persistent and obnoxious adversary of the imperial system. Examples are the Jesuits in South America or the Church of England in South Africa. During the nineteenth century, the witness of the church was significant in ending the slave trade throughout the British Empire. Clusters of faithful Christians did oppose evils which dehumanize the person during an era of heady Western imperialism.

Of course, the church did not always and consistently function as a conscience. There were many tragic compromises with the colonial powers. For example, the strong anti-Christian bias of the first decades of the Chinese communist revolution was grounded in a century of obnoxious alliances between Christian missions and Western economic and political imperialism in China. The Enlightenment sometimes rightly critiqued the church for having a blind eye on human rights.

Global Secularization

This exploration accepts a divergence between secularization and secularism. As mentioned occasionally in previous chapters, secularization is the process of change, movement, and development in a humanizing direction. Secularism is a commitment to human development with little or no recognition of the Creator. In secularism humanity is at the center of the stage. Thus secularization may become secularism. This is what happened in the mainstream of the Enlightenment.

Yet the secularization process does not need to drive a culture into the embrace of secularism. Too often commitments to human development go to seed when that happens. The experience of Western culture suggests that secularism cannot sustain authentic secularization. Secularism lacks the moral and spiritual energy needed to sustain dynamic wholesome human development.

An astonishing phenomenon of the nineteenth and twentieth centuries is that a secular worldview similar to the Enlightenment has spread around the globe. This profound transformation is working like a leaven in the worldview of peoples everywhere. This is especially true of global urban culture. English is becoming the language which unites this universal urban secular culture.

There is a universal revolutionary change let loose which functions at a far deeper level than merely borrowing "ideas" or "practices" from Western culture. Western culture may have assisted the transformation process, but mere cultural transfer is hardly an adequate explanation for the pervasive worldwide disenchantment with the status quo so characteristic of the modern global community and especially urban culture. From whence has this disenchantment come?

Bishop Lesslie Newbigin[17] and professor Arend Theodoor van Leeuwen,[18] writing from different vantage points (India and the Netherlands) refer to this disenchantment with the status quo as the phenomenon of "secularization." They describe this as a powerful and irreversible process which is more and more attracting the whole community of humankind. They affirm that secularization is the conviction that there is movement and purpose in human history and that human development is right and possible.

Both Newbigin and van Leeuwen observe that secularization does not develop or spread through societies before the witness of the church is present. On the other hand, secularization occurs wherever biblical faith is present. That basic observation leads these scholars to conclude that the presence of the church is the seed which creates secularization. They are convinced that secularization is the progeny of biblical faith.

The presence of the Christian gospel in a society is the yeast which creates the conviction that history and the person have significance and purpose, that history is moving toward a future glorious fulfillment. The gospel is the yeast which functions to turn a society away from worldviews which believe that history is a meaningless cycle or that it hangs without real or significant movement.

Biblical faith informs a culture that the good heavens and earth are not divine, nature is understandable, and the earth can and should be made better through human enterprise committed to the well-being and progress of people. Even though only a few people in a culture may explicitly embrace the Christian gospel, nevertheless, as the lifestyle, perspectives, and biblical narratives emanating from the Christian community begin to penetrate the culture, a serendipitous result is secularization. Once a people have glimpsed this invitation to human freedom and development, there is no turning back.

The Dyak chief of West Kalimantan described in chapter seven is an excellent example of the relationship between the Christian faith and secularization. For centuries these people of the rivers had functioned in an ontocratic worldview which believed that capricious spirits caused natural phenomena. Life revolved mostly around the need to pacify these spirits through sacrifice and entreaty. Squawking birds were the omens of the spirits. At least annually human sacrifice was required by the spirits.

Now all of this was changing. The sacrifices were offered no more. Squawking birds were hardly noticed. The developing Christian congregation had developed a thriving medical clinic and agricultural development project. Literacy was being introduced. As the village chief explained it to me, the church had brought enlightenment to his people in just a few years.

The words of this goateed man with his large straw umbrella hat; this illiterate Dyak chief of a small clan of three hundred river people in the isolated jungles of West Kalimantan; this man whose words were accompanied by the croaking of frogs from the flooded river which flowed around and under the village homes elevated on wooden piles cut from the forest; this man who was interested in knowing how large the river is which flows past my village, for he could not conceive of traveling from village to village without a river highway—the words of this man seemed to have come right from the mouth of the eighteenth-century French interpreter of the Enlightenment, Voltaire.

This is what the Dyak chief said to me: "Now we think, plan, and do our work. In this way we experience progress. It is much easier being a chief now than it used to be because we don't worry about the squawking of the birds any more."

The philosophers of the Enlightenment would have substituted "religion" for the "squawking of the birds." Yet the meaning is the same. The Dyak chief and his people have begun drinking from the stream of secularization. And the waters of that stream are refreshing. The power of the "birds" of religion who inhibit human development have been broken forever. Reason has usurped the role of the "birds" in human planning. There will be no turning back.

Nevertheless, the Dyak chief has not really become Voltaire, at least not yet. Although he is drinking from the stream of secularization, he has not yet become a secularist. The Dyak Christians include worship and prayer in their planning and life together. The church and the Christian gospel have revealed to them that God loves them and invites them to become part of his family who are committed to joyous human development. They have discovered that God is opposed to all forms of superstition. They have become a people inspired by the gift of hope.

However, the boundary between a commitment to secularization and secularism can be easily traversed. At the church-operated riverside medical clinic in West Kalimantan, I observed no praying for the ill children who received medication from the Indonesian Christian nurse. They received only pills. That act of healing through science without any prayer was surprising in this Dyak society where the spiritual dimension of existence had always been so central.

I could almost feel the thought processes of the Christian nurse. If the natural laws related to healing are understandable and reliable, why pray? Once enlightenment happens, why consider God? Do people really need God to understand and subdue the good, reliable, and understandable earth? Does humanity really need to know and obey God to establish a just, righteous, and harmonious society? Does Jesus have any relevance to a people who have been freed from the bondage of "religion" or the "birds"? As for spirits and gods, were they always only imagination anyway?

Global Secularism

The manner in which a people answer those questions determines whether God or humankind will be at the center of the secularization process. When a society places the person in the center of the stage and nudges God into the irrelevant and unnoticed periphery, that is secularism, and that is what has happened in the European Enlightenment. Marxism has been one of the most powerful expressions of secularism; that will be the theme of the next chapter.

A characteristic of modernity is that secular perspectives, which are skeptical of the dynamic involvement of God either in the natural order or in history, pervade the global community. These perspectives are packaged in various philosophical wrappings. Some examples are atheism, deism, agnosticism, humanism, New Age movement. Although the Christian faith may have originally planted the seeds of secularization, these and other such ideologies which prevail in the modern global village are not biblically grounded.

The spirit which induced Thomas Jefferson to scissor from the biblical gospels all references to the miracles of Jesus is now a global phenomenon. The conviction that nature and history function autonomously of any divinities, spirits, or God is present in societies around the world. Although the biblical accounts of God's acts in history have nurtured and sustained the perspectives which originally formed the secularization processes, now that the phenomenon is under way, secular ideologies often replace faith in God. A big bang formed the universe with all its complex intricacies. The God of biblical theism is irrelevant.

Recounting his wartime travels, Curzio Malaparte tells of a conversation at a 1943 diplomatic dinner in Helsinki. The guests were conversing about a communist prisoner who had killed the prison chaplain because the pastor had challenged the prisoner's atheism.

A guest commented, "He had tried to kill God in the pastor."

The Turkish ambassador elaborated, "The murder of God is in the air; it is an element of modern civilization."[19]

Free Enterprise

The Enlightenment gave birth to the free enterprise theory of economic growth. It also birthed Marxism, which the next chapter explores. Both systems are committed to the accumulation of material wealth through human enterprise. In a free enterprise or capitalist system, the individual entrepreneur gains freedom to acquire personal wealth. The right to private property is a cornerstone of the free enterprise system. Market forces determine prices and wages and which products shall be produced.

Adam Smith (d. 1790) was the seminal philosopher of the free enterprise system. His *Wealth of the Nations* was published in the same year as the United States Declaration of Independence. Adam Smith perceived that greed is a natural law and should be the engine which empowers the economies of nations. Of course, Smith and his fellow economists gave greed a more respectable name—self-interest. He worried about the evil consequences of a capitalism not grounded in ethics; the system could only function wholesomely in a healthy ethical environment.[20] Greed with no ethical moorings would be a cataclysm.

The fundamental theory is that if people are encouraged to function in accord with their natural inclinations of self-interest, market forces will bring about good for all. Smith spoke of the invisible hand which functions in market forces, blessing the whole society

when an economy is structured in accordance with natural laws.[21]
The ideal system is free enterprise, which provides opportunity for
individual initiative. In such a system, self-interest produces incredible wealth which benefits the society as a whole.

In a free enterprise economy, market forces will temper the inclination of greedy people to exploit others. For example, the insensi-
tively greedy merchant will lose customers. Yet self-interest empowers the whole system. It creates dynamic economies.

The free enterprise capitalist system has produced enormous
wealth in the global village. It has also created ecological disaster.
Market forces cannot control the rape of the sea and land by greedy
people. Natural law as championed in the free enterprise system is
not enough to rescue our planet from destruction. The quest for immediate wealth must be tempered by concern for the well-being of
the earth and the survival of future generations.

Future hope and responsibility must temper greed. Responsible
governments everywhere are discovering that greed must be controlled. Otherwise the planet will be devastated. Nations and governments must incorporate future hope into their laws governing human
economic enterprise. Governments and societies must set boundaries.

It is also evident that the invisible hand is not working well in
bringing blessing to the global village as a whole. This hand,
thought to distribute the fruit of self-interest in a manner which benefits all, has in many circumstances become the hand which takes
from the poor and gives to the rich.

During the 1980s, the people living in absolute poverty in our
global community increased from 500 million to 1,100 million. Huge
disequilibriums are developing between the rich north and the poor
south. By the beginning of the 1990s, the huge region of Africa south
of the Sahara was producing an annual gross national product equal
to that of tiny Belgium. Much of this poverty-wealth disparity has
developed in free enterprise global systems.

On a recent flight to Peru, my nighttime reading included a section
in the *New York Times* describing the economic plight of that country.
I learned that the median income for a government civil servant in
the capitol, Lima, was one-tenth of what was required to support a
family of four at poverty level in that city! At that time Peru was paying $50,000,000 monthly in interest rates to Western banking systems.

In 1990 the poorest countries, in the global community transferred
$38,000,000,000 to the wealthy countries through interest payments.
In most impoverished countries, the net flow of wealth is away from

the poor and into the banks of the wealthy. Self-interest, which functions without restraints in a free enterprise global system, contributes to poverty, suffering, and death for one-fifth of the global community.

The Problem of Evil

The pioneers of the Enlightenment were optimistic about human nature and enthusiastic about the capabilities of reason to discover and apply the good. They encouraged decision makers to form social institutions so as to give the individual freedom to think and do as she chooses. Then all would be well.

This basic optimism concerning human nature was not sufficiently alert to the persistent reality of evil.[22] The twentieth-century German experience shook the confidence of Western culture. By the first third of the century, Germany had developed one of the most sophisticated and open-minded intellectual establishments the human family had ever enjoyed. Yet that is where the Holocaust happened. A characteristic of the Enlightenment and of all subsequent Western culture is that there is an unwillingness to recognize or deal with the very real phenomenon of evil.

Yet what is evil? What is good? The pioneers of the Enlightenment believed that human reason alone could discover and apply the good. However, three centuries ago they functioned in a Christianized society which had a fairly clear consensus regarding the nature of the good. That consensus has weakened in modern Western and global society, where pluralism abounds.

In earlier chapters we referred to Allan Bloom, a twentieth-century U.S. philosopher who stands firmly in the tradition of the Enlightenment. His popular book *The Closing of the American Mind* describes the easy drift into relativism which characterizes modern North American society. Bloom insists that relativism is a betrayal of the clear, reasoned thinking which the Enlightenment demanded. Nevertheless, he seems to flounder in his quest for a way out of the quicksand of our moral relativism.[23]

For Americans of the last half of the twentieth century, the only real virtue is nonjudgmental openness to all values, no matter how contradictory they are. In the face of pluralistic national and global communities, the highest virtue proclaimed throughout the societies in which the Enlightenment has triumphed is this: be open-minded! Both the absence of clear moral perspectives and a philosophy of life which exalts the individual pursuit of happiness are inviting Western culture into hedonism.

Recall that Hindu philosophy and religion also embraces relativism. In this regard, Hinduism, or movements derived from Hinduism, are attractive to modern Western societies. The Hindu option does not place on the person with philosophical inclinations the requirement to discover and apply universal morals. Neither does it accept the biblical orientation which insists that, although cultural diversity is right, there is one righteous God, one humanity, and one morality grounded in self-giving love and commitment to the well-being of others.

The fathers of the Enlightenment would be appalled that their idealism has been distorted into an easy-going relativism. They, just as their ancient Greek counterparts, were confident that rational thought and intuition could perceive clear, universal moral virtue. Alas, instead of continuing the quest for that universal good, the new morality celebrates pluralism in the global village with only two foundational commitments: Enjoy yourself. Be open-minded.

a hopeless state of being

The American Crisis

The U.S. experiment with a democracy grounded in the principles of the Enlightenment is an instructive example of the dialogue between faith and secularism in a secularizing society. In the mid-1980s, Robert N. Bellah and a team of social scientists at the University of California published a study, *Habits of the Heart*, which described and interpreted case studies of mainstream American culture.[24] The intention of this study was to develop a profile of the American worldview some two centuries after launching this experiment in democracy.

The study demonstrates that there are two major themes which inform American commitments. First is the biblical covenantal theme. The Pilgrims landing at Plymouth Rock is the archetype of that theme. They came to the New World seeking religious freedom. In the Massachusetts Bay Colony, they formed a covenant community in which they intentionally sought to apply the principles of biblical faith (especially Old Testament). They lived with an awesome awareness of the transcendent authority of God. A biblical covenantal theme has always been a significant influence in the American worldview.

The second theme comes into American culture from the Enlightenment. The archetype of this theme is the Declaration of Independence. In that declaration there is one particular theme which has become dominant in American society—the pursuit of happiness! The study demonstrates that in American culture the pursuit of happiness is largely interpreted in individualistic terms.

The several centuries in which Americans struggled with the con-

quest of the Western frontier significantly enhanced the individualism theme. By the late twentieth century, freedom and individualism
had become the dominant theme in American culture. Americans believe the purpose of life is the pursuit of individual happiness.

The Enlightenment theme of individual freedom has overwhelmed
the biblical covenantal themes in American culture. There is almost no
awareness of God from the perspective of biblical faith. This is not to
say that Americans are atheists. Indeed not! But the function of God
in the American worldview is different than in biblical faith.

For most Americans, God's function is to assist them in the pursuit of individual happiness. Largely absent in the culture is any
awareness of God, the transcendent one, who confronts the person
calling for repentance and righteous living. There is almost no
awareness of the church functioning as a covenant community. Few
people would consider seeking specific moral guidance from the
church, because such decisions are exclusively an individual matter.

The individual pursuit of happiness overwhelms other values
and commitments. Enduring covenantal relationships are incomprehensible in a society where individual self-fulfillment is paramount.
Even a relationship as intimate and significant for the well-being of
society as the family is expendable in the interest of the individual
pursuit of happiness. At every level, relationships take on a contractual character. They endure only as long as the individual is experiencing self-fulfillment.

Surely this individualistic development in American culture is a fulfillment of Jean-Jacques Rousseau's worst fears. Just over two centuries ago, he worried that the Enlightenment could self-destruct on the
shoals of individualism. His *Social Contract* was an attempt to bring a
corrective into the movement. He argued that personal fulfillment
could develop authentically only in communities of accountability.

Just over two centuries later, Bellah and his colleagues lament the
way individualism is sabotaging precious qualities in American culture. They worry that American society cannot endure without a revival of covenantal commitments.[25]

Commitment to the individual pursuit of happiness, when combined with the power over nature which scientific technology offers,
is creating ecological disaster. Bellah and his colleagues lament
modern American culture, in which there is only a whisper of
awareness of accountability to the Creator. In biblical faith, humanity is commanded to subdue the earth—but with accountability to
the Creator. The biblical mandate is for humankind to work in part-

nership with God to preserve, care for, and develop the good earth.

The Enlightenment encouraged Western culture to ignore these foundational commitments of biblical faith. Creation became nature, which is governed by natural laws. These laws function independent of any relationship to a creator. Accountability to the Creator has been severed.

Is the Enlightenment Helpful?

The second chapter in our exploration of global gods identified issues of global human survival and well-being. Each subsequent chapter has reflected on aspects of those issues. The Enlightenment has been a powerful influence in the global community and yeast permeating responses to global issues. These summary statements identify ways the Enlightenment informs global culture.

1. The Enlightenment has been supremely an urban movement. Modern global urban culture is really Enlightenment culture. It undergirds a worldview which nurtures the technological commitments required to sustain modern urban societies.

The English language is a significant medium of communication in this global urban culture. Modern communication systems link all these urban centers of global culture. Television and radio are significant facilitators of global Enlightenment values.

2. The Enlightenment desacralized creation. The universe is now referred to as nature rather than as creation. While it may seem awesome and exhilarating to assume responsibility to use nature for human desire without reference to the Creator, the consequence is often ecological disaster.

Perhaps the ultimate crime against creation has been the development of nuclear weapons. If they are ever used on a massive scale, the good earth will be ruined. If there is no Creator to whom we are accountable, then the destruction of the earth is our right if we so choose.

3. Hope for a better future may help to inhibit irresponsible use of the good earth. Yet a deficiency of modern Enlightenment culture is the crisis of hope. Is it possible for a culture to sustain a sense of hope and purpose without awareness of transcendent reality?

If the universe consists of only more and more galaxies to be discovered, but there is no God providing purpose to the whole phenomenon, then human existence really has no ultimate purpose. The consequence is malaise. Why be concerned about the future?

4. The Enlightenment championed the worth of the person. A positive development has been increasing global concern for human rights. This includes the affirmation of pluralism in the context of secular government.

5. Global Enlightenment culture has now come to the place where it cannot conceive of universal truth. Human reason has been enthroned as the center of the universe. Reason left to itself is capable of absorbing enormous quantities of data and developing fascinating philosophical speculation. Yet coherent universal truth eludes modern Enlightenment societies.

The test of time has demonstrated that the parents of the Enlightenment were misguided in their assumption that rational reflection would bring forth self-evident truth. Enlightenment culture celebrates personal values, but it cannot comprehend universal truth claims. The consequence is moral, cultural, and religious relativism.

6. However, Enlightenment culture has created several "scientific" ideologies that have claimed universal political validity. Politics became ideological; so-called rational ideas become ideologies that transcend the parameters of the nation. American manifest destiny is one expression of the synthesis of ideology and the political in a mission that moves far beyond the constraints of a national political system.

Ideology married to politics was the root inspiration that catapulted the global community into World War II. This was a war of political ideologies—Nazism, Stalinism, and American manifest destiny—in collision. All were inspired and nurtured by the rationalism of the Enlightenment. Each was an ideology firmly grounded in scientific self-evident truth. Let the world be aware. Rational ideologies married to political systems can be treacherous![26]

7. The Enlightenment in its primal vision was a champion of human freedom. This theme has powerfully contributed to the movements for independence among colonized nations, beginning with the United States in the late eighteenth century.

In more recent times, the freedom theme threatens the fabric of nation-states as ethnic-national groups seek greater autonomy. In some circumstances the Enlightenment notions of the social contract have been revived, as for example in the nations of the former Soviet Union. The perception is that ethnic-national communities should have the right voluntarily to decide the issues of participation in a nation state or community of nations. Such ideas place enormous strains on the political and economic fabric of nation-states.

8. The Enlightenment also affirmed the integrity of the person. Commitments such as universal education for all are one of the consequences. Even in the poorest nations, universal education for the children has become a reasonable expectation. Yet it is important to recognize that in the developing world, the church has often been in the vanguard of facilitating that commitment.

9. The Enlightenment has sown the seeds of individualism in cultures. Some social scientists warn that Western societies are in danger of disintegration because of an overemphasis on the right of the individual to seek individual self-fulfillment.

10. The application to economic theory of the individualism and self-interest which the Enlightenment fostered in Western societies has produced astonishing wealth. Yet those same theories have contributed to tragic decline into deep poverty for hundreds of millions of people.

11. The individual self-fulfillment theme in global culture is creating havoc with the family. For too many people, covenantal relationships are sacred no more. The thought of self-sacrifice and self-discipline for the well-being of the family is an echo from a distant past for many who are drinking from the wells of modern global urban Enlightenment culture.

12. The Enlightenment has not done well in reducing the frequency or fury of war. In the wake of the Enlightenment, France experienced a bloody revolution. The United States was the first nation created in the glow of the Enlightenment. That nation was born in bloodshed.

The quest for individual freedom which the Enlightenment championed has too often inspired war against oppressors. Other wars have been fought to extend the wonderful fruit of Enlightenment culture to those less fortunate. During the nineteenth century, colonial wars were too often justified under the mandate of extending the benefits of Western civilization.

The humanization themes of the Enlightenment may have helped to instill conscience in the liberal democracies of the West against the use of excessive violence in their colonial empires. Or was it the conscience of the church? In the twentieth century, England surrendered much of her vast empire, in most cases through amicable agreements with the leadership of freedom movements in the colonies.

13. The Enlightenment has been a powerful movement for change. It is a desacralizing movement which encourages the replacement of

religious or faith perspectives with secular commitments. In modern times these perspectives have become adversarial to religious institutions and beliefs. This is especially so when those institutions or beliefs are perceived to restrict individual freedom.

14. The Enlightenment critiqued superstition. It has also been critical of religion as a whole. It is especially ruthless against religious expressions which are superstitious and dehumanizing. In this way, the critical spirit of the Enlightenment may actually be a gift to religions by inviting them to rid the movements of superstitious beliefs and dehumanizing practices.

The Enlightenment perspective demands that people of faith be prepared to give account of the basis of their belief. Evidence is required if the believer is to function with credibility. On what basis do Hindus believe in the reincarnation of the soul, or Muslims that the Qur'an has been revealed by God, or Christians in the bodily resurrection of Jesus? What is the data on which belief is founded?

Is the data credible? The Enlightenment worldview is intolerant of belief not grounded on reliable evidence. This questioning approach to the truth claims of believers might also be a gift of the Enlightenment to the global community. Authentic religion requires evidence; otherwise it might be only illusion.

15. It appears that in relationship to theistic faith, the Enlightenment worldview has become a closed-minded system. The modern spirit of the Enlightenment seems to have developed a bias against considering that God might act in history or creation.

A Secular Gospel

The global village is entangled in a paradox. On the one hand, there is universal intrigue with the humane and technological qualities of the Enlightenment culture. A sign of this intrigue is the voracious quest throughout the world for learning a European language—English, French, German, Spanish. English is especially attractive around the world. English has become an important window through which a non-Western person can observe Enlightenment culture. That is the chief reason for the quest for a European language such as English.

On the other hand, there is apprehension concerning the quality of modern Western societies. Other peoples perceive that Western culture is becoming decadent. There is anxiety concerning the ecological disaster which uninhibited technological growth has created.

There is dismay that it is hard to discover hope in Western culture. The individualism and moral relativism of late twentieth-century Western culture nurtures a debilitating hedonism. The huge U.S. budget deficits which commenced in the early 1980s appall the world community. Our friends ask why the United States is digging her own grave. Western culture is squandering her economic and moral capital.

It is true that seventeenth- and eighteenth-century church structures and hierarchy often opposed the humane, political, or scientific aspirations of the Enlightenment. Nevertheless, it is also true that the presence of biblical faith contributed significantly to the invigorating foment and worldview which enabled the Enlightenment. The synergistic interaction with Greek philosophy was also important.

A salient quality of the Enlightenment was hope. The original taproot of that hope was the conviction that God is working in history to bring about the fulfillment of the kingdom of God. However, Western culture now ignores and even denies these spiritual roots which have nurtured the flowering of scientific methodology, the sense of hope and anticipation which is the essence of commitment to human and economic development, and the humane qualities, rights, and freedoms which intrigue so many others in the global community.

It might be that others from non-Western societies will become the true preservers of an enlightenment and secularization which nurtures the qualities of human dignity, freedom, hope, and development which the European Enlightenment sought. These are the people who, like the Dyak chief, seek expressions of secularization nurtured by faith in the Creator.

An example are the Quechua Indians in the Cusco region of the high Andes of Peru. They are descendants of the Incas. Recently I met with a medical and economic development team serving in Christian congregations of Quechua people.

"The worldview of these mountain people is perplexing," confided the North American development team.

"We will invest half a day planning for community uplift. Then they conclude the discussions with prayer, singing, festive worship, climaxed with exuberant informal conversation."

I queried. "Could it be that their faith is forming them into an authentic development community?"

Theirs is an enlightenment whose taproot is faith in the Creator of the good earth who loves them and energizes with hope.

Interestingly, the Quechua now want to learn Spanish. Why?

Spanish is the official language of Peru. Yet there is more to the quest for Spanish than integration into national society. Spanish will open a door for Quechua participation in global Enlightenment culture!

Reflection

1. In what ways had biblical faith and the church planted the seeds in European soil which brought forth the Enlightenment?

2. Assess the effect of the Enlightenment on the global community.

3. What might be the danger to the ecological well-being of the earth of humankind considering the earth as "nature" rather than "creation?"

4. Account for the persistent interest the global community has in understanding Western culture. What is attractive about Western culture? What aspects are not attractive?

5. Account for the changes taking place in the village of the Dyak chief.

12

Utopia Without the Gods

Marxism

CLANKING METAL on pavement and the rumble of powerful internal combustion engines awakened me. It was just after midnight on October 21, 1969. Dawn revealed the source of the ominous sounds in the night. A military tank blocked the entrance to our compound; the muzzle of its huge gun faced our home. The commander ordered us to remain in our homes.

We obeyed.

The morning news from Radio Mogadishu revealed that overnight all major population centers in the Somali Republic had been liberated by the military. We were informed that a revolutionary council now governed the nation. Marxism-Leninism was the ideology which would guide the new revolutionary government. Somalis could now boast of an October revolution, as did their Russian communist comrades. Parliament was dissolved and the name of the nation was changed from Somali Republic to Somali Democratic Republic.

In time the direction of the new revolutionary government became more clear. The principles of scientific socialism were to replace those of bourgeois democracy in governing this nation in the northeastern Horn of Africa, which generated a gross national product of less than $100 per capita per year.

Nomads mused in astonishment at the radio broadcasts from their nation's capital explaining the nature of scientific socialism.

Rumors wended through the oral news grapevines that even the camels would be socialized. This was a startling possibility in a nation in which 90 percent of the three million inhabitants were nomads, some of whom followed their precious camel herds on circuitous grazing patterns of two thousand miles annually.

The differences are enormous between nineteenth-century industrializing Europe, which nurtured the worldview of Karl Marx, and the nomadic culture of contemporary Somalia. The mainstream of Somali nomadic culture is similar to that of the biblical Abraham of four thousand years ago. Furthermore, the Somali culture is thoroughly Islamized. Muslim faith runs deep throughout this culture, for the process of developing the Muslim community in this region had already begun during the lifetime of Muhammad. In contrast, Marxism is a modern atheistic secular philosophy

Why should a poor preindustrial nomadic Islamic society be attracted to the nineteenth-century atheistic ideology of Karl Marx and Friedrich Engels? It is evident that the Marxist vision of global community enticed the imagination of a significant cadre of Somali decision makers. That same attractiveness has appealed to many underdeveloped societies globally.

A Discredited Global System?

However, as the decade of the 1980s came to closure, Marxist ideology began to suffer significant discredit. This was especially true in Eastern Europe. The swiftness of the dismissal of Marxist governments in Eastern Europe in 1989 and 1990, and even in the Soviet Union in 1991, sent tremors throughout the earth. The transformation was surprising and astonishing.

"Do West Germans ever consider the possibility of the unification of East and West Germany?" I queried a West German friend as we drove the autobahn between Munich and Stuttgart.

That was late September 1989. My driver companion looked at me in disbelief at my naivete. He responded forthrightly, "Any thought of East and West German unification is so far from possibility that we never speak of it. Marxism is a powerful ideology. We see no possibility of change in East Germany."

Only weeks later the Berlin wall came down! Three months later on Christmas 1989, my wife and I listened in our home in Pennsylvania to a live broadcast of the East Berlin and West Berlin orchestras playing together. I wept with joy during the final movement. It was Beethoven's orchestral and vocal crescendo of hope, the German national anthem celebrating the brotherhood and sisterhood of humankind.

Two years later, on Christmas Day 1991, the hammer-and-sickle flag of the Soviet Union was lowered from its pole above the Kremlin where it had flown for over seventy years. The Soviet communist system had been discredited and abandoned. On that same day, Mikhail Gorbachev resigned as president of the Soviet Union. The Soviet Union itself was officially dissolved.

All these events had global reverberations. It is difficult to assess direct causality linking the various developments in global Marxism during this period. Yet it was not only in Eastern Europe and the Soviet Union that there were astonishing transformations. One other example will suffice.

During that same Christmas season that the West and East Berlin orchestras played together, Somalia was also caught in a swirl of change. Apocalyptic economic catastrophe and interclan violence had thoroughly discredited the twenty-year Marxist regime. During the closing days of 1990, the regime was violently overthrown. The destruction was unbelievable, for the regime turned its artillery on the capital city, Mogadishu. The Soviet ambassador fled for his life to the fortified U.S. embassy and was helicoptered to the safety of an aircraft carrier offshore in the Indian Ocean. Hundreds of other expatriates escaped in a similarly undignified manner.

The aftermath of the overthrow of the regime was anarchy, destruction, death, hunger, and utter collapse. In the north over one million mines were buried in the sands in scattered locations by the retreating troops. For several years no political entity emerged with sufficient credibility to lead the nation in reconciliation. Only anarchy remained in the wake of the discredited Marxist regime.

This does not suggest that Marxism has no further attraction. The discrediting of Marxist ideology should not delude us with the notion that Marxism is dead. Several Asian Marxist governments dug in for a holding action; they sought to preserve their versions of a modified Marxism.

Marxism still possesses a fascinating attraction for many of the world's dispossessed poor. Through electoral processes socialists (communists) have regained control of several formerly communist governments, although these communist political parties are now committed to democratic rather than revolutionary processes. However, there is little indication that revolutionary violence inspired by communist ideology has ameliorated in other areas of the global village. This is especially true in regions where the poor are hungry. Inspired by Marxism, they may use revolutionary violence in the struggle against the rich for food. An example has been the Shining Path guerrillas of Peru.

Marxist Ideology

Marxism has been especially attractive to societies whose religious or worldview orientation did not seem to encourage economic development and justice. Whenever religious systems are indifferent to the felt needs of a people for authentic human development, Marxism provides an attractive solution to the human predicament. This has been especially true if key decision makers in the society have been influenced by the winds of secularization. If religion seems to get in the way of human progress, the Marxist disdain of religious faith can become a tempting alternative.

Marxism is a secularism. Recall that the last chapter contrasted the phenomenon of secularization with that of secularism. Secularization is the conviction that the person is exceedingly significant and that human and economic development in history is right and feasible. Secularization is the notion that history has purpose, that it is moving toward a good goal. Secularization is the conviction that the good gifts of nature should be understood and marshaled in a manner which blesses both humankind and nature.

On the other hand, secularism takes the commitments of secularization and transforms them into an ideology in which faith in God is irrelevant or disparaged. Marxism is such an ideology.

During the last half of the twentieth century, until the discrediting of Marxism in at least a dozen communist nation-states, Marxism had become the most influential and widespread secular ideology of modern times. A third of humanity lived in societies governed by communist political institutions.

Revolution the Solution

The early conceptualists of communism, Karl Marx and his later associate Friedrich Engels, were sensitive spirits troubled by the appalling injustices spawned by the European industrial revolution. They lived and wrote during the heyday of the early industrial revolution. This was the era of which Charles Dickens wrote; recall *Oliver Twist*. Such thinkers were distressed by the evils the industrial revolution spawned.

At that time European Christianized society as a whole was too insensitive to the exploitation of the working class poor. Marx and Engels were angered because too many Christians in power used religion to solidify and justify their privileges and wealth. They were convinced that a religious system, which used the promise of heaven after death to justify a lack of concern for poor children working long hours in dangerous factories, was evil and cruel. The journey into atheism for Marx and Engels was a reaction against God-talk and religion which had no concern for the poor.

Karl Marx was a child of the Enlightenment. He was also a child of Judaism and the Christian faith. His lawyer father was the descendant of a long line of Jewish rabbis. Nevertheless in 1817 his father was baptized into the Lutheran church, probably to escape the repression of the Jews in Prussia. It is likely that he became a Lutheran to gain the right to practice law in Christianized Prussia. However, Karl's mother continued her practice of Judaism.

An essay in his high school graduation thesis discussed John 15:1-14, in which Christ is described as the vine and the believers as the branches. Marx described the union of believers with Christ. Yet the essay shows little comprehension of Christian faith; he portrayed Christianity as the highest moral development of humankind. The thesis reveals that as a high school student Karl Marx was already headed toward the conviction that human moral self-development could bring about the perfect society.[1]

Marx's university studies introduced him to the philosophical streams which had formed the Enlightenment. He was also influenced by the later German philosophers Georg W. F. Hegel and L. Feuerbach, who built on themes which were developing in the Enlightenment.

Hegel fully secularized the biblical vision of the kingdom of God. In biblical faith, God is acting in history to bring about the fulfillment of his eternal kingdom at the *eschaton* (end). The kingdom has already begun, especially in the life of the covenant people. All history is being influenced by and receives its purpose from the drama of God's initiative to bring to pass his intention to establish his kingdom of righteousness and peace forever. Hegel's philosophy took this biblical vision and replaced God with the notion of the ideal.

Hegel agreed with the Christians that history was on the move. However, for him the inspiration and power behind that forward movement is not God; it is a human vision of the ideal. The ideal is always counter-balanced by the real situation, which represents an antithesis to the ideal. The tension between ideal and antithesis is eventually resolved by a synthesis of the two. This synthesis is progress. The new synthesis in turn becomes the antithesis to a fresh ideal, which eventually creates a new synthesis. Thus history moves forward empowered by the creative tension between the real and the ideal, the antithesis and the thesis.

Through the pen of Marx, Hegel's notion of the tension between the ideal and the real became the revolutionary tension between social classes. For Marx historical materialism is the driving force in history. The scientific analysis of history demonstrates that the story of humanity consists of the struggle between economic classes. Revolution is the method through which the struggle between classes is resolved.

Religion an Illusion

Feuerbach provided Marx with the intellectual equipment for his atheism. Feuerbach perceived the belief in God as a person's need-inspired psycho projection. Marx agreed, but modified Feuerbach's notion by viewing belief in God as a projection of the felt needs of social classes.

In high school classrooms around the world today, students learn that Marx believed religion to be "the opiate of the people." This is to say that social classes project a concept of divinity which gives them comfort. The god whom the privileged classes invent promises to reward those who help themselves. The god whom the impoverished classes invent promises to give them heaven when they die. For both the rich and the poor, God-talk is comfort-talk. It is an opiate which enables social classes to escape from taking responsibility in the real world

Marx observed that the church and religious institutions tend to ally themselves with the status quo. They seem to promulgate images of God which induce the various social classes to accept their state in life. Karl Marx proclaimed that all of these divinities are nonsense. For Marx, "the exercise of critical judgment shifted from heaven to earth, from religion to natural right, from theology to politics."[2]

Biblical faith would agree with Feuerbach and Marx that the divinities or the perceptions of God which are the psycho-projection of the person or social classes are false. They must be denied any authority over a person or society. God in the Bible is the God who calls people to pilgrimage and movement, not the status quo. He is the God who requires societies to seek justice, not the comfort of the privileged. God in the Bible confronts, calls for repentance, urges people to leave the false gods whom their minds have invented. In Marx's righteous rage against the false divinities who bless the impoverishment of the masses, he missed the God of biblical faith who identifies with the poor and confronts those who exploit the oppressed.

Friedrich Engels became a friend and associate of Karl Marx. For twenty years he lived amid the cotton mills of Lancashire, England. Although he was the son of a wealthy industrialist, he identified with the working class poor among whom he lived. He bitterly opposed both his father's Christian pietism and his capitalism. He rejected the faith of his father, which seemed to ignore the plight of the poor.[3]

Marx and Engels radically secularized the biblical vision of the kingdom of God. Marx's thought is clearly developed in his writings over a period of forty years. Engels assisted Marx in writing many of these statements, the most noteworthy of which is *Das Kapital*, which they developed over thirty years. Their brief *Communist Manifesto* is a succinct, readily understood statement of communist ideology. The kingdom Marx and Engels wrote about is a classless society, created not by the power of God, but by the revolutions of people.

The eventual universal triumph of the classless society is inevitable, because natural laws determine the course of history, just as they determine the functions of nature. The laws of history are economic forces which can be analyzed and understood through the study of dialectical materialism. The triumph of communism was certain because the philosophy was founded on scientific truth.

> In the confident spirit of the Enlightenment, Marx was convinced of the ultimate triumph of science and reason in history. The purpose of his life and work was to establish a science of society as reliable as the natural science already triumphantly interpreting the nineteenth-century material order.[4]

A Global Plan
Marxism is skeptical of democracy, for the wealthy classes influence and distort the democratic processes. Only revolution can really bring about the classless society and justice.

The blueprint for a Marxist revolution is clearly developed in the writings of Marx and Engels. Other communist theoreticians and practitioners further developed and applied the theory. They include revolutionaries such as V. I. Lenin who led the October Revolution of 1917 in Russia, or Mao Tse-Tung who led the Long March of the Chi-

nese communist revolutionaries from Manchuria south to eventual
victory over the Nationalists in 1949. These Marxist revolutionaries
describe similar themes for the establishment of a communist society.
The communist plan is straightforward. After the revolution the
proletariat (laborers) must establish a dictatorship. Reeducation of
those with bourgeois (capitalist) tendencies must commence. Those
who resist reeducation must be dealt with. Property must be redis-
tributed with the goal of achieving equality.

As equality is achieved, people will benefit from all that is needed for a wholesome, happy life. Communism will create a good and
generous society, for it is the quest to acquire property which feeds
evil and avarice. Once the personal quest for property and wealth is
impossible, society will become increasingly good and generous.

This beneficial situation will lead to the decline of religion, which
feeds on the material and social needs of people. When a society
provides for all human material and social needs, there will be no
further function for religion. It will wither away.

The goal of communism is revealed in this statement of fundamental communist commitment: from each according to his ability
and to each according to his need.[5]

The proletariat must remain the governing class until the collective mass of people really does function in accordance with the communist ideal. As this goal begins to be achieved, the governing proletariat can begin to relax its dictatorial responsibilities. Gradually
government can diminish, until its role becomes only that of a regu-
latory function such as directing traffic and managing the flow of
goods. This is the "withering away of the state." Engels wrote,
"Government over persons is replaced by the administration of
things and the direction of the processes of production."[6]

The withering of the state and religion may be the ideal. Yet Marx
and Engels never clearly spelled out how to achieve these transitions.
Mao Tse-Tung thought of an ongoing revolution. That is what the Chinese cultural revolution was all about. Religious and political institutions where attacked. Mao perceived that any relaxation of firm guidance from the proletariat ruling class would be a long time coming.

Marx and Engels writing in the mid-nineteenth century were de-
lighted because in some regions of Europe the processes of revolution had reduced the classes to only two—the proletariat and the
bourgeoisie, or the laborers and the owners of capital. After thousands of years of human history, the laws of dialectical materialism
had set the stage in this region of the world for the final revolution,

which would enable the establishment of the classless society. This is the inevitable destiny of history.

Dangers of Compassion

Yet Marx and Engels sometimes worried that the evolution of socialism in the industrialized democracies might soften the alienation between the proletariat and the bourgeoisie, thereby eroding the revolutionary furor of the working classes. That fear was justified. Especially in England, the nineteenth century was marked by periods of significant renewal in the churches which produced a deepened social conscience.

Recall that our earlier exploration of biblical faith described specific social and economic institutions in ancient Israel. These practices put a check on the greed of the wealthy and provided opportunities for the poor. The Jubilee is one such institution. The Jubilee ideal in biblical Israel was an attempt to soften the disparities of wealth through leveling devices such as the forgiveness of all debts every fifty years. At the same time, slaves were given their freedom. Another example is the prohibition against the charging of interest in the Hebrew Torah, a prohibition Islam also upholds. This commitment to the well-being of the poor and oppressed permeates the biblical Scriptures. The renewed churches of nineteenth-century England and Europe discovered in the biblical Scriptures great concern for the plight of the poor.

Even before Karl Marx could begin to dream of communism, Christian social conscience was prodding government and business to provide more humane working conditions for the poor. William Wilberforce was a key leader in this movement for Christian compassion, both in Britain and beyond. He is especially remembered for awakening Britain's conscience on the evils of slavery and the slave trade. This social conscience reached far beyond Britain. After the 1807 action by the British parliament to outlaw the slave trade in the empire, the British led and prodded the whole world toward the universal abolition of the slave trade and slavery.

In England, which had pioneered the industrial revolution, Christian compassion for the poor was translated into public policy. Active compassion softened the harsh edge between the bourgeoisie and the proletariat. For this reason as the nineteenth century progressed, the workers in industrialized Britain and Europe did not desire a revolution. They were receiving increasing benefits from the capitalist system which was becoming more humane.

The growing and transforming influence of compassion in Western Europe seems to have saved these societies from communism. It is not in these industrialized regions of the world, which seemed most ready for the final revolution, that communism has thrived. Rather the original revolution began in Russia, a repressive, feudal, agrarian society.

Sometimes the Marxist uneasiness concerning compassion by religious people has had tragic consequences for faith communities. Marxist governments have always restricted expressions of compassion by religious communities, whether Christian, Muslim, or Buddhist. All social service institutions must be controlled by the dictatorship of the proletariat. Faith communities may be permitted to worship, but they are not allowed to express compassion in the larger society.

The Shining Path revolutionary movement in Peru has been an example of the communist phobia regarding Christian compassion. During the 1980s, these revolutionaries destroyed billions of dollars of infrastructure, thereby seriously crippling the entire economy. Then they began targeting persons and institutions ministering among the poor.

Why would a Marxist movement fighting for the cause of the poor attack those institutions who serve the poor? The reason is that the revolutionaries fear that any expressions of compassion may soften the revolutionary spirit of the poor. People may worship God, but not serve humankind. Marxism fears compassion.

Global Utopia

There has not been sufficient zest for developing economic structures which benefit the poor throughout the world. There have been too few Wilberforces awakening the conscience of the industrial powers during the twentieth century. Consequently, especially during the last half of the twentieth century, the standard of living in the poor nations has declined significantly. A fundamental reason for this decline is the self-interest of the wealthy industrial nations, whose debt policies do impose usury on the poor and whose trade and financial regulations benefit the wealthy at the expense of the poor.

For example, the wealthy nations have determined that international trade must be conducted in "hard currency." This money is the currency of key industrial states. Therefore industrial states may operate with a significant annual trade deficit. This is especially true of the United States. These American trade deficits flood the world with hard currency dollars which nations need for international trade. However, the poor are forbidden to operate with trade deficits.

The poor nations cannot import more than they can sell abroad, unless they get special permission to do otherwise from financial institutions such as the International Monetary Fund (IMF). That rule does not apply to the rich nations. The United States has frequently operated with an annual trade deficit of over $100,000,000,000. However, if Peru has a trade deficit, the IMF will cry, "Foul!"

If a poor nation has a trade deficit, the IMF will require a tax on the price of imported goods such as petroleum in an attempt to decrease the demand for imports. This is the reason the cost of gasoline in some of the world's poorest countries has been four times as much as Americans pay. Furthermore, the IMF will likely require that the currency be devalued. This will trigger another round of escalating prices. These pressures on the poor nations place incredible strains on democratic governments.

Justice for Exploited Nations

Thus not so much workers in wealthy industrial societies but rather in oppressed societies have been attracted to twentieth-century Marxism. These oppressed workers now function as the proletariat of the wealthy nations. In other words, the revolutionary tension between the bourgeoisie and proletariat, which intrigued Marx and Engels in nineteenth-century industrial Europe, has in the twentieth century become a global revolutionary situation between nations. From the perspective of Marxist ideology, the bourgeois are the wealthy industrial nations who set the rules for global finance and the proletariat are the poor nations, whose labor and resources serve the whims and needs of the wealthy nations.[7]

These dual realities were juxtaposed at the close of 1988 in two statements issued in the same week. In his last formal press conference as president of the United States, Ronald Reagan stated that one of the great personal satisfactions of his presidency had been the good growth in global prosperity. That very week the World Bank issued a statement indicating that during the 1980s the standard of living among the world's poor nations had declined by 20 percent. Marxist ideology offers a solution to this juxtaposition of wealth and power: revolution.

Marxism has been an enticing ideology for nations caught in the hopeless web of international economics, a web which guarantees that next year they will be poorer than this year. Consequently during the post-World War II era, most Marxist revolutions have been internationalized. This was also true of the early communist revolution in Russia. Nevertheless, a distinctive characteristic of most communist revolutions in the last half of the twentieth century was that they were fueled by the anger and frustration of the poor states suffering from economic domination by the wealthy nations.

Most local revolutionary conflicts involved the communist powers and the capitalist powers supporting opposite sides. A few examples include Vietnam, Cambodia, Nicaragua, Angola, Afghanistan, El Salvador, Korea. The capitalist-communist polarization contributed to incredible suffering in nations experiencing revolutionary conflict, while the great powers who contributed resources to the conflict remained largely unscathed. Some conflicts continued for several decades; the great powers provided weapons generously.

Peace Among the Nations

Marx believed that once the proletariat gained power in different nations, they would become a transnational community of peace. Marx believed that wars are caused by bourgeois nationalisms. Capitalist interests create wars. However, once the proletariat gained power in the global community, international animosity and warfare would cease.

In Marxism, the political power of the proletariat unites the nations who have undergone a communist revolution. The term "communist bloc nations" was appropriate. The ideal was that the various governments of the proletariat cooperate in a manner that developed mutually beneficial transnational relationships among the communist states.[8]

Marxist ideology has a plan to bring international peace into the global community; Muslims, Buddhists, and Christians also have a vision for international global peace. Each of these four visions are different, in relation to the nature of the vision as well as the means for achieving the goal.

Some expressions of the Buddhist sangha seek to function as a transnational community of peace. However, the focus of Buddhism is personal peace.

The church is a transnational community which ideally contributes to international peace through its life and witness. It is a universal community present among local communities. When the church is consistent with the New Testament vision, it does not need or seek political power to effectuate its mission. The church in its original [Ch + state — handwritten margin note] vision is a community which seeks to influence rather than control political systems. The faithful church functions as an advocate for justice and peace.

The Marxist dream has intriguing parallels with the dar al-salaam in Islam. Recall that the mission of the Muslim ummah is to extend its political control from region to region around the world. States which have come under the political authority of Islam are united by this transnational community of faith.

Several years ago I served on an African high school social studies curriculum project. We were Muslims, Christians, a free enterprise American, and a communist Russian. Our different perspectives on the meaning of history made it almost impossible to work together.

The American pedagogist was certain that the essence of history was the spread of democracy and free enterprise. "In all my studies of global history, I have discovered that personal freedom is the universal wave of the future," the American expounded with indiscreet insistence.

The Marxist knew that scientific objectivity demonstrated that the wave of the future was proletariat revolution. He was eloquent as he described the coming era of peace, when all the earth would be ruled by the proletariat, who would bring about unity and cooperation among the nations.

The contribution of the Muslims and Christians could not be heard above the clash between the two secular Enlightenment ideologues. The committee dissolved when a communist revolution overthrew the Islamic government!

Marxism and Other Faiths

Marxist ideology has been exceedingly attractive to masses of the earth's dispossessed and poor. Yet it seems that the ideology connects especially with particular perspectives.

Christianity

For example, almost without exception, the leaders of Marxist revolutions since World War II have received at least some of their formal training in Christian schools. This does not mean that their societies were necessarily significantly Christianized, but the leaders of the movement *were* mostly persons who had significant exposure to biblical faith.

This suggests that the secularization which the Bible encourages is often the seedbed for the development of the secularism known as Marxism. Yet this does not suggest that Marxism will develop everywhere the church is present. In Christianized societies, communism has been mostly attractive where the church in the main has encouraged a spirituality with little relevance to the hard issues of poverty and oppression in this life.

A fundamental attraction of Marxism is the notion that history is moving toward a just social order, and no social institution, including religious systems, should get in the way of this movement toward inevitable human progress. This ideology justifies a radical surgery of institutions or persons which seem inimical to human development.

Marxism introduces its secular commitment through violent revolution, which attempts to enforce a radical break with the past. Although in the initial stages communist regimes are usually ruthless and violent, the revolution is nevertheless often received as a liberation by those who seek change. This may be especially true in cultures where centuries of tradition or superstition have chained the society to a past which discourages human development.

The methods by which biblical faith secularizes a culture are very different. The transformation which the church brings into a culture is two-dimensional. The first is through the conversion of people to Christ and a worldview consistent with the Christian gospel. The second is through the secularizing influence of biblical perspectives in the culture. They are like yeast in the bread dough, to use a metaphor from Jesus.

Buddhism and Confucianism

Marxism has been especially attractive in a number of non-European societies whose worldview was traditionally Confucian, Buddhist, or Muslim. Marxism provides a welcome break with the past for those who seek change as well as a better life for the poor. Did the worldview of some of these societies also help to make Marxism enticing?

Probably so. For example, recall that both Buddha and Confucius considered divinity irrelevant to the real issues of life and human destiny. Thus the atheism of Marxism is no worldview shock to persons in touch with the original beliefs of Buddha or Confucius.

However, popular Buddhism and Confucianism have always been attuned to the supernatural dimension of existence. This includes ample overlays of superstition and ancestor worship. The change agents in these societies, who wish to break free from the accretions of religiosity and superstition which have distorted the original teachings of Buddha and Confucius, will see an ideological ally in Marxism.

In a number of Buddhist societies, Marxist governments have been ruthless with the Buddhist sangha (monasteries). This has been especially true in Tibet, China, and Mongolia. A secular ideology such as Marxism considers the sangha worthless; it contributes nothing to the secular life of society or the development of the economy. By closing monasteries, communist governments have slowly strangled the life from Buddhist societies, for authentic Buddhism cannot survive without the sangha.

There are interesting areas of convergence between Confucianism and Marxism. Both believe that right political structures and education can form a good society and good people. Each ideology is exceedingly optimistic about human nature. Each dreams of creating the ideal person. For Confucius that person is the superior human; for Marx he is the communist human. The fundamental quality of both the superior and communist person is a generous spirit.

Both ideologies believe that laws and principles determine history. For Confucius the present needs to conform with the way of the ancestors; for Marx the laws of economics determine the destiny of history. Although the ideal political and educational mechanisms Confucius and Marx dreamed about were vastly different, both believed that the right political and educational environment would create ideal humans.

It would be interesting hearing the philosophers Marx and Confucius argue the pros and cons of using coercion and violence in bringing about the just political order and combating evil. On that issue they surely would have disagreed. Recall that Confucius did not believe that violence and coercion are constructive instruments for creating a good and harmonious society.

Maoism in China

Mao Tse-Tung took the doctrines of communism and adapted them to Chinese Confucian society. He functioned as a twentieth-century Confucius hoping to remold Chinese culture in accord with the thought of Mao. His Chinese brand of Marxism became Maoism.

However, the violence and suffering of the great leap forward and the cultural revolution turned the heart of multitudes of Chinese away from Maoism. The June 1989 massacre of students in Tiananmen Square in Beijing deepened the malaise. Consequently it might be that the time-tested thought of Confucius will outlive the radical challenge of Marxism and Maoism. Yet significant aspects of the radical secularization which Marxism and Maoism enforced on a whole generation of Chinese people will endure.

China also struggles with Hong Kong, a British crown colony that challenges the assumptions of Chinese communist ideology. Britain's ninety-nine-year agreement with China extended colonial rule over Hong Kong only until 1997. The consequential process of absorbing Hong Kong into the People's Republic of China has been an extensive and traumatic experience for both Hong Kong and China.

Hong Kong's economic dynamism is creating new developments throughout China. Even five years before the 1997 event, an avalanche of Hong Kong factories had relocated in China. The leaven of Hong Kong free enterprise, finance, and know-how has permeated China. China's gradual absorption of Hong Kong's free enterprise economics has stimulated enormous economic growth. During the 1990s, China's gross national product was growing at more than 10 percent per year!

Perhaps it is more accurate to say that Hong Kong is absorbing China rather than that China is absorbing Hong Kong. The merger of these two systems is inducing China away from purist communism to a socialism which embraces free enterprise.

Today there is often considerable interest in faith, especially faith compatible with human and cultural development. The disillusionment in China with Maoism and Marxism opens the door for a renewed spiritual quest for a faith for secular people.

Islam

We now explore a few of the convergences and divergencies between Islam and Marxism. Islam, like Confucianism and Marxism, teaches that the good society and good person can be developed through political and educational mechanisms. When necessary, the Muslim community is not averse to using the mechanisms of violence to secure the integrity of that community. In both Islam and Marxism, the freedom of the person must be restricted in the interest of the collective humanity.

Both Islam and Marxism are concerned for the poor. Recall that Muslims cannot forget the manner in which God provided for the orphan Muhammad through the generosity of family and community. This primal story in Islam nurtures the institution of almsgiving and other expressions of compassion for the poor. The prohibition against usury is an attempt to inhibit the exploitative power of the wealthy over the poor. Muslim and Marxist societies experience affinities in their concern for justice for the poor.

Islam and Marxism value the person as a worker. In Islam the person is caliph, a caretaker of this earth. Marxism takes the work theme further by declaring that the value of the person is his work.

Another convergence/divergence is the ideal of equality. The equality of all before God is a central conviction of Islam. A visual demonstration of this fact is the annual hajj (pilgrimage) to Mecca, where all participants dress in the same kind of white cloth. The theme of equality is evident in the daily prayers, where all stand in rows, bowing together with faces to the ground before God. Anyone can lead the prayers, even a child. Even in death the equality of all is revealed. Muslim graveyards are not ornamented by ostentatious tombstones. All the markings are the same. (In some communities the graves of saints are an exception.) All are equal before God.

Marxism also proclaims the goal of equality in a classless society. In Islam equality is necessary because only God is sovereign over all. In Marxism it is the dictatorship of the proletariat which facilitates and even enforces equality.

Both Islam and Marxism perceive that they have a mission in the world—to extend the region of peace to the ends of the earth. For both communities the region of war, confusion, and injustice are the societies which have not yet come under the respective rule of either Islam or communism.

In Islam peace is that region which has come under the political control of the Muslim community (ummah). The sovereignty and will of God guarantee that the faithful ummah will be successful. As the community above the nations, its rule brings peace.

Marxism is a secular ideology with similar themes. The areas of the world ruled by the proletariat are the regions of peace. The economic laws of dialectical materialism guarantee that eventually the entire earth will come under the rule of the proletariat. That will be the era of universal peace.

Both communities have similarities in their views of government in the community of peace. In both movements the respective communities of peace must be governed by those who are faithful to the primal vision of the community. The rights of minorities and other religious communities are guaranteed, yet always in the confines deemed appropriate by the Islamic or communist authorities.

In both systems there is great concern about revisionism, which is known as *bidah* (innovation) in Islam. Both insist that the governing authorities avoid any revision of the primal ideology which created their respective movements. In societies governed by Islam, that responsibility rests with the Muslim community which, guided by the theologians, is the final arbiter of government policy. In societies governed by Marxism, it is the communist party which is the final arbiter of political power and protector against revisionism. Revisionism is dangerous!

The basic assumption in each is that all alternative religious or ideological perspectives are only a passing phase. Each system is certain that given time all peoples enjoying the benefits of their respective regions of peace will eventually also subscribe to the faith or ideology of the rulers. Consequently, in both systems the norm is to relate to alternative communities as aberrations.

For this reason both Muslim and communist governments find it exceedingly difficult to tolerate conversions into an alternative religion or ideology. For Muslims, the movement of peoples under their rule should always be toward the true faith of Islam, never in another direction. The state is responsible to guarantee this. In a communist state the movement of the peoples must always be toward Marxist ideology, never in the other direction. It is therefore not surprising that alternative religious groups living under either Islamic or Marxist gov-ernments often lament that the authorities do not really support the Universal Declaration of Human Rights.

The common commitment of both these post-Christian movements of Islam and Marxism to establish an expanding global community of peace is astonishing. That peace is established through political power.

Yet there is a great divide between the Islamic and the Marxist vision of the region and era of peace. On the one hand, the Muslim is keenly committed to submission to the will of God who guarantees the triumph of the faithful ummah. In contrast, Marxism is atheistic. For the Marxist, it is the will of the proletariat who function in accordance with the natural laws of dialectical materialism who bring about the triumph of the socialist revolution. In Islam the region of peace is grounded in theism; in Marxism the communist society is grounded in secularism.

The similarities and differences between the Islamic and Marxist sense of mission have contributed to the love-hate relationship between these two communities. For many years Muammar Khadaffi of

Libya worked toward what he called the third way. He described a vision of a theistic communism, a merger of the revolutionary ideals of Marxism with the faith perspectives of Islam. This experiment demonstrated an intriguing attraction between Muslim and communist societies.

A Great Debate

Both Islam and Marxism reveal a commitment to their respective missions which is a reinterpretation of the biblical vision of the eventual triumph of the kingdom of God. The biblical prophet Isaiah poetically describes the coming era of peace.

> He [the Lord] will judge between the nations
> and will settle disputes for many peoples.
> They will beat their swords into plowshares
> and their spears into pruning hooks.
> Nation will not take up sword against nation,
> Nor will they train for war anymore.[9]

World peace is the hope of both Islam and Marxism. Yet the biblical manner in which the peaceable kingdom is established is radically different from both Marxism and Islam.

In Isaiah it is a "little child" who shall lead the nations into the community of peace.[10] This is a picture of a universal voluntary community of peace established gently, unobtrusively, surprisingly through the leadership of a child, the metaphor of one who is vulnerable. In the New Testament, this theme of peace through vulnerability is historicized in Jesus of Nazareth.

The New Testament description of the peaceable kingdom parts ways with both Islam and Marxism at the cross of Jesus Christ. Jesus avoided using the instruments of political and military coercion in his ministry. He perceived that these devices do not establish genuine peace. Quite the opposite, the community of peace is created through a confrontation with evil which leads to the suffering of the cross. Participation in this kingdom is voluntary.

The Marxist ideal to create a global community where the disparities of wealth are obliterated has been attractive to the world's desperately poor one billion people. Yet Marxism is far more than an ideal. It is also an analysis of the causes of poverty; the people with capital use that power to exploit those who labor. Furthermore Marxism is a plan of action to remedy the tragedy of hunger and poverty in an opulent world. The plan is violent and coercive revolution.

There are biblical nuances in Marx's commitment to truth-in-action, yet in the convergencies there is divergence. Marx considered the cross nonsense.

> Truth for him was quite inseparable from praxis, from its consequences in action. "The philosophers have only interpreted the world in one way or another; the thing now is to change it." The political revolution which he foresaw and wanted to prepare for was for him the expression of an overture to total revolution which would give rise to a new type of men. . . . [I]n this new order the dehumanizing process is brought to an end and man fully receives his identity. This is a secularized biblical eschatology in which the proletariat has assumed the broad features of the Servant of the Lord, whose vicarious suffering for the whole creation inaugurates the new age.[11]

Like Jesus, the proletariat sought justice. But it was coercive and violent justice. The vulnerability of the cross was considered foolishness; violent revolution was the only way.

Nevertheless, the communist revolutions have brought a greater sense of well-being to oppressed masses in some societies. Few Russians would want to return to the prerevolutionary days of the czars, when the masses were oppressed under the heavy-handed exploitation of opulent landowners. The Marxist revolution in China finally broke the power of the warlords whose abuse of power is legendary. Few in Cuba would desire to return to the massive illiteracy rates or the neglect of health care which was a characteristic of the pre-revolutionary era. The Marxist ideal, analysis, and plan provided hope for many of the world's oppressed poor.

Disaster in the Global Village

Nevertheless, the Marxist plan has also been implemented at enormous human cost and suffering. V. I. Lenin, who founded the Soviet communist regime (1917-1924), and Joseph Stalin, who carried forward the revolution as president of the Soviet Union (1929-1953), orchestrated unbelievable atrocities. Who will ever know how many died in the genocides wrought by Lenin and Stalin as they imposed the dictatorship of the proletariat on the peoples of the Soviet Union?

In a December 1991 conversation between several Russian Orthodox Church leaders with a small gathering of American church persons, we heard that evidence now indicates sixty million people died during the first decades of the communist revolution in the Soviet Union. In China estimates are that thirty million died during the great leap forward. No figures can adequately communicate the horror of death on such a scale.

"Please, tell me your story," I invited a variety of people who hosted me, during several visits in the region. I sometimes wept as I listened.

"When I was a child, they came through my town and killed all the men. I grew up in a village without men."

"They separated my family. No communication was possible. For fifty years my mother never heard from my father. It is a miracle of the grace of God that this week my parents finally made contact. Both are now in their eighties. My father had remarried, thinking my mother was dead."

"Eighty-five percent of my church community were killed."

"They dynamited 193 church buildings in my city. Only seven churches still stand."

"They expelled me from the university when they learned that I was a believer."

"They asked the children in school, 'Does your father or mother have a Bible, or ever pray?' If the answer was 'yes,' the parents went to prison for seven years."

"Spouses could not trust each other; one out of three people was an informer."

The statistics are about people.

Banishment, torture, and massive executions characterized the first three or four decades of Soviet communism. Stalin was discredited by later Soviet leadership, but not until Mikhail Gorbachev introduced the winds of change known as *glasnost* (openness) and *perestroika* (restructuring) did human rights as described in the United Nations' Universal Declaration of Human Rights become a significant consideration in Soviet domestic policy. For three generations the Soviet experiment in communism was cruel and ruthless in its response to dissidents.

Soviet communism has not been the only Marxist society involved in human rights abuses. The secret police system, imprisonment for political or religious dissenters, torture or use of mind changing drugs, public or secret executions of those who differ with the revolutionary regime, curtailment of free speech and the press, or reeducation centers which attempt to change the minds of people accused of having bourgeois inclinations have been far too common patterns in revolutionary Marxist societies.

I have lived through the horror of an African Marxist regime in which the bullet-riddled bodies of dissenters helped to secure the revolution through the powerful weapon of fear. Some Marxist systems have been more ruthless than others. Yet the revolutionary phase of the dictatorship of the proletariat is universally characterized by the abridgement of personal human rights in the interest of the well-being of the new collective communist peoplehood.

How can it be that the communist movement which was intended to bring freedom and happiness to the suffering masses has most often become a secularism that brutalizes? One factor is the communist view that the person does not have intrinsic or eternal value. The person is only a highly intelligent material being whose value is measured by the work he produces. Therefore, any values must be eradicated which inhibit collective work. The collective party of devoted workers is the absolute authority. There is no other authority.

"There is no Erma's Diner or Pete's Butcher Shop," I thought as I walked the streets of Halle, Bucharest, East Berlin, Tirana, and Moscow.

The communist system determined to erase all wrinkles caused by an entrepreneurial spirit. The collective strangled the ego identity of the person.

"A friend came over one evening and cut my hair," a Romanian friend mused over a late night cup of coffee in his home in Hateg. "I gave him a few lei for the favor. The next day the security police fined us a whole month's wages for this crime against the collective community. Hair-cutting was exclusively the responsibility of the state. Any personal initiatives in hair-cutting were prohibited."

The strangulation of the personal ego extended into a brutalization against cultures, nationalities, minorities, the proprieties which oil social relationships, and nature. Even though the culture is spoiled, the creativity of the human spirit is smothered, faith is dismissed, nature is raped, minorities are oppressed, and dissenters crushed—let the people produce goods and services. That is the reason for human existence.

In Marxist governments the dictatorship of the proletariat becomes the cohesive force throughout the entire region controlled by the communist authority. Ethnic identities are of no consequence. The new identity is the laboring classes who transcend ethnic considerations.

However, disrespect for the integrity of ethnic societies in Marxist governments builds up enormous counter-pressures. We observe that in time those ethnic aspirations can become explosive. The fabric of the state has been threatened or destroyed by ethnic resurgence and anger in post-Marxist societies as diverse as Ethiopia and Yugoslavia. The lesson is obvious: healthy national or global systems must respect ethnic identity.

Marxism, like all secularisms, views nature as an entity independent of a creator. The person and society have no accountability to a creator for the use of nature. Too often a worldview which denies any accountability to God for our use of nature leads to ecological irresponsibility. If nature groans under the exploitative hand of human enterprise, so be it.

Let the people wrench from nature all the riches possible! Such attitudes encourage people to destroy the land. Material progress is right, regardless of the ecological tragedy which that progress may produce. Ecological disaster is the consequence.

In their book *Ecocide in the USSR*, the authors observe,

> When historians finally conduct an autopsy on Soviet communism, they may reach the verdict of death by ecocide. . . . No other great industrial civilization so systematically and so long poisoned its air, land, water, and people.[12]

How does one comprehend the ecological catastrophe in Eastern Europe and the Commonwealth of Independent States where societies struggled to achieve utopia on earth? At the beginning of the 1990s, when the curtain of secrecy parted, a ghastly apocalypse was revealed. Thirty percent of all foods contained hazardous pesticides. A third of Polish farmlands were so contaminated with industrial wastes that geneticists feared damage to the human genes. In the Russian Republic, seventy million people living in 103 cities inhaled air which contained five times the allowable levels of hazardous chemicals.

Pediatric hospitals throughout the region struggled to sustain the lives of children suffering from bronchial problems directly related to breathing noxious air. Five million acres of Siberian forests were vanishing every year. Mercury was present in 70 percent of the fish in the Volga. Erosion had ruined six million acres of farmland. Scores of nuclear power plants were not safe, and the nuclear waste problem had acquired catastrophic dimensions. These are some of the dimensions of the disaster.[13]

In his *Gulag Archipelago*, Aleksandr I. Solzhenitsyn weeps for his country, the Soviet Union. This book earned him a one-way ticket away from his motherland. This Nobel Prize-winning literary genius describes the horror of a good vision gone evil. He struggles with the reality that such evils have happened in the wondrous twentieth century of enlightenment, socialism, progress, and scientific technology.

He asserts that the root cause of this tragic distortion of humane values is that spirituality was neglected and despised. The communist party and ideology replaced God as the ultimate authority. No other transcendent power was recognized as having the authority to invite people or government to another way, to repentance. This "scientific" system despised and discredited any alternative perspectives. Solzhenitsyn comments,

> Power is a poison well-known for thousands of years. If only no one were ever to acquire material power over others! But to the human being who has faith in some force that holds dominion over all of us, and who is therefore conscious of his own limitation, power is not necessarily fatal. For those, however, who are unaware of any higher sphere, it is a deadly poison. For them there is no antidote.[14]

After his enforced exile from the Soviet Union, Solzhenitsyn moved to the United States, where he lived for two decades until his country was ready to welcome him home again; he returned home in May 1994. His song of lament also embraced Western culture. He perceived that in both Soviet and North American societies, the quest for things had supplanted spiritual values. The secularisms of the twentieth century have nudged God to the periphery of life. This has been true both in Western capitalist societies and in communist societies.

Solzhenitsyn believes that the neglect of spirituality in both cultures has contributed directly to dehumanization and decadence. Can hope which creates authentic, wholesome cultural dynamism be sustained and preserved for multiple generations in any society which does not cultivate a relationship with the God who gives hope?

Faith for the Future?

A friend who knows Russian fluently visited the Soviet Union in the summer of 1988 to participate in celebrations remembering one thousand years of Christianity in Russia. One evening in Leningrad, he was hosted in the home of a local family. The hostess was a communist party official. The conversation centered on faith and especially on the relationship between faith in God and morality.

At her initiative, the conversation became an exploration on the relationship between Christian faith and ethics. She observed that believers seemed to work hard, had integrity and strong families, and avoided alcoholism. Her conclusion was that believers, whom communism had attempted to discredit, had done a better job than communism in creating the personal qualities necessary to develop a dynamic economy and culture. The ideal communist might be a believer rather than an atheist.

At the close of the evening, the hostess astonished my friend with the comment, "You will be interested in knowing that in the various levels of the communist party leadership in the Soviet Union today, there is discussion concerning faith in God. The moral crisis of our people is contributing to that interest. Some have even become believers."

My amazed friend replied, "How can that be? Faith in God and communist ideology are incompatible."

She replied. "This evening you have been talking with one of those believers. We must look beyond communist ideology for help. We have no idea where this will take us!"

Only three years later on August 29, 1991, the Soviet legislature overwhelmingly voted to suspend all activities of the communist party in the Soviet Union. Through this astonishing legislative act, the Soviet Union's experiment with communism ended. On Christmas Day, only four months later, the flag of the Soviet Union was lowered from the Kremlin flag pole. The Union had been dissolved.

Why did the authorities lower that Soviet flag on the day when much of the global church celebrates the birth of Christ? Was this only a coincidence? Or was it a symbolic gesture of recognition and appreciation for the church by the leaders of the newly emerging regimes? The church confesses that the child is Lord who was born in the cattle shed in Bethlehem on Christmas Day.

In subtle and mostly unobtrusive ways, the church had been significant in cracking open the monolithic communist systems of the region. It was the churches, although discredited and often oppressed, who persisted for seven decades, with amazing resiliency, as the only enduring alternative thought communities.[15]

The first significant fissure in the system began in Poland. From that tiny Polish fissure, a fatal crack began to spread throughout the communist systems of Eastern Europe and the Soviet Union. From whence did that fissure in Poland commence?

The 1985 election of Mikhail Gorbachev as president of the Soviet Union was important. However, another election of great significance preceded that of Gorbachev. Ask anyone in Poland, and the answer is always the same: the beginning of the crack in the communist system began in 1978, when Karol Wojtyla was chosen as pope by the Roman Catholic Sacred College of Cardinals.[16] He was chosen in October 1978; by June 1979, this Polish pope, John Paul II, made a pilgrimage to his homeland.

Hundreds of thousands gathered for the masses he conducted. He applauded the role of labor. Then in gentle yet obvious contradiction to communist dogma, he insisted that labor should be a servant to humanity rather than a dominating force.[17]

In the center of Warsaw, the heartland of Polish communist power, Pope John Paul II proclaimed to a congregation of hundreds of thousands, "Christ is at the center. Christ cannot be kept out of history in any part of the globe. The exclusion of Christ from the history of humanity is an act against humanity."[18]

The crowd was amazed by the boldness of the statement. Then slowly the throngs began singing songs of faith. Finally, in a crescendo of affirmation they began chanting, "We want God! We want God!"[19]

From that time a drama of suffering, disappointment, pathos, courage, hope, faith, and persistence gained momentum in Poland. Only a decade later, the communist regime in Poland was crumbling, and the shock waves of that collapse had become global. All communist systems in Eastern Europe were beginning to experience the kinds of fissures which had begun in Poland.

"Words cannot communicate what we experienced at this place." With tears of wonder, two Romanian youth, Ioan and Livia, described the origin of the December 1989 Romanian revolution which overthrew the communist regime.

We were standing in Opera Square in the heart of Timisoara, Romania.

"The authorities demanded that Pastor Laszlo Tokes leave his parish in the Reformed Church here in Timisoara. The congregation was dismayed, and so they held an all-night candlelight prayer vigil on the night of December 16, 1989. By the next day Christians from churches throughout this city joined in the vigil, and the gathering moved into the center of town here at Opera Square.

"Soldiers surrounded the people and using machine guns, killed many people. Even children trying to escape were shot. That was December 17.   *effective peaceful resist.*

"When the nation heard what had happened, vigils and demonstrations spread throughout the country, including huge demonstrations in Bucharest. Even the killings in our town did not prevent the vigils from continuing right here. More and more people joined the gathering in Opera Square which continued day and night. By December 22, the vigil had grown to two hundred thousand people.

"Again the soldiers moved in with machine guns. In that moment of terrible crisis, the Baptist pastor, Peter Dugulescu, mounted a platform and motioned for quiet.

"Then Peter spoke, 'Soldiers, it is the will of God that you lay down your arms and desist from violence against your own fellow country-persons.' "

With tears of wonder, Livia said softly, "And the soldiers obeyed."

She continued, "Pastor Peter called on those two hundred thousand people to kneel in prayer. And they did. Even the soldiers knelt in prayer as the pastor led those throngs in prayer for the healing of the Romanian nation."

While this was happening in Timisoara, President Nicolae Ceausescu was fleeing his palace in Bucharest. He was killed three days later.

Multiple forces converged in bringing about the demise of these regimes. A February 24, 1992, feature article in *Time* magazine described involvement of the United States Central Intelligence Agency. Analysts document that Western political intrigue helped to destabilized the communist governments. Others elaborate on the economic malaise or the stifling bureaucracy. Such pressures did contribute to the transformation.

Yet we are wise not to ignore the role of the local churches in inspiring and guiding the mostly peaceful and nonviolent revolution that brought about the demise of communism. Only days after the *Time* article, Gorbachev wrote a tribute to the role of Pope John Paul II and the church in bringing about the transformation of Eastern Europe and the former Soviet Union. He said,

> What I have always held in high esteem about the pope's thinking and ideas is their spiritual content, their striving to foster the development of a new world civilization. . . .

Now it can be said that everything which took place in Eastern Europe in recent years would have been impossible without the pope's efforts and the enormous role, including the political role, which he played in the world arena. . . . Everything that can serve to strengthen man's consciousness and spirit is today of much greater importance than ever before.[20]

Pope John Paul II responded to Gorbachev. "It is the church, and not the pope which has counted in this process. If something can be ascribed to the pope, it is the fruit of his devotion—his devotion to Christ and to mankind."[21]

We join with Mikhail Gorbachev and Pope John Paul II in pondering the meaning of it all.

Reflection

1. Consider this statement. Marxism has reinterpreted the biblical kingdom of God as a secularism.

2. Reflect on Solzhenitsyn's critique of Marxism and Western culture.

3. Compare Marxism with Confucianism and Islam.

4. Account for the atheistic orientation of Marxism.

5. Why is Buddhist, Muslim, or Christian compassion a problem for Marxist idealists?

6. Describe the Marxist plan for global peace and justice.

7. How does Marxism cope with pluralism?

8. Account for the demise of Marxism in the former Soviet Union and Eastern Europe.

13

Global Gods and Human Choices

I S ATHEISM better than religion?"Singh, the turbaned youth flying from Nairobi to London via Athens, was pondering that question. The first chapter in our exploration describes Singh's quest. His religion was Sikhism and his community intermingled with secularists, Marxists, Jains, Hindus, Buddhists, Christians, Muslims, Zoroastrians, and Confucianists. He had already devoured volumes of scriptures and philosophies in his quest for a way to build peace among the peoples of his motherland. The interreligious violence of the Punjab propelled his inquiry.

"What is truth?" Singh and I had reflected on that question together during our night flight to Athens.

The baffling complexities of the modern global village give Singh's quest urgent poignancy—the interdependence of people and communities, the juxtaposition of wealth-hunger-poverty, economics and ecology, human rights and pluralism, our kind of people versus their kind of people, the nation-state and the ethnic community, ethics, freedom and responsibility, cultural change, the meaning of the person and history, war and peace, family and children, the relationships between women and men, and the city. Modernity has forced these issues into the consciousness of people everywhere.

One Global Village

The manner in which the person and the global community respond to these issues is dramatically affecting the quality and the survivability of all human society and each person as well. The religious pluralism of Singh's Indian Punjab is a microcosm of the whole world. We are now one pluralistic global village.

The issue is not whether our choices will affect the quality of the global village. Of course they do. The blitz of plastic bags I saw along the railroad on the edge of Jakarta in Indonesia is the direct result of millions of personal decisions to toss plastic bags from train windows. Our "insignificant" individual turnings amplified throughout the whole network of local and global village relations is affecting the entire human family, as well as the well-being of the earth. Our choices are important!

Apparently Confucius was right as far as he went. A good emperor does contribute to blessing within the entire cosmos; an evil emperor creates trouble. He could have added that the same is true of each of us. Each person has some responsibility for the well-being of the cosmos. The directions in which the person and society turn affect us all. That being the case, it is important for each of us as well as our communities to consider carefully our choices, those little turnings in the road of life. Yet in what direction shall we turn?

How do we find the way among the cacophony of global gods? And that brings us right back to Singh's question in the late twentieth century, "What is truth?"

We seek truth not just because we find philosophy or religion interesting. We seek truth because we need a trustworthy direction for life. Surely truth is the way of well-being for the person as well as the local and global village.

We have reflected on a variety of global gods and their fascinating contribution to the choices we make. Each offers perspectives on truth. We have explored ways several religions and ideologies affect the well-being of humanity and the earth.

Religions and Modern Societies

We have described ten religions and philosophies which influence modern communities—African traditional religion, Hinduism, Buddhism, Platonism, Confucianism, Judaism, Christianity, Islam, the Enlightenment, and Marxism. We have especially considered the primal vision or norm of each religion or philosophy.

We have also identified distortions, modifications, or paradigm shifts of the primal vision or norm in response to the exigencies of history or the pressures of modernity. We have been conscious of the dialogue and occasional tension between the primal vision and modern realities.

Our exploration has been evaluative. The question which has guided the exploration is this: how do these global gods—these various perceptions of God, these faiths, philosophies, and religions—affect the quality of the global and local village as well as the well-being of the person?

We have explored religions which are local or national—African religions, Hinduism, and Confucianism. We have struggled with these faiths and philosophies, empathizing with the internal tensions which globalism presents. Group relativism and ethnocentricism are enduring characteristics of national and tribal faith systems.

We have discovered that global realities often nudge tribal and national societies toward participation in a universal faith or ideological community which enables them to transcend the relativisms of small-scale ethnic or national society. People often discover that the gods of tribe and nation are in themselves not adequate for realistic and wholesome participation in the global village.

We have found that there are three world religions which specifically invite involvement in transnational universal community—Buddhism, Islam, and Christianity. Alongside these three paths are smaller divergent trails, such as the Unitarians who skirt off to the side of the Christian path, or the Bahai who parallel the Islamic road.

We have explored Buddhism, which is a winsome, sensitive, and growing missionary movement. The Buddhist negation of the significance of material reality and the person runs counter to the aspirations of a secularizing world. Nevertheless, Buddhism will continue being attractive in societies where people are disenchanted with secularism and materialism.

Our exploration gave considerable attention to the nuances of the faiths who view Abraham has their beginning. We have probed the meaning of the biblical faith communities of Judaism and Christianity as well as Islam. It is these movements which most widely affect modern global community, for half the people on earth consider themselves the faith descendants of Abraham.

We discovered that biblical faith has contributed to the phenomenon of secularization and secularism. We have reflected on secular philosophies and ideologies which provide global perspectives. Of these only Marxism has provided identifiable access into a global community. This is the community of the proletariat, whose ideology is materialistic secularism. We recognize, however, that about 1990 there were the beginnings of a surprising discrediting of Marxism in vast regions ruled by communist governments through much of the twentieth century. We have explored the discrediting process.

Many of us have been surprised that the global community hosts only four significant faith or ideological communities which genuinely transcend ethnic or national boundaries—Buddhism, Christianity, Islam, and Marxism.

Our exploration has been especially concerned with the manner in which these universal communities respond to the phenomenon of pluralism. We recognize that a wholesome global village requires a healthy respect for diversity. How do these universal faiths cope with ethnic, national, and religious diversity? We have assessed the way these save-the-world movements affect the quality of pluralistic relationships within the modern local and global village.

Welcoming the Good

We have discovered that each of the religions and philosophies we have explored have something precious to share with the world community. All have their gift. We mention several examples.

The Buddhist fortitude in times of suffering may be a special gift to societies everywhere.

The *ahimsa* nonviolent theme in Hinduism has stirred the conscience of the world during the mid-twentieth-century struggle for Indian independence. In subsequent decades that theme has lived on in freedom movements far from India.

The African insight into exuberant person-affirming community is a blessing to communities wherever African people are present.

The Marxist concern for the poor has in some instances pushed Christians to rediscover the need for the church to be committed to the well-being of the poor and oppressed.

Our exploration has revealed attractive and constructive contributions to human well-being within each of the ten perspectives described in this book. That would also be true of other faith or ideological systems we might explore. We have discovered that the phenomenal cross-fertilization which characterizes modernity enables many local communities to benefit from various values and insights of different faiths or philosophies.

There are various ways in which a faith or ideological community can benefit from the perspectives of another community. We have learned that Hinduism or Buddhism are especially adept in syncretism. Islam and Christianity, on the other hand, would invite their respective communities to evaluate the gift which other communities of faith offer in the light of the truth center to which they are committed. Ideally these faiths would resist syncretism. So does Marxism; revisionism has always been anathema to Marxist systems.

Regardless of the stance a faith or ideology might take toward others, modern mobility and pluralism are providing amazing opportunities for the beneficial sharing of gifts with one another. A Western Christian family living in London might be enriched by learning from the respect for the elderly that their immigrant Confucian neighbors from Shanghai demonstrate.

We discover that conversations between religious and ideological communities can encourage a spirit of mutual cooperation for the human and community good. In recent years, global interreligious conferences have developed fairly significant common statements on issues such as human rights, justice and peace, or ecological responsibility.[1] Left to themselves, a religious or ideological community might not pay attention to such global human concerns.

It is, for example, likely that the communist regimes of Eastern Europe and the Soviet Union would not, on their own initiative, have sought to remedy human rights abuses in their societies. The Helsinki Agreement (1975) between the West and East block nations and the follow-up conversations after that conference nettled these Marxist regimes toward more sensitivity for human rights.

In the interreligious or interideological conversation itself, fresh perceptions and commitments can emerge, which are fostered by the requirements of global well-being. We learn from one another.

Worrying About Evil

Our exploration has worried about evil. We have observed that religious systems can cause great harm. We have struggled to discern the source of these evil inclinations. Occasionally we have discovered tendencies among the gods which are destructive to personhood and global community.

The disciplines of psychology also help us understand potentially destructive dimensions within the person. Sigmund Freud (d.1939) fretted about the pleasure principle as the fuel which empowers the human person. Alfred Adler (d.1937) worried about the will-to-power as the primary force within the person. Later B. F. Skinner developed theories of determinism—the normal person experiences the abdication of ego identity and personal responsibility. The environment determines the choices a person makes. Religions often nourish such inclinations in the human psyche which can become destructive of human well-being—pleasure, will-to-power, or ego-abdication.[2]

When religion provides no critique, corrective, or constructive outlet for harmful inner drives or inclinations, it becomes an accomplice in evil. Although we did not explore the ideology of Nazism or the patriotism of Shintoism, these are modern examples of global gods which became diabolical in the mid-twentieth century; these religio-ideological systems stoked the flames of the uninhibited will-to-power.

Even universal movements for global salvation such as Christianity, Islam, or Buddhism might become distorted and evil through a quest for self-aggrandizement. We will save the world by tramping underfoot all others. On the other hand, these same faiths might nurture evil through encouraging the abdication of the ego—misdirected humility in Christianity, avoidance of personal responsibility through submission to the will of God in Islam, or ego-emptiness in Buddhism. A healthy faith must constructively critique the pleasure principle, the will-to-power, or the inclination toward the abdication of ego identity.

We have observed tendencies inimical to the well-being of the person and the global or local village. These harmful inclinations might be present in the soul of the primal vision and norm of a religion or ideology. The primal norm of a religion is not necessarily good; the same is true of philosophy or ideology.

For example, the Marxist use of revolutionary violence to initiate utopia is hardly a distortion of the primal vision of Marx and Engels. The violent expression of the will-to-power is in the soul of Marxist ideology. So is the Marxist insistence that the personal ego be abdicated in favor of the collective ego. The loss of ego identity was one of the great tragedies of decades of communist domination in Eastern Europe.

Our exploration has taken note of the tragic dimension of such ideological or religious gods. We have tried to assess to what extent such distortions of human well-being and quality community are an aberration of the movement or within its essence. What are we invited into when we embrace the primal norm of Moses, Plato, Confucius, Buddha, Muhammad, Jesus, Rousseau, or Marx? Is the primal norm in essence healthy?

Our whole exploration has been the search for those enduring qualities which really do provide a way for joyful and full personhood in authentic local and wholesome global community. Our expectation has been that the journey toward healthy personhood and the well-being of the local and global village is also the answer to Singh's question, "What is truth?"

Alternatives and Commitments

We shall now sharpen the issues and alternatives we experience as we explore life in global societies. We shall use the analogy of walking through the woods where we encounter divergent paths.

There is the fork in the path in the woods of life between agnosticism, which assumes that the truth is unknowable, and the conviction that the truth can be known. Is it wise at any time, and especially in times like these, to avoid the real issues of personal and global realities? Does not the agnostic fork in the path offer just that sort of cop-out? To say that there is no answer to Singh's question is to doom the human enterprise to futility. Is it not wise to seek that universal truth which enables and empowers us to realistically address the life-and-death struggles in our modern global village?

Paradoxical as it might seem, I believe the gift of truth invites a spirit of humility and an attitude of respect for the other, regardless of her point of view. I believe the truth invites commitment, but it does not need defenders.

Another fork in the path of life is between a universal faith and a local tribal or national religion. The phenomenon of the modern global village reveals that entrusting the nation or the tribe with the responsibility to define truth on its own terms is relativism. We have explored the Hindu philosophical defense of relativism. We have discovered that in folk Hinduism, relativism is nurtured by millions of gods. I believe it is no accident that classic Hindu philosophy considers that human existence is a tragedy.

I agree with the late twentieth-century U.S. philosopher Allan Bloom who says that moral relativism dooms the human experience to futility.[3] Is it not true that relativism, like agnosticism, does not provide us with the spiritual, moral, or intellectual undergirding for the tough, painful, and sacrificial choices we must make if we wish to cultivate humanization and quality global community? I believe the quest for universal truth is in the best interest of the person as well as both the local and the global community.

Then we come to four forks in the trail of life branching off in different directions—Buddhism, Christianity, Islam, Marxism. These are the four faith or ideological options in the global village proclaiming universal "truth" which have, on the basis of their respective truths, created significant identifiable international global communities.

There are tiny trails which skirt off alongside one or the other of these four main movements. There are also philosophies such as the Enlightenment or religions such as the New Age Movement which "salt" societies with ideas. Yet these "salt" movements have not created identifiable global communities. Thus we discover that there are four options before us as we consider universal communities which have been created by universal truth claims.

Our exploration has probed the core convictions of the four paths and communities which offer universal peace and well-being for global humanity. We summarize, in the chronological order in which these global communities have emerged in the history of humankind.*

First, there is the path of individual intuition and enlightenment which is the Buddhist way. This is the way of the Four Noble Truths and Three Refuges as taught by Gautama Buddha. This conviction has created the *sangha*, which has become a global monastic community. The Buddhist path requires developing the disciplines necessary for the enlightenment which leads one into personal peace through escape from suffering and the allurements of the material world. The goal of Buddhism is emptiness (nirvana).

Second, there is the path of faith anchored in the conviction that God reveals himself to humankind through his acts in history and supremely in his act of self-revelation in a man who grew up in a town called Nazareth in Palestine. This path has created the church. It is the way of faith nurtured by the Bible. This path requires making a U-turn away from all other local or global gods, as the believer confesses that Jesus from Nazareth is Messiah and Master.

Third, there is the path of peace through submission to the revealed sent-down will of God. This is the conviction that God reveals his will through prophets and in sending down several books of revelation. This path requires submission to the will of God as revealed

---

* The church as a movement growing out of the covenant community known as Israel is the oldest and most enduring of the four communities. The church as an after-Christ movement is a more recent global community than is the Buddhist sangha.

through all the prophets, but especially in the final book of revelation, the Qur'an. The prophet Muhammad is considered to be the seal of the prophets and an ideal example of authentic submission to God. This is the Islamic path which sustains the Muslim ummah. Muslims seek to bring every aspect of human society under the will of God through personal and political effort.

Fourth, there is the path of secular philosophy. This philosophy claims to base its authority on scientific facts. Marxism is the only modern secular philosophy which has developed an identifiable global community. This so-called classless society of peace is established by the dictatorship of the proletariat. Although Marxism has been discredited in vast regions of the global village, it has nevertheless continued as an attractive option and viable system for hundreds of millions of people.

A Confession

This exploration begins with a question Singh and I pondered, "What will truth look like when you find it?"

Singh believed, "The truth will replace hate with love."

However, love cannot overcome hate without suffering. Such love requires active personal engagement and involvement among those wherein hate and brokenness reigns. Christians believe that personal, suffering, active love is not futile. The conviction that God raised the crucified Jesus of Nazareth from the dead gives believers that hope.

The man from Nazareth invites a life orientation radically different from pleasure, the will-to-power, or ego abdication. His invitation is to a life empowered by unconditional love.

I believe in times like these there is need for a community of faith among the nations who joyfully confess their surprising conviction that the truth center of the universe is revealed in a man from Nazareth who forgave his enemies, even while they crucified him on a wooden cross on a hill called Golgotha. I believe there is need for a community which confidently and humbly express that truth center in sacrificial, joyful service in and among the nations.

As I see it, when we discover our Creator as one who personally, actively, unconditionally loves us and all others, including our enemies, that is empowerment for personal healing as well as "healing for the nations."[4] That healing process becomes reality as people are empowered to love, forgive, and serve one another in the same spirit as that man from Nazareth.

These last comments are a confession of faith and commitment. Yet it is not easy for me to believe that our Creator loves us as keenly as that man from Nazareth loved. I experience faith as a gift to be cherished, not an achievement to boast about.

Each of us possesses the precious gift of choice. We meet divergent trails during the pilgrimage of life. The personal and global consequences of the paths we choose are often more significant than we expect. The words of Robert Frost express the mystery and exhilaration of choosing a trail among the trails (a God among the gods) that invite us as we stroll through the woods (of the global village):[5]

> I shall be telling this with a sigh
> Somewhere ages and ages hence:
> Two roads diverged in a woods, and I—
> I took the one less traveled by,
> And that has made all the difference.

Notes

Note

Biblical quotations are from the *New International Version*, 1985.
Qur'anic references are from the Abdullah Yusuf Ali interpretation, *The Holy Koran*.

Preface

1. David B. Barrett, *"Annual Statistical Table on Global Mission: 1993,"* International *Bulletin of Missionary Research*, 17/1, 1993, 23.

2. F. M. Cornford, ed., *Greek Religious Thought from Homer to the Age of Alexander* (London: J. M. Dent and Sons, and New York: E. P. Dutton and Company, 1923), 85.

3. Hans Küng, *Global Responsibility: In Search of a New World Ethic*, Projekt Weltethos, trans. (New York: Crossroad, 1991), 62-64, 89.

Chapter 1

1. Emile Durkheim, *The Elementary Forms of the Religious Life* (London: George Allen & Unwin, 1976), 102-156.

2. Sigmund Freud, *The Future of an Illusion;* W. D. Robson-Scott, trans.; revised and edited by James Strachey (London: Hogarth Press), 1973.

3. Jeremiah 10:3-5.

4. Emil Fackenheim, *The Presence of God in History: Jewish Affirmations and Philosophical Reflections* (New York: New York Univ. 1970), 8-14.

5. John P. Kealy and David W. Shenk, *The Early Church and Africa* (Nairobi: Oxford Univ. Press, 1975), 206

6. John B. Noss, Man's Religions (New York: Macmillan, 1956), 426.

7. Ibid., 427.

8. Thomas S. Kuhn, *Structure of Scientific Revolutions* (Chicago: Univ. of Chicago Press), 1970.

Chapter 2

1. Marshall McLuhan and Bruce R. Powers, *The Global Village: Transformations in World Life and Media in the 21st Century* (New York: Oxford Univ. Press, 1989).

2. For a more thorough discussion of the present crisis, a helpful document is *Justice, Peace, and the Integrity of Creation*, the World Assembly of the Christian Churches, Seoul, Korea, March 5-13, 1990.

See also Hans Küng, *Global Responsibility*.

3. Küng, 89.

4. John N. Akers, editorial, "Evangelism's Search for Tomorrow," *Christianity Today*, 9-2-88, 11.

5. Lesslie Newbigin, *Foolishness to the Greeks* (Grand Rapids: Eerdmans, 1986); *The Gospel in a Pluralist Society* (Grand Rapids: Eerdmans, 1989).

Chapter 3

1. Arend Theodoor van Leeuwen, *Christianity in World History*, H. H. Hoskins,

trans. (New York: Charles H. Scribner's Sons, 1964), 158-165.

2. John S. Mbiti, *An Introduction to African Religion* (London: Heinemann, 1975), 78-81.

3. W. B. Anderson, *The Church in East Africa, 1840-1974* (Dodoma: Central Tanzania Press, 1977), 27-32.

4. Samuel G. Kibicho, "The Gikuyu Conception of God: His Continuity into the Christian Era and the Question It Raises for the Christian Idea of Revelation." Unpublished Ph.D. dissertation (Nashville: Vanderbilt University, 1972), 33.

5. Ibid., 57.

6. David W. Shenk, *Peace and Reconciliation in Africa* (Nairobi: Uzima, 1981), 21.

7. Alec Smith, *Now I Call Him Brother* (Basingstake, Hants: Marshalls, 1984), 119.

8. Shenk, 13.

9. Julius K. Nyerere, *Freedom and Development* (London: Oxford Univ. Press, 1973).

10. John S. Mbiti, *Concepts of God in Africa* (London: S.P.C.K, 1970), 177.

11. Anderson, 97-98.

12. I. M. Lewis, ed., *Islam in Tropical Africa* (London: Oxford, 1966), 58-75.

Chapter 4

1. The Upanishads, Swami Prabhavananda and Frederick Manchester, trans. (New York: The New American Library, 1957), 68-71. John B. Noss, *Man's Religions* (New York: Macmillan, 1956), 132.

2. Stephen Neil, *Christian Faith and Other Faiths* (London: Oxford Univ. Press, 1970), 71-73.

3. K. B. Rokaya, letter to Miriam Krantz (Tribhunan University, Pulchowk, Kathmandu, Nepal, Nov. 25, 1997).

4. Dor Bahadur Bista, *Fatalism and Development: Nepal's Stuggle for Modernization* (Calcutta: Longman, 1992), 6.

5. The Song of God, Bhagavad-Gita, Swami Prabhavananda and Christopher Isnerwood, trans. (New York: New American Library, 1951), 31-34.

6. Ibid., 45-46.

7. Ibid., 47.

8. Virginia Fabella, Peter K. H. Lee, David Kwang-sun Suh, eds., *Asian Christian Spirituality: Reclaiming Traditions* (Maryknoll: Orbis, 1992), 66-72.

9. Ibid., 68.

10. Allan Bloom, *The Closing of the American Mind* (New York: Simon and Schuster, 1987), 25.

11. Bhagavad-Gita, 53.

12. Bista, 6.

13. Noss, 128-134.

14. The Upanishads, 123.

15. Rabi Maharaj, *The Death of a Guru* (Eugene, Ore.: Harvest House, 1984).

16. S. Radhakrishnan, *Eastern Religions and Western Thought* (New York: Oxford Univ. Press, 1940), 313.

17. The Upanishads, 126.

18. E. Stanley Jones, *Gandhi: Portrayal of a Friend* (Nashville: Abingdon, 1948), 66-73.

19. S. Radhakrishnan, *East and West in Religion* (London: Allen and Unwin, 1933).

20. Kenneth Kaunda, *The Riddle of Violence* (San Francisco: Harper & Row, 1980).

Chapter 5

1. B. de Kretser, *Man in Buddhism and Christianity* (Calcutta: YMCA Press, 1954), 38.

2. *Sacred Books of the East*, vol. X, *The Dhammapada*, trans. from Pali by F. Max Muller (Delhi: Matilal Benarsidass; reprint of original text, Oxford: Clarendon Press, 1881), 1:2-5.

3. *The Buddha's Way of Virtue,* a translation of the *Dhammapada* by Wagiswara and Saunders, Wisdom of the East Series (London: John Murray, 1912), 44; cited in John B. Noss, *Man's Religions,* 179.

4. Hans Küng with Josef van Ess, Heinrich von Stietencron, and Heinz Bechert, *Christianity and World Religions: Paths to Dialogue with Islam, Hinduism, and Buddhism,* Peter Heinegg, trans. (New York: Doubleday, 1986), 404.

5. Stephen Neil, *Christian Faith and Other Faiths* (London: Oxford Univ. Press, 1970), 117.

6. Küng, *Christianity and World Religions,* 384.

7. Ibid., 398.

8. A. C. Bouquet, *The Christian Faith and Non-Christian Religions* (London: Nisbet, 1958), 289.

9. Küng, *Christianity and World Religions,* 337.

10. Trevor Ling, *Buddhist Revival in India: Aspects of the Sociology of Buddhism* (London: St. Mary's Press, 1980), 67-69.

11. Küng, 352-353.

12. Melford E. Spiro, *Buddhism and Society: A Great Tradition and Its Burmese Vicissitudes* (New York: Harper & Row, 1970).

13. Somnuk Montrelerdrasme, a Thai resident in Bangkok.

14. Noss, 164.

15. Ron Moreau, "Sex and Death in Thailand," *Newsweek,* 7-20-92, 50.

16. Küng, *Christianity and World Religions,* 347.

17. Ibid., 351.

Chapter 6

1. *The Way of Life: Lao tzu,* a translation of the *Tao Te Ching* by R. B. Blakney, (New York: New American Library, 1955), 54.

2. Ibid., 126.

3. Noss, 320.

4. Ibid., 350.

5. Luke 6:31.

6. *The Sayings of Confucius,* James R. Ware, trans. (New York: New American Library, 1955), 84.

7. Noss, 82.

8. Sigmund Freud.

9. Walter Wink, *Unmasking the Powers* (Philadelphia: Fortress, 1989).

10. Acts 17:16.

11. W. H. C. Frend, *The Early Church* (London: Hodder & Stoughton, 1972), 95.

12. *St. Augustine, City of God,* an abridged version from the translation by Gerald G. Walsh, S. J.; Demetrius B. Zema, S. J.; Grace Monahan, O. S. U.; Daniel J. Honan; ed. Vernon J. Boubke (New York: Doubleday & Co., 1958), 148.

13. Frend, 93.

14. Virgilius Ferm, *A History of Philosophical Systems* (New York: Philosophical Library, 1950), 48.

Chapter 7

1. Van Leeuwen, H. H. Hoskins, trans. 46-67, 158-165.

2. Ibid., 13-196.

3. Lesslie Newbigin, *Honest Religion for Secular Man* (London: SCM, 1966).

4. "The Global Poison Trade, How Toxic Waste Is Dumped on the Third World," *Newsweek,* 11-7-88, 66-68.

5. Romans 8:21.

6. Romans 8:19-21, Revelation 5:9-10, 13.

7. Genesis 1:1.

8. Genesis 3:8-10.
9. First John 4:16.
10. Matthew 11:28.
11. John 17:20-29.
12. M. Scott Peck, *People of the Lie* (New York: Simon and Schuster, 1983), 182-253. Wink, 9-53.
13. Joshua 24:15.
14. Genesis 11:1-9.
15. Genesis 12:1-3.
16. Morris Jastrow, *The Civilization of Babylonia and Assyria* (Philadelphia: J. B. Lippencott) 1915, 358. J. H. Hertz (ed.), *The Pentateuch and Haftorahs*, 2d ed. (London: Soncino), 5734/1973, 201.
17. Genesis 26:22.
18. Exodus 20:1.
19. Exodus 20:8-17.
20. First Samuel 15:22.
21. Hosea 6:6.
22. Second Samuel 12:7, 13.
23. Isaiah 49:6-7.
24. Genesis 3:15.
25. Isaiah 11:9-10.
26. Hans Küng, *On Being a Christian*, Edward Quinn, trans. (New York: Simon and Schuster, 1978), 226-238.

Chapter 8
1. Genesis 12:1.
2. Genesis 12:7.
3. Genesis 13:14-17.
4. Genesis 26:4.
5. Genesis 16:10.
6. Genesis 17:20.
7. Genesis 21:13.
8. Genesis 21:20.
9. Genesis 17:18.
10. Genesis 17:21.
11. Genesis 22:16-18.
12. Fackenheim, 8-14.
13. Deuteronomy 6:4-5.
14. Deuteronomy 16:12.
15. Deuteronomy 16:14-15.
16. Amos 5:11-12.
17. Exodus 23:27-28.
18. Genesis 12:3.
19. Second Chronicles 20:15.
20. Second Chronicles 20:21.
21. Isaiah 12:1-4.
22. Nehemiah 8—10.
23. Jacob Neusner, *Judaism and Christianity in the Age of Constantine: History, Messiah, Israel, and the Initial Confrontation* (Chicago: Univ. of Chicago Press, 1987).
24. Noss, 538.
25. Genesis 12:3.
26. Isaiah 11:2-5.
27. Arthur Hertzberg, "Waiting for the Messiah," *Commonweal*, New York, 5-8-92.
28. Jimmy Carter, *Keeping Faith: Memoirs of a President* (New York: Bantam Books, 1982), 273-403.

Chapter 9

1. Zechariah 9:9-10.
2. Matthew 21:9.
3. Matthew 1:18—2:23; Luke 1:26-38; 2:1-20.
4. Luke 19:45-48.
5. Mark 14—15.
6. Matthew 28:1-7.
7. Matthew 28:18-20.
8. Acts 2.
9. Acts 11:26.
10. Luke 1:3-4.
11. Küng, 145-165.
12. Jeremiah 10:1-16.
13. Luke 4:18-19.
14. Luke 4:21.
15. John 14:9.
16. Colossians 1:19.
17. Luke 1:32.
18. Luke 3:38.
19. Matthew 5—7.
20. John 13:1-17.
21. Küng, 410, 437.
22. Luke 23:34.
23. First John 4:8.
24. René Girard, *Violence and the Sacred*, Patrick Gregory, trans. (Baltimore: Johns Hopkins Univ. Press, 1972), 1-67, 250-273.
25. Ephesians 2:13-18.
26. First Peter 3:18.
27. Matthew 18:20.
28. Matthew 26:26-30.
29. Ephesians 2:19.
30. Matthew 19:5-6.
31. Ephesians 5:22—6:4.
32. Acts 15:1-35.
33. Romans 13:1-7.
34. John 6:15.
35. John 17:14.
36. Revelation 22:2.
37. Matthew 6:10.

Chapter 10

1. Qur'an, Proclaim: 96:1-2.
2. Ibid., The Glorious Morning Light: 93:6-11.
3. Ibid., The Heifer, 2:256.
4. Badru D. Kateregga and David W. Shenk, *Islam and Christianity* (Grand Rapids: Eerdmans, 1981), 76-78.
5. Qur'an, Iron: 57:16.
6. Ibid., The Night of Power: 97:1-3.
7. Ibid., Those Who Set the Ranks: 37:99-110.
8. Ibid., Fatiha: 1.
9. Ibid., Jonah: 10:94.
10. H. A. R. Gibb, *Mohammedanism* (New York: Oxford Univ. Press), 1962, 49.
11. Ibid., 77.
12. Fazlur Rahman, *Islam* (Chicago: Univ. of Chicago Press, 1979), 212-265.
13. Ibid., 236.

14. J. Spencer Trimingham, *The Sufi Orders of Islam* (London: Oxford Univ. Press, 1971), 199-200.

15. Qur'an, The Heifer: 2:143.

16. Ibid., The Heifer: 2:122.

17. Abdullah Yusuf Ali, *The Holy Quran: Text, Translation and Commentary* (Beirut: Dar Al Arabia, 1958), commentary and notes, 52.

18. Qur'an, The Roman Empire: 30:30.

19. W. Montgomery Watt, *Muhammad: Prophet and Statesman* (New York: Oxford Univ. Press, 1969).

20. Bernard Lewis, *The Political Language of Islam* (Chicago: Univ. of Chicago Press, 1988), 25.

21. Ibid., 29.1.

22. Kenneth Cragg, *The Call of the Minaret*, 2d. ed. (New York: Orbis, 1985), 189.

23. William Pfaff, *The Wrath of Nations* (New York: Simon and Schuster, 1993), 125.

24. Salman Rushdie, *The Satanic Verses* (New York: Viking, 1989).

25. Qur'an, The Spoils of War: 8:45-46.

26. Ibid., The Table Spread: 5:36-37.

27. Ibid., The Heifer: 2:143.

28. Philip K. Hitti, *History of the Arabs* (London: MacMillan, 1973), 441.

29. Qur'an, The Cow: 2:223.

Chapter 11

1. Ferm, 89.

2. John Foster, *Church History: The First Advance, A.D. 29-500* (London: SPCK, 1972), 82.

3. Lars P. Qualben, *A History of the Christian Church* (New York: Thomas Nelson and Sons, 1958), 177.

4. A. N. Whitehead, *Science and the Modern World* (Cambridge: Cambridge Univ. Press, 1926), 18.

5. Lesslie Newbigin, *Truth to Tell: The Gospel as Public Truth* (Grand Rapids: Eerdmans, 1991), 62.

6. John Chester Miller, *The Wolf by the Ears, Thomas Jefferson and Slavery* (New York: Free Press, 1977), 168.

7. Edward Gibbon, *Rise and Fall of the Roman Empire* (New York: Modern Library), 1932.

8. Abb, Raynal, *The Philosophical and Political History of the Indies*, 1st ed. (Amsterdam, 1770).

9. Alf J. Mapp, *Thomas Jefferson: Passionate Pilgrim* (New York: Madison Books, 1991), 264.

10. Sharon Begley, Daniel Glick, Debra Rosenberg, Donna Foote, "Heavens," *Newsweek*, 6-3-91, 50.

11. Paul Davies, *The Mind of God: The Scientific Basis for a Rational World* (New York: Simon and Schuster, 1992).

12. David J. Bosch, *Transforming Mission* (Maryknoll: Orbis, 1991), 499.

13. Davies, 139.

14. Ibid.

15. Jean-Jacques Rousseau, *The Social Contract*, trans. and introduced by Maurice Cranstor (Harmondsworth, Middlesex: Penguin, 1968).

16. Pfaff, 233-234.

17. Lesslie Newbigin, *Honest Religion for Secular Man* (London: SCM, 1966), 7-43.

18. Van Leeuwen, 16-17, 329-334.

19. Pfaff, 230.

20. Newbigin, *Truth to Tell*, 76.

21. Arthur Hugh Jenkins, *Adam Smith Today: An Inquiry into the Nature and Causes*

of the Wealth of Nations, Simplified, Shortened, and Modernized (Port Washington, New York: Kennikat Press, 1948), 380.

22. M. Scott Peck, *People of the Lie.*

23. Allan Bloom, 25-61.

24. Robert N. Bellah, et al., *Habits of the Heart* (Berkeley: Univ. of California Press, 1985).

25. Ibid., 142-166.

26. Pfaff, 233, 234.

Chapter 12

1. David Lyon, *Karl Marx: A Christian Appreciation of His Life and Thought* (Herts, England: Lion Publishing, 1979) 25-30.

2. Arend Theodoor van Leeuwen, 335, quote from Karl Marx, 'Die Fruhschriften,' Landshut and Mayer, ed., *Der historische Materialismus,* I (Leipzig, 1932), 279.

3. Lyon, 63.

4. Pfaff, 64-65.

5. V. I. Lenin, *State and Revolution* (New York: International Publishers, 1932), 80.

6. Ibid., 16.

7. Van Leeuwen, 337.

8. Joseph Stalin, *Marxism and the National and Colonial Question,* ed. A. Fineberg, (New York: New York International Publishers, n.d.), 20-30.

9. Isaiah 2:4.

10. Isaiah 11:6.

11. Van Leeuwen, 336.

12. Murray Feshbach and Alfred Friendly, Jr., *Ecocide in the USSR* (New York: Basic Books, 1992).

13. *U. S. News and World Report,* 112:14, April 13, 1992, 40-52.

14. Aleksandr I. Solzhenitsyn, *The Gulag Archipelago, 1918-1956,* Thomas P. Whitney, trans. (New York: Harper & Row, 1974), 147.

15. Niels Nielsen, *Revolutions in Eastern Europe: The Religious Roots* (Maryknoll: Orbis, 1991). J. Martin Bailey, *Churches in the Rebirth of Central and Eastern Europe: The Spring of Nations* (New York: Friendship Press, 1991).

16. Bailey, 58.

17. Ibid., 60.

18. Ibid.

19. Ibid.

20. "Gorbechev, Pope: Two Who Changed the World," *Intelligencer Journal,* Lancaster: Lancaster Newspapers, 3-9-92, A-6.

21. Ibid.

Chapter 13

1. Hans Küng, *Global Responsibility, 63.*

2. John Powell, S. J., *Unconditional Love: Love Without Limits* (Allen, Texas: Tabor, 1978), 18-22.

3. Bloom, 25-140.

4. Revelation 22:2.

5. Laurence Perrine, *Literature* (New York: Harcourt Brace Jovannovich, 1978), 624. From Lathem, Edward C., ed., *The Poetry of Robert Frost* (Henry Holt and Co., 1969).

Select Bibliography

Ali, Abdullah Yusuf. *The Holy Quran, Text, Translation and Commentary*. Beirut: Dar Al Arabia, 1958.

Bailey, J. Martin. *Churches in the Rebirth of Central and Eastern Europe: The Spring of Nations*. New York: Friendship Press, 1991.

Baron, Salo W., and Joseph L. Blau. *Judaism: Postbiblical and Talmudic Period*. New York: Bobbs-Merrill, 1954.

Belford, Lee A. *Introduction to Judaism*. New York: Association Press, 1961.

Bellah, Robert N., et al. *Habits of the Heart*. Berkeley: Univ. of California Press, 1985.

Bista, Dor Bahadur. *Fatalism and Development: Nepal's Struggle for Modern ization*. Calcutta: Longman, 1992.

Bloom, Allan. *The Closing of the American Mind*. New York: Simon and Schuster, 1987.

Bradley, David G. *A Guide to the World's Religions*. Englewood Cliffs: Prentice-Hall, 1963.

Brown, Robert McAfee. *Religion and Violence*. Philadelphia: Westminster, 1973.

Campbell, Joseph, and Bill Moyers. *The Power of Myth*. New York: Doubleday, 1988.

Carmody, Denise Lardner and John Tully Carmody. *Peace and Justice in the Scriptures of the World Religions*. New York: Paulist, 1988.

Carter, Stephen L. *The Culture of Disbelief: How American Law and Politics Trivialize Religious Devotion*. New York: Basic Books, 1993.

Cassidy, Michael. *The Passing Summer: A South African Pilgrimage in the Politics of Love*. London: Hodder and Stoughton, 1989.

Chacour, Elias, with David Hazard. *Blood Brothers*. Grand Rapids: Zondervan, 1984.

Chang, Jung. *Wild Swans*. London: Flamingo, 1993.

Chapman, Colin. *Whose Promised Land? Israel or Palestine?* Belleville, Mich.: Lion, 1985.

Clasper, Paul D. *Eastern Paths and the Christian Way*. Maryknoll: Orbis, 1980.

Cohn-Sherbok, Dan, ed. *World Religions and Human Liberation*. New York, Maryknoll: Orbis, 1992.

Collins, Larry, and Dominique Lapierre. *Freedom at Midnight*. Glasgow: Harper Collins, 1975.

Coomaraswamy, Ananda K., and Sister Nivedita. *Myths of the Hindus and Buddhists*. New York: Dover Publications, 1967.

Covell, Ralph R. *Confucius, The Buddha, and Christ, a History of the Gospel in Chinese*. Maryknoll: Orbis, 1986.

Coward, Harold. *Pluralism: Challenge to World Religions*. Maryknoll: Orbis, 1985.

Cragg, Kenneth. *The Call of the Minaret*. 2d ed., rev., exp. Maryknoll: Orbis, 1985.

_____. *The Christian and Other Religion*. London: Mowbrays, 1977.

_____. *The Event of the Quran: Islam in Its Scriptures*. London: George Allen & Unwin, 1971.

_____. *Muhammad and the Christian: A Question of Response*. Maryknoll: Orbis, 1984.

_____. *To Meet and to Greet, Faith with Faith*. London: Epworth, 1992.

_____. *The Wisdom of the Sufis*. London: Sheldon Press, 1976.

Davies, Paul. *The Mind of God: The Scientific Basis for a Rational World*. New York: Simon and Schuster, 1992.

D'Costa, Gavin, ed. *Christian Uniqueness Reconsidered: The Myth of a Pluralistic Theology of Religions*. Maryknoll: Orbis, 1990.

Donovan, Vincent J. *Christianity Rediscovered: An Epistle from the Masai*. Notre Dame: Fides Claretian, 1978.

Durkheim, Emile. *The Elementary Forms of the Religious Life*. London: George Allen & Unwin, 1976.

Ellis, Marc H. *Toward a Jewish Theology of Liberation*. Maryknoll: Orbis, 1987.

Ellul, Jacques. *The Presence of the Kingdom*. New York: Seabury, 1967.

_____. *The Subversion of Christianity*. Geoffrey W. Bromiley, trans., Grand Rapids: Eerdmans, 1986.

_____. *The Theological Foundation of Law*. trans., Marguerite Wieser, New York: Seabury, 1960.

Epp, Frank H. *The Israelis: Portrait of a People in Conflict*. Toronto: McClelland and Stewart, 1980.

Esposito, John L., ed. *Islam and Development: Religion and Sociopolitcal Change*. Syracuse: Syracuse Univ. Press, 1980.

_____, ed. *Voices of Resurgent Islam.* New York: Oxford Univ. Press, 1983.

Fackenheim, Emil L. *God's Presence in History: Jewish Affirmations and Philosophical Reflections.* New York: New York Univ. Press, 1970.

Ferguson, John. *War and Peace in the World's Religions.* New York: Oxford Univ. Press, 1978.

Ferm, Virgilius. *A History of Philosophical Systems.* New York: The Philosophical Library, 1950.

Freud, Sigmund. *The Future of an Illusion.* W. D. Robson-Scott, trans.; rev., ed. James Strachey. London: The Hogarth Press, 1973.

Friesen, Duane K. *Christian Peacemaking and International Conflict.* Scottdale: Herald Press, 1986.

Gibb, H. A. R. *Mohammedanism.* New York: Oxford Universrity Press, 1962.

Girard, René. *Violence and the Sacred.* Patrick Gregory, trans., Baltimore: John Hopkins Univ. Press, 1981.

Goldston, Robert. *Next Year in Jerusalem.* New York: Fawcett Crest, 1978.

Grimm, George. *Buddhist Wisdom: The Mystery of the Self.* Carroll Aikins, trans. Delhi: Motilal Banarsidass, 1978.

Guenther, Herbert V. *Buddhist Philosophy in Theory and Practice.* Baltimore: Penguin Books, 1971.

Guillaume, Alfred. *Islam.* New York: Penguin, 1979.

Haddad, Yvonne Yazbeck. *Contemporary Islam and the Challenge of History.* Albany: State Univ. of New York Press, 1982.

Hitti, Philip K. *History of the Arabs.* London: MacMillan, 1973.

Hooft, W. A. Visser't. *The Fatherhood of God in an Age of Emancipation.* Geneva: World Council of Churches, 1982.

Jones, E. Stanley. *Gandhi: Portrayal of a Friend.* Nashville: Abingdon, 1948.

Kateregga, Badru D., and David W. Shenk. *A Muslim and a Christian in Dialogue: Islam and Christianity.* Nairobi: Uzima, 1985. Scottdale, Pa.: Herald Press, 1997.

Kaunda, Kenneth. *The Riddle of Violence.* San Francisco: Harper & Row, 1980.

Kenyatta, Jomo. *Facing Mount Kenya.* London: Heinemann, 1961.

Knitter, Paul F. *No Other Name? A Critical Survey of Christian Attitudes Toward the World Religions.* Maryknoll: Orbis, 1985.

Kuhn, Thomas S. *Structure of Scientific Revolutions.* Chicago: Univ. of Chicago Press, 1970.

Küng, Hans. *Global Responsibility: In Search of a New World Ethic.* Trans. Projekt Weltethos. New York: Crossroad, 1991.

_____. *On Being a Christian.* Trans. Edward Quinn. New York: Simon and Schuster, 1978.

Küng, Hans, with Josef van Ess, Heinrich von Stietencron, Heinz Bechert. *Christianity and World Religions, Paths to Dialogue with Islam, Hinduism, and Buddhism.* Trans. Peter Heinegg. New York: Doubleday, 1986.

Lapp, John A. *The View from East Jerusalem.* Scottdale: Herald Press, 1980.

Lewis, Bernard. *The Political Language of Islam.* Chicago: Chicago Univ. Press, 1988.

Lind, Millard C. *Yahweh Is a Warrior.* Scottdale: Herald Press, 1980.

Ling, Trevor. *Buddhist Revival in India: Aspects of the Sociology of Buddhism.* London: St. Mary's Press, 1980.

_____. *A History of Religion East and West.* New York: Macmillan, 1968.

Lyon, David. *Karl Marx: A Christian Appreciation of His Life and Thought.* Herts, England: Lion Publishing, 1979.

Marx, Karl, and Friedrich Engels. *On Religion.* Intro. by Reinhold Neibuhr. New York: Schocken Books, 1971. (Repr. 1957 ed., Foreign Languages Publishing House, Moscow.)

Mbiti, John S. *African Religions and Philosophy.* London: Heinemann, 1971.

_____. *Concepts of God in Africa.* London: S.P.C.K, 1970.

_____. *An Introduction to African Religion.* London: Heinemann, 1975.

McLuhan, Marshall, and Bruce R. Powers. *The Global Village: Transformations in World Life and Media in the 21st Century.* New York: Oxford Univ. Press, 1989.

Michael, Aloysius. *Radha Krishnan on Moral Life and Action.* Delhi: Concept Publishing Co., 1979.

Naisbitt, John. *Megatrends.* New York: Warner Books, 1984.

Neil, Stephen. *Christian Faith and Other Faiths.* London: Oxford Univ. Press, 1970.

Neusner, Jacob. *The Death and Birth of Judaism: The Impact of Christianity, Secularism, and the Holocaust on Jewish Faith.* New York: Basic Books, 1987.

_____. *Judaism and Christianity in the Age of Constantine: History, Messiah, Israel, and the Initial Confrontation.* Chicago: Univ. of Chicago Press, 1987.

Newbigin, Lesslie. *A Faith for This One World.* London: SCM, 1961.

_____. *Foolishness to the Greeks.* Grand Rapids: Eerdmans, 1986.

_____. *The Gospel in a Pluralist Society.* Grand Rapids: Eerdmans, 1989.

_____. *Honest Religion for Secular Man.* London: SCM, 1966.

Nielsen, Niels. *Revolutions in Eastern Europe, The Religious Roots.* Maryknoll: Orbis, 1991.

Noss, John B. *Man's Religions.* New York: Macmillan, 1956.

Nyerere, Julius K. *Freedom and Development.* London: Oxford Univ. Press, 1973.

O'Flaherty, Wendy Doniger, trans. *Hindu Myths.* Baltimore: Penguin, 1975.

Parrinder, Geoffrey. *Upanishads, Gita and Bible: A Comparative Study of Hindu and Christian Scriptures.* New York: Harper & Row, 1972.

Peck, M. Scott. *The Different Drum: Community Making and Peace.* New

York: Simon and Schuster, 1987.

_____. *People of the Lie.* New York: Simon and Schuster, 1983.

Pfaff, William. *The Wrath of Nations: Civilization and the Furies of Nationalism.* New York: Simon and Schuster, 1993.

Radhakrishnan, S. *East and West in Religion.* London: Allen and Unwin, 1933.

_____. *Eastern Religions and Western Thought.* New York: Oxford Univ. Press, 1940.

Rahman, Fazlur. *Islam.* Chicago: Univ. of Chicago, 1979.

Ranger, T. O., and Isaria Kimambo. *The Historical Study of African Religion.* London: Heinemnn, 1972.

Rauf, M. A. *The Life and Teaching of the Prophet Muhammad.* Washington: Islamic Center, 1964.

Renou, Louis. *Hinduism.* New York: Washington Square Press, 1961.

Ruether, Rosemary. *Faith and Fratricide: The Theological Roots of Anti-Semistism.* New York: Seabury, 1974.

Sanneh, Lamin. *Translating the Message.* Maryknoll: Orbis, 1989.

The Sayings of Confucius. James R. Ware, trans. New York: The New American Library, 1955.

Scharf, Betty R. *The Sociological Study of Religion.* New York: Harper & Row, 1970.

Shari'ati, Ali. *On the Sociology of Islam.* Trans. from Persian, Hamid Algar. Berkeley: Mizan Press, 1979.

Sharma, Arvind, ed. *Our Religions.* San Francisco: HarperCollins, 1993.

Shenk, David W. *Peace and Reconciliation in Africa.* Nairobi: Uzima, 1981.

_____ and Ervin R. Stutzman. *Creating Communities of the Kingdom.* Scottdale: Herald Press, 1988.

Shipler, David K. *Arab and Jew: Wounded Spirits in a Promised Land.* New York: Penguin, 1987.

Sivaraman, Krishna, ed. *Hindu Spirituality: Vedas Through Vedanta.* New York: Crossword, 1989.

Smart, Ninian. *The Religious Experience of Mankind.* London: Collins, 1971.

Smith, Alec. *Now I Call Him Brother.* Basingstake, Hants: Marshalls, 1984.

Solzhenitsyn, Aleksandr I. *The Gulag Archipelago, 1918-1956.* Thomas P. Whitney, trans., New York: Harper & Row, 1974, 147.

Spiro, Melford E. *Buddhism and Society: A Great Tradition and Its Burmese Vicissitudes.* New York: Harper & Row, 1970.

Swami Prabhavananda and Christopher Isnerwood, trans. *The Song of God, Bhagavad-Gita.* New York: New American Library, 1951.

The Teachings of the Compassionate Buddha, Early Discourses, the Dhammapada, and Later Basic Writings. Ed., commentary, E. A. Burtt. New York: New American Library, 1955.

Tempels, Placide. *Bantu Philosophy*. Paris: Presence Africaine, 1969.

Thomas, Edward J. *The History of Buddhist Thought*. London: Routledge and Kegan Paul, 1971.

Toynbee, Arnold. *Christianity Among the Religions of the World*. New York: Charles Scribner's Sons, 1957.

Trimmingham, J. Spencer. *The Sufi Orders in Islam*. Oxford: Clarendon, 1971.

Tylor, Sir Edward Burnett. *Religion in Primitive Culture*. New York: Harper and Brothers, 1958.

The Upanishads. Swami Prabhavananda and Frederick Manchester, trans. New York: The New American Library, 1957.

Van Leeuwen, Arend Theodoor. *Christianity in World History*. H. H. Hoskins, trans. New York: Charles H. Scribner's Sons, 1964.

Watt, W. Montgomery. *Muhammad: Prophet and Statesman*. New York: Oxford Univ. Press, 1969.

The Way of Life: Lao Tzu. A new translation of the Tao Te Ching, by R. B. Blakney. New York: The New American Library, 1955.

Weber, Max. *The Sociology of Religion*. Boston: Beacon Press, 1972.

Weifan, Wang. *Lilies of the Field*. Hong Kong: Foundation for Theological Education in Southeast Asia, 1988.

Wilson, Monica. *Religion and the Transformation of Society*. Cambridge: Cambridge Univ. Press, 1971.

Wink, Walter. *Unmasking the Powers*. Philadelphia: Fortress, 1989.

Yoder, John H. *The Original Revolution*. Scottdale: Herald Press, 1971.

Zaehner, R. C. *Hinduism*. New York: Oxford Univ. Press, 1972.

The Author

DAVID W. SHENK was born and grew up in Tanganyika (Tanzania), East Africa. His parents were pioneer missionaries among a tribal people moving toward modernity. *Global Gods* is the culmination of his many years of living and working internationally amidst the religious pluralism of the global village.

An Eastern Mennonite College graduate in biblical and social studies, David has also studied at New York University, where he earned a doctorate in anthropology and religious studies education. He has authored nine books related to interreligious dialogue, religion and culture, world religions, peace, and African church history.

Themes of *Global Gods* appear in two of his other books: *Peace and Reconciliation in Africa* (Uzima, 1983) describes peace themes in traditional African societies. *A Muslim and a Christian in Dialogue* (Herald Press, 1997) is an earnest conversation between Shenk and a Muslim friend, Badru Kateregga.

David is an international educationalist. He has taught elementary through graduate school in the United States and Africa. He participates in leadership training seminars and events on six continents. He has directed international ministries with Eastern Mennonite Missions, with opportunities to facilitate interfaith conversations and relations in some forty countries.

As a global churchperson, David is keenly interested in the function of the church and other religions within the global village. His is not a theoretical concern. On an occasional evening he may be found sitting on the floor of a mosque in Philadelphia or elsewhere in deep conversation with Muslim friends about fundamental faith questions and the ways faith affects personal, local, and global *shalom.*